FRAGMENTS

MY LIFE AND DEATH IN A CULT

ELISABETH FRASER

'One million people commit suicide every year'
The World Health Organization

Published by
Chipmunkapublishing
PO Box 6872
Brentwood
Essex CM13 1ZT
United Kingdom

http://www.chipmunkapublishing.com

Forward

I first met Elisabeth Fraser at one of my talks in Edinburgh. I noticed that she had an indescribable graceful dignity, which some truly mature people have. Her ancient little house and her well-kept garden also displayed the same harmony.

Elisabeth in her long and interesting life encountered many spiritual traditions and teachers. She was able to see the harmony in their varieties of approaches.

Fragments is a story about how she managed to unify the essence of many different paths of traditions into a harmonious understanding and practice, I am sure we can all learn a lot from her experience and insight.

Ringu Tulku
Samyeling, Scotland

Contents

Foreword—by Ringu Tulku Rinpoche   *iii*

Preface—by Edward Averill   *vii*

Acknowledgements   *xii*

Introduction

1   Before I was Born   *1*
2   My Birth   *17*
3   Growing Up   *27*
4   The War Years   *59*
5   My Predicament   *76*
6   My Dilemma   *89*
7   Group Life in the Temple   *106*
8   Awakening   *147*
9   Awareness   *179*
10 Conditioning and Indoctrination   *192*
11 Leaving the School   *210*
12 Life with Alexander   *250*
13 A New Life Opens Up   *280*
14 Challenging Changes   *302*
15 My Scottish Experiences   *337*
16 Meeting Krishnamurti   *356*
17 Learning to Understand Who We Are   *391*
18 Penetrating Awareness of The Now   *418*

Epilogue   *444*

Glossary   *458*

Bibliography   *475*

Preface

By Edward Averill

My sister's story interweaves two complementary and interacting themes. One captures a charming, honest, and surprisingly accurate description of her actual life, which of itself has significant historical interest concerning the last eighty years of the Twentieth Century. The second theme concerns her struggles to make sense out of the traumas and upheavals that she encountered. Through her efforts to understand how it could be that she had the experiences that she had, and through the writing of this book, she gained an inner peace that she had never experienced before and at the same time became a greater human being in consequence. The lives of perhaps many readers will be comparable, and hopefully this completely open account of her life and struggles will provide them with a meaningful rationale for their own lives, just as it has for my sister.

As a child, she wondered why she was who she found herself to be and not someone else. As she grew to adulthood she gradually became aware that this 'me,' whom she found herself to be was at the very centre of her activties. She discovered that everyone else had a similar 'me' that behaved in a way equivalent to hers. By facing herself within the midst of her difficulties and catastrophes she gradually gained an awareness of how her 'me' behaved. The pursuit of self-knowledge began to change her life and its experiences—both outwardly and inwardly. She recognized a link between her difficulties and her 'me' and later she traced her 'me' to being built upon a foundation of pictures that she had made of herself since childhood.

The first dramatic step within her life-story occurred fifteen years after her marriage, when she was caught in a shattering upheaval and crisis for which she was completely unprepared. It led to her becoming totally separated from her family of four children to whom she was deeply attached and it catapulted her into being trapped in a school of philosophy that she later came to realise was a cult. However, the absolute darkness and suffering of those times did result for her in what she later came to appreciate was of enormous value—the realisation of the part that her 'me' played in her life.

In her fifteenth year of marriage, she was struck by a totally unexpected and unforeseen tornado of happenings that drastically changed her life. It took many years for her to recognise what was perhaps the underlying dynamics that brought about these happenings. For her it was an all-consuming passion to find Truth, as she then perceived it. What transpired so alienated her husband that when the opportunity suddenly presented itself, he cut her off instantly and absolutely from both himself and her children. In retrospect this underlying passion, which had been semi-dormant but simmering in the background, until it forcibly surfaced after the birth of her fourth child. At this time in my sister's life she had no conception or idea concerning the effect that this reawakened part of herself would have on herself, her children or her husband.

She became completely separated from her family against her will and wishes, and totally unable to escape from the School that later both my sister and I realised must have always been a cult. Her very traumatic experience forced her to embark on an exploration into the understanding of self-knowledge, in spite of the cult's teachings. My sister's response to her situation gradually became the most important activity and purpose in her life. It took many years for her to realise that there are no absolutes in Truth, but that specific aspects of Truth may be glimpsed at certain moments. However, it was her life at the cult that convinced her that beliefs, authority or persuasions of any kind do not lead to inner peace. She learned that the pathway toward Truth starts with self-knowledge and a focus on what is happening within ordinary everyday behaviours.

The more she persevered and had the courage to face the part that she played in shaping and forming her everyday life—which led to each day and its happenings—the more she became aware of the influences that others had over her self-ignorant self. Further, through her perseverance, she found that interactions with others presented her with the most significant opportunities to understand herself. Through that she began to recognize the importance of the part played by her attitudes and intentions. This led her to make meaningful contact with not only the inner spiritual side within herself but also within others.

Later, as she reviewed this passion she had for discovering Truth, she recounts her upbringing as a Christian until thirteen, after which her parents introduced her to esoteric teachings. This led her to become an avid reader of other teachings, such as Taoism, Buddhism, Sufism, and especially and much later to the teaching of Krishnamurti.

There was one particular occasion when listening with great intensity to a talk given by Krishnamurti at Brockwood Park that she gained a more complete insight into the significance of self-knowledge. Through this talk she became aware that there was a very strong connection between herself—as the observer of what was happening at any point of time—and that which she was observing. This insight showed her that action without conflict meant that there was no separation of 'the observer'—herself—with what she faced—as the observed. The observer created the conditions that were being observed, and thus what-was-observed reflected the observer.

Over time, she learned that everyone has a part to play in everyday human life, and that no one is more important than another, whatever the part is that we seem destined to play. She now feels that nothing, not even our insights, can be properly and fully understood and assessed through our limited everyday minds, nor is anyone in a position to judge another whatever they may have done or may not have done in their lives. She keeps coming back to the fact that it is her response to each moment—the now—where there is 'a power fashioning the shape and substance of the unborn hour'. She recognizes that her 'me' belongs to the past, and that unless she deeply realises this fact of life, the past—her 'me'—overwhelms the *now*, and then of course she is reliving memory rather than experiencing what is actually happening in the *now*.

Thus, she has learned the importance of constant vigilance to be alert and attentive to prevent the past from distorting each new situation and each relationship with others, and once this vigilance becomes fruitful it leads to greater conscious awareness and understanding of the opportunities within each new moment.

She felt herself compelled to write *Fragments*, within which compulsion was a recognition that we all belong to the same human family, diverse and unique as we are. She saw that her basic emotions of fear, hurt, anger, hatred, jealousy, sorrow, joy and happiness are more or less the same as those of the rest of mankind. Underlying her writing is the conviction, as she puts it, that 'My story is your story and your story is my story'. Hopefully her story will help others to discover within themselves a greater inner peace.

In everyone's life there are times when we meet tragedy head-on and meet dead-end entanglements that push us to lose heart. But, as my sister's story shows, by honestly facing our failures and difficulties they can become opportunities to uncover the gifts concealed within them. She was comforted in her struggles to know that nothing can last forever and that, by acceptance of where she was, nothing is so awful that it becomes all consuming. Thus, her story is about discovering self-knowledge, and how it helped her to cope with her 'failures' and wring out of them positive benefits. We, my sister and I, do not believe that any of us are left alone. There is an Unseen Spirit within us that is always there to guide us if we look for it; and for us that is what underlies Jesus' saying, 'Seek ye first the Kingdom of Heaven within, then all else shall be added unto you'.

Edward Averill

Acknowledgements

I would like to acknowledge my appreciation to the many friends who have encouraged me to write this my autobiography. In particular, my thanks are due to my Literary Agents, Susan Mears and Julian Robbins, for their immense support and encouragement. In particular I am most grateful to Chipmunka Publishing, who have been tremendously helpful and patient with me during the production of this book. I particularly want to express my deep appreciation to my friend Mark Rowden, for his willingness to help me at a time when I needed his expertise to bring everything together.

Especially would I like to mention that I have received immeasurable help during my life from Krishnamurti's Teachings, which have been instrumental in changing my understanding of what in means to be a human being.

I hope that what I have been able to glean from my life, will not only be helpful to readers, but will be a form of historical interest. Above all I hope it will encourage those who have had to meet suffering and deep sorrow in their lives to find some sort of solace in reading this my story. I would like to add that I hope my experience in a cult reveals that devastating experiences are often the very means of bringing out the best in us.

Not forgetting my dear friend, Ken Kerr, who not only designed the front cover, but also chose the title. He made it possible for me to use a computer, without which I could not have managed.

Lastly I owe much to my beloved brother, Edward Averill, who very generously helped me by going through my text so patiently and encouraging me in a way that no one else could.

Introduction

THE BEGINNING CHAPTERS set the background and conditions of my life that led me to becoming part of a cult in January 1956. At that time, totally against my will, I found myself permanently separated from my children. In the cult I had to conform to the protocols set by the Principal. And to survive in that close-knit community of some twenty-five persons from different backgrounds, became quite a challenge for me.

I discovered during my stay in the cult that the Principal imposed her hypothetical vision of 'hidden' Masters as a means of psychologically controlling the group, creating an undercurrent of fear that if we disobeyed her, The Masters would punish us. This caused us to succumb to whatever she commanded us to do, however bizarre. By her method of 'divide & rule' we learnt to keep our thoughts to ourselves, thus mistrust developed between us. Hence, it was that I experienced a 'death' to my own identity.

I recognise now, that cults attract vulnerable religious people, who are persuaded that they have been chosen to do God's work. It was not until I escaped from this environment, some eight years later, that I realised that all the hard lessons experienced in the cult, were the very means of preparing me to be more open within myself to respond to the Teachings of Krishnamurti.

On hearing Krishnamurti talk for the first time at Brockwood Park in 1969, some six years after I had left the cult, I was profoundly moved by his radical approach to human psychology. It revolutionised my outlook on life and gave me my first real glimpse of why my life had been so fragmented. Over the years listening to him, I began to realise just how conditioned I was, causing a continual misuse of psychological thought resulting in a perpetual conflict within my actions and reactions. Above all, it became absolutely clear that no one could help me, but myself; nor could I find Truth except through my own heart.

After many years of struggling within myself to find a deeper meaning to life through self-knowledge and self-awareness, I became conscious of the operational interdependency and interconnectiveness that abounds everywhere within our Universe. Indeed, I felt instinctively that human kind had a vital roll to play in the development of Creation. Thus it was that I found myself challenged to live my Life as it is and to meet the 'what is' steadfastly, which enabled me to discover an inner guiding principle that comes with clear 'insights'. I was confronted with a realisation that there was absolutely nothing to find. I pondered over this awareness of nothingness as it persisted with me. I felt that there needed to be a greater awareness of what that nothingness meant. So I said to myself, surely there is no security in nothingness? But certainly, I felt that there was no security in following the conceptional views of the Christians about God and the Creator that I had been conditioned to believe, which now seemed to me to be only conjecture! In spite of such conjecture, I felt that the sayings of Jesus were true; especially His declaration. '*Seek ye first the Kingdom of Heaven within and then all else shall be given unto you.*' (Luke Chapter 12, Verse 31.)

Strangely enough, a deep insight penetrated an absolute clarity to my conception of nothingness. I could see that what I had thought was nothingness—was a total revolution within the known—an emptiness to all my yesterdays—and in that emptiness, was a stillness and within that stillness, the mind was silent—cutely aware and sensitively alert for any changes. And in the light of that awareness there was a quietening of the brain that brought forth a transformation to my psychological make-up, which in turn revealed a totally different meaning to my understanding of the known. In that new awareness of the known I felt there was a freedom for the unknown to emerge, whereby there's a possibility for a Union between the known and the unknown.

A further penetrating insight revealed a deeper awareness, which seemed to coincide with what Jesus referred to as 'The Kingdom of Heaven within'. Suggesting the utmost importance of living in the immediate present—the Now. For it seemed that Now represented complete Freedom—whereby there is no 'self' or 'me'—no space or time—to interfere with The Absolute Supremacy of The One Dynamic Energy that is the Liberating Truth of The Universal Law.

And within this compelling Presence of the Now, I feel there is a true Oneness of Being—wherein Love and Compassion—sparkles beauty into Life and harmony into Peace, so that there is an immense joy in Living.

Elisabeth Fraser, *Edinburgh 2008*

Chapter One

Before I Was Born

Ah, Love! Could thou and I with Fate conspire?
To grasp this sorry Scheme of Things entire,
Would not we shatter it to bits and then
Re-mould it nearer to the Heart's Desire!

The Rubáiyát of Omar Khayyám
Translated by Edward Fitzgerald (1809–93)

I THINK THE YEARS BEFORE ONE IS BORN ARE IMPORTANT, mainly due to the influences they have on our parents, which are bound to reflect on any forth-coming child. Two years prior to my birth in 1920 the First World War had just ended, leaving privation and social upheavals all over the world, although there was a new spirit of freedom and adventure beginning to make itself felt. This was the environment into which I was born. Although born in England, I was in fact conceived in the USA, which often made me wonder if this was why I always felt so attuned to the Native North American way of life, for I can so easily understand their sacred ways and their love and respect for nature.

The war devastated the world by the loss of millions on millions of servicemen, whose horrendous deaths lingered in the background of everyone's life. The figure was 10 million dead around the world: for Britain, three-quarters of a million and 200,000 from around the Empire, plus 1.5 million over-all seriously injured. It is extraordinary to think that on the 11th November 1918, in a railway carriage in the forest of Compiègne, at dawn, two German Generals and a Catholic politician put their names on the armistice document. By 11.00 a.m. all fighting had ceased on the battlefields. But the settlement was so poor that it led to another World War just twenty years later. In the aftermath of this appalling war, apart from the terrible devastation, countless loss of life and injuries—unemployment everywhere greeted servicemen returning home from the trenches, and from sea and air.

Strangely enough, in Great Britain just after the First World War, more than 150,000 deaths were recorded due to the virulent 'Spanish 'flu' epidemic. Apparently, troops and displaced persons carried this bug home with them causing the disease to spread like wildfire around the world. Many more deaths occurred worldwide during this period than the total number of deaths during the entire First World War.

The coalition government in Great Britain during the First Great War had established a firm control over all industries through food rationing and pub licensing hours, deeply affecting everyone's lives. However, there were some hopeful signs. Class distinction, that for so long had stifled the emancipation of the majority, had begun to decline. There was increasing opportunity in education, and the school leaving age was raised to 14 years; social services and transportation facilities were improved, to cite but two examples. In spite of all the suffering there was a feeling of renewal, stimulated by the few who had a clearer vision of what was needed to build a new society.

After this war, a new social order gripped the world, which was particularly evident in Great Britain. Women started to be more independent of men in a way that they had never been able to before the war. Women, who had been supporting the war effort by temporarily doing men's jobs while they were engaged on active service, had gained a new spirit of independence, which spread throughout all classes.

At this time, there was a continuing increase in technological devices. As a result it brought unrest among workers, whose jobs appeared to be in jeopardy; but it had not yet affected the low pay that the workers received. All through this period there was general unrest provoking many strikes, culminating in the General Strike in 1926. Unemployment and destitution added to the widespread suffering and misery that were the hallmark of the situation following the war.

Naturally, my parents were caught up in all these changes. My father, who had volunteered for service in the army in 1914, had been wounded in Gallipoli at the end of 1915 along with many courageous servicemen of the Commonwealth that included some of father's relatives in New Zealand and Australia. Later, my father returned to duty only to be badly wounded again on the Western Front, where the Germans made a major withdrawal. He was one of the casualties to be sent home, having to remain in hospital for months. I remember, as a child, seeing father wind a crepe bandage round his left leg and foot for support, which he continued to do every day of his life.

Whilst father was recovering from his wounds, he met my mother, who was a nurse. Their romance blossomed in an unexpected way. Mother's friend, who was also a nurse, had asked mother to 'stand in' for her date with my father. It had been a last minute decision by my mother's friend, as she had but recently met a tall dark handsome officer, who had asked her out on the same evening. Caught between the two dates, my mother's friend chose her tall dark handsome officer.

Mother says she reluctantly agreed to keep this date for her friend, and turned up half-an-hour late, only to become rather flustered when she looked around at the chosen meeting place, and could not see her friend's dating partner. Suddenly, she spotted him standing by a lamppost on the other side of the road, leaning on a stick. She felt sure it was her friend's date—an officer in uniform, and he was also looking around as if expecting someone. Mother claimed that she fell head over heels in love with father from that very first moment she saw him standing there leaning on the lamp-post. She was captivated, and stood watching him for some time before crossing the road to introduce herself. My mother had luxurious auburn hair caught up in a bun at the nape of her neck. Her large dark brown eyes, that were usually full of merriment, shyly watched my father as she explained why she had taken her friend's place. She had a lovely fresh complexion, accentuated by her beautiful hair and eyes. She had just turned twenty-five and did not have a boyfriend.

True, father was not very tall, but he was nevertheless a very handsome man and his dark hair contrasted well with mother's; and although the injury to his leg caused him to limp for a year or so, mother said it did not seem to make him at all self-conscious. After hearing mother's explanation as to why she was there, he greeted her with delight on this their 'blind date'. Father took mother's arm in his and quietly suggested that he knew exactly where to find a very good restaurant near by, and if she would care to accompany him, he would be glad to take her there. Mother bashfully agreed, at the same time hiding her face from father's direct gaze. Before the evening had come to an end mother said she felt she had known father all her life. They had a wonderful evening, at the end of which, mother said, father kissed her goodnight and immediately made another date.

After a whirlwind romance of six weeks they married, and as soon as father received his discharge papers from the army he applied for two passages to America paid by the British Government. Surprisingly, he was successful at a time when only a very few privileged passengers were allowed aboard ship. They sailed on S.S. Mauretania on the 17th July 1918. My father was 29 years old and my mother was 25. Thus, they were able to leave Southampton, just before the end of the war. In spite of the somewhat hazardous route taken, they landed safely in New York on the 25th July. During the voyage they were obliged to move away from the shipping lanes to avoid being hit by torpedoes from the German submarines. As children we loved to hear father tell us the story of how he was forced to exert his authority over our mother during their voyage to America.

Father said that mother was a very headstrong young woman, although he was always quick to add as he delved deeper into the story that she had indeed mellowed over the years! Our little faces would turn swiftly to watch mother's expression, never missing a thing. As we glanced at mother, it was obvious to us that she, too, was enjoying the tale as much as we were. The story went that one day out of sheer exasperation, father had picked mother up bodily and while she was still fully clothed, dropped her into a bath full of water! As children, we became very excited at the very thought of our mother receiving such a punishment. We never tired of hearing this tale over and over again. And father, who thoroughly enjoyed relating to us just how severely he had dealt with mother, would exchange meaningful and amused glances with mother as the story unfolded. I suppose it fired our imaginations to think that father had actually put mother into a bath of cold water while she was fully clothed! For us, it was a total surprise, for father was such an easy-going man. I suppose in hindsight we all felt secretly appeased to know father had actually got the better of mother, for we never could. We had all suffered from the sharp end of mother's tongue and the rough side of her hand—many a time.

My sister, Marguerite, was born in 1918 on the 25th February in New Orange, New York State, where they had taken a small apartment. We never heard very much about their time in America, but I gathered that they were both homesick for England and that when father was offered an opportunity to return to England in 1920, he jumped at the chance. The Graphite Company, which employed father in America, had asked him to return to England to represent their Graphite interests in the U.K.

Excitedly, my parents booked their passage for home. Mother's pride and joy was her baby perambulator. It was hand-made of tightly woven basket weave, with a rounded basket hood and a pale natural coloured pram apron. It looked very special and mother was very proud of it. She wanted to bring it onto the ship that was taking them to England, but the regulations did not permit and mother was refused. Nothing daunted, my mother, with total unconcern and much to my father's utmost embarrassment, wheeled my baby sister in the perambulator onto the ship with a look of: "Don't dare try and stop me bringing my baby aboard," that so flabbergasted the bursar, that he waved my mother through, not daring to look up at the Captain on the Bridge.

My mother was nearly six months pregnant with me, and behaved in such a way as to defy argument. The pram lasted satisfactorily for all her five children and I can well remember, with some of mother's pride, wheeling my baby brother up and down the street. The pram was so totally different from English prams that it hardly ever ventured out without some comment. People would ask mother where she got it, and when mother proudly said from America, it gave her self-esteem a great boost. For in those early days of the early twentieth century, travel was mostly for the well to do or businessmen or service personnel. No one envisaged that by the end of that century there would be such an enormous revolution in our travel.

Shortly after landing at Southampton, my father took my mother and baby sister to Great Witley in Worcestershire, which in those days was considered a long journey by train. Worcester was the nearest country railway station to where his parents lived. Grandfather met them at the station with his pony and trap. Although my mother was pregnant, she was none the less a very comely young woman and was straight away very much admired by my grandfather.

However, my mother had never lived in the country before, let alone on a farm, so she found it disconcerting and foreign to her. Most of all she hated living away from father, who had to leave her with his parents whilst he set up his business in London, which meant that mother was left alone with her baby in a strange atmosphere away from father. She felt very insecure, not only because she was pregnant, but also because father was not with her, for being unused to farm life she found everything very primitive.

The homestead was, even by the standards of that day, very old-fashioned, which made it very challenging for mother to look after her baby, especially as she had been used to a far more modern life-style in America. Moreover, she had always been accustomed to living in towns where there was running water and loos that had pull chains.

Grandfather managed eight farms as Farm Bailiff to the estate of Lord Dudley, which included the farm where they lived. In the 1920s there were few places in the country that had telephones or motorised vehicles, as they were still considered a very great luxury. Once a week grandfather was obliged to visit all the farms. In those days, the only means of transport in the more remote farming areas was on horseback. He had to look after all his fellow farmers and if there were any problems he had to sort them out or report their troubles to the Steward. Grandfather had to report daily to the estate office, which was next to the great house, at Witley Court. The Steward looked after the whole of the large estate owned by Lord Dudley.

Grandfather loved his farm with its large farmhouse where all his family grew up. The house was made of stone and had a moat that ran all the way round both it and its outbuildings. It was by far the largest farmhouse on the estate, and quite close to Witley Court, which overlooked a small lake, where I seem to remember, as a child, seeing lots of kingfishers. They had impressive long blue tail feathers and feathers of blue and green on their backs, which glistened in the sun. They were adorned with beautiful head crests and had long stout beaks and to me they seemed to be quite large shy birds. The small lakes around the estate provided a natural habitat for them. The kingfishers loved the small fish that were plentiful in the lake and they could often be seen silently and patiently watching at the edge of the lake, ready to pounce on an unsuspecting fish.

In the early days the round tower on one side of the farmhouse accommodated the loos. But the tower had two floors, so one can imagine it was not a very practical arrangement! Therefore, over time, the loos were removed and the recesses were replaced with round, independent window seats. I remember, these round seats were heavily curtained off from the main room and provided me with an ideal hiding-place. I have a distinct memory of curling up into a small ball waiting for mother to call me, and

Grandfather.

when she did, I never answered her call just in case she found my hiding-place. Of course in the end she did find me and I recall it became a game thereafter.

Grandfather thought that in days gone by, the farmhouse had originally been the main house of the estate, but this was long before Witley Court was built. Mother thought so too, for it was not long before she discovered one night that the old farmhouse was definitely haunted. This is what she said happened. While father was busy setting up his business in London, mother said she was awakened one night in the early hours of the morning to see a distraught-looking man enter her bedroom, dressed in very old-fashioned clothes. Terrified she pulled the bedclothes up to her eyes as she watched him cross the room, gliding past the end of her bed, to vanish through the chest of drawers and disappear through the wall behind it. Unable to bear this for more than two nights, mother left her room to seek grandmother. On her way to find her, mother said she saw another apparition gliding toward her. Mother described her as a most beautiful lady, exquisitely dressed in the palest of blue. Mother said she did not look in the least unfriendly. Suddenly the lady stopped and smiled at her, and before mother could collect herself she had vanished through a door.

Feeling more reassured by the friendly ghost mother went back to her own room, wondering if she had dreamt seeing the man gliding through the wall behind her chest of drawers. The next day, she asked grandmother about the lady in pale blue. "Oh," said grandmother dismissing the incident as if it were of no purport, "She's Elisabeth—you don't have to worry about her—she has always been here and has always been a happy ghost, never causing us any trouble." Mother always said that is how I came to be called Elisabeth. I was, I'm told, a very happy baby and so

I supposed I deserved the name. Nevertheless, mother remained unhappy with the distraught gentleman that every now and then invaded her privacy. In the end grandmother allowed a maid to sleep with her whilst father was away. What made mother even more, uneasy was the fact that the maid never saw the ghost and thought mother was making up the whole story. In the end grandmother did too. This infuriated my mother.

The farmhouse felt like a nightmare to mother, particularly without father. The farm's loos were constructed next to the corn bins, in an adjoining wooden shed, some yards away from the farmhouse; each of the five loo seats had been carved out of wood by grandfather. They were constructed over a deep hole and joined together by wood, sized respectively to suit the family. All these five seats were together, two somewhat smaller than the others, except for one very small seat, which I can vaguely remember using. These loo holes were 'flushed' with lime powder, instead of water. They were mother's particular daily horror and totally unbearable to her sense of propriety; in spite of the fact that grandfather would every now and then do what he called 'a digging job' to refresh the 'loos'. I remember that they had a peculiar smell no matter what grandfather did to them. It was rather like the smell of damp earth with something akin to a mixture of farmyard manure and rotting potatoes!

Mother told me that one day grandmother asked her to fetch a hen for the boiling pot from the chicken house. Mother said that as soon as she opened the door of the chicken house, all the cockerels fluttered all over her head. She tried to grab one, but the other cockerels flew all around her until she felt quite defeated. But not wanting to return to her mother-in-law without a chicken, she sat down on a ledge and waited until all the chickens had calmed down.

Suddenly she grabbed the nearest cockerel by its legs. Feeling very flustered, she left the hen house hurriedly, quickly shutting the wooden wire-netted door behind her, as she clutched the indignant cockerel. She triumphantly returned to the kitchen, where grandmother was busy. Mother said that grandmother critically eyed the cockerel, and as she did so she turned to mother saying, "Now wring its neck out in the yard." Mother was absolutely horrified, and positively refused to do so.

It did not take grandmother very long to ring the cockerel's neck, and with a curt wave of her hand she told mother to follow her into the fowl house, where the feathers and guts were removed to prepare the chicken for the boiling pot. Feathers were kept in a special bag for eventually filling pillows and mattresses. The guts were slung away in a bucket for the pigs. Every task that was required was made even more difficult by the fact that there was no running water or electricity or gas. All the water had to be carried in pails from the well, after it had been pumped up by hand. Mother's first lesson on preparing a fowl for the table, caused her to be so flustered that she begged to be spared such a task again. But Grandmother was ruthless and said, "However do you think you are going to manage a turkey at Christmas, if you aren't able to pluck a hen?" Mother said her only answer was to give grandmother a look of utter horror. But nevertheless, grandmother was a wonderful cook and taught mother all she knew about cooking. Mother said it took her a long, long time to get used to the preparation that the farmhouse meals required, especially as the oven range, which was a nightmare to her, had to be polished every day with some kind of blackening material.

Heating and cooking were by fires and all lighting was obtained from oil lamps. Mother found these old-fashioned methods deeply distressing. She tried to cope with my sister, under conditions that she was not used to nor could ever get used to. Mother told us that the old farmhouse kitchen had a huge oven where the bread was baked. She said that she became quite used to kneading the dough for grandmother and watching it rise before the old-fashioned range, until grandmother pronounced it was ready to be placed into the bread tins. Then after it had risen again, it was kneaded and cut into sizes and placed into the baking tins to rise for the last time. Grandmother always kept small pieces of dough to put on a tray for rolls, which grandfather loved, especially when they were hot. When they were ready she would ring a little bell to call him. Soon that became my sister's job. My sister was still very small, being only eighteen months when I was born.

Mother felt that the moat all round the farmhouse was very dangerous, and she said she was always afraid my sister might stray from the farm-house, and fall into the water below the wall and drown in the moat.

In the early 1920s in the country, one must remember, there were hardly any telephones, or running water, and very few motorcars. Buses were horse drawn. Electricity and gas installations were practically non-existent on farms or cottages. All the larger country estates had to do as they had always done for generations—rely on local girls to help them to do the entire household work etc. In fact, country estates were the main source of employment for both young men and women, living in the country area.

Despite the changes that occurred after World War One, it took yet another World War to totally revolution-ise most of our world. New technology was developing at an alarming pace and country folk found it hard to keep up with it.

In my grandfather's day there was little or no farm machinery to help farmers to plough their fields. But farms were gradually obtaining modern machinery after the First World War, which made life easier for farmers. I know that my grandfather always used the farming methods that his father and grandfather had used and grandmother managed the dairy in much the same way as it had been run for generations. In fact, many people preferred the tried and tested methods of farming, finding the new modern ideas difficult to get used to; but changes wait for no one.

Nobody went for holidays abroad in those days, and many people never left their villages. I know that grandmother and grandfather were never able to take holidays, because of the responsibility of the farms. But sometimes relatives from Dudley and other parts of Worcester would visit them. I remember my great-aunt Bessie, whom my sister and I loved, often came to stay. She would cuddle us on her voluptuous lap as she sat on the bench outside the farmhouse in the back garden. She always wore an overall tied round her plump waist over her black dress, for she was in mourning. I recollect that when the weather permitted, she would take a little walk with us.

Grandmother said that even though the local people were cut off from the cities or towns before the railways came, everybody made sure that once a year they would attend the local fair. Everybody in the country looked forward to this annual event, which usually took place after the harvest, on the open 'village Green' in the middle of the village. The local squire always opened the fair, whilst the vicar and his wife would organise the entertainment, such as the egg and spoon races, horse riding and competitions for local arts and crafts. Local ladies would bring needlework and woodcarvers exhibited their wares. Everyone wore their best Sunday clothes and before the end of the day, Grandmother told us, there was dancing to the local band on the village 'Green'. It was an occasion for merriment, especially for the young men and women, who would come together for the dancing and courting.

But grandfather said times were changing and things were no longer as they used to be in his young days. Before all the modernisation that arrived with the railways, he said, he could remember the big parties given by the gentry at Witley Court, and the elegant carriages bringing aristocrats from miles around. He said that he sometimes caught a glimpse of a motorcar driven by one of the young men from the 'big house'.

Grandfather would tell us how he was expected to account to the Steward for the yearly progress of his farm and all the other farms. Sometimes he had to meet Lord Dudley to discuss any big changes. Grandfather said on those occasions he was expected to wear his bowler hat and Sunday best clothes. And the Steward always accompanied him. However, in the countryside changes were hardly noticeable, as they occurred so gradually. There seems a strange oddity about human nature that resists change, especially people in the country, who are slow to accept changes and always think their old ways are best.

When father managed to find time to come home, grandfather and mother would meet him in the pony and trap at Worcester station, while grandmother stayed behind to look after my sister, who slept in her pram. It was my mother who told me what an exciting time it was when the pony and trap transported her through the country lanes to the station to meet father. She told me that as her time drew nearer for my birth, she longed so much for father to stay with her and not return to London.

Grandfather would take him to the station in the very early hours of a Monday morning in the pony and trap.

Father had to work hard in London setting up his business and did not always find it easy to come home every weekend. Mother began to worry as her time drew nearer to have me, in case father would not be there to look after her. In those days there were no telephone boxes and grandfather did not have a telephone. But somehow he managed to keep father informed, and as soon as my mother felt the first twinges of labour, father came home, and as the hour of my birth approached he took mother to the nursing home in Kidderminster by pony and trap. I am told there was much excitement and happiness at my birth.

Chapter Two

My Birth

Every baby born is an expression of absolute purity.
Anyone who has been present at a birth must
acknowledge this. Each new birth is a bursting
out of life-itself. Each baby is a container for the
emergence of the raw life-energy—unadulterated,
undifferentiated.

'Abd Al-Haqq Sayf al-Ilm
The Nature of Man

I WAS BORN ON THE 9TH SEPTEMBER 1920 in a nursing home near Worcester, some ten miles or more away from the farm, at l0.30 p.m. It was a leap year—a lucky circumstance. Afterwards, my mother returned to the farm. Also, mine was a unique birth in that I was born with a caul, an extra layer of thin foetal membrane covering the head of a baby at birth. Sailors used to pay good money for cauls, as they were supposed to be lucky as they protected them from drowning. My mother sold mine for £25—a lot of money when I was born!

The first two to three years of my life were spent on the farm. I was walking at nine months and caused much consternation. I am told I would often escape to the orchards to gather apples or cherries or plums from the ground. Mother said that one day I bit into an apple where a wasp was busily feeding, which gave me a nasty sting on my tongue, and in order to make me feel better, grandfather had taken me to feed the chickens. This opened up an exciting new world for me. Once I saw a mother hen and seven little chicks in the hollow by a hedge, much to my delight and grandfather's pride, especially when the mother hen walked up to grandfather, followed by her brood of seven little fluffy yellow chicks. The hen was making all kinds of clucking noises, which I tried to mimic. Grandfather made a hencoop for them and it was my pride and joy to help grandfather feed the mother hen and her chicks and to watch them grow. Grandfather would move the coop nearly every week to give the hen and her chicks fresh feeding-ground. They loved pecking at the new grass.

Often grandfather found what he called a broody hen. Then he took a square of turf he called a 'sod', and placed it under the broody hen with several eggs, which he had stolen from other laying hens. Sometimes one of these broody hens would hatch those eggs, but at other times they rejected them.

Grandfather had two dogs and grandmother had three cats. The dogs were too big for me and grandfather would call them off, but I loved the cats. One day I found one cat with four little kittens. Grandmother would not let me keep the kittens; she said she had too many cats already. She told me that she was going to give them away, but I knew this was a big fib, because I peeped through the curtains and saw grandfather putting them all in a pail of water. When I went to bed that night and while grandmother was helping me say my prayers as we came to the part to forgive our trespasses, I said, "Forgive gran'f'her for putting all the kittens into the pail of water so they couldn't breaf." Grandmother forgot to say the rest of the prayers and hastily kissed me good night!

When I was well over two years my grandfather would let me help him collect the eggs. I remember, very vividly early in the morning being awakened by grandfather, who would throw a pebble against my window to tell me he was off to feed the hens. I dashed out of bed, putting on my clothes in a higgledy-piggledy way as I ran down the stairs to find him. He was in the corn shed mixing food for the hens from the three corn bins. He would tie my shoelaces and ruffle my hair. Then he would hand me a small pail of hen food and off we would go, all around the farm calling to the hens. Grandfather would throw the food about as he called to them and I, of course, did the same, only I couldn't make the hen noises that grandfather made, however hard I tried.

In the late afternoon I loved taking the eggs that grandfather and I had collected to the dairy. There were various egg bowls, into which the eggs were placed, according to size. As I stepped down into the cellar room I saw large wide shelves everywhere. The stone steps were very uneven and grandfather always held my hand.

The cellar was strictly grandmother's domain. There were rows and rows of bowls that held milk, on the top of which the cream was settling—whilst other bowls of milk were for cheese making. They had white muslin covers over them with little beads at their edges to hold them over the bowls. Some bowls had milk in them for making butter; these were kept separately. Under the main shelf in the dairy, grandmother kept a white bucket containing button mushrooms, soaking in a special concoction of spice and vinegar. Beyond this bucket were enormous great jars in which hams were soaking in a preserving mixture of brine, raisins and nutmeg—the family recipe. I learned much later that the brine had to be turned over the hams every day, but never by a woman if she had her period. It was simply considered to be enough to turn the hams off!

In another corner of the dairy over a side shelf, huge muslin bags were hanging on large hooks that had been driven into the ceiling. These muslin bags contained the cheeses that were grandmother's pride, for she was considered to make the best cheeses in the Worcester market. The whey from the cheese was collected in a bowl beneath the bag. Grandmother used this whey to make delicious scones, which had raisins and peel in them. Sometimes she put cheese into them instead, especially for grandfather, who loved cheese scones. Often she took several dozen scones to the market, to give them away to storekeepers. In one corner of the largest dairy slab, jugs were standing, filled with fresh milk covered with muslin, edged with beads. Grandmother used to make these muslin-edged bead covers. I helped her by passing the beads to her, while grandfather would tell my sister and me a story before we went to bed.

Often I helped my grandmother churn the butter, which she did in another adjoining cellar. Grandfather would put the milk that had been kept separately into a large butter churn. Grandmother closed the lid and then began turning the handle at the side of the barrel, causing the barrel's contents to turn over and over. The continual movement eventually separated the whey from the butter. It always seemed to take a long time before we heard the plopping sound inside the churn, which grandmother said was the butter beginning to form. She added that it would soon be ready. I was allowed to turn the handle of the butter churn sometimes, but mostly grandmother took charge. When the butter was ready grandmother took the butter from the churn with two large butter pats and placed it into a very large bowl. She then poured all the buttermilk left over from the butter making into jugs from a tap at the side of the barrel. She added a small amount of salt to her butter, which she had placed in the big bowl. Then with a large wooden spoon she would stir and press the salt into the butter. It was at this time that I was always allowed to drink a glass of buttermilk, which I loved.

Grandmother lifted another pair of smaller wooden butter pats off the shelf from a jar of cold water. She then cut off a slice of butter from the huge lump with her butter pats and began patting the separated butter into a square. Then she weighed the square, which usually made up to a pound. If there were too much or too little in the square, she would add or take away accordingly with her butter pats, until the correct weight was achieved. Grandmother was nearly always accurate in her judgement, and seldom had to change the amount. She would then place the butter square onto some greaseproof paper, and after wrapping up the butter in a special way, she finally placed the packet into a basket marked 'butter'. The leftovers from the pounds of butter and the buttermilk were taken into the dairy ready for our use. The butter in the basket was for the market, which she kept cool in the dairy.

I remember my grandmother distinctly. She was of regal appearance, her dark hair swept up into a bun at the nape of her neck. She was gracious and kindly, albeit very severe-looking. Her most remarkable feature was her beautiful skin, more often than not highlighted by the softest pink colouring on her cheeks, which was both startling and attractive. She had a well-formed oval face with lovely bright blue eyes that could pierce you with a haughty disapproving look or be madly mischievous. She always wore high-necked blouses with a cameo brooch. Her aprons were worn with such elegance that they accentuated her slender waist and comely figure. She was totally committed to my grandfather, and ran the farmhouse as efficiently as she did her marketing ventures.

I never got tired of hearing my grandfather proudly recall an event one Sunday, which took place close to their local church. With ritualistic regularity my grandfather would walk my grandmother to church from the farm every Sunday, both dressed in their Sunday best—particular fashion, which in those days in the late nineteenth and early twentieth century still remained a token of respect for the Sabbath, and a custom obeyed by all who attended Church. The Church was almost a mile away from the farmhouse.

"One Sunday," my grandfather would begin in his accustomed manner, proudly eyeing his wife as she sat by the range fire mending his socks, "your grandmother and I were walking to Church as was our custom. She held my arm as I escorted her proudly along the country lane. A man passing by turned to his lady companion saying, in a loud derogatory tone of disapproval: 'Painted! By God!' "

Without the slightest hesitation, grandfather had raised his hat and turned to face the gentleman. Politely but firmly he said in a very loud voice, loaded with pride, "Indeed, sir, she *was* painted by God!" Giving my grandmother a roguish look, my grandfather would continue: "After this episode, your grandmother's high colour became the talk of the village, for indeed she is a very beautiful woman."

On market days my grandmother would take my sister and me in her pony and trap to sell her eggs, milk, butter and cheese. On those occasions my sister and I would be made to wear, beneath our dresses, long frilly knickers, which was the fashion. I tried constantly to pull up my knickers, because I found them very bothersome round my legs, but my sister did not seem to mind the fashion. Our bonnets were tied under our chins and our dresses were beautifully ironed. It was very exciting riding in a pony and trap with grandmother going to the market. But I was never allowed to hold the reins however many times I begged grandmother to let me. She would always firmly say 'No!' and that would be the end of it. When we started off, she would call, 'Gee up!' as she jerked the reins, and grandfather would give the pony's backside a slap that sent her trotting down the farm track to the bye-road, which in those days was hardly more than a narrow country lane with little or no traffic.

The Worcester market place was crowded with stalls of all kinds and descriptions. I remember my grandmother unloading the baskets of butter and cheese, and the bottles of milk and baskets of eggs from the pony carriage onto a broad trestle table, which she had covered with a spotless white tablecloth. After unloading all the goods, grandmother would take off the pony's bridle to free her from her harness and the carriage. At one end of the village green there was a trough of water for the ponies and horses. When the pony had enough water grandmother would tether her to a post where she happily grazed until we were ready to return home to the farm.

There were so many stalls, most of which held some sort of home produce. Some stalls had articles such as homemade rugs or wood containers for logs. Everyone would be busy unpacking their goods onto their tables and arranging them to look attractive. Grandmother would place the scones she had brought onto a plate and allow my sister to take them round to the storekeepers near our stand, and in exchange grandmother would receive a cup of tea, which my sister would carefully carry back to her. The men would raise their caps and smile there thanks to my grandmother, and the women would bob a curtsy. Grandmother would allow us to drink the apple juice we were offered and take some of the homemade sweets.

Sometimes grandmother would bring some of grandfather's homemade cider, which did not last very long on the stall—they soon sold out. It was exciting being at the fair and everyone seemed happy. Some stores held fresh flowers, others sweetmeats, cakes, pies and freshly baked bread; while other stores had all kinds of cooking utensils and farm pails, jangling on hooks, under which were cups and saucers, plates and dishes. There were all kinds of clothes and towels hanging in rows, jumpers and underwear were laid neatly on the top of the trestle tables, while other stalls sold bedding, linen and sheets. There was a large vegetable stall, next door to ours that was always busy. Turnips, cabbages, cauliflowers, potatoes, carrots, onions, lettuces and beetroots were piled up on the table in baskets, next to many other vegetables. I remember this store well, it was owned by a farmer with very red cheeks and bright blue eyes, like my grandmother's.

Sometimes a potato would roll off the pile on his table, and I would scramble down over the grass to pick it up. The farmer would always swop it for an apple or plum for helping him as he smiled at my grandmother.

The stall keepers kept very strictly to their own wares. Grandmother's stall was near the cake and bread stand, so she never sold her scones. Grandmother was always greeted kindly by her fellow stall-keepers, who would often give my sister and me a homemade sandwich or a small cake with icing on top. The noise and commotion thrilled me—everybody with a stand was shouting his or her wares. But grandmother never shouted, she didn't have to, as everyone crowded around to buy her eggs, butter, milk and cheese. There was also a large stand, where you could buy homemade sweetmeats and meat pies, tea, sandwiches, and glasses of fresh milk.

The trip back to the farm was just as exciting. The farmer next to our stall always helped grandmother to harness the pony to the carriage. Soon we were all packed up and away we'd go. On the way home grandmother would sing to us and we'd try to join in. The pony would trot along, pleased to be going home to her stable. When we arrived home grandfather was always there to greet us. But we were tired and glad to see mother again for we were already nearly asleep!

Grandfather's speciality was his cider. He would collect from the orchard huge mountains of apples, and place them in the yard onto a stone slab surrounded by a wooden frame. Then when the apples were decayed enough he would take off his shoes and socks and pull up his trouser legs and start pressing the apples. In no time at all, I was in beside him, having pulled off my shoes and socks and stuffed my dress into my knickers. We had lots of fun treading the rotting apples the juice would run in channels into large tubs sunk into the shed, where grandfather made his cider.

Many years after we left the farm, when we came to visit our grandparents, grandfather asked me to run down into the cellar and draw him off a jug of cider. I had watched him so many times before, turning the tap and knocking the top, so I knew just what to do. But he would never let me have a taste when he drew the cider. On this particular day, I was just about six or seven years old, I remember so well running down the steps of the cellar in great glee to the barrel of cider. Of course I had a good drink of the cider. After all the apple pressing, I was curious to know what cider really tasted like. After another good cup full, it was not long before I was sound asleep and I remembered no more until I woke up in my bed.

My mother found it increasingly difficult to manage on the farm with two young children and longed for a home of her own. It had been helpful to father to feel mother was being cared for by his parents while he was setting up his business. But the time had come to find mother a home of her own. However, houses were not easy to come by, father was lucky to lease a cottage on a farm in Saffron Walden, so we moved into our new home just before my brother Charles was born.

The cottage at Saffron Walden was a great joy to my mother after living on the farm. It was conveniently located near a railway, although in the midst of the country. It was much easier for mother to manage and it had all modern conveniences, which pleased her. But she was especially pleased, as father was able to come home every night.

Chapter Three

Growing up

"The time has come," the Walrus said,
"To talk of many things:
Of shoes—and ships—and sealing wax—
Of cabbages and kings—
And why the sea is boiling hot—
And whether pigs have wings."

Lewis Carroll
Through the Looking-Glass

AFTER WE MOVED into our new home, there was great excitement for my sister and me. We had a large garden to explore and a railway close at hand to watch the infrequent trains go by. But in our new home there were loos with pull chains, and running water and gas lighting. Mother was in her element. I remember that she used to  light the gaslights with long tapers as soon as it was getting dark. It was much brighter than the oil lamps at the farm. Father would come home every night and mother seemed much happier.

If I awoke crying in the middle of the night, I soon found my father close beside me asking me what was the matter. On most occasions I sobbed 'that my leggies ached'. Then I remember that my father spat on his hands and rubbed my legs, saying that would make me all better. I did not like him putting spit on to his hands and then rubbing it into my aching legs, but I was sure I really felt better as he settled me down into bed and kissed me good night. I remember hiding my face in shame on his shoulder, because I did not like his spit on my legs. Nevertheless I felt the comfort and reassurance that he was there when I needed him. I remember burying my face into my bedclothes after father had gone, and silently crying myself to sleep.

As a very small child, I knew, too, that I could see people others could not see, and hear music others did not hear. If I mentioned it, I was told I had a good imagination, which as I look back I am sure was true, although that did not stop me believing that I saw these people and heard their music, for I felt a strong connection with what was unseen. What it really meant I did not know, but to me it was very real. Those far-off days of my childhood still hold a magic memory for me.

Sometimes mother would take us into the nearest market town to shop. Whenever mother went shopping we always went by train, just one stop away. I remember my mother running up the side of the bank and waving frantically to the Station Master to hold up the train. She would be carrying our brother and dragging a pushchair, while my sister and I trailed behind. The Station Master would greet mother in a most respectful manner, in spite of the fact that he nearly always had to hold up the train for us. Mother was very beautiful, her long auburn gingery hair held in a neat bun at the nape of her neck, her red cheeks and large brown eyes caught the station master's eye as he bustled her and her brood into the carriage, touching his hat before blowing his whistle. Then away we'd go.

It was at Saffron Walden that I had some of my most vivid recollections. I remember we were never allowed to go near the duck pond close to the farm up the lane. Apparently, the year before, the farmer's only daughter aged 18 months had drowned in the duck pond. We were told that the little girl had wandered away from the farmhouse and had fallen face downwards into the pond and could not get out again. The tragedy was not discovered until it was too late. The horror of such a tale caught my imagination and made a great impression on me. Thereafter, I was very protective of my little brother, who had been born after we had moved into our new home.

I recollect that the cottage had a long garden and there were lots of hedgehogs. We use to poke these hedgehogs with a stick to make them curl into balls, and then we'd push them with the stick all the way down the hill. They were so prickly that you could not touch them. There were always plenty of play areas in the garden and we were safe enough from harm, or so my mother thought, until one day the milkman arrived and left the garden gate wide open while he delivered milk at our back door. His pony was grazing outside the garden gates where he had left her, but I suppose the pony must have thought that the grass looked greener on the other side of the gate because she pushed her way through our gate into the garden driveway dragging the cart after her. She munched the grass greedily. I eyed the pony with curiosity. Being afraid of nothing, I advanced toward her, but unfortunately, I got in the way of her legs, and in her fright she kicked out, luckily only grazing my head with her hoof. But it gave the milkman an awful fright to hear my cries. Mother came rushing up calling to the milkman to take his horse and cart out of her garden. She gathered me up in her arms, frightened to see the blood pouring down my face. The doctor soon put some stitches in my head and said what a lucky girl I was not to have been killed by the pony.

One night my father came home early bringing a puppy in his pocket. We were all in the bath. My father suddenly opened the door and stood looking mischievously at the scene that met his eyes. Mother was kneeling beside the bath, all splattered with soap, washing a bath full of babies! Father suddenly pulled out a wee puppy from his pocket and to our squeals of delight and mother's utter horror put it in the bath. With, "Oh Charlie, how could you?" Mother grabbed the puppy, indignantly giving the wet little chap back to father who promptly put it on the floor, not wishing to get wet. Soon we were all out of the bath trying to get hold of the puppy that just kept shaking the water off its coat. My mother cried, "Oh Charlie, what a mess you've made!" as she gathered up the youngest in a towel, giving up the unequal struggle against my mischievous father. I just adored this little doggie. We called him Bonso. We had enormous fun with him in the garden. Unfortunately, one day I was running up the garden path calling 'Bonso!' without looking where I was going, and tripped and fell over a stone, catching my head on a rock. I remember the doctor stitching my head up, only because I was proud of the fact that the stitches were put in on my mother and father's bed!

At Christmas time father dressed up as Santa Claus. He did all his preparations away from the cottage in an outhouse, down at the farm. He would come up to my mother as he arrived at the front door with a sack over his shoulder and a red cloak covering his body and in a loud Santa Claus voice would say: "Well mother, have they been good children?" All our little faces would turn anxiously to mother waiting for her reply. "Well, on the whole, yes, they have been good children," said my mother as she gently stroked her youngest child's head, who had climbed onto her knee for protection against the funny man dressed in such a large red cloak and tall red hat edged with white, and wearing huge boots. Santa Claus would then open his sack to give each one of us a present.

After the excitement had died down and we had all been given our presents Santa Claus would say rather hurriedly, "I must away now, I have hundreds of other children who are waiting for me." We waved him goodbye through the window until he was out of sight down the driveway. My sister always asked mother why daddy was not with us, because she said she did not like him missing Santa Claus or his present!

It is funny how one associates happenings with places. It was here that I had my first experience of a violent thunderstorm. I remember so well how frightened I was. We all got into mother and father's bed. Afterwards the villagers blamed my mother for the storm, because the day before mother had driven our Wolseley car all the way to Southampton to meet my father off the Cunard Liner from America. The car had a roof that opened up, which mother always left open, unless it was raining. She was very proud to drive, as very few women drove cars in those days. Father had arrived from America after attending a business conference. Our Aunt Maggie, mother's sister, was looking after us, so that mother could fetch father. Mother was pregnant at the time with my brother John and was near her time. She told us she could hardly get into the car or out of it! Cars in those days did not have reclining or adjustable seats and it was all that she could manage to squeeze herself between the front seat of the car and the steering wheel.

Cars were only just coming into fashion, and they were still very unusual to be seen in such a small village, especially driven by a pregnant woman. The villagers considered it quite indecent for mother to drive at all, particularly in her condition! They blamed the dreadful thunderstorm that had done so much damage to the countryside entirely on mother driving our car!

We were always having adventures with mother. One day in the summer I saw a man coming up the driveway to our front door. I ran to tell mother. In those early years after the war there was a great deal of unemployment and poverty. The man had been in the army. He asked my mother if she had a photograph that she would like to have enlarged or painted, as he was an artist. He added that he and his family were starving. My mother knew that father had a small treasured photograph of his mother in a frame by his bedside. Wanting to please father and at the same time to justify her own emotions at beholding such poverty, she passed the photograph in the frame to the man, who promised to bring it back to her the very next day.

Mother remained in agony of suspense, as two days passed with no return of the supposed artist and knowing what the photograph meant to father; mother was beside herself with worry. She did not dare to tell father what she had done. After three days, mother said, the man returned with the photograph and a large painting of grandmother. Mother was so relieved and pleased that she gave the man much more money than he had asked for. I can still see the surprised look on the man's face and the tears in his eyes as he thanked her profusely, bidding my mother a 'Good day!' Father, needless to say, was totally delighted. My father left the painting to me at his death.

Sometime after this episode mother told us that on one dark night, she had made father bury a duck in the garden. It transpired that mother had thought that the duck, which had been given to her by the farmer, needed hanging like a game bird. After a while she discovered to her horror that the duck was crawling with maggots. She immediately asked father to take it away. Reluctantly father buried the duck in the garden, unaware that a nosy neighbour had witnessed the scene. To my father's horror and mother's consternation, before very long the entire village was gossiping about father burying one of his children in the garden!

During the next few years we moved houses several times. Usually it was mother who coped with moving, as father was always busy. The next house that I remember was somewhere in Surrey. It was, I felt at the time, an enormous house, but when I revisited it again, years later, I found it was very much smaller than I had remembered! The house was close by the river and my mother always felt the house was damp. Those early years in the late 1920s were very unsettling times in Great Britain, which continued all through the early 1930s, when our parents would talk in hushed whispers about the slump. Father still had his own business, which eventually developed into a paint-manufacturing company.

Mother believed in having her children whilst she was still young, thus they tumbled out and before long she had four children under the age of four years. It was a blessing in many ways, as garments could be handed down from one child to another. Needless to say, my sister and I were taught the art of motherhood at a very tender age.

We grew up lacking nothing. In fact, years later, I remember our cook and maid of all works saying that 'we slipped on butter and swam in milk'. My mother had absolutely no idea of money, although she could spend it with an ease that was tantamount to extravagance; at least my father thought so when the monthly bills were presented to him, causing him many headaches.

Mother never seemed to think she was extravagant and would say, "Well, Charlie, you would have a large family!"—as if it had absolutely nothing to do with her. She would add quite unconcernedly with the sweetest smile, "Besides, it always pays in the end to get the best." She would say it in such a way that my poor long suffering father gave up instantly and paid all the bills with no further reprimand. My mother knew how to discipline her children but she could not manage to transfer this effective principle onto herself or her buying habits. As children we adored our mother, for she took us into all kinds of adventures.

Nothing pleased my mother more than our half-yearly visits to the Great Metropolis. London in those days did not have the traffic problems that we have today. Mother drove father's Wolseley up to London with the greatest of ease. Indeed, she drove it almost as soon as father had bought it, imagining it was entirely for her benefit and practically before father had time to try it out for himself. In those days you did not need to pass a driving test. Perhaps that was just as well, because mother would always say to us in gay abandon during our visits to London, "Keep a sharp look out for Bobbies!" as Policemen were called in those days. A bobby was short for 'Sir Robert Peel's boys in blue.' At Christmas time we would be taken to London to see Father Christmas. By then mother had another child on the way.

Mother chose Oxford Street to do her shopping. She held the little boys by their hands and kept a sharp look out for my sister and me, who were made to hold hands as we trailed hurriedly behind her. We dodged people right and left in order not to lose sight of mother. When we took the underground to Oxford Circus we had to go up a moving staircase. This definitely frightened me.

At the bottom of the moving staircase I positively refused to put one foot onto it. My sister had managed very well and had nearly caught up with my mother, who was holding on to her two little boys. She was powerless to do anything about her troublesome daughter who refused to get on the moving staircase. Mother was being taken further and further away from me, and by now I was screaming and my mother was distraught. She shouted for help, and drew attention from all sides by her state of alarm. Several people tried to lift me up, but I was in such a frightened state that I held my ground, refusing to move. Suddenly a kindly gentleman, seeing my mother's dilemma, swept me bodily off my feet before I could protest any further. He talked to me all the way up to the top of the moving staircase. I remember this man had a long beard with sidewhiskers and a pronounced voice of kindness, soothing all my fears away with his tale about his dog Squeaky. I was sent into raptures as I clung closely to him. When we got to the top of the moving staircase, I remember I did not want to let him go, and hung onto him with all my might, much to my mother's dismay. She had by now recovered herself and was giving the gentleman one of her flustered looks. He swept his cap from his head, after putting me down, laughing at my mother's confusion. In no time at all, he had disappeared.

Something always caught my mother's eye on those trips. On one occasion she bought one of the first Hoovers on the market; positively no one in my mother's neighbourhood had such a cleaning contraption that ran off electricity. Naturally my mother bought it and of course it was put onto her account; something she avoided telling father until the monthly session of accounts came up! I remember how proud she was when it eventually arrived by carrier. The whole house was immaculate when father came home. The same thing occurred when she bought her first washing machine, when they came onto the market. Positively everything washable went through the stages of being cleansed in the wonder washer. In those days a separate dryer had to be purchased. Nothing daunted, my mother had that article lined up for her next trip to London. She tried to convince father she had saved up for it, but my poor long-suffering father knew differently and would only nod his head despairingly.

He had learned his lesson years ago, when my mother had her first son. She positively refused to get up from her bed after his birth. In those days normal births usually occurred at home. She cried so hard that father begged her to tell him if anything was seriously wrong. However, he knew that nothing really intimidated my mother. With immaculate timing, and between loud sobs, she confided in father the reason for her unhappy state by pulling from beneath her pillow, one at a time, the many bills she had collected and hidden away from him. By now she was sobbing in real earnest, handing the bills reluctantly over to father. By this time father, who was nearly beside himself trying to cope with two young children and a new-born baby, barely gave the pile of bills a glance, pausing only to ejaculate nervously, "Is that all, Edith?" My mother, with a heart-rending sob, pulled out the last bill, which naturally was the worst, as she eyed father nervously from her pillow over heaving sobs. "I'll take care of these," said father magnanimously. With a huge sigh of relief, my mother, to father's utter astonishment, immediately climbed out of bed to cope with her new-born baby and her two other children. Nothing more was ever mentioned about the pile of bills!

My memories of *Pentyre*, Broxbourne, where we moved next, remain vividly in my mind. I can distinctly recall an occasion when we had recently returned from holiday, and my little brother John had come in from the garden. He crept up to mother shouting gleefully, "Which hand mummy?" his roguish smile portraying his intent. I am sure my mother thought he was up to something. He was such a tease. After a few playful moments my mother pointed to his right hand, never guessing what he held in his chubby little hands. John could hardly contain himself as he jumped up and down, at last producing handfuls of baby frogs! With cries of, "Oh, Johnnie, take them away quick, please!" Mother covered her head with her apron, while John mischievously tried to place them on mother's lap. But father stopped him just in time, chasing him back into the garden together with his frogs!

Oftentimes, I remember, John would sit on the big gatepost in front of our house. How he climbed onto it nobody knew, but early every morning all kinds of people on their way to work would stop and say, "Good morning I's John, and how are you today?" He had collected this name 'I's John' after people had asked him what his name was and he had replied, "I's John!" He was a lovely little boy with freckles all over his face, especially around his dear little snub nose. Crowned by a mop of ginger curly hair and the most roguish smile, he soon became the pet of the street and would come into the house with many a present.

Another recollection I have is when I used to play with a little girl, whom nobody else seemed to see, at the bottom of the garden. She was about my own age, with golden curls down to her waist and a funny-looking apron over her dress. Her clear blue eyes matched her faultless skin. We used to play for hours together, especially with the red mud that was a part of the vegetable garden. When our old gardener offered me some sweets, I'd say, "Please let Jane have some too!" But the gardener would look all around him, asking where was Jane, in spite of the fact that I knew she was standing right beside me. In the end, as I persisted, he shook his old head and gave me some more sweets for Jane. I never did understand, until years later, why he never saw Jane.

There were four other occasions I remember very well after we moved into *Pentyre*, Broxbourne. The first was May 14th 1926. We were all waiting in the hallway for the doctor to arrive. Suddenly there was a loud Rat-tat-tat-tat on the front door. We stood rigidly together as the maid opened the door. The doctor had arrived with his little bag. He ran past us all, laughing, telling us he would shortly have a surprise for us. He ran up the stairs two at a time to mother's bedroom, where we were not allowed to follow, which troubled us very much. After what seemed ages, the doctor came down the stairs to say we had a new baby brother. This must have made a great impression on me, for one day much later, when we were all betting each other how far we could remember back, I called out that I could remember being swung in the doctor's bag to keep me quiet before he took me up to Mother's bedroom!

Another memory, which was not so pleasant, occurred when my sister and I had taken my baby brother Edward in his pram for a walk along the riverbank. My sister made me hold on to the side of the pram. Suddenly she became aware that a man was following us, which frightened her. She immediately commanded me not to look round, which of course I did. This considerably upset my sister, who was by now running as I held on to the pram. Eventually the man caught up with us and started suggesting 'rude' things to my sister. She was only about seven or eight years old, but for all that, she kept her head and began running hard for the gate, warning me to hurry. We were both very frightened, but arrived home without mishap. When we told mother she was horrified and called the police immediately. My father arrived home just at that moment, and I remember being taken with my sister and father in the police car to see if we could spot the man. Needless to say we never found him. We were never allowed out alone again.

My sister and I slept on the top floor in the room next door to our Irish cook. Many a night I used to see a large figure with a cowl over his head, leaning over my bed. My recollections are that it felt as if my head was expanding, getting larger and larger, until eventually I was looking at my body far below me. Apparently, I would sleepwalk down the stairs and mother, who was a light sleeper, would hear me and be ready at the bottom of the stairs to catch me in case I hurt myself. I never woke up, and mother would bring me back to bed. After repeated episodes mother says she put a night light in our room, which seemed to put an end to my sleepwalking. I learned years later when I visited Broxbourne that our terraced house had been the site of an old monastery.

Yet another memory stands out very vividly. My mother had been opening one of the windows in the basement when the window cord snapped, trapping her fingers in between the two frames of the window. In agony she called to people passing by, but they did not hear her. She turned to me and told me to run upstairs and open the front door and call for help. But I was so horrified that I was rooted to the spot and could not move. Eventually my poor mother coaxed me by saying she would soon be all right, if only I would call for help. I ran upstairs, and with great difficulty opened the front door, calling for help to a man passing by. He came immediately. Unfortunately, he pulled the frame of the window the wrong way, to screams from my mother. When it was all over and the doctor had gone, I remember, I clung to her in terrified silence.

We used to attend a small school a little way away from Broxbourne called Bolt School, close to Hoddesdon Village. To reach this little school we had to go by way of Holly Walk, so called because holly hedges lined the route on either side. We often pulled leaves off the trees and would point to the sharp prickly edges of the leaves saying, "Will we be late for School? Yes, no, yes, no." until we had covered all the prickly spikes on the leaves. If it ended in 'yes' we'd run all the way to the end of the walk. If it ended in 'no' we would just dawdle. At the end of Holly Walk there was always an old soldier, with a wooden leg, who sat by the gate. He would pull the gate open with a long thick piece of string as we came near to the gate, then he would say, "Hurry up, or you'll be late for school!" We'd sometimes put a farthing in his cap if we had one.

Bolt School, which was only round the corner from Holly Walk, was run by a middle-aged teacher with a bun at the back of her neck and pince-nez glasses on the end of her nose. I remember learning a lot from her. She taught us French by pointing her stick to a poster that she placed over the blackboard. The poster was in French and there were all kinds of figures on it, plus kitchen utensils and farmyard animals. She would point with her stick to the gentleman with a slight stoop and say, "Qui est-ce que c'est?" We would all shout, "Le Grand-père!" I can still see her face full of delight when we got it right. That takes me back a good many years.

The next move we made caused great excitement. My parents had bought a most beautiful house on the Essex Estate, near the old stables that once belonged to a large mansion, outside the new town of Watford. Much of the country estate, with its extensive parklands, contained many old rare trees. Part of it extended to the Grand Union Canal, which had been purchased by the Watford County Council and renamed Cassiobury Park. It had been made into a recreational area for the town and thus many of the magnificent trees were preserved. Property developers had bought the rest of the estate. I was told that the Earl of Essex was unable to meet the heavy death duties, which forced him to sell his beautiful heritage.

It was true that my parents needed a larger house to accommodate their growing family, now numbering five children, together with our cook and a maid. The house stood in its own grounds of about an acre, well back from the road—not far from the Essex stable buildings. Later, father established a tennis court, vegetable garden, and a long rose garden. The property contained four magnificent trees that were originally a part of the Essex Estate. Next to the house was a garage and behind it was a yard, which had a drain in the centre for washing the car. Our new home was mother's delight and appropriately called Essex Lodge.

The house had been especially built for an elderly lady, who wanted a Tudor style design. Oak beams covered all the downstairs ceilings, and there was parquet flooring throughout, with oak panelling three quarters of the way up the walls. The old lady had personally supervised the construction of the house stage by stage. On the ground floor there were three large reception rooms, a large kitchen with a boiler for the hot water system. There was a smaller kitchen area for cooking and washing-up. Beyond this was a boiler house for the central heating, a back loo, and a large coal shed. By the greenhouse, adjacent to the back of the house, was the open-sided sun porch that led from the morning room into the garden. From this sun porch one had a good view of the huge Mountain Hemlock, with its large sweeping branches that in places touched the ground. Father had a neatly constructed nine-hole putting green placed around the old tree, and propped up all the branches with stout wooden stakes.

From the kitchen there was an oak door that led into a large dining room, which had a double bay window that held diamond-shaped leaded panes of glass. A special oak seat had been constructed to fit all around the base of the bay window, concealing central heating radiators. It was one of my favourite escape areas, for I could conceal myself in the corner behind the velvet curtains to read my weekly *Girl's Own* magazines. The comfy red velvet cushions matched the curtains, so it was an ideal spot to hide from mother who was always calling me to help her with one thing or another. I would stay as quiet as a mouse whenever she called.

Another door from the dining room entered the lounge. It was in here that our grandfather clock took pride of place. It chimed cheerfully every quarter of an hour. From the other side of the room there was a door that entered into the morning room. A glass-panelled door led from the lounge which mother called the drawing room. There was a cloakroom in the hallway on the left as you entered the front door. The oak-panelled staircase to the right of the front door led upstairs, where there were five bedrooms off a landing. There was a spacious bathroom with exciting tiles covering the walls. A large linen cupboard lined the corridor next to a front bedroom where my sister and I slept. There were basins in all bedrooms—a truly luxurious house by comparison to our former homes—extremely modern for the 1930s, with its built-in central heating and internal water pipes.

As I look back on those far-off days, I realise we were very lucky in so many ways, especially having such caring parents. Mother's mother lived with us. I recall vividly how much I adored my granny and being the only one at home while I was waiting for a space to become vacant at the boarding-school where my sister was, I got to know my granny much better than the rest of the family did. We often chatted about this and that. She had no one to talk to except my parents, who were always too busy to have much time for her.

Mother decided that granny looked best in purple, as her hair was snow-white. After she came to live with us, a dressmaker was called to make new clothes for her. I always thought she looked beautiful, except that she had only one eye. She had to take her false eye out at nights, and it was my job to fetch it from the bathroom every morning. Only once did I peep under the lid of the container in which the glass eye rested. I never did that again as I did not like the eye staring up at me.

Granny's tales intrigued me, for she always had a story for a good listener with a vivid imagination like myself, particularly as her stories transported me into another intriguing era. Granny had married a widower with four children and then had had six children of her own. She was born in the 1800s, and her early childhood had been spent in London within the sound of the Bow Bells. At that time there were only horses and carriages to take people from

Grandmother.

one place to another. Street hawkers would shout their wares. Men with organ grinders would sharpen knives. Beggars and pickpocket thieves robbed unsuspecting people. Roads in some areas were unclean and prostitutes roamed the streets openly at night. All of them, granny would say, had stories to tell.

One of granny's tales was so unusual that it remained vividly in my mind. Through one of the coachmen, who had once lodged with her parents, granny had got to know an old woman who had once been a 'flower girl'. She could not remember her name, but said that she had had a very strange story. It transpired that this flower girl had once had a flower stand at the corner of Leicester Square, quite close to where granny used to live as a little girl. When this flower girl was only seventeen, she had been working for her Auntie and Uncle, who had a flower stand off Covent Garden. One day they had a bad accident and were both killed. Through no fault of her own, the flower girl found herself caught by the bad debts left behind by the aunt and uncle, which her uncle's creditors said she was responsible for, as she was looking after the flower stand. No one in her family was able to help her to redeem the debt, so she was seized by the creditors and thrown into the dreaded Newgate debtors' prison.

The authorities had no respect for persons who incurred debts. It did not matter which class they came from, they were all treated in much the same way. They were thrown into a large filthy prison cell, infested with lice and rats. It so happened that the flower girl found herself next to a real gentleman, strangely enough in much the same predicament as herself; or at least that was his story. He looked so ill and was obviously in need of medical help. His illness caused the flower girl such concern that she called the guard, who reluctantly pulled the shutter open.

He asked her roughly what was the matter. On being told that the gentleman was ill, the guard promptly closed the shutter and nothing more was forthcoming. All night the flower girl cradled the sick man's head in her lap, covering him with her shawl. The following day the door of the jail was thrown open, a tall well-dressed gentleman, holding a kerchief to his nose to avoid the stench, stood in the doorway looking around as if searching for someone. Suddenly the gentleman next to the flower girl called weakly, "Hello, Michael!" Michael turned sharply, stepped quickly to his side, and began pulling him to his feet. As Michael hurried him out of the door, the sick man asked the flower girl her name, then supported by Michael, he walked unsteadily through the prison door, which closed immediately with a bang.

Two days later the door of the prison swung open once again. This time the jailer called the flower girl by name. He said to her, "You're lucky, yer debts 'ave been paid! Quick, make 'aste, away with yer!" And as she followed the gaoler to freedom, she discovered that it was the gentleman who had come for the sick man two days before who had paid her debts.

At the door of the prison the flower girl saw her benefactor. "Oh sir, I am very grateful to you for your 'elp!" she cried. With no more ado the gentleman told her to shut up and hastened to tell her he was expecting 'blood money' for getting her out of that hellhole. There was a carriage waiting by the curb, and she was unceremoniously pushed in, where she found herself confronted by the sick man from the prison. Michael ordered the coachman to take them to a certain destination and then sat down in the seat opposite the flower girl.

Michael spoke in hushed tones: "I expect you have been wondering what all this is about. Do not be frightened, we mean you no harm, but we need your help urgently. "This," pointing to the sick man, "...is James. He is in trouble and he is ill and needs a chaperone to escort him to friends in France. You are to act as his sister and take him to an address I will give you. I have bought you some new clothes, and I will take you to a coach house where you will be able to wash and change into them. Then you will come with us to Dover. I will pay you handsomely for your services. Will you agree?"

"Please sir, I have no choice," she replied, "I'm a good girl and wish nobody no 'arm, and I'll be glad to 'elp you, if you'll do me no 'arm!"

Michael hastened to reassure her and their bargain was clinched.

Soon, granny continued, the flower girl found herself standing next to the sick man dressed in her beautiful new clothes, which she had changed into at the coach house, having first had a good wash to get rid of the dirt and the lice. James and the flower girl now stood side by side leaning over the railings of a boat docked at Dover. They waved goodbye to Michael, who was leaning on his stick on the pier. They were bound for Calais, in France. Michael waved his kerchief with a relieved look on his face. The sick man had a reserved cabin and was soon sound asleep in bed. The flower girl sat by his side during the crossing, watching for any sign of relapse. He groaned several times and once shot up into a sitting position, crying in distress.

When they reached Calais, a coach and coachman were waiting for them by the quayside. The flower girl noticed that there was a crest in gold and blue on the side of the carriage door. Words in French highlighted the top of the crest, and there was a golden eagle entwined in a halo of blue and gold. Soon they were on their way. They travelled for the rest of that day and all through the night until the next morning, going far into the depths of the French countryside. They only made one or two stops for refreshment. At last they reached an enormous pair of wrought iron gates with two massive eagles in blue and gold over the top of two columns either side of the gates. The coachman jumped down and called loudly, "Open up for the Prince!" as he rang the bell. The gates were soon opened by a burly-looking man, the coach passed through the gates and the coachman whipped up the horses into a trot, bound for what looked like a huge castle in the far distance.

On arrival at the massive front door, the coachman jumped down and pulled on the huge bell handle, which hung beside the carved oak door that was enclosed in an open porch. The sound of the bell could be heard peeling through the building. The door swung open softly, a servant dressed in rich livery had obviously been expecting the visitor. Immediately he called to an attendant to help the sick man from the coach. The flower girl got out of the coach to assist the attendant, but the richly dressed attendant waved her back with a nod of his head saying, "We can manage your grace." Between them they proceeded to half carry James up the huge marble stairway, and that was the last the flower girl ever saw of him. The next moment she was being bustled back into the coach by another attendant, who placed a rug over her knees. Before she could utter a word a packet was placed into her hands by a lady gorgeously attired in the palest of blue with a magnificent Indian shawl around her shoulders. The glimpse, the flower girl had of her face made her gasp, for it was incredibly beautiful, although deathly pale. The lady whispered her thanks in broken English as the coach door was closed. The coachman saluted the lady as he climbed into the top seat. Soon the carriage was racing away at a breakneck speed, through the grounds of the castle in another direction from the one by which they had come, and away from the huge castle gates.

The flower girl noticed that they were taking twice as long to get out of the grounds of the castle. She began to feel nervous. At last they reached a gate, which was being held open by two rough-looking men. She caught a glimpse of one of the men, who eyed her in a strange manner. Then she opened the packet that had been given to her by the beautiful lady, and sat more comfortably on the cushions of the seat. Her name was written on the outside of the packet, in bold letters. In it she found a return ticket to England, and to her surprise and joy there was enclosed in an envelope five hundred guineas! "That is how," said granny, finishing her tale, "she was able to buy a flower stand at the corner of Leicester Square and become a flower girl of distinction, buying her flowers in Covent Garden at four in the morning and creating a good business for herself, which made her independent for life. She never found out, who the sick gentleman was or what sort of trouble he had managed to get himself into. Nor did she ever meet Michael again," concluded my granny quickly, before I could ask her any further questions.

My grandmother fell silent. "O granny!" I cried. "Have you another story like that one?"

"My dear child!" my grandmother replied, beaming with delight, because she could see that I loved her stories. "There are many tales I could tell you, but my poor old head cannot remember any more today." But like all grandmothers she liked to talk of her early years and I was a good listener. I found it so interesting to hear what happened when she was young.

One day, granny slipped on the highly polished parquet flooring at Essex Lodge and broke her wrist, which took a long time to mend. My mother would sit outside her bedroom as poor granny struggled to do up her corsets. She kept grumbling as she cried out, calling my mother a cruel daughter for not helping her. But it was my mother's way of making her use her wrist, and in later years granny had reason to be grateful.

When I was young I was always asking questions and saying 'Why?' but no one seemed to give me any satisfactory answers to my questions. However, I do remember an uncle who came to stay now and then, whom I regarded as definitely different from most grown-ups. He actually listened to my questions, for which I loved him. He did not tell me to stop bothering my head about such absurdities, at my time of life. Instead he would take my hand in his large one and suggest we walked as we talked. He had a slight limp and always carried a stick, which he would suddenly poke into the air as he exclaimed in a deep-throated tone, "Have you ever noticed that the cloud patterns are never quite the same, no matter how many times you suddenly remember to look up at them?" He would scratch his head and look at me with his large black eyes, wriggling his bushy eyebrows with such a quizzical look that I would stop and gaze at him, wondering if my eyebrows would ever grow as thick as his, and if so, if I would be able to wriggle them like my uncle.

Of course our family had the usual ups and downs like most families, though I remember my childhood days were mainly happy ones. On Sundays my parents took us to a special village church some distance from home. The reason this village church was chosen was simply because mother had heard that the parson was a free thinker. He certainly turned out to be a most tolerant one. My mother would shepherd us into our special pew, a little too near the front I always felt, and indicate our seats, which were hard and with no cushions, for there were only flat cushions for mother and father and my elder sister, Marguerite. My mother would send each of us a warning look, that plainly said, "Now, no nonsense!" as we arranged ourselves in the pew, all looking trim in our Sunday clothes.

When we reached the stage in the service for the sermon to begin, my father would always settle himself more comfortably on the flat cushion that rested on the hard pew. He would pay respectful attention at the beginning of the sermon, but soon sleep would take over and he would inevitably nod off. We children knew only too well what was coming next, and waited in frigid anticipation. Sure enough, very soon father snored loudly, completely oblivious of the stern reproving eye of the parson or the deadly hush from the congregation. We all smothered our giggles as mother sharply nudged my father into wakefulness.

These events continued more or less the same week after week, but father had no idea at the time why mother should nudge him so meaningfully, nor why we children, except for my elder sister, would be smothering our giggles. Indeed, he never appreciated the exact nature of the nudge from my flustered mother, until he caught sight of the parson's stony stare. Once the penny dropped, my father would glance sheepishly at my mother, reshuffle himself into a more attentive position, and stare at the parson as if nothing untoward had happened. All the while his expression would become more and more bewildered as he tried to follow the sermon, much of which he had missed. Nothing escaped our notice, for we were storing every particle of evidence with which to tease him on our way home.

Regularly my mother attacked my poor father unmercifully immediately we were out of range of the parson's hearing. She reprovingly said, "Charlie, how could you, and in front of the children too?" She never seemed to worry about the parson or the congregation, for they could hardly be counted; it was always 'just family' with my mother. My younger brother, John, who was the clown of the family, very soon imitated father's snores, and so realistically that we all burst out laughing. This put an abrupt end to mother castigating father, and she was soon laughing with all of us, all our pent-up feeling from sitting so long in church gave way to uncontrollable giggles. My little brother John, with his unruly, auburn-red head of beautiful curls, was a fine mimic. He would find fantastic ways of imitating the shocked congregation, using his dear little freckled face to make absurd contortions and all kinds of expressions, as he depicted the various horrified facial grimaces made by the congregation as they listened to father's snores.

First he was an old lady, then he was father snoring, then he was the old lady's shocked expression—all within seconds—with such expertly fast changing expressions that naturally our screams of laughter encouraged his imagination, until my mother begged him to stop as she was hurting herself with laughter. Father only managed a sheepish grin, until John suddenly remembered the stranger in the corner pew who had arrived in church that very day for the first time. He gave another realistic imitation. This time my father really had to laugh outright!

My mother was quite a taskmaster and disciplinarian, though I recollect that she never managed to discipline herself. I never recall hearing my father swear, for mother had very definite views about swearing. However, when father was exasperated he would curse by saying, "Christopher Daisy!" (Whoever that was) rather than use a swear word. Or he would say, with emphasis, "You children; get my goat!" None of us knew why it should be a goat and not a cow, but then father was very adaptable over his use of swear words to accommodate mother, who never minded his 'By Jove!' which would often express his feelings of delight, especially when the Christmas pudding came to the table all alight.

The Sunday ritual of religious learning continued after the lunch dishes had all been cleared away. Father would begin by asking us questions about what we thought of the parson's sermon, but he never got very far. All his five 'thinking' children would have none of that. Laughing, we all turned on father to ask him what he thought about the sermon, knowing of course that he had hardly heard a word of it. This created more laughter. John would suddenly snore loudly from his seat next to mother. Thus we were all laughing again, which relieved us of the burden of talking about the sermon. Instead we began to ask serious questions about God and Jesus. I managed to ask some of my pent-up questions about other matters of religion, and soon we were all off into a deep animated discussion. Mother and father began to treat us, on those occasions, more on their own level, for our questions were not easy for them to answer, and soon we forgot about all else.

Suddenly our youngest brother, Edward, the quietest of us all, would come up with the most profound question of the day. We would gaze in wonder at him, and my elder sister would hug him affectionately, for he, I remember, was only six at the time. We all loved those Sunday after-lunch sessions and would often forget all else, until it was well past teatime. We all talked seriously, and when discussion became too deep and father was having a hard job to answer our questions, John, our clowning brother, would say something so uproariously funny that the whole family would collapse into laughter, until our sides ached. This would usually put an end to the religious session.

One thing I remember so well about our Sunday lunches is that if any member of the family was in bed ill, the ritual was that another member of the family would take up a glass of the Sunday joint 'juice' that had leaked out into a little cavity in the huge meat dish. Whoever was the lucky one to take this 'elixir of life' up to the invalid, in a special wine glass, would be moistening his or her lips as the glass was filled to the brim. Then with the warning: 'Don't spill it!' from mother, the lucky one would gingerly mount the stairs, and walking very slowly into the invalid's room would cry, 'Look what I've brought you, you're lucky, we've saved all the juice for you!' If we happened to be really very lucky our invalid would decline the potion. Then with a quick, 'Are you quite sure you don't want it?' the elixir was swallowed with enormous relish and then the culprit would mutter, 'Don't tell mummy!' as he (or she) dashed down the stairs into the dining room to tell the waiting family how much the invalid had enjoyed it. The little liar seldom got away with it.

When my father was away in America my brothers were all packed off by my mother to a Boys' Preparatory Boarding School, a mile or so from home. She had passed the responsibility of her boys onto Mr Campbell, the Headmaster. I think she was finding the boys too difficult to manage without father. My poor grandmother was kept busy from morn till night sewing on nametapes and I was made to help her. My three brothers, after a while, ran away together from the School. This of course created a huge rumpus.

I remember the occasion well; it was the time when I was the only one who was at home, as my sister was away at a boarding school. One day out of the blue, Mr Campbell telephoned my mother to ask if her boys were with her. Mother became very flustered and agitated, assuring him they were not. The Headmaster told her that he had decided he would call the police if mother or the school could not find them within the hour. Mother went out immediately in the car to search for her boys, taking me with her. Unluckily for the boys I spotted them in one of the Cassiobury Park side entrances, a few minutes walk away from home. Mother braked sharply, and I climbed out of the car to call to them. They had seen me and were scurrying away. Mother was close on my heels, and shouted to them to stop running away from her. The boys were all very frightened, but stopped and came sheepishly up to mother. Without a word mother bundled them into the back of the car. She turned on my eldest brother, Charles and demanded an explanation. It appeared that they did not like being away from home in a boarding school and wanted to be reassured that mother was not following father to America.

My mother found this a satisfactory explanation and announced that she was taking them straight back to school, much to the boys' dismay. They begged her not to, but mother reassured them that she would explain everything to the Headmaster. Mother believed in doing things immediately, but I could see she was very relieved to have found her boys. The Headmaster, although very worried, saw my mother immediately. After apologising, mother spoke up for her boys and said she was quite satisfied that they would never run away again, and asked the Headmaster to give them another opportunity to settle down. She explained the whole situation to him, emphasising that their father was in America but would soon be coming home and would be sure to visit the school on his return. In the meantime she begged him not to punish her boys, saying she felt they had been frightened enough already. I think this satisfied mother far more than the Headmaster, who had naturally been very worried.

He was well aware that mother had packed her boys off to his boarding school in the absence of her husband, and he felt that she had done so without father's permission. He had more sympathy for the boys than their tiresome mother. Mother hugged all her boys and hurried me out of the room with no more ado, leaving everything in the hands of the Headmaster.

As I grew up I was considered to be rather a tomboy. I loved nothing better than playing with my three brothers. We would climb the old Yew tree in the garden searching for birds' eggs, and we even managed to make quite a good hiding place amongst its branches. We often played clock golf around the huge Mountain Hemlock at the back of the house. The tennis court ran alongside the house between the huge Oak tree and the old Yew tree. We spent a lot of time playing tennis on that fine grass court.

As I grew older I was obliged to help my mother with the ironing and other jobs, which I desperately tried to duck. I would hide under the bed when I knew mother wanted me, and I never answered her call. Then I would hear her coming up the stairs to find me, and when she entered my room I would lie as quiet as a mouse under the bed. But she always caught me, pulling me out from under my bed by my legs. Grumbling, I'd follow her downstairs to the ironing board. My reward was always some chocolates, which my mother knew I loved.

After we had all been at boarding schools for some time, we began to go our separate ways, but we still spent

Out riding with father.

part of our summer holidays together as a family by the sea. Father would rent a large bungalow at Selsey Bill, the garden of which backed down to the steep cliffs, where a narrow pathway led to the beach below. We more or less had our own private beach, where mother and father would rest on rugs or deck chairs on the sands, whilst we all amused ourselves.

Sometimes we went swimming with father, who taught us to swim and cope with the big September breakers. Father would always accompany us, as we had to wade out some distance to be clear of the big waves. Father also taught us riding, and I remember our first lessons were spent in a paddock. Father would not allow us to ride along the sands until he considered that we were all sufficiently capable of riding our ponies or horses in his strict military style. He had been in the cavalry during World War One, and was an excellent horseman.

When we were allowed on the hard sandy beach, his favourite command would be 'Ride your horses!' as he lined us all up behind him. First we'd walk slowly along the sands, then father would wave his hand, which was a command to 'trot!' then to 'canter!' and then to 'gallop!' as we followed his example. We loved galloping along the hard sandy beach, but on our way home to the stables we often had a job to control our ponies; especially when we trotted them close to the sea, for they loved nothing better than splashing in the cool waters, especially after their strenuous galloping. One day, my brother John's pony did not just paddle in the sea, it rolled right over, splashing about. John was thrown into the sea and as he picked himself up, he moved away, as disgusted as father; while we watched in delight, glad that our ponies had not disgraced us.

When the sea was calm, father would hire a rowing boat in the early hours of the morning and take us out fishing. We would all get into the boat, and then father would push the boat out to sea and hurriedly climb in, grabbing the oars as he sat down. He never rowed very far away from the shore, and after putting down the anchor he handed us all some worms as bait for our fishing-lines. We held the lines over the side of the boat, silently willing a passing fish to grab our bait. I think it was as much fun bringing the fish triumphantly back to mother, who cooked them for our breakfast, as it was to catch them. We loved those happy summer days by the sea.

When we grew older, father considered that it was only his boys that required further education by going to university, so when we left school he placed my sister and me under mother's care. Mother believed the proper place for her girls was at home with her, so that she could prepare us for marriage. When my sister and I rebelled, father eventually compromised by allowing my sister to train as a teacher at the Rudolph Steiner College in Birmingham, whilst I took a six months' course at St James Secretarial College in London. In those days, preference was given to boys with regard to careers, as it was considered that they would eventually be solely responsible for their own households.

In the 1930s life was very different for girls, who did not have the same opportunities as they do today. Girls were conditioned to believe all kinds of assertions about the superiority of the male sex, and were naturally influenced by the environment set by their parents. Girls were persuaded by unsavoury tales of those who had disobeyed their fathers or husbands, and sometimes were threatened even with being confined in asylums or other harsh disciplinary conditions. Thus girls would enter marriage somewhat diffidently. World War Two gradually changed most of these conventional ways. But conditioned beliefs and inbred habits can take a very long time to change; particularly was this so with regard to the conventional belief that females needed to rely totally on males to protect and support them.

Me in the sand and the family
with father all round.

Chapter Four

The War Years

Weapons of strife, however beautiful,
are emblems of ill omens and incentives of ill feeling,
The servant of Tao does not employ them.
He who walks in peace,
the path of the blessed doth honour.
He who walks in strife,
the path of the unblessed doth follow.
Weapons of strife confer no blessings.
The wise man prefers tranquillity
and peace before them.

From: *The Simple way of Life according to Lao Tzu.*
Wu Wei is a paradox in which is contained the secret of the Simple Way,
which is the middle path between all extremes.
By ceasing to strive, we overcome strife.

SINCE THE EARLY 1930s my parents had been interested in searching into Truth. This brought them in contact with the interesting and informative character Mrs Kathleen Barkel, a trance medium whose guides spoke on esoteric subjects and the furtherance of inner religious esoteric teachings. Right from the beginning my parents were captivated by Kathleen Barkel's sincerity. They attended several of her lectures in the Queen's Hall, London. Thereafter, they were invited to attend a course of weekly lectures held at the headquarters of *The Marylebone Spiritualist Association.* Kathleen Barkel's guides addressed the audience. She had two guides: White Hawk, who brought teachings on Initiation, the work of the Hierarchies and Love, both Human and Divine, and I-Em-Hotep, who spoke on

Hermetic Philosophy. Both gave talks on various other subjects at different times.

After a while my parents began attending further meetings held regularly by Kathleen Barkel at her home outside London that were held in a specially constructed building at the bottom of her long garden, which she called her Temple. Kathleen Barkel also conducted talks at 72, Queen's Gate, London and at the Queen's Hall in London, besides giving private inner esoteric teachings on Astrology and other more advanced esoteric teachings to members of her group, *The Order of the Dawn*.

As a teenager in my school holidays, I remember being allowed to accompany my parents to these talks given by Kathleen Barkel's guides. I was so impressed by the teachings that I attended them whenever I could—they affected me greatly. I had always had an inquiring mind and I immediately felt a deep inner connection, which drew me toward these teachings. Over time our family grew very fond of Kathleen Barkel and visited her home on numerous occasions, getting to know her so well that we children called her 'Grannie'.

Kathleen Barkel wrote a number of books, which I still have. One of them was called *The Dawn of Truth* and subtitled *The Masters by I-Em-Hotep*. The book consisted of recorded talks held during the winter of 1935–36, although originally the talks were not intended for publication, since each student was given a transcript. I remember that the guide I-Em-Hotep spoke during one of those talks about the importance of the role that women could play in centuries to come. I found what he said particularly interesting, and the following remained in my memory long afterwards:

To such women who can become mothers,
a wonderful world is opening out before them.
For with the knowledge that the
Masters of Wisdom are living,
loving Great Ones, who are able to
contact and guide them aright, that
the Angel world is close beside them,
and that they are God's chosen,
they can so prepare themselves
that children may be born to them
who can be used by those who
will redeem the world.

From, *The Dawn of Truth.*

Kathleen Barkel was highly thought of by The President of *The Marylebone Spiritualist Association*, Mr. George Craze, who spoke of her as being: 'A lady of culture, with an engaging personality, vivacious, yet with almost a distaste for publicity, but devoted to her mission of comforting the distressed, aiding the searcher for truth, healing the sick, serving her guides and their co-workers, whom she regarded as servants of the Hierarchies of Heaven.'

Sixty interested members of *The Marylebone Spiritualist Association* in 1935–36 wanted to form an esoteric branch of the Association, initially for the furtherance of the teachings given by Kathleen Barkel's guides. As a result, the Association formed *The School of Esoteric Thought*. Eventually most of the sixty members were also initiated into the first degree of *The Order of the Dawn*, an order that had been established by Kathleen Barkel in 1922, and had once been affiliated with the *Golden Order of the Dawn*, consisting of more than 5,000 members. My mother and father were initiated into *The Order of The Dawn*, and later my youngest brother, Edward and I. Due to these teachings our understanding and attitude toward orthodox religion underwent a radical change.

The School of Esoteric Thought and *The Order of the Dawn* were in turn associated with the worldwide organisation of *The Theosophical Society*, co-founded by Helena P. Blavatsky and Col. Henry S. Olcott. Interestingly enough, it was spiritualism that had united and inspired these two unusual and influential characters to form *The Theosophical Society* in 1875. Later Annie Besant became friendly with Madam Blavatsky and supported *The Theosophical Society*. She was eventually elected as its President. Annie Besant, ex-wife of a clergyman, played a significant part later in helping India to become free from British rule. She was a very heroic character, who earned a reputation through her acute understanding of the caste system in India.

Later, in 1911, Annie Besant introduced Jiddu Krishnamurti to the world as the World Teacher for the New Age, who in turn eventually broke away from *The Order of the Star of the East* organised for him by Annie Besant. In 1929 Krishnamurti disbanded this Order saying:

I have only one purpose: to make man free, to urge him toward freedom, to help him to break away from all limitations, for that alone will give him eternal happiness, will give him the unconditioned realisation of the Self.

After Kathleen Barkel died, my parents and I were deeply distressed. But this did not deter our interest in the esoteric teachings. My mother searched to find someone to whom she could turn, in the same way that she had turned to Kathleen Barkel. After a while mother found *The School of Universal Philosophy and Healing in London*, and requested the Principal for a horoscope reading. Several years were to pass before any further contact was made with this School.

When the news of the outbreak of war was announced on September 3rd 1939, we as a family were all staying on a farm in Devon on a horse-riding holiday. We had stopped for a bite to eat at a local country pub to meet our mother after our early morning ride over the moors with father. We were all sitting in the lounge having a sandwich lunch when there was a sudden announcement over the radio stating that the Prime Minister, Neville Chamberlain, had a message for the nation. In a solemn voice he declared that it was his 'painful duty to inform the nation that we were now at war with Germany'. He then called for volunteers. There was a terrible silence. Then there was a burst of conversation. Mother was crying as she looked at her boys. Father was looking rather strained. We were all so young and did not know what the horrible implications of war meant, but our parents did. We felt generally excited, although we were silenced by the shock of such an announcement. We mounted our ponies and returned rather more soberly to the farm.

At the beginning of World War Two, in spite of our parents being very worried, life went on in the beginning very much as usual. My sister continued her training at the Rudolph Steiner College and I finished my secretarial course at St James' College and the boys went back to school.

The government decided to evacuate thousands of children to Canada and America, especially from London and the very large cities, each child bearing his or her name printed on a disc tied around their wrist or neck. It was very sad to hear that so many children were forcibly parted from their parents.

Soon ration books were issued to everybody, which was also an additional burden for mother, I remember, as food queues inevitably followed. Father joined the Home Guard, a voluntary organisation responsible for protecting the Home Front during the war. Mother made blackout curtains for all the windows and doors, to prevent any light from being seen from the air during enemy air raids. One often heard the wardens shouting, 'Put that light out!' as they patrolled the streets. Warning sirens echoed loudly whenever enemy aircraft approached our shores. If we were out in the street we would dash for the nearest shelter, where we would huddle together until the all clear sounded. We all dreaded those nerve-shattering experiences of hearing the drone of the enemy aircraft overhead and then the sudden shriek of the bomb as it whistled to earth with a thud, before exploding. Sandbags were placed in many areas, especially along the coast, in preparation for an expected invasion. We all thought that the sandbags did more for our morale than our safety.

As the months went by I personally witnessed some horrific scenes and tragic deaths during the heavy bombing raids over London. I vividly recall seeing the whole of one side of a house, which had fallen to the ground, exposing on the third floor an old man still in bed. His bed was held precariously against a wall by some rafters protruding from it. Firemen were trying to rescue him, their huge ladders propped against the wall that looked none too safe. They were shouting to him to remain very still by encouraging him to feel that he would soon be safe. He was finally bought down, amidst cheers from the crowd, and apparently none the worse for his horrific experience.

Before the war was over, I saw many, many more dreadful scenes. Especially I remember the bomb that went off just outside the entrance to Marble Arch Tube station. I was there and personally witnessed the terrible devastation. Many people died, most of them so badly blasted within the station by the bomb, that they were unrecognisable. The horror and desolation lived with me for many years, as I am sure it did for all who were caught up in the war. I also remember being able to read in my bedroom in Kensington from the light of the fires created by the bombing of London Docks, in spite of being several miles away.

At King's College Hospital where I was nursing, I often arrived on duty to find bomb-shattered people sitting around the central fire in the Nightingale Ward. Most of them had no homes left and were in terrible states of shock; some had minor injuries and others were totally apathetic. All these experiences helped me to become more aware of the devastation human beings can cause to one another through wars.

Just before World War Two was declared, I completed my secretarial course at St James College in London. I remember being inspired by the war effort, and soon after war was declared I applied to King's College Hospital for a position as a nurse. I travelled by train from Watford to London with my father for my first interview. Father's paint manufacturing business, which he had established in the early 1920s, was located in Duke Street, off Stamford Street. We parted company when I took a tube train to Denmark Hill, and we arranged to meet again on the return journey. Father was very protective towards his daughters.

In early 1940, on a particularly hot day, I was at home reading a book in the garden, waiting for my acceptance papers for King's College Hospital, where I was hoping to take a four-year training course in nursing. Quite unexpectedly, the maid called me into the house, announcing that an army officer was waiting in the drawing room to see my parents. I went into the house, wondering who this officer might be, thinking he must have come from the Home Guard to see my father, who was organising the local Home Guard. But I was mistaken. This tall handsome officer was apparently on leave, having just returned from active service overseas, at Dunkirk. His uncle, who was a member of the same West Herts Golf Club as my father, had given him some names and addresses of a few of his friends, together with letters of introduction, one of which was for my father. Apparently, my father was the last one on his list. On hearing that my parents were not in, the officer insisted that he would like to wait until they returned home, but I could not tell him when they were expected. At a loss to know what to do with him, I took him into the garden to meet my grandmother and to await the return of my parents. Little did I think at that time that he was to become my future husband?

When we reached my grandmother, who was sitting in the rose garden, the officer immediately introduced himself as Raymond, and we were soon enjoying an afternoon cup of tea. As we chatted about this and that, I became more and more aware of his penetrating attention. I was deeply embarrassed. I was eighteen and had little or no experience of the opposite sex, having just left Malvern Girls' College in Worcester. As the afternoon wore on we walked around the garden, stopping while Raymond stooped to cut a rose and place it in my hair as he complimented me on my good looks. I blushed deeply, shyly looking up into his face. Thankfully, just at that moment my parents called from the house, which saved me from further embarrassment.

For several days after our first meeting, Raymond was a frequent visitor. My parents began to suspect that his interest in coming to see them was in fact mainly to see me. I found myself falling in love with this tall, dark, handsome officer. He was my first love, and although he was sixteen years older than I was, our romance blossomed quickly.

In the meantime, I received word from King's College Hospital to say my application had been accepted and that I had to report immediately for duty. Strangely enough, Raymond's Regiment was moving to Norfolk. I took up my nursing appointment, so we corresponded. Eventually Raymond asked me to meet him in London's West End for a weekend to see a show and afterwards go to a dinner dance. My mother arranged hotel accommodation for us, and we met Raymond in the bar of the hotel. Raymond promised to take care of me and mother left us. This was my very first date and I felt nervously excited.

In 1941 after a whirlwind courtship, Raymond asked my father for my hand in marriage. I knew if I married it would put a compulsory stop to my nursing career, since married women in those days were not allowed to continue their career in nursing. So my nursing training transpired to be a little over nine months,

It seemed natural to me when I became engaged to Raymond to ask Grannie Barkel if she would officiate at our marriage ceremony on June 21st 1941. Much to my delight, my fiancé made no objections; despite the unorthodox nature of the marriage ceremony, which took place in Grannie's Temple at the bottom of her garden. We had registered our marriage at the Kensington Marriage Registry Office in London before we took our marriage vows in Grannie's Temple. She conducted a moving and beautiful service. My sister-in-law and my husband's parents were present, together with my family. It was a unique private wedding ceremony.

After the wedding, a grand reception was arranged at my father's Conservative Club in London, where over 220 guests were invited. Considering it was a wartime wedding, the Club produced a wonderful wedding banquet. Two long tables were set on either side of the top table in the Club's Banqueting Hall, where the bride and bridegroom and their respective families presided. A large three-tiered wedding cake, beautifully displayed, rested on a centre table in the area between the long tables. Magnums of champagne were set on all the tables. All the silver cutlery and glassware sparkled, and there were little sprays of red roses wrapped in silver paper tastefully arranged in heart shapes. All the tables looked very attractive with flowers in the centre, and around the banqueting hall there were huge vases of flowers.

In one corner of the room a large table was set aside displaying the wedding gifts? My younger brother John, who had recently joined the Rifle Brigade, was asked to be the bridegroom's best man; the bridegroom's own brother, who was serving in Egypt as a Major in the 50th Division, Royal Engineers, was unable to obtain leave.

My father and mother had given me a magnificent send-off into our new life. I was very conscious of the fact that it was during my early teens that Kathleen Barkel had been the central focus for my deep interest in Esoteric Thought, which meant so much to me in the way that I conducted my life. The fact that she had also officiated at our marriage enhanced my idealistic expectations for our future married life.

Soon after our wedding and honeymoon I returned with my husband to Swaffham, where his regiment was stationed. After we had settled into an old-fashioned farm-house, I met the other officers and their wives. I remember feeling very nervous, as I was very unused to being with so many army personnel.

The only method of cooking in this old-fashioned farmhouse was by oil stove; there was no electricity or gas laid on. I remember it was very cold, especially after I had been used to a centrally heated home. Soon I was expecting our first child and when the baby was due I moved north to stay with my parents-in-law.

On June 24th in 1942 our first son was born. Some weeks after the birth of the baby I moved into a little semi-detached house in the village of Wolsington, within walking distance of my husband's parents' home. They were very kind to me and helped me furnish the house. Raymond came as often as he could obtain leave. Although I was very near my husband's people, I did not know anyone else. I missed Raymond and my family very much.

Shortly after moving North, my husband's 19th Field Regiment was once again called overseas on active service. I was not to see him again until 1946. I cannot help but feel, on looking back, that I was in no way prepared for what happened thereafter. I remember feeling very disconcerted at being left on my own, with no husband to take care of my baby and me. I felt the effect of living in unnatural circumstances due to the war, and worried that my husband might be killed. I tried to make something of my life, but being on my own felt very strange. Somehow, I felt that I had to move away from the isolation in Wolsington, since I missed all my friends and family. But it was wartime and so I tried to accept the situation. I swallowed my loneliness in my pride at being married to a Captain fighting for his country in the armed forces overseas. It is true my parents-in-law helped me all they could, but when darkness descended and I had locked the doors for the night, I felt very much alone and sometimes frightened. In those days there was no television, and with a young baby I was compelled to remain in the house alone every evening.

At the beginning of 1943 I remember feeling particularly lonely and isolated. I had received very little news from Raymond and was worried that all was not well with him. In the middle of the night I awoke with a start, I felt a vivid premonition that he was in danger. Inside me I felt strongly that he had been wounded in the stomach. Early the next morning the front door bell rang loudly. I rushed to the door, and as I opened it I saw the telegram boy holding a telegram toward me. My heart sank to the pit of my stomach as I took the telegram from him, read it, and closed the door. Slowly I re-read it. It stated that my husband had been wounded in his leg. I was relieved, thinking my premonition had been wrong. But several weeks later I received a letter from my husband saying he had narrowly escaped death as a bullet had grazed the wall of his stomach, and that the surgeon had said he was very lucky to be alive.

He was nursed back to health locally and eventually, after several months, he reported back for duty and was again caught up in the skirmish of the troops' landing on the Anzio Beachhead off the Toe of Italy.

A few months later two friends, whom I had met just before my husband went overseas, visited me and persuaded me to stay with them in Prestwick, Scotland. I jumped at the chance, and after renting my house, started another kind of life with my little son in a busy manse. They were very kind to me and I loved being with them. Yet, again after nearly a year, I felt the need to see my family, so I returned to London to stay with my parents. But the bombing was so severe that my father arranged for his brother to invite me to stay on his farm in Worcestershire.

One instant of our short stay in London stands out in my memory. By now my little boy was about three years old. I was taking him to the shops to buy him some Wellington boots for the farm. I thought it would be a new experience for him to go by underground tube instead of by bus to the West End. He was standing close beside me on the seat and I was supporting him in case he fell, when at the next station, more than a dozen America G.I. soldiers boarded the train. They sat down in the empty seats around us. One of the G.I. soldiers turned to my little son and said: "Well sonny! And where is your daddy?" Without the slightest hesitation my son replied, "I have one daddy in Tunisia and the other daddy fighting in Italy." A prompt reply came from another G.I. as he looked at me with a twinkle in his eyes: "Oh my! Oh my! What a lucky boy you are to have two daddies! Most people have only one. You must have a very special kind of mummy." Blushing to the roots of my hair, I hid my face in my little son's back, wishing I was anywhere else but there. It was, I suppose, quite understandable for the little chap to get muddled, when his daddy was in Tunisia one day and the next day in Italy, so I suppose it seemed natural for him to think he must have two daddies!

At the end of 1943, after a month or so on the farm, I began to yearn for my own independence, but did not relish the idea of returning to the North of England, or for that matter to bomb-ridden London. Therefore, I answered an advertisement in a local Worcester paper that gave details of a cottage that was for rent in Great Malvern. Much to my astonishment, I discovered that the Games Mistress of Malvern Girl's College, where I had been a boarder, owned the cottage. She had been my favourite Games Mistress, who had trained me for her first hockey team. To my delight she agreed to let me rent her cottage, and in no time at all I had settled in with my little son.

Shortly after, I applied for a job at a local nursing home. I shall always remember the reception I met with when I arrived for my interview. The matron gave me one penetrating look, and then with tears in her eyes, she impulsively drew me into her arms saying, "God must have sent you to me." She told me she had very few staff and engaged me on the spot. She told me where there was a little nursery school, just two blocks down the road, where I could leave my little boy during my working hours. I found the experience in this large nursing home, enthralling. Besides a number of permanent residents, there were a variety of other patients. We were always short-staffed and very busy. Operations were performed, babies were born, and there was never a dull moment. The cottage was a joy to live in, and I have many, many unforgettable happy memories of those days.

In 1945 the war ended, at least for the Europeans, but it was some months before my husband returned from overseas. He was obliged to wait for his demobilisation papers before he could leave the army, which took a few more months. He eventually returned in March 1946.

Soon after, we moved to the North of England, where we set up home and began to enjoy family life together. We had two more children—a girl and a boy. Although my husband did not share the same interest as I did in esoteric thought or unorthodox religions, our children, whom we loved dearly, filled our lives. But I never lost my urge to seek after Truth.

I suppose the fact of not having the usual start to married life provoked certain uneasy situations that arose between us after my husband returned from the forces. I found it very difficult to restart my married life, especially after living so independently for more than four and half years whilst my husband was away fighting. In those days things were very different from the way they are today. When I married, husbands were very much the head of the family, and consequently I never thought of disobeying him. But the independence that I discovered through having to cope on my own caused me to feel resistance against being again held under my husband's controlling influence. Nevertheless, under the circumstances, I thought I had yielded very well to restarting our married life, in spite of the freedom that I had experienced during my husband's absence.

It is true I missed my family very much, and living up North seemed such a long way away. My sister Marguerite had married and settled in Kensington, London, and my brother John had left the army and was called to the bar, practising as a criminal barrister in the Law Courts in London. My brother Charles had returned from being a prisoner of war and was working in my father's paint manufacturing business. He was married and had a young baby. Edward, my youngest brother, was studying Geology in Montreal, Canada.

In the early 1950s my parents had to leave London and decided to move to North Wales. The move included reinstating my father's paint manufacturing business, the cost of which I remember him saying was prohibitive.

Some time after the move, in 1954, my mother became very ill with a massive stroke. After seeing my immediate family taken care of, I left for North Wales to look after her. I found my mother in a very disturbed condition. The whole of her right side had dropped, making it impossible for her to climb in or out of bed or to talk or walk properly. It was very sad to see her in such a state. We were all worried about her, especially father, who never did find it easy to cope with anybody who was ill, particularly my mother. My youngest brother, Edward, who was in his early twenties, was living with my parents to help my father with his business. He had broken his studies at McGill's University in Montreal, Canada, where he had been studying and working as a geologist, They were both pleased and relieved to see me, as they were not finding it easy to manage both mother and the business.

Very soon after arriving I noticed that mother was very disturbed and frustrated by something. She was finding it difficult to convey to me what she wanted. She kept pointing to the bottom of her chest of drawers. I opened the bottom drawer, and after searching found nothing. But when I put my hand underneath the white lining paper of the drawer, I discovered a large brown envelope. My mother sighed with relief. When I opened the envelope, I found a delineation of a horoscope addressed to my mother, dated some years previously. It was from the Principal of *The School of Universal Philosophy and Healing*. I read it over carefully to my mother and to my complete astonishment, I found her present stroke had not only been forecast, but precise details were disclosed about my mother's character that pointed out exactly how it was possible for her to ignore the signs leading up to her stroke. Mother pointed to the letter heading. I asked her if she wanted me to contact the School. She nodded her head as best she could.

Thus it was that we became involved with the Principal of *The School of Universal Philosophy and Healing*, and it was entirely due to mother's illness that my father, my two younger brothers and I all became very interested in the activities and teaching of the School. Before long we were all involved in long discussions with regard to the recommendations made by the School to help mother back to health. Besides the herbs and healing, the School also sent us lectures, which I read to mother.

The School advised an immediate change of diet, which mother followed meticulously, and through the healing and herbs that the School administered to her, she made a complete and miraculous recovery. This left a big impression on me, and affected my two younger brothers so strongly that they both eventually joined the School.

In those days of nearly half a century ago, the medical profession generally did not take diet into consideration as a means of treating patients' illnesses, in the way that they are beginning to do today. My mother weighed nearly fourteen stone (82 kilos) at the time of her stroke. After eighteen months on the diet prescribed by the School, she reduced her weight by more than three stone and was once again fit and well, much better, in fact, than she had been for many years. She continued to lose weight until she weighed ten stone. We were all very impressed by what the School had done for our mother, and we soon all became more involved with their activities.

Chapter Five

My Predicament

The Moving Finger writes, and having writ
Moves on; nor all thy Piety nor wit
Shall lure it back to cancel half a line,
Nor all thy Tears wash out a Word of it.

The Rubáiyát of Omar Khayyám, stanza 51,
Translated by Edward Fitzgerald (1809–93)

HAVING NURSED MY MOTHER for two or three weeks through the worst of her stroke, and seeing that she was now on the mend, I left Wales by car to return to my family. I was unable to forget what the School had done for my mother. I found myself ruminating on the connections between Kathleen Barkel's teachings and those of *The School of Universal Philosophy and Healing.* As I thought about the School's lectures I could see many similarities with the teachings of Grannie Barkel. They also fitted in very well with the philosophy set out by P. D. Ouspensky in his book *In Search of the Miraculous*, which a friend of my husband had given me, and which I had been reading just before I left my family to nurse my mother. Ouspensky vividly described the esoteric teachings of G.I. Gurdjieff, a Greek-Armenian mystic who had rediscovered the Fourth Way[1] during his long travels in the East. The Fourth Way of the Sufi esoteric teachings is based on an individual understanding of in-depth self-investigation. Gurdjieff transmitted and guided his pupils by way of a series of disciplined sacred dances and courses on self-remembering

[1] *The Fourth Way* by P. D. Ouspensky,
 published by Routledge & Kegan Paul, 1957.

exercises, whereas Ouspensky, a Russian mystic, followed a more formal intellectual approach for his pupils that was nonetheless rigorous to the extent that in-depth training of the mind involved self-knowledge and self-responsibility in relationships.

My mind was so absorbed by the spiritual development that was once again invigorating my life that I had not noticed how time was passing and that I would soon be home again with my family. As I thought about the vegetarian diet recommended by *The School of Universal Philosophy and Healing*, I wondered how I could adjust our family to such a diet. I felt sure that the diet that had worked so well for my mother would benefit my family. The thought of this brought me back to the School and their activities, particularly to their lectures, which I found so helpful at this particular point in my life. I returned home in a leisurely way.

It was good to be with my children again. They seemed to have grown in the short while that I had been away. There was great excitement as I had remembered to bring each of them a present. I told my husband about *The School of Universal Philosophy and Healing* and their activities and how their suggested diet had helped my mother and how well she was responding to their healing and herbs. I explained to my husband what a miraculous recovery my mother had made and that she was now on her feet again and would soon be back to normal. She had already gained most of the feeling to her right side, and although her speech was hesitant it was not so slurred.

Now I was back at home, I investigated more fully the benefits of a vegetarian diet. I had seen my own mother return to health by changing her diet. I discovered many things: firstly, that more than half the population of the world is vegetarian; secondly, the human digestive system absorbs vegetarian raw food more readily than animal products; and thirdly, that unlike Vegetarians, Vegans do not include any dairy products in their diet. Whilst I was with mother, we had all decided to follow a vegetarian diet to make it easier for her to adapt. I do not think father was very happy with his change of diet, but I had already begun to feel the benefit, which made me determined to continue eating vegetarian food, in the hope that the fibrosis's I had been suffering from for so long would never return.

Once I could prove to myself the benefits of being a vegetarian, I knew I would want to pass this changed diet on to my children. I told myself that if I believed it promoted better health, I would be a hypocrite not to provide it for my children. My husband was not interested in changing his diet, and seemed very much against it, but I hoped that would change over time.

Once again I settled down to married life, realising that the interest I had always had in the teachings of Grannie Barkel were now being revived by my recent connection with *The School of Universal Philosophy and Healing*. I recalled how impressed I had been in my teens when I used to listen to Grannie Barkel's talks on esoteric philosophy. But after I had married, living so far away from London I had felt cut off and I now realised just how much I had missed those talks, which I had always found so very stimulating and important to my well-being.

I was very absorbed with my family life, and the urge for another baby became much stronger. I prayed this could happen, but my husband felt we had enough with our three children. My youngest child was then nearly five years old. My persistent desire to carry a child again arose, as I remembered a talk given by Grannie Barkel's guide, I-Em-Hotep, during his lectures on Master Jesus.

His words remained strongly in my memory, expounding the idea that women who prepared themselves could bring into birth children who would help the world. I felt ready now to carry out this mission, which I suppose was strengthened by my contact with *The School of Universal Philosophy and Healing.* Thus, when we were very close one night in bed, I whispered to my husband my longing for another baby. In spite of my husband's reluctance to have another baby, that night he must have forgotten for he used no precautions; this worried him, but it was too late. I snuggled down in bed feeling blissfully contented and happy and was soon fast asleep.

Some hours later, conscious of being in a half dream-like state, I became aware of a vision of an ancient Greek figure coming toward me. The Greek wore a blue tunic; his face was expressionless, although his eyes penetrated into mine. His dark hair was short and curly, and swept away from his face. He walked slowly toward me with out-stretched arms, holding across them a limp form. I felt drawn towards him and the limp form he proffered, the dream faded before my eyes. In wonder, I felt sure I was going to have a baby.

I must have fallen asleep again almost at once, only to wake up with a start to see before my eyes what seemed to be the oldest face in the world, smiling from ear to ear. I watched him, entranced, as I pinched myself to see if I was awake and whether what I was watching was real. He was Chinese, clad in a gown with a mandarin collar. His face was very old, as old as Methuselah; his smile covered the whole of his beautiful face, which was wrinkled with age. His white hair was drawn up into a topknot on top of his head and his long white beard stretched down to well below his chest. His eyes were as deep as the ocean and his demeanour was one of great love and joy. I was spellbound. Slowly this beautiful face began to fade. I did not want him to go away; I could feel an extraordinary emanation of divinity coming from him. As the vision faded before my eyes and I was left alone, I now felt certain that I was going to have another baby, and sank into a deep blissful sleep. The vivid recollection of that face remained with me for many years.

Thus, the next nine months were of untold joy to me. I made all the baby clothes, even the nappies. I kept rigorously to my newly changed diet, and took the herbs recommended by the School. I stopped smoking and drinking and was divinely happy. My next-door neighbour said to my husband, "If I thought I could bring such a beautiful radiance to my wife's face as your wife is portraying, I would make her pregnant tomorrow!"

In spite of my positive experience of the vegetarian diet, and now that I felt in much better health and my fibrosis's had completely gone, I still gave a great deal of consideration to the matter before finally deciding to change the family's diet. I explained to my husband that if he wanted to eat meat or fish he could easily have whatever he wanted for lunch at his club. It was only much later that I saw how this change to a vegetarian diet was upsetting my husband's whole life style. He greatly valued eating the game he reared for shooting and all that went with it. He loved entertaining his friends at home—eating meat, smoking, and drinking—so it was quite understandable how he felt, although at the time I did not notice how much such change was affecting him. I suppose, for a man of his age and inclinations he was very set in his ways, and I am sure that he had no desire to make such changes. However, at the time, I had optimistically felt he would soon see the benefit—health-wise—to the changes that I felt sure would help him too in the long run.

Whilst I was with my mother, I had promised the Principal of the School that I would make her a new gown to wear during the lectures as a thank-you for helping my mother back to health. To do this work I got up very early in the morning, which upset my husband. But it was the only way I knew whereby I could have the peace to study the lectures that the School had sent me and at the same time make the new gown.

As my time drew nearer for the birth of my baby I made arrangements with my local doctor so that I could have my child at home. I engaged a nurse to look after me during the confinement. I did not want to go into any nursing home or hospital to have this baby. Just before the baby was due, I recall cleaning the house from top to bottom and washing everything in sight. I was extremely tired, but relaxed and happy when the baby began to show signs of coming. My nurse had arrived, and to help the delivery along she suggested a hot bath. After this, whilst I was resting in bed, the pains began coming every half-hour; then every ten minutes—this was when the nurse called my doctor. My husband had gone down to the local pub leaving the nurse in charge. The two younger children were already in bed and were very excited about the coming of the new baby. It was the quickest birth I had experienced: only five and a half hours. I am sure this was due to my change of diet. It was a much easier birth, made easier by my waters breaking for the first time. With the other three children the births had taken between thirty-six to forty hours and I had always had a dry labour.

Sometime later, at the moment of birth, my husband opened the door of the dining room, where I was in labour. He was in time to witness the birth of our fourth child, a son. It was the only one of our children he had witnessed being born. I remember being aware that he was standing by the door rooted to the spot—unable to move—with his eyes riveted on the baby who was coming into the world. This was about 10.30 p.m. on the 22nd November 1955.

Shortly after the birth, my husband and I were invited by the Principal of *The School of Universal Philosophy and Healing* to bring our baby son, then only one month old, down to London for the Christening. My husband made no objection whatsoever to this arrangement, so our flight to London was booked. The ceremony was to be held at the School on Christmas Day. We both took part in the ceremony and enjoyed the vegetarian luncheon arranged for us that followed. I was glad to see my brothers again, who enthusiastically showed us over the School. Then we flew back to the North of England to spend the rest of the Christmas festivities with our three other children.

For some time I had been experiencing difficulty within myself with regard to our physical intimate relationship, and after the baby was born I found it difficult to respond to this side of our married life. I do not know if it was that it was too close to the birth of our child, or if my concept of marriage was too idealistic since, as with all ideals, things never happen that way in real life. I prayed repeatedly for guidance, but I just did not know how to handle such a dilemma without upsetting my husband.

It was about a month later that I started having real difficulties with breast-feeding. I drank quantities of water but to no avail. My doctor had advised me to substitute my breast-feeding with bottled milk, but all of the brands I tried upset the baby, including the Ostermilk that my husband had especially collected one night from the chemist. My husband became very exasperated with the way I was handling the difficulty I was experiencing with the baby's feeding problems. He said that if I did not pull myself together he would put me away so that I could get some help—by which I was sure he meant an asylum. There were no psychiatric hospitals in those days. This frightened me very much, as I knew that he had a doctor friend, whose wife had turned religious after her baby was born, and the doctor had put her away into an asylum and no one heard anything more of what happened to her.

The next day my husband was away with a shooting party, and I was desperate to solve my feeding problems with my baby who was crying so much. In my desperation I telephoned the School for their advice. They suggested that I bring my baby down to London so they would be able to help me and at the same time give both of us some healing.

I decided to go to London, thinking I would soon be home. I arranged for my mother, who was by now fully restored to health, to be at my home to look after my husband and two younger children, who were both of school age, my eldest son being away at boarding-school. My mother said she would arrive in time to be at home when the children returned from school in the late afternoon. I telephoned my husband's agent to reserve my seat on the train leaving for Kings Cross, London, and said I would meet him on the platform to collect my ticket. I left messages in various places for my husband, whom I could not reach personally as he was out on the moors with his shooting party. I ordered a taxi and began getting ready for the journey, I quickly packed a few things for myself and attended to my baby.

At Newcastle Central Station I met the agent and obtained my first class ticket. As I was walking slowly towards the platform to find my seat on the train, holding my baby in a carrycot beside me, my husband suddenly appeared before me. He was absolutely furious. I began to cry in distress, begging him to understand why I had arranged to go to the School. I tried to put my free arm around him, but he shrugged me away telling me not to make an exhibition of myself in front of other people. By now I was crying openly. Abruptly my husband turned to face me. His words made such an impact on me that I clearly remember him angrily exclaiming: "If you insist on going down to London to that place, our life as it stands will be finished! I will buy a semi-detached house for you and the children, and I will come to see you all whenever I like." I cried in anguished disbelief: "Please don't say such things; I must feed my baby he's crying so much and they have promised to help me, please dearest, understand and let me go. Besides, you have never said you were against the School before." He brushed my words aside with, "I forbid you to go!" In desperation I cried, "You cannot mean what you have just said!" "Indeed I do!" he replied, fuming as he looked angrily at me. I cried in utter disbelief: "I must go, as our baby's feeding problems are serious, so you leave me no choice!" And with a final pleading look, I began walking slowly toward the train with my baby. I felt very shocked and choked at my husband's angry outburst, but I was far too concerned with the feeding problems I was having with our baby to be stopped by his words, or even to take them literally, or believe that he really meant them, or even dream that he would carry out such threats.

My husband followed me down the platform saying authoritatively, "If you go away now, you need not come back unless you stop having any more contact with that place, where your two stupid, crazy brothers have gone." Horrified by his words I found myself shrinking away from him as he helped me into the carriage with the carrycot. He slammed the carriage door, and noticing Lord Berry sitting in the seat opposite to me, said through the open window, "I see you are in good company!" I came to the window, staring at him incredulously as he swept off his shooting-hat and with a mocking bow turned on his heel, striding off down the platform without a backward glance. The train moved slowly out of the platform. For the first time in my married life I had challenged my husband's authority over me. As the awful events of the past few moments sank into my consciousness, I was suddenly mortally afraid of what he might do. But I quickly consoled myself that I was sure he was only trying to frighten me.

The train gathered speed as I sank back into my seat feeling very shocked but totally unaware of the other passengers in the first class carriage. I was unable to think coherently. Then it slowly dawned on me that my husband's outburst at the station might have resulted from his pent-up feelings over the birth of our baby. In my anxiety over the feeding problems I had not observed how my husband truly felt or what he really thought about *The School of Universal Philosophy and Healing*. Now that he was so angry he must have thought that I had over-ridden his authority as head of the household in contacting the School for their advice. I quickly told myself that he had been away shooting, so I could not have asked him. I was so desperately worried over my baby's feeding problems that I could think of nothing else. Thoughts were going round and round in my head in a whirl.

To me it had been the most natural thing to do, to contact the School for their advice, since they had been instrumental in my mother's recovery from her stroke. I had the greatest respect for my husband and loved him dearly, and I had no intention of slighting his authority in any way. The train was lulling me into a more relaxed state of mind. I wondered why my husband had never given me the slightest indication of his objection to the School or the Christening until this moment. So when he displayed his disapproval so emphatically and dramatically to me on the platform, it came as a very great shock, quite dumbfounding me. Numbed, I was unable to take his words seriously.

An hour or so later, the train stopped at a station and more passengers came into our carriage. I moved the carrycot closer to me and attended to my little baby son. I nursed him for a while until the train moved out of the platform. Then the turmoil in my mind began whirling around in my head all over again. As I put the baby into his carrycot, I wondered if my enthusiasm for a vegetarian diet had blinded me to the disastrous effect it might have on my husband, in spite of my improved health. Having this baby had meant so much to me, and when the feeding problems had become acute, all else had faded from my mind. But I knew I desperately needed to have my husband's support, especially as I was so sure that breast-feeding was very important for the baby's health. I never intentionally tried to create antagonism between my husband and myself by going to the School for help. The constant crying of my baby had made me feel so upset that I was unable to think of anything else but getting my baby better. These thoughts kept tumbling about in my mind as I tried to justify my actions.

Later, as I became calmer, the dream that I had had the night before came once more vividly before my eyes. It was as if I was watching a cinema screen. The dream seemed to have occurred between waking and sleeping. I now watched it unfolding before my eyes again. 'I was holding my baby in my arms, when I suddenly became aware that Jesus was walking near me—on the other side of a fence—with all his disciples following him. I called out. "Please, Jesus don't go by, I have always wanted to see you!" As I said these words I appeared to be putting my baby into a car before running towards Jesus and his disciples. His disciples were saying to Him, "Don't go to her, she is that kind of a woman." But Jesus said, "She called me." As he came toward the gate, all of a sudden I seemed to be two people, one dressed in black and the other in white. Jesus placed his hands on both my heads, as he drew me through the gate toward him. One thing I do remember distinctly is that Jesus was nothing like the pictures you see of Him. He was vibrantly alive and his eyes shone with a depth of sincerity and divinity.'

As the dream faded I sat very quietly. I was still in shock. In my naivety I had not been aware of any impending crisis. I had only been half-aware that I had arrived at a period in my life when I seemed to be driven by a deep inner prompting. Consequently, I did not see the oncoming dangers of a crisis looming ahead. Furthermore, looking back now and judging from my husband's behaviour during the crisis, I realise that he, being much older and wiser than me, must have realised already that the relationship in our marriage had reached an impasse.

When the train pulled into King's Cross Station, my brother John, now renamed James was on the platform waiting for me. I began crying. He asked me what was the matter as he carried my baby in the carrycot. I told him all that had happened since I left home. He remained quiet while he hurried me into a waiting taxi. We were taken straight to the School. James took me to the basement 'meeting-room' to attend to my baby whilst he informed the Principal I was there. After a while, Mrs Spearman-Cook came down to see me. She was very kind and said she was sure things would work out all right and that I must not upset myself or it would affect the baby's milk. The expected telephone call from my husband did not materialise, which made me feel very anxious and isolated.

My predicament was that after I had been unable to obtain help from the usual medical practices and had turned to the Principal of *The School of Universal Philosophy and Healing*, I was now placed in an impossible position from which I was unable to turn back. It was from that time onward that I found myself totally trapped and under the domination and control of the School. I suppose my husband must have felt that he had lost all control over me—hence his outburst at the station. Having arrived at the School, to my unutterable despair I was unable to believe what was happening to me. The group, who surrounded me, influenced me to obey the Principal.

Torn between my baby's feeding problems and my own traumatic state, I found myself caught by my own actions and quite unable to decide what to do. But I did begin to recognise that my actions in coming to the School for help had taken me into a different environment, where I was cut off from my husband and seemed to have lost control of my life, no doubt due to my naivety. I could not understand how things had come to such a pass. It all happened so quickly. I felt that nothing I did would ever bring things back to the way they were. I was completely trapped by my own actions in turning to the School for help. My husband seemed to have deserted me, and I became desperately afraid to return home. My tears flowed copiously. My heart ached for my children. In my horror I found I could not face the actuality of what was happening to me; in my terror I clung more and more to my true feelings, weeping bitterly—not knowing what to do.

Chapter Six

My Dilemma

To see a world in a grain of sand,
And a heaven in a wild flower,
Hold infinity in the palm of your hand
And eternity in an hour.

William Blake
Auguries of Innocence

As I looked back over the part of my life, which I
have just outlined, I came to realise that the dilemma in
which I found myself had been accentuated by the birth of
my baby—his inability to feed properly and his perpetual
crying. In my ignorance and naivety I had not perceived
that I must have been suffering from postal natal depression, which in those days was not recognised as such. But I
now feel it must have blinded me from realising that there
was any real rift between my husband and myself. Perhaps,
if I had not been so caught up within myself and the crying of my newborn baby; I might have been more aware of
the crisis that was developing within me due to my inner
searching's for Truth and the change of our diet. Thus I
did not perceive the gulf beginning to divide my husband
and I from each other. Looking back, it now occurs to me
that our marriage was definitely undergoing greater strain
than I had realised; a strain that I only recognised after it
was far too late to do anything about it.

Much later, I wondered if the deep underlying cause
of the strain in our relationship was due to the images I
had built of my husband and myself—images that I had
created in my mind, bearing little or no resemblance to

the actuality of who we really were. It is more obvious to me now as I observe the influences that most of us fall under, living in little worlds of our imaginations. We hold subjective pictures of each other in our minds, images that leave out far too much of reality. In the early days of my marriage I had not recognised that I entertained such images, let alone that they were interfering psychologically with the reality of my daily life—or even that they were causing separation from the husband I had married or the person that I really was. I am sure that had I recognised the significance of what those images were doing, I would never have allowed them to persist. In consequence, my approach to life would have been vastly different. But in those days I was ignorant and did not have enough self-awareness to sustain me.

My beliefs, my background and my environment had created certain unrealistic attitudes and predispositions towards married life that I feel we all unconsciously tend to have, and I am sure that these self-images produce an unrealistic, romantic view of what marriage represents. No wonder so many marriages break down, I thought. On looking back, I think I had never come down to earth, so to speak, to see things in their proper perspective. I suppose I was always trying to fit my husband into the preconceptions that I had of him, perhaps based on a false premise. I can only speak for myself with regard to this image making. But if my husband had perceived me equally through a set of images, and we were both unconsciously coming down to earth at last by recognising that those images were unreal, then we would inevitably be meeting a very different situation in our marriage. Unaware of our image forming, neither of us could have realised what was happening until the crisis hit our marriage. Hence, once it occurred, neither of us was able to meet the reality of it nor even would have been able to help the other through such an impasse.

I feel sure that married couples remaining together often do so because one of the partners suppresses his or her feelings and drifts apart into his or her own world. Thus the pair behave like two images living together, neither able to appreciate what is happening, and in many cases neither willing to acknowledge that there may be deeper issues that need addressing. Be that as it may, in my later years I now feel strongly that the circumstances that brought about my difficulties are common to many marriages that break down. Situations can come to a head so quickly, and before we know where we are things are out of control. Nonetheless, the changed lifestyle I was forced to experience during and after my predicament and dilemma eventually forced me to face myself as I really was and not as my self-images had made me think I was. I have therefore related in depth the way that I felt and how I found my way to cope with the situations that followed in the wake of my family crisis.

On my arrival I was given a temporary room in the School upstairs on the same floor as the Principal's bedroom. A few days later I was invited to join the group in their evening meeting. I had just fed my son and put him down for the night and he seemed to be comfortable. The group and the Principal had gathered together waiting for me to join them. I found them sitting in a circle. A space had been left for me almost opposite the Principal, next to her son John. The Principal explained to me that they always came together each evening at this time before retiring, to receive a benediction from the Great Spirit by joining together in singing and chanting to soft music from the gramophone. We all held hands and were asked to give our utmost attention to the music. Before the Principal said her prayer she told us that it was very important to keep a joyful, uplifting frame of mind in order to provide the right atmosphere for the benediction.

I do not know how long we had been singing in a chant-like fashion, before I became conscious that my feet were beginning to go numb. The numbness began to creep up my legs and body. I continued singing, being uneasy about stopping, until I found myself only conscious of being the smallest dot in my heart. I felt an intense, hushed peace overwhelm me. It was a peace that is not possible to describe. Then I heard a Voice close beside me say: *"I bring to you my peace. I will come again and tell you what happened at the last supper; that no man knoweth, but you must work hard. You must work very hard."* More words were said, but sadly, I could not recall them.

All the time I was conscious of myself as the smallest dot within my heart. Then from a different part of my consciousness, there descended on me the most mysterious and profound state of awe. It seemed to come from a great way off. Silently the wondrous experience overwhelmed me and then gradually withdrew from me. But I was still left with an incredible feeling of peace and awe. As I came back to myself I heard—accompanied by awesome, unearthly music—the words of the hymn Onward Christian Soldiers:

> *"Onward Christian Soldiers, marching as to war*
> *with the cross of Jesus, going on before.*
> *Christ, the Royal Master leads against the foe*
> *forward into battle see his banners go..."*[1]

When I opened my eyes my brother James was kneeling beside me holding my hands. The Principal asked him to

[1] Sabin Baring Gould.

take me to my room, and said that she thought a Sister of Mercy had come over me. I did not know what she meant by her remark, but I did know that what she said was not true. The baby was asleep when I got to my room. In a daze I went to bed glad, oh so glad, that I had the bed to myself. The mystical experience had greatly affected me and was still with me as an extraordinary presence.

As I lay in bed, I vividly recalled one of the last times my children and I were altogether. I had been feeding my baby, with the other three children all standing around me. I had thought, 'These, are my most precious children. I have nothing I regard as so precious.' As I looked at them an insight flashed through my mind, a presentiment that in my innermost desire to serve God—I was about to lose what was most precious to me.

Now lying quietly in bed, in this strange house in London. I was feeling awe-inspired by the experience I had just received during the singing and chanting. I became conscious of a deep realisation that the insight I had received when I was with my children altogether, was now an accomplished fact by which I was being asked to abide. Tears rolled down my cheeks. What had I done? I now knew no one would ever understand the spiritual dilemma I was in. Unless someone had received a similar experience, no one would ever understand or believe what it really felt like, or even believe such an experience was possible. I was in a terrible inner agony, especially as I had now experienced the very Presence of Divinity—a Presence of whom I knew that it was possible for anyone as devastated as I was, to receive. Anyone going through such an experience translates just as I did, from his or her own point of view. Just as the Principal had done after my experience when she said that a Sister of Mercy had come to me. How could I convince anyone of the enormity of what had happened to me, especially as I had now made a conscious connection with such an awe-inspiring Presence? At the time, I was very moved and unable to comprehend the full significance of the visitation. To my dismay, I knew there was nothing I could do but work hard, as I had been told.

As I lay in the silence, the words of the hymn I had heard, as the extraordinary Presence was withdrawing, returned to me. The words kept reverberating through my head. 'Onward Christian Soldiers, marching as to war...' Suddenly, it ceased to matter whether people believed what I had experienced or not. I knew it was true and I treasured it. In fact, it kept me stable, and enabled me to face the horrendous circumstances that were to follow. Soon I fell into a blissful sleep, and slept peacefully until the early hours of the morning when the baby's cries awakened me. It was the best night's sleep I had had since the baby was born.

Unfortunately, my son was not responding any better to my breast-feeding, and he continued to be very restless and cried a lot, in spite of the extra bottled milk he was having, along with the warm water with the smallest amount of honey. After a day or two, the Principal asked a member of the group, Myrtle, who had been a nanny, to take care of the baby for me in her room, in order to give me some rest. I did not want this to happen, and begged to be allowed to care for my baby myself, but I was told firmly by the Principal that Myrtle would take care of him and that this was the best way for him. Anyway, I would see him when he needed feeding. I could often hear the baby crying and many times I tried to go to him, but a member of the group always stopped me. As I was so distressed, James, my brother, suggested I go to the Temple room to pray. The Principal said that I must remember that if

I let the emotional upheaval with my husband affect me, it would upset my breast milk. They said they would increase the bottled milk with a new special brand of easily digested milk, which they had obtained from the chemist, although I was still feeding him. They also said they would give my son some healing.

Throughout this very distressing time, I wanted to contact my husband, but the Principal reiterated again that it would be unwise for me to do so as it would be sure to upset my milk and would not be good for the baby. I kept wondering why my husband had not telephoned, if only to find out how the baby was.

Now that there was such a distance between my husband and myself, I began to be frightened that he meant to keep to every word he had said on the platform—especially as he had made no contact with me and I had not heard from him by letter or telephone. I felt distraught—trapped—as if my world had crashed down over my head. I had only come to the School because they said they would help me with the feeding of my baby. Now they told me that my milk was upsetting the baby because of my fear of what my husband would do. All I really wanted was reassurance from my husband and for him to fetch me home, and then I would be home once more with my children. I had no money or any means of getting any since my husband kept all accounts and I had never had anything to do with that side of our marriage. I felt completely trapped.

My eldest brother Charles, who never had anything to do with the School, came one day to try to persuade me to return to my family. The group tried to prevent him from seeing me, but my brother insisted and I understood that he said that he would call the police if they did not let him see me. A member fetched me and pushed me forward so that my brother could see me. I did not have a proper conversation with him, as the group told me that the Principal had sent a message to say I must not talk with my brother and I was to tell him to go away from the School. As the door closed I felt bitterly disappointed that it was not my husband.

Throughout this whole crisis I had a lurking fear that would not go away. What frightened me the most was that I knew my husband had a close shooting friend, a doctor living in Newcastle, whom I remembered well because I had never liked him. The doctor's wife had religious leanings of which her husband did not approve. He maintained she was mentally deranged after the birth of her baby, and had placed her into an asylum. I never heard what happened to her, but I could not understand his cruelty. Since my husband had not telephoned me, I did not know what to think. It made me feel very uneasy, frightened and disowned, although I was conscious that the School afforded me protection against his wrath, even though I felt totally abandoned and unable to realise the full purport of what was developing. Nevertheless, the fear of being sent to an asylum if I returned home was uppermost in my mind.

One day the Principal sent for me. She was very kind and said that she had that morning received a message from her guide Chang-Fu, to inform me that I had been chosen to do the work of the Great Ones, and that I was to become a leading member of the School. She said to prove my allegiance to The Masters I must go to my home and fetch all my belongings, my jewellery and anything else that was mine, and bring them back in my car. She added that it was a good time to go since my mother was still looking after the two younger children. I felt I was being pushed into doing something I definitely did not want to do, but I could feel her power enveloping me, stopping me from thinking properly. At the same time I wanted to do the bidding of The Masters, and she kept insisting that it was their will to do as she declared. I knew I had very few clothes with me, and that encouraged me to agree. She persuaded me, she kissed and hugged me and told me I was a good girl and that she knew I would do what The Masters wanted. I fell under her spell, as I was reminded of the mystical experience that I had had and the feelings that I experienced when I first joined their evening circle. Also, I was fearful of being caught by my husband and placed into an asylum; however, the Principal reassured me by saying that The Masters would protect me.

Arrangements were made for my departure, and the Principal told me that her son, John, would go with me. We were to fly North to my home and John was to bring all my clothes and personal belongings back with him in my car. I was to take a taxi to the airport and return by air. I was given money, for I had none. We set off very early by air, arriving in what I thought was plenty of time to avoid meeting the children coming home from school. My mother was at home and she helped me to gather everything into boxes and cases. Mother told me how angry my husband was and added she did not like to think of what the outcome would be if he found me at home. When she saw my distressed state, she hugged and kissed me saying she was sure everything would work out for the best for all of us in the end. Being in my home pulled at my heartstrings. I felt as if my world was shattered to pieces and that there was nothing I could do to stop it. I was mortally afraid of meeting my husband. I did not want to be whisked off to a mental home like my husband's doctor friend's wife.

I had an arrangement with our next-door neighbour to keep my car in their spare garage, so I went over to collect it and bring it round to the front of my house. Before I went I telephoned for a taxi to take me to the airport. John packed the car, as mother and I brought him the luggage and boxes. Unfortunately, we had to wait a long time for the taxi. John told me he would drive behind the taxi and that the taxi must not stop for anything! When it arrived John helped load some of my hand luggage into it and then he said something to the taxi driver that I could not hear. We left the house in a hurry, and as we approached the hill going up to the main road, to my utter dismay, I saw my two younger children coming down the hill. I wanted to get out of the taxi, and tried to do so, but John kept hooting and the cab driver must have been told by John not to wait for anything, because he continued to proceed up the narrow hill in spite of my pleas for him to stop. I sank back into the taxi feeling completely defeated.

Thereafter, everything escalated into a nightmare. I missed the flight back to the School and had to wait for another plane. I thought about ringing my husband, but I felt far too frightened of what he would do. When I eventually arrived back at the School I was not consulted any more about the feeding of my baby and the child was kept totally away from me.

Everything was taken out of my hands. When I objected, I was smoothed over with: "But you asked us for our help and we know what is best for the baby and you. Please trust us, we know what we are doing." I was moved to a small attic bedroom away from the baby. I was no longer allowed to see or have anything to do with him. I felt so distraught. My brothers tried to soothe me and told me to go to the Temple Room and pray.

One day, after I had been back at the School for nearly a week, I was coming down the back stairs when I saw my baby being carried in the carrycot by Myrtle. She was going out of the back door. I ran to her demanding to know where she was taking my baby. She said to St Mary Abbot Hospital in Kensington, not very far away from the school, and that there was a taxi waiting. "Why?" I demanded. "Because his feeding problems are getting worse," she replied. I was absolutely distraught. I pleaded with her to let me go with her to the hospital. She refused, but I followed her to the taxi and got in before she could stop me.

At St Mary Abbot Hospital we waited to see the doctor who said, after examining the baby in front of us, that he thought the child looked healthy enough, although he was very thin. Then he said he felt it would be best to keep the baby in hospital for a day or two, so that he could assess what was wrong with his feeding problems. He was very kind and assured me the baby would be all right, asking me if I would like to stay awhile. But Myrtle said we had better return to the School. I was beside myself with worry and felt very unhappy about leaving the baby in hospital. Nothing was turning out as I had hoped. My mind was in a complete turmoil.

Then the School without my knowledge informed my husband that the baby was at St Mary Abbot Hospital, and would he come down to London to fetch him. I only heard about this after my husband had collected the baby. I was shocked and outraged. I wanted to go home to my children. I was in a dreadful state and kept wondering if I had been right to come to the School for their help. I was forced to face the fact that since my husband had not come to see me when he collected the baby that he was keeping to every word he had said at the station, and as far as he was concerned our marriage was over. I thought of all the reasons why I had wanted this baby so much, my revealing dreams and my mystical experience, and I was totally unable to comprehend why I was being forcefully parted from my children.

That night as I was undressing to go to bed in my little attic bedroom, I remember again feeling glad I had the bed to myself. I was suddenly aware of little voices calling for their mother from the next-door house. The children's room was adjacent to mine. The division between the two large detached houses was very narrow, only a little alleyway. One little voice was urgently calling to his mother loud enough for me to hear every word that was being said. As I listened I heard the little voice saying, "Mummy, mummy, please wipe my botty." I cried, wishing it were one of my children calling to me.

At no time since I arrived at the School had I heard a word from my husband after he had left me at the station, and I did not know what he was really thinking, or what he was going to do. I knew it was only he who could reassure me that he was no longer angry and would never put me away. I knew he would be even angrier when he discovered I had fetched my clothes and taken my car. So after he had fetched our baby and not come to the School to take me home with him, I finally knew conclusively it was all over. The terrible imposition that was being placed on my children was all I could think about. My dilemma was that I was no longer there for them when they needed me. It was the horror of the permanent parting from them that cut deeply into my heart.

Unable to face what was happening, I climbed into bed. I knew that this was the moment that I finally understood the depth of the dilemma I was in. I pulled the bedclothes over my head in desperation, unable to do anything to change the fate that gripped me with its icy cold reality. Neither the circumstances nor the reasons why it had all happened seemed important any more compared with the fact that I was no longer there for my children. My deepest grief was that I was unable to comfort them, or love and cuddle them in their predicament. I knew my children could do nothing to change the situation that they found themselves in. Years later, I discovered that they had sent letters to me with little toys I'd given them, begging me to return. I also discovered, many months later, that the School had kept all the letters away from me ever since I had come to the School, even the little toys, which mysteriously appeared one day years later, on a table in the office. Toys, that I instantly recognised as presents I had given to my children. They had all been kept away from me. When I inquired nobody knew anything about the toys or letters and told me I must be mistaken. I was informed emphatically that whatever had come for me I would have received. But I knew I had not been mistaken about the toys, although I could prove nothing. By the time I discovered them I had already begun to suspect that the Principal had played a large part in engineering me into a position from which I could not extricate myself, in order to keep me in the School. Nevertheless, in spite of all my misgivings, I felt that the Principal was only doing what she thought was right and that her motives were for the best.

For now, all I could think about was my children. What could I do? In my anguish I turned to James, my barrister brother, who said he had already taken steps to apply to the Court for my children to be made Wards of Court. As Wards, the Court would have charge over them whilst the case was pending and before the Judge eventually decided which parent should have custody. In desolation I finally realised my marriage was really over and that my husband and I would soon be fighting for the custody of our own children, something that was absolutely abhorrent to me.

A week before the Court Case was due I remember feeling so low that I took a walk in Holland Park, which was not far from the school. I was walking along in a mood of utter despair when I saw a woman sitting on a seat rocking her pram backwards and forwards. As I passed her, I suddenly found myself asking if she would mind if I picked up her baby for a moment. She said she did not mind, asking me if I had lost my baby. I made no reply as I picked the child out of the pram and gently drew her close to me. The little darling did not cry as I rocked her back and forth, then a smile began to spread across her lovely little cheeks. She began talking to me in her baby talk, her large blue eyes all the while watching me as I drew her ever closer. My tears fell on her soft little cheeks. After a while I placed her back carefully in her pram. By now tears were flowing down my cheeks. I thanked the mother and hurried away.

When I arrived back at the School I went straight to my room. I remember hating everything about the School, my husband and most of all—myself. Then I turned to a book I had brought with me, which a friend of my husband had given me some months before all this had happened. It was entitled *In Search of The Miraculous* by P.D. Ouspensky. The book fell open at the chapter relating to group life. It pointed out that living in a group was a very good way to discover oneself, since it helped to reveal weak character traits. I read also that in groups members could help each other in 'remembering', especially when they placed all their energies in one direction, and particularly if they were searching for Truth. Ouspensky was referring to the Teachings of George I. Gurdjieff, who had investigated hidden Sufi truths and secret societies for many years. He had travelled all over the world, meeting various sages, who had shared their truths and understanding with him.

Rereading this chapter helped me to pull myself together, so I went downstairs to see if I could be of any help.

I vividly recollect that just before the Court Hearing I used to hear vendors calling in the street below my little attic bedroom. They were selling strawberries, shouting, 'Anyone want to buy my Kent strawberries?' repeating it over and over again until I could hear their voices fading into the distance. Whenever I eat strawberries now I think of that little attic bedroom. The street vendors brought me back to the 'outside world' and the everyday things that I had once been so used to; memories of my children flooded back into my mind making me feel desperately alone and completely cut off.

Early one morning, about 3 a.m., the group were summoned and told to gather in Zamiar's bedroom. Zamiar, the name by which the Principal of the School—Mrs Spearman-Cook—was always known, had a special message for the group. But before she started, she told me that Chang-Fu wanted my name changed from Betty to Elisabeth, one of my Christian names, which my father had shortened to Betty. I was pleased, as strangely enough I never really liked being called Betty. My barrister brother had already had his name changed from John to James, and all the rest of the group had their names changed soon after they joined the School. The one exception, I remember, was my brother Edward, who retained his name.

Eventually, after some weeks, the case between my husband and I came before the Court. It was held in London before Judge St John. It was heard *in camera* and no reporters were allowed into the Courtroom because of the ages of my children. My brother James, who was a barrister, was acting for me. My husband was in Court and as I looked at him, he turned his head away.

As the case progressed I was very nervous, as I could see that it looked very much as if I would be allowed to keep the baby and that the other three children would remain with their father. I did not want the children separated on my account, as I truly felt that it would be better for them all to remain together to support one another. I felt a further division in the family would only produce more conflicts and complications, which would not be good for my children. I whispered my feelings urgently to my brother. In consequence, before any judgment could be made, I stood up in court and begged the Judge not to separate my children. In a very quiet voice, I said, 'I would rather give up all the rights to my children if it meant that they would have to be separated from one another.' When I had finished speaking I sat down very near to tears. There was a deathly hush in Court. I recall vividly the words Judge St John said as he rose to address the Court. First he looked straight at me with his piercing eyes, then he turned to the Councils and said: "I want what I am about to say to be recorded on your briefs. This woman is a very brave woman, and I stipulate that she can change her mind any time that she wishes to do so within the next three years. In the meantime…" He hesitated, first looking again hard at me and then directly at my husband. He repeated the movement swiftly several times as he continued, "the judgement has been taken out of my hands and I have no other course than to give custody of the children to their father." Judge St. John turned toward me and bowed his head low as he withdrew from the Court. His words were imprinted on my heart. I treasured the way he had bowed his head to me as he had closed the proceedings. I was very, very forlorn and lonely, and I desperately yearned for my children.

That night after the Court case, back in my little attic bedroom, my tears flowed. I turned in prayer to Jesus. I called for him to come to me as he had done the night of the chanting, I prayed to him to help me find faith and courage. I sobbed out my feelings to him, begging him to look after my children. I cried in the agony of my sorrow. I reviewed what had happened in Court, as the full realisation began to sink in that I would never see my children again. I was torn to the very depth of my heart as I pulled the bedclothes over my head and wished that I would never wake up again. The year was 1956.

Chapter Seven

Group Life in The Temple

*Those who create an image of someone or something
in the spiritual realm which evaluates people's lives
and behaviour and then bestows blessings
or punishments upon them,
lead others down a dead-end road.
This is the kind of thinking that is used to
manipulate small or large groups of people
into surrendering themselves to an established
social force that controls their lives
from beginning to end.*

Taoist Master Ni, Hua-Ching

IN THOSE FIRST FEW MONTHS AFTER THE COURT CASE
when I knew I would never see my children again, nothing seemed to appease my sorrow. I missed my children
so much that I found it impossible to settle down. I was
living within a group of some twenty- five fellow students
in a large mansion house that had a full basement, three
main stories, plus a full attic space with several bedrooms.
The house, which we called The Temple, was detached and
situated in a good locality in Kensington, London. There
was an imposing main mahogany stairway leading out
of the hall to the bedrooms above. The hallway and the
Temple room overlooked the back garden. The back door
of the Temple was entered from the basement, which was
always used by the students. The house could be said to
be a mansion by London standards, and although it had
a very small front garden, it led to an impressive-looking
front door.

The Inner Temple was a big room chiefly used for prayer, meditation, healing, and weekly services to which the public were invited. It consisted of rows of chairs with a central aisle through which Zamiar walked to the altar. Her Victorian chair with its side arms was large and upright, and placed on the right hand side. Zamiar used the chair exclusively for her trance mediumship. On the other side of the altar was a gramophone, used to play uplifting music prior to the start of the weekly service. John, Zamiar's son, swung an incense burner from side to side as he walked up and down the room before the service began. The aroma of incense lingered in the room throughout the week.

Healing services were conducted twice a week in the Temple room. They were open to the public and usually lasted from 2 p.m. to 5 p.m. every Tuesday and Thursday. We would clear the room of chairs, placing a few in the centre of the room. Zamiar would usually put on a long white overall, and would be assisted by her son, John, who also wore a white jacket. She always had two further helpers, also in white overalls. Ruth would answer the door and usher in the patients. Zamiar would sometimes go into trance if it were thought necessary for Chang-fu to assist in the healing. Herbs were administered from a cupboard in the hall, which Myrtle and I packed under John's direction and priced according to the variety of herb and the amount. Zamiar never charged for the healing but there was a donation box directly outside the door of the Temple room.

Our normal working day started at 5.30 a.m. seven days a week. Every morning we collected together for a study class. Before we entered the study room we lifted a small glass of lemon juice from a tray on a nearby table. Zamiar would come to join us, and nobody dared be late. She would come into the room commanding immediate attention as she sat down in the chair that James offered her. Sometimes she was accommodating and sometimes distinctly aggressive. Although she was short in stature, her bearing was of one of authority that brooked no inter-ference. All the time we were studying *The Zohar*[2] under the supervision of Zamiar, she would dart questions at us and if we could not respond she would either be cross or say nothing. Sometimes we found it was better when she was cross than when she said nothing, because she would pounce on us later to see if we had given the question some consideration. If we hadn't we suffered the sharp end of her tongue. The name Zohar translates as *The Book of Enlightenment*, which first appeared in thirteenth cen-tury Spain. We learned that *The Zohar* is an esoteric and immensely complex work.

Sometimes Zamiar had something to tell us before starting the study period or on other occasions she would reprimand one of the group. We usually finished the study session at 7 a.m. At 7.30 a.m. we met in the Temple room for prayers and meditation, which lasted until 8.15 a.m. Then we all went about our daily jobs, and those who were employed outside the School left for the day. Their wages helped support the cost of running the School. At night at about 6.30 p.m. we all met together in the basement com-munity room for our evening meal. Everyone prepared his or her own meal individually. Our diet was very strict. We ate only raw food, plus some Rye-Vita biscuits, tomatoes and fruit. We drank herbal infusions only, which were con-sidered important to keep us healthy. Incidentally, during all the time I was at the School I was never once ill or even

[2] *The Zohar,* the major work of the *Kabbalah*, means 'receiving'. Its central theme is the interplay of human and divine realities. The teachings of the Kabbalah are acknowledged to be profound and powerful.

had a cold or 'flu'. I was very healthy and so was the rest of the group. Tea and coffee were banned, and of course no drugs or alcohol of any kind were allowed.

Eating together lasted until 7.30 or 8.00 p.m. and was a relaxing time. We could watch television, usually the news. After this break we continued our Temple duties. Before going to bed, we gathered at 9.00 p.m. for our evening singing and chanting, which took place in the study room and lasted for about an hour or more. Some of us continued working or studying before retiring. There was always a great deal to do in the running of the School. Often Zamiar interrupted our work in order to force us to follow her dictates or to simply call us all to a meeting in her room.

My youngest brother, Edward, was responsible for going to the fruit market to buy crates of apples, pears, oranges, tomatoes, dried and other fruits. He sometimes purchased other things for the School that were obtainable in bulk, such as Rye-Vita biscuits, office equipment, soap powders, and so on. We always saved the soft tissue-like paper in which the apples and oranges were individually wrapped in those days. We spent time together flattening each piece of paper and putting them into boxes to be placed in the numerous loos in the house.

Flowers for the altar were obtained by Myrtle from the flower market, which was adjacent to the fruit market. Edward left once a week at about four in the morning and sometimes James or I or Myrtle went with him. We bought our herbs in bulk too, but they were delivered at the back door by a London wholesaler.

As time went by, like all member of the group, I soon called the Principal Zamiar and looked on her as the voice of The Masters. By living in the School I became aware of the necessity of instantly obeying all commands coming from Zamiar; which involved discarding all what I thought I knew, particularly about trance mediumship, to which I had been accustomed through my experience with Grannie Barkel. I found myself enclosed within a group that was manipulated by a very strong and dominant leader, who accentuated all our emotional feelings of fear to a far greater extent than ever anyone would have done in the 'outside world'.

Gradually, I noticed that Zamiar used our weaknesses to frighten us into obeying her least command; although at the time one was so emotionally caught up within oneself that one was totally blinded to what was really happening. The very fact that members of the group had no possible redress against her or any part of her authority, I felt was her saving grace. For us, there was no one to turn to, since Zamiar exercised a method of 'divide and rule' that kept all of us strictly apart from one another. She was, in fact, a real despot.

I tried to settle down to my new life and become familiar with my position within the group, but I found that nothing made any sense to me anymore. I could not understand why seeking for help to feed my baby had caused my life to make such a radical 'about-turn'. I went around like one in a trance, doing the jobs I was asked to do as I clung to my faith in God and the mystical experience I had had soon after I arrived at the School.

I remember thinking about the early days before I was married. Like many young girls of my age, after we left school we were captivated by the thought of marriage, without giving any due consideration to what it really entailed. Being very young and naive when I married I did not know what to expect. Parents in my young days expected a daughter to marry as soon as she came of age. It was looked on as being the proper thing to do. Parents felt there was something odd about their daughters if they were not married by the age of twenty-five.

In consequence, my conceptual views on life were very limited. I did not envisage the kind of influences that the Principal and the group would have over me. I still had a long way to go before I realised that in or out of the School I was still very unaware of how naive I was. By that I mean how automatic were my reflexes and how unaware I was of the way that I copied everybody and joined the group's habit of blindly following Zamiar, who controlled us through her ideal of The Masters, which she imposed over us. The shocks I received just before and after I entered the School made me realise that the self-knowledge that I had read about in Ouspensky's book *In Search of the Miraculous* was the first real means of my breaking away from my limited views on life. However, it took me a very long time to comprehend that I could never learn what it really meant to be a human being until I became fully conscious of the way in which Zamiar used her power over me through my belief systems.

I recalled that in my younger days I had never been encouraged to make anything of my life other than to prepare for marriage, so that when I eventually settled down to married life I was confined to a very insular family environment with my husband and my four children. This was my world before I turned to *The School of Universal Philosophy and Healing* for help and advice over the feeding problems I was encountering with my baby son. I never thought for one moment that I would become part of the School or that my life would be so radically changed. However, I can now see in hindsight that in spite of my lack of maturity, the school allowed me to find a greater clarity toward understanding how needful it is to be more open within and about one's self. The severity meted out by Zamiar and her ideas was in fact a way of teaching us lessons about ourselves that could never have come any other way. For that I shall always be grateful.

Nevertheless, in my ignorance I was easily enticed to believe all that she impressed on me. Once inside the School things became very different. I saw that I was out of my depth. Although I could see that I was being forced to experience an environment of which hitherto I had no conception, I later came to realise that it was in fact not a School at all, but rather a very strict religious cult, expressing esoteric notions fabricated from Zamiar's own ideas. Nevertheless, I had not fully realised what it would mean to live under such totally isolated conditions that were completely alien to what I had been used to among my family.

I slowly discovered that she was an entirely different kind of medium from Grannie Barkel, not only because her character was completely opposite in almost every respect, but also because her behaviour patterns were foreign to me. I was unable to distinguish between Zamiar as a person and the role she assumed as medium to the Master—or indeed a further role she held as the teacher/master of the group. All group members looked on her with the greatest respect, blindly following her dictates and loyally supporting her every venture, and soon I found myself responding in the same way. In the beginning I tried to understand her on a personal basis, which was a mistake, as I found such a relationship did not really work between student and master. I was so caught up with the emotional aftermath of my crisis and the subsequent court case that I had not noticed the power strategies that Zamiar used to discipline her group.

Zamiar's method of dealing with my emotional upheaval over the loss of my children came as a complete surprise to me. After about a month of being in the group she reminded me in no uncertain way that my wandering around the house looking destitute was having an effect on everyone in the group. She admonished me to forget my former life and concentrate on serving The Masters in the same way as the rest of the group. I was frightened by the severity of her manner, which hitherto I had not noticed. But I did not know how to handle my emotions or keep them covered up, and she never gave me any indication of a way forward, except to force me to recognise the importance of serving her via the masters. It did in the end force me to cope with the over-whelming loss of my children, by hiding my feelings away in the back of my mind.

One day merged into another, and my life with the group felt very different from the life I had been leading at home. I found it difficult to adjust to having no family to look after around me, nor a baby son to care for. At the School everything circulated around Zamiar. It was not unusual to be called two or three times in the middle of the night to assemble in her bedroom to hear a message from one of her guides or for someone to be reprimanded.

When I was unusually down hearted, members of the group would encourage me by saying that I had been chosen by The Masters to do God's work, as they had been. In spite of their encouraging words I was sometimes conscious of uneasy feelings of doubt creeping in, which I hastily buried at the back of my mind, too afraid to face them. Later, I was left in no doubt that Zamiar had sensed my feelings, for on one memorable day I was called by James to come at once to the communal room, as Zamiar wanted to see me. I was having a bath at the time, but I was ordered to come downstairs immediately and wrap myself in a towel. I was very frightened. As I entered the room Zamiar screamed at me, 'you bitch! After all we have done for you, you go around crying, not caring about anybody else in the group except yourself!' She continued shouting at me, pointing her finger accusingly, "You are upsetting the whole group, moping around the house as if you are the only person to be considered!" She was very angry. The whole group were present to support Zamiar, with comments that were either true or half-true. I was one against so many. The result of the onslaught, which was a devastating shock, was to shatter me. I could hardly believe it was happening to me. I found myself trembling in fear. It was the first time in my life I had been addressed in such a fashion. I had never been told by anyone before that my self-centred behaviour was affecting other people and that I had to change or be punished.

The impact of this onslaught did not break my inner resolve to follow the mystical message I had received soon after I came into the School. Although I felt completely unnerved, I did not cry. I think I was far too frightened and uncomfortable in only a bathrobe. I felt that my pride was wounded beyond repair. My punishment was to paint the downstairs lavatory. The group was informed by Zamiar that no one must speak to me until she lifted the ban. Before I was sent to bed that night I was reminded once again in no uncertain terms by Zamiar that I was there to do the Master's work and not to think about myself. She said the High Spiritual Beings whom she was serving were in constant communication with her and that they were very concerned that my selfish vibrations were affecting the Temple's work. Later, I realised that the term 'The Temple' was often used to apply to the School, as well as the room where our Sunday services were held each week when the 'outside world' was invited to attend lectures. Calling the School 'The Temple' seemed to impress on us an added importance of our work as a special group.

I found Zamiar's method of bringing me face to face with my behaviour through authority and pressure both nerve-wracking and frightening. I could not fathom whether she was using her personal invective to uphold the Master's power in order to substantiate her authority, or whether she was distinguishing herself as a master in her own right. Whatever it was, she made me feel terrified of putting a foot wrong. I realised that most of the group responded to her in much the same way that I did. Zamiar repeatedly emphasised that she had a mission to serve 'The Great Ones' and that nothing was going to stand in her way. She kept saying The Masters had chosen her to be their vehicle for 'The Voice of God.' I felt at the time that I had to believe her, as she seemed so totally committed: committed, I felt, into believing entirely in her calling to serve The Masters. It would have been impossible for any of us in the group to remain, had she been unable to exercise such a power over us. Besides, she seemed so very genuine in her behaviour, often raising our spirits with her sense of humour and merriment. Thus no one in the group would have dreamt of questioning her motives, not even her husband, who was a staunch supporter. We all accepted whatever she brought forth from The Masters.

It slowly sank into the depth of my being that I had trapped myself in the School with no means of escape. Zamiar made it quite clear to all of us that if we escaped from the School The Masters would find us and take revenge on us for evading our promises to support the School, promises we had to make when we took our initiation vows into the School. I gradually had to accept her methods of discipline, and was forced to look to her to help me sort out my grief over the loss of my children. Zamiar could be so wonderfully kind on occasions, which always made us long so much for this kindness that we would do almost anything to gain it. She often referred to these Spiritual Beings she was in touch with as 'The Masters', which I realised gave the group the uplifting feeling of actually having been chosen to do The Masters' work. But it could also engender within us feelings of abject fear, especially when she picked on any of us for a reprimand for not living up to that purpose. I certainly did not want a repetition of the ghastly scene I had experienced in the communal room when I was wrapped in my bath towel. Unfortunately, I was often in trouble; it turned out to be only a beginning,

Nobody in the group could anticipate when Zamiar might be disposed to treat any one of us with kindness or be unexpectedly angry or pick on anyone or all of us for a severe reprimand. I must admit, when it was someone else's turn and not mine I felt relieved, although I found it difficult to speak out in support of Zamiar against any member of the group who were being reprimanded. We knew if we did not do so, she would give us a far worse reprimand than the member who was in trouble. Even if anyone felt like supporting or making excuses for a member, no one dared to do so. If we did not support Zamiar against the victim, she forced us to do so by turning on the one who said nothing in her support, causing a far worse scenario. Looking back, I feel sure she used these methods of divide and rule to force her authority over us, just as dictators do.

Strangely enough I found there were unexpected benefits to group life. After a while one sensed that there was a certain comradeship gained from living and working together for a cause that lifted us up out of ourselves. Those who came to the lectures referred to us as the 'initiates'. One or two added that from their personal experience, they thought we had 'the look of nuns and monks'.

The School forced me to recognise my own inadequacies with regard to my personality. I found that I was still very susceptible and naive. Learning about myself was not easy, as I did not know where to begin, since self-knowledge was not included in the teachings of the School. I suddenly realised that what I thought was learning about myself was not really self-knowledge, but rather how to fit into a group without creating conflict. However, it was the very fact of living in such a tight-knit community that caused me to be confronted by my own mannerisms, which the group soon forced me to recognise. I think I was helped during this time by the teachings of Gurdjieff portrayed in Ouspensky's book *In Search of the Miraculous*. I studied the teachings minutely and began to be more aware of myself as a human being.

During my life at the School so many unanswered questions kept coming into my mind such as: 'Who am I?' 'Why am I here on earth?' ' Why have I been parted from my children?' And the repeatedly tantalising question of my childhood: 'Why was I born to be me and not someone else?' I felt unable to be at peace within myself or with others, so my questions remained unanswered. Even so, I came to realise that life meant so much more than I had ever thought possible. But that came later, bit by bit, after and as I received many more unexpected confrontations with myself.

In the beginning, as I probed into myself, I was frightened of the very thought of the path that lay ahead of me. As I continued to watch others, and myself I began to see much to my surprise just how fundamentally alike all the members of the group were. We were all very easily frightened, having shut the door on our former lives. None of us wanted to get into trouble with Zamiar. Yet I felt that we were all trapped by our initial search for Truth and our inability to see our own weaknesses, which came to the surface more quickly through group life.

I recognised much too late that leaning on others was not only a mistake but a form of escape, in that there was a certain in-built refusal to face oneself. And learning to live in the School was not easy. Yet I had only myself to depend on to keep attentively 'awake' and 'aware' in order to survive the very strict discipline meted out by Zamiar.

I felt that it was because all human beings are unique that it was possible for there to be a sustainable group; a realisation that alerted me to my responsibility towards the group. At the same time, I recognised that whoever we are and whatever we may have done individually, we are important to the whole of any organisation we may join, and in consequence we are accountable to the whole.

During the summer not long after I had become a group member, Ra-Men-Ra, another guide of Zamiar, announced at the service that he wanted the presence of The Masters to be felt all over the British Isles through the presence of his instrument. This meant that The Masters would be with Zamiar, bestowing their power through her as she travelled around in the car with certain members of the group. Blindly we accepted this. Zamiar repeated these trips many times in the years that followed, and we were all glad to be chosen. Zamiar selected different parts of the country, and the name of whoever was chosen to join her was announced by Ra-Men-Ra at the weekly service. Directly after the service those selected departed, using my car—or more correctly speaking, now the Temple car.

On the first occasion my brother James, Myrtle and I were chosen. We started off, with James reading the map, I was to drive and Zamiar sat in the front seat next to me. Zamiar directed me to drive to Scotland as I had been there with my husband years before. I suggested that we should make our way north via the Lake District. Zamiar agreed. The weather was good and we camped the first night by one of the lakes. Zamiar and James slept in the car, while Myrtle and I slept in the tent, which James helped Myrtle and me to erect. We took six days to do this journey to Scotland and back to the School. When we arrived in Scotland we made our way to Glasgow and then followed the Loch Lomond road that leads to Arrochar and on to Inveraray and Crainlarich. We took the road just before Glencoe that forks off to Oban, which is a particularly beautiful part of Scotland. We eventually spent the night on the Oban pier overlooking some of the Isles.

The next day we took the road out of Oban to Fort William, where on rare occasions the road is flooded. Especially is this so on the low-lying areas alongside the Firth of Lorne, when the tide can sometimes be higher than usual due to the weather or the time of the year. Unfortunately for us, we were unaware of this situation, so when we arrived along this stretch of road we suddenly came on this flooded area without any warning.

Horrified, I looked at the water in front of us, which was covering the road and rushing in on us. James and Myrtle hurriedly jumped out of the car and started to push it clear of the flooding water and with my efforts at the wheel we managed to get onto higher ground. Zamiar did not want to get out of the car because of the level of the water. I really was scared, but I think James was even more frightened than I was, as the water was swirling all around beneath the car. The tide was coming in very fast. Finally we managed to manoeuvre the car from the flooded area by driving onto a private road, which eventually led us back onto the main road again.

After this event we made our way further along the coast, where all around us arose a majestically beautiful range of mountains. Arriving at Fort William, we made our way through the town to Glencoe, where we camped the night amidst its rugged, awesome mountains. Glencoe is a very special area not only because of its awe-inspiring atmosphere, but because it is steeped in the lamentable history of the MacDonalds.

The next day we set off for the North of England. Zamiar decided that I must take her to see my home. I was appalled at this idea in case my children might be there. I could not understand why she wanted to torture us so. It was a dreadful thing to be forced to go there so soon after I had left them. I was sure she must have known the pain it would cause the children if they happened to be there. I knew Zamiar would not let me stop even if the children were there. When we arrived I saw the pram outside the front door, and two of my children's faces at the upstairs window. A strange woman came to the front door, which was open. As the two older children came out of the house, Zamiar and James screamed at me to go. I hesitated, but in the end I was forced, much to my consternation and agony, to drive away just as the children came towards the car. My precious children were left by the roadside—horror-stricken.

I was in a terrible state, full of resistance and resentment toward Zamiar. I loathed her action, which soon brought her wrath down on me. I was in deep trouble, with Zamiar shouting at me and creating a dreadful fear within me. I was horrified and totally mortified as I thought about the effect our visit would have on my children. I felt it was a very cruel thing to do and it created immediate feelings of deep resistance and resentment in my mind towards Zamiar. I could not understand why she behaved in such a way, especially as she proclaimed that she was in touch with The Masters. I wondered what her motive could be for doing such a thing to me and why she involved my innocent little children.

When we were clear of the village, Zamiar ordered me to stop the car and told James to drive. I climbed into the back seat unable to shut away the scene of my beloved children, who had so recently come before my eyes. I could not remove it from my mind. I remained silently crying, and inwardly terribly confused and devastated for my children. I knew they would never understand what had caused such a cruel action any more than I did, or realise that at the time and under the circumstances, I could do no other than what I was told. Tears choked me. I was devastated as I realised the total devastation inflicted on my children.

We returned to London in time for the Sunday service. Meanwhile, I knew I was in deep trouble for behaving as I did and resenting and resisting Zamiar for what she had made me do to my children. But in the enclosed confined environment of the School nothing was the same as in the 'outside world'. The punishment I received from Zamiar, besides being told off again in front of the group, was to clean all the inside windows in the house and all the downstairs windows outside. There were about twenty-five large windows and they were all mostly double-bayed. The whole mansion had very high ceilings, which meant that I had to carry around tall steps in order to reach the higher parts of the windows. In spite of my aching heart, I suppose the punishment forced me into action, an action that helped to me to control my utter despair. I remember the task took me all day.

Later, by contrast, I was made to feel Zamiar had a real affection for me. I know it may sound odd to say this, but I too felt certain affection for her, in spite of what she had just done to my children and me. She had such endearing ways when she was not in one of her frenzied or dominating moods. I suppose I looked to her for my security. I thought that perhaps Zamiar was training me in some way of which I was not yet aware, or that The Masters had influenced her to act in the way that she did.

However, for all the time that I was in the School she remained a complete enigma to me. I never knew how to take her. She had a unique way of wiping away all the hurts and starting again, especially when she told me how pleased The Masters' were with me. Her clever psychological ability to channel my mind in a completely new direction broke the spell of any rigid conceptions of what should or should not have happened, wiping from my mind the abject despair. Had Zamiar not had this ability she could not have kept control over her group. At the same time, she was able to keep everyone in the group loyally supporting her bizarre actions. This was done by her divide and rule technique, at which she was undoubtedly very adapt. I never really knew for certain how she managed it, but I suspected it was due to our fear and her authority over us. However, there was no doubt she knew exactly how to control her group psychologically.

One could not keep up any sort of resentment or pretence with her—she simply refused to allow it. I could not help feeling that she was sincere in her own way. I had to force myself to maintain my belief in her. By coming to the School for her help in the first place I had burned my boats and there was no turning back; and I was much too afraid ever to call my husband, or escape from the School.

Days passed into weeks, and months into years. Gradually I discovered that if I did not resolve the hurts and the fears I felt, as they arose, they would accumulate around me, forming blocks that prevented me from seeing the truth about myself. At first I was unaware that, in my search into self-knowledge, I needed to face the problems that came my way by myself, and not hide behind them or escape from them or expect someone else to resolve them for me. But later in my search for truth, I discovered as I watched myself carefully, that the problems arose from within myself, and therefore needed to be sorted out by my own inner being. This to me was the beginning of the learning of real self-knowledge that eventually led to self-awareness.

However, when Zamiar forcefully pointed out my failures in front of the group, I began to recognise that I was hiding behind my hurts and fears, quite unable to know how to face them. As I looked into myself further, I began to doubt Zamiar's absolute authenticity. Yet when I carefully examined these doubts, I could see that they arose from my own doubts about myself. The more I delved into myself, the lonelier I felt—mainly—I suppose, because I was being forced to face my behaviour patterns. Funnily enough, the more I was able to understand my new life, the more my memories of my former life began to fade into the hidden recesses of my consciousness.

Zamiar appeared to me to be shaping and moulding the group into a pattern that suited her; for what purpose I was unaware. I did not know if this was to fulfil her own ambitions of spirituality or whether it was that she was really obeying the 'Voice of The Masters' with specific instructions as to how we were to be trained. Sometimes it appeared to me that Zamiar held us captive by her persuasive and powerful personality. Yet at other times, I felt she was blinding us by her powerful use of the Master's Voice and often I simply did not know what to make of her. I was

sure she played on my emotional feelings of righteousness, and at the same time, I felt she was manipulating me
into religious servitude. Unable to fathom her intentions, I
placed all my attention on working to the best of my ability as hard as I could at whatever task I was asked to do. In
this way I was able to accept the position I found myself
in.

As the years passed, I needed a few more clothes, so I
wandered down to Bayswater Road or Earls Court Road
to the second-hand merchants, who placed their garments
for sale on long trestle tables, perched on the pavement
leading from doorways outside their sales room. I would
spend some time sorting through the collection of 'soiled
clothes' until I found a reasonably new garment, and if it
was my size I would pick it up and then continue to search
to see if I could find another garment. If I was lucky enough
to find another suitable garment, I would try and bargain
for a lower price, and more often than not, I was lucky.
Whatever I bought, it only cost me a few shillings[3], and
when I got the clothes back to the School, I washed them
in vinegar to dispel the smells of other people—something
that my grandmother used to say 'took away the vibrations
of people who once owned them'. If at the Sunday service
someone would happen to mention how nice I looked
in one of my new purchases, I was well rewarded with a
feeling of satisfaction, far in excess of anything I used to
feel when I purchased expensive clothes.

It felt extraordinary to begin with, going through
clothes that were none too clean, especially when I recalled
the days that I would never have been seen dead in them
or considered going down such a street, let alone buying
a second-hand garment from a second-hand merchant.

---

[3] At that time Bitish currency was still in pounds, shillings and pence,
with twenty shillings to the pound and twelve pence to the shilling.

But it is truly amazing just how quickly one's attitude can change when the wherewithal is not available. Over the years I have noticed that charity shops have sprung up all over Great Britain. I am never tired of going into these charity shops where so much is offered at such reasonable prices and the garments are often unused. At least I proved to myself that my attitude of snobbery had undergone a remarkable change over the years.

These experiences enabled me to recognise that by living in the School in a group I had gained a totally different set of values. I began to see myself in a new light. I learned so much about myself and the other members of the group, becoming aware of what I did and the way in which I behaved, as well as the way in which my snobbish attitudes had deprived me of seeing that there was so much more to life and people. I found closeness to others that I had never experienced before, even to people who were complete strangers. I could not help feeling that being at the School had some benefits. All people now mattered to me. It did not make any difference who they were or what they may have done. To me, now, they all came from one human family and I felt a part of them.

After I had been in the School a few years one member of the group said to me, "Elisabeth, don't you ever feel, as I do, that you want to be normal again, as people are in the outside world?" I had not exactly felt that way, but I understood exactly what she meant. Not that we felt in any way superior to others who were not in the School; but being in the School cut us off from the normal everyday activities of the 'outside world', which at times made us feel committed to a mode of behaviour that was not accepted in the world at large as being normal. But we had to be very careful about what we said to each other in case at a later date it was used against us. Not that it would have been intentional, but Zamiar had a way of extracting information out of us to add strength to any particular situation in which she was involved.

At times Zamiar treated me with great kindness and singled me out to be her companion, nurturing me and making me become more aware of the purpose of her group. She asked my brother Edward to fix a bell next to my bed, and often called me several times during the night. I don't know why I was glad of this extra attention, but I suppose I felt pleased just to be singled out from the rest of the group to gain Zamiar's full attention. My righteous emotional feelings had always been captivated by the thought of serving God and even as a very small child I had been drawn towards a spiritual outlook. The whole purpose of the group was to serve The Masters, but because of the loss of my children and the doubts that kept creeping over me from time to time, I could not help feeling that my present world seemed to be unnatural.

I observed that Zamiar was forced to meet changes even as the group were, but our subservient attitude toward Zamiar often prevented us from sensing her real need. I suppose living in such a tight-knit group had a very powerful effect on us. No wonder the group, restricted as they were to raw food and a rigid vegan diet, sometimes broke the rule. Even Zamiar did not escape from the pressure that such an atmosphere had over us all, and would bend the rules herself.

Being 'in favour' with Zamiar could often last as long as several months. On rare occasions she would take me to Lyons Corner House where we could help ourselves to as much as we could eat from the 'Salad Bowl' for two shillings and six pence. Zamiar's 'off the diet' favourite was deep-fried potato chips, and she had little or no difficulty in persuading me to indulge as well. But these little episodes filled me with concern that Zamiar was not living up to my expectations of her as a teacher. At times like these I found the only way to resolve my concern was to tell myself that she must be doing this because she had observed that I was developing an unbalanced ascetic state, and she was demonstrating her role as Master by sacrificing herself to show me balance.

However, I found out later that most of the group were susceptible to occasional binges, but we never openly discussed such behaviour and nor did Zamiar. Instead we pushed such episodes under the carpet as if they never happened. We could not 'let our back hair down' very often for the simple reason that we only received fifteen shillings a week as pocket money, and that had to pay for all our toilet requisites and clothes, or anything else we needed. This restriction was indeed a deterrent to our self-indulgences, but temptations always lurked around the corner.

One particular incident to do with 'off the diet snacks' stands out in my memory. It occurred after I had been at the School for about three years. My divorce papers had just come through and I was feeling particularly low. As it so happened, I was again in trouble and out of favour with Zamiar and expected some form of punishment. I sneaked out to Lyons Corner House in Earl's Court Road for a cup of coffee. I joined the queue to pay for my coffee and to my astonishment, when it was my turn to pay; I found I was holding an empty cup in my hand. I must have been drinking the coffee without being conscious of what I was doing while I waited in the queue. The girl at the pay desk looked at me and then at my empty coffee cup. She did not know what to say, nor did I. I was so shocked I could not speak. Someone in the queue offered to pay for another cup of coffee for me, but the manageress stepped forward and ushered me through the pay desk with a fresh cup of coffee, whispering to me that I need only pay for one cup. I tried to hide my tears. I was beginning to see how many good people there were in the world willing to help others who were in need. It made me realise just how hateful class distinction was and how much our true values in life can so easily be distorted by conventions or other people's opinions.

When I returned to the School, somewhat humbled by this little episode, I did not feel quite so frightened of what to expect as a punishment, which usually accompanied my being out of favour. Mostly, I never knew what I had done to upset Zamiar, but her explosive remarks would always leave me in shreds. On this particular occasion I had managed to do something to greatly annoy Zamiar. I forget what it was, but she kept me on tenterhooks before administering her disapproval. The following morning she came into the study group and told us that during the night she had received from The Masters a message of their disapproval of one of the group, without naming who was in disgrace. It soon became quite obvious to everybody and to myself that it was indeed me that Zamiar was referring to, since she continued to make pointed remarks that could only have been meant for me. Instead of directly addressing me, she implied my misdeeds. Suddenly, I reached a pitch where I could stand it no longer and asked her why she did not name me, since all her remarks were quite obviously aimed at me. She was absolutely furious and stalked out of the room. James left the room to attend her.

In the utter silence that followed I cringed. All day I could feel things boiling to a climax. That night everybody was ordered to assemble downstairs in the communal room in the basement. Zamiar immediately singled me out. I was very, very frightened. The group all came down on me. How dare I question the Master! Such a thing was unheard of. No one ever questioned the Master, who was of course—Zamiar. But I had no means to distinguish The Masters from Zamiar, which at times made me suspicious. But I simply could not possibly say so, even though I may have thought so. I was told it simply was not done to speak as I had spoken. Whatever had come over me, they all wanted to know. I was in utter disgrace. The attack continued until I was made to feel the lowest of the low. I hung my head in utter dejection and shame.

My punishment was to lay a floor covering of a smooth material, backed by a heavy hard wearing under felt; over the spiral stone steps, which led from the hall on the ground floor through a closed door into the basement below. The next day in dead silence I surveyed my task. I cried. It appeared to be so impossibly difficult. I had no idea how to do it. Every time anyone came up or down the stairs I was so flustered that I had to start measuring all over again. I had to move promptly, especially when Zamiar came up or down the stairs. Everybody ignored me. I was so afraid of cutting the material incorrectly, because I was told that if I made a mess of the fabric the replacement cost would be taken out of my pocket money! I began again with more tears. But my nature does not give in very readily so I eventually responded to the challenge. Once it was cut, I had to stick it to the stone steps of the spiral staircase. The glue had to be just right and the stone steps scrupulously clean or it would not stick. If I begged someone not to come down when I was at a crucial part of the process, they ignored me. In despair I stopped laying the stair carpet, determined to do it at night when everyone was in bed.

But by doing it at night I received a further punishment and had to clean and paint the kitchen as well. At last the staircase and kitchen were finished. I am a very fussy person and like things done correctly and I knew that I had made a good job of both the staircase and the kitchen. All the succeeding years that I was there the staircase covering never moved. Astonishingly enough Zamiar's extreme methods of putting people in and out of favour did not make me dislike her. In fact, in some peculiar way it did the exact reverse, for I longed to be back in favour again. But I dreaded the disapproval of Ra-Men-Ra. Eventually I began to find myself more and more nervous every time I was brought back into favour. In spite of feeling relieved that I was no longer out of favour.

I was slowly made aware of the divisive opposites in my nature, something that I had never taken very much notice of before. I now became aware of descending into the depth of despair one week, and being happy the next, one time hating my life at the School, another time when things changed, I enjoyed it. I could see myself swinging from one extreme to the other. I could not understand myself. Within seconds, people or circumstances could have the effect of making me feel exactly the opposite of the way I had been feeling two seconds before. This discovery was another step in becoming more aware of myself.

I recall a particular incident after my mother and father had joined the School that made me feel utterly wretched, when only seconds before I had been feeling happy enough. It was so sudden and unexpected, that I was taken off my guard. I was coming down the spiral staircase into the basement, when I had a sudden feeling that the soldering iron that I could see in the workshop had been left on. The room was directly opposite the last step on the stairway. I was unable to see if the soldering iron was on or off, for it never showed a light or glow when it was on. I refused to pay any attention to the warning voice that said within me, "If you don't turn the soldering iron off some-one will burn his or her hands." I had scarcely got into the kitchen before my father came to me with one hand red raw from a large burn that he had received by grasping hold of the soldering iron. I was horrified and felt terribly guilty. I remember that I swore there and then, by all that was holy, that I would never ever again block my ears to the inner warning voice, which had been with me since I was a very small child.

Many of these sudden warnings had saved me from all kinds of difficulties, such as knowing when someone was lying to me or when something was about to happen or had happened. The premonitions were always unpre-dictable and would come to me with no prior warning. I remember one particular occasion when I was staying in London with my parents, while my husband was abroad fighting. I was crossing a road holding tightly to my lit-tle boy's hand. Suddenly, I was conscious of a strong force holding me back. A second later a motorcycle sped past us both, with only inches to spare. Often these warnings appeared to be out of all proportion to the circumstances I was encountering at the time. But I discovered over time that these premonitions were hardly ever wrong. Since the incident of the soldering iron I have never again ignored that inner voice, no matter how trivial the warning may seem.

When we had the healing sessions I often felt what was wrong with the patient, although there was no clear means of proving that what I felt was correct. I realised that my logical mind could interfere with my perceptions, so I never felt like pressing my point or being absolutely defi-nite, especially when giving a diagnosis to a patient. I just voiced my feelings. Sometimes it was not wise to relay to a patient what I felt, so I did not do so, because I felt I should not. Then I would feel from within that a particular herb would be beneficial for the patient, which nearly always did prove helpful.

I remember an incident when I was taking the healing session on my own, after John and his wife had left the Temple and Zamiar was away on one of her trips. Two patients came into the room together, a mother and daughter. The mother was speaking for her daughter, who was apparently unwell and in her teens. I was beginning to find it difficult to gain any insight to help her. But the very fact that the mother was there gave me an instant insight to the girl's problem. She was feeling inhibited in herself due to the over-loving care of the mother. Afraid to say what she felt about her own indisposition, she was suppressing the feelings inside that were creating her indisposition. In an instant I saw what to do. I asked her mother if she would allow her daughter to go away on her own, perhaps with her granny, as an experiment to see if the daughter could discover what was making her feel so unwell. The daughter immediately asked her mother to agree. Reluctantly, the mother agreed. Several weeks later they came again, this time all smiles. The girl was quite different and so was the mother. The girl had been hiding something away from her mother, which she was afraid to tell her about. The granny had been able to extract the trouble from her granddaughter and convey it to the mother without causing any unpleasantness. I was never informed as to the details of the difficulty and never asked, for it was enough to see two happy faces. We all had a good laugh and they went away with some herbs and healing.

As the years went by I suppose my unbounded energy and business sense enabled me to improve many aspects of Temple life, especially with regard to the packing and selling of herbs and arranging the lectures. James called me in one day to tell me that my efforts had brought a profit of five hundred pounds to the School that year. This was a direct result of my taking over the management of sales and lectures. It was in the late 1950s.

In spite of my close associations with Zamiar, I never realised just how much she was manipulating me. If I may have unconsciously suspected it, I simply did not think about it. Even so, like the rest of the group, if we were ever aware of her manipulation, we did not attempt to combat it, for we all recognised that Zamiar's word was law. Being in Zamiar's good graces gave me a feeling of uplift, which I believe she recognised. But it never occurred to me at the time that it was my own ignorance of myself that made it possible for Zamiar to hold power over me.

Looking back later, I realised that it was the skilful way in which she used her powers of clairvoyance and psychological manipulation that had blinded me to her intent. On a number of occasions she easily trapped me by asking a question, and in answering her I was unaware that I was revealing how I was feeling. Sometimes after revealing my feelings, much to my dismay, she exposed me to the rest of the group in an early morning session before our studies.

One night about this time, Zamiar heard on the television that the Cambodian Ambassador's wife had beaten one of the young concubines. Apparently the wife of the Cambodian Ambassador was jealous that he was paying too much attention to this attractive concubine, who had recently given birth to a beautiful baby son. The concubine in desperation had run away with her baby from the Embassy and the cruelty of the Number One wife. The next day this story made headlines in almost all the newspapers. Zamiar suddenly decided to give the concubine refuge at the School. She instructed James to get in touch with the newspapers to find out where the concubine was hiding. One of the newspapers managed to trace her. The concubine agreed to come under the protection of the School. To establish Zamiar's case for her protection, she arranged for James to marry her immediately. It was to be a celibate marriage. Zamiar gave her the name of Sekuntala, and we all looked forward to the marriage ceremony, which was to be arranged in the Temple room as soon as possible.

In her own right Sekuntala was a princess of the Royal Household of Cambodia. On the day of her wedding she looked lovely in her deep blue sari. She was so petite, her long dark hair falling over her shoulders. Her sparkling eyes looked shyly at James. She was now a number one wife, and no longer a concubine. This meant more to her than being in the group or a concubine of the Ambassador of Cambodia. James and Sekuntala registered their marriage in Kensington Registry office. Sekuntala and her baby were delegated to sleep in my room, which was now on the first floor facing the street. She was a strikingly beautiful girl with a lovely nature. Her baby was absolutely adorable. The Ambassador sent for Sekuntala, but she proudly announced she was now married. In consequence we never heard any more from the Embassy. Nevertheless, having the baby in my room brought back all my memories over the loss of my children. I felt very uncomfortable, but in some odd way I accepted their presence and really loved having them both in my room.

Some weeks after when we had all settled down to our routine work, I noticed that Sekuntala was behaving in rather a sulky way. I asked her what was the matter. She had no hesitation in telling me that she had asked James for an alarm clock and he had refused to give her one. Much to my amusement I discovered Sekuntala was giving James a really hard time. For one so small and unpretentious, I was very surprised to note how much she was subtly making James suffer. Most of the group never got away with anything from James as he was directly in control under Zamiar. No one dared disobey him. After a week of this battle of wills between Sekuntala and James, I was very much astounded to find that the atmosphere had suddenly lifted, for Sekuntala was all smiles as she proudly showed me her new alarm clock. When I saw James the next time I thought he looked a little sheepish. Of course, I never said a word.

I remember a night when I was in bed and out of favour. I lay crying softly to myself, when suddenly I became aware that Sekuntala was kneeling by the side of my bed. She whispered, 'We have a saying in my country that right is might, not might is right.' I have always remembered her kind words. She was so full of love. Perhaps it was just as well that Sekuntala slept in my room, because before she came, when I was miserable I used to slip out of the window at night. The room being on the ground floor overlooking the street, made it comparatively easy to climb out of the window. I used to go to the coffee bar in Earl's Court Road, which was open all night. The coffee lady was kind and in her cockney way she would say, "Ello ducks, I sees summink's up! Paw lass, 'ere's a cuppa!" and she would add, "No, 'tis on the 'ouse!" when I attempted to pay. I could always count on feeling better after I had visited her and she never asked me any questions, she just took me as she found me. Yet she was always kind and motherly. She had large brown eyes that twinkled as she retorted slyly to her customers, who in return gave her back as good as they got. It was so down to earth that it brought me back to my senses more effectively than anything I had experienced before.

As I recall the risks I ran being out on the open London streets alone at that time of the night, a shiver runs down my spine. Crawling cars often stopped near me. Late at night with no one about it was really a very foolish thing to do, but I was so desperate that I took the risk. However, as soon as I saw a crawling car I would hide in doorways where no one could see me. I was lucky to get away with it, but somehow at the time the reality of the danger never really occurred to me. I was too bent on getting a cup of coffee or tea to relieve my troubled feelings. My friend at the coffee bar used to make me laugh and I helped her out if she was busy. Then I would creep back to the window that I had left slightly open and silently lift it up wide enough to climb inside and so back into my bedroom, then after quickly undressing clamber into bed.

A few years after Sekuntala joined us the School purchased a boarding house, just a short walk from the Temple. Lily, a member of the group, was sent over to take charge and I was sent over to help her. There were about nine to ten rooms to let. We had to make breakfast and clean the house. It was hard work but we were in touch with the 'outside world' again, and although the rooms were constantly re-letting, I found I quite enjoyed the change from being under Zamiar's constant supervision. Eventually, I was moved over to the Guest House and I slept in one of the attic bedrooms next to Lily and Diana, both of whom had joined the School after myself. Diana and Lily were very staunch supporters of Zamiar but I had no means of knowing how else they may have felt. Diana was lovable and kind, but could be the exact opposite given the right opportunity; whereas Lily was a law unto herself and a person whom one would not want to cross in any way. But sometimes I felt she was inclined to be that way to cover up her real feelings, especially those of doubt.

I was asked to cook the meals for the guests. My temptations were increased a thousand-fold for 'an off the diet snack', which I sometimes succumbed to. I would hastily devour a slice of toast whenever an opportunity presented itself. But I had to be very careful in case Lily caught me, as I knew she would report me to Zamiar.

I could see the back garden of the Guest House from the kitchen window as I cooked the breakfast for the guests. The chief feature of this small-secluded garden was a magnificent Magnolia tree close to the back of the house. It was a truly beautiful and a fully mature tree, and in the spring the aroma from the blossom was exquisite. I never fail to think of the Guest House when I see a Magnolia tree in full blossom.

My mother and father, who had joined the group just after we had bought the Guest House, were given a room in the basement. Mother was asked to do the washing and ironing for the guests. My father was relegated to look after the gardens. He loved the Magnolia tree and would sometimes sneak mother a spray of the blossom, which he would place in their bedroom next to mother's bed, much to her delight. I remember smelling the exquisite perfume when I entered their bedroom one day. Father had clumsily placed the sprays of those beautiful blooms in a tooth tumbler, which I remember changing for a small vase that I found.

My mother worked hard. There was always much linen to wash and iron. I helped her fold the sheets and bring in the laundry from the clothesline, which my father had erected for mother in the back garden. I recall an incident that is indelibly etched on my mind. My mother had fallen and hurt herself. All my nursing instincts made me certain she had broken her hipbone or femur, so I put her to bed. Zamiar was told of the incident, but she immediately ordered mother back to work, saying that she did not think she had broken a bone and that she must be made to continue working. I stood firmly out against this decision. I had been a nurse long enough to know that she could not stand on her leg without the gravest risk of danger and acute pain. I said as much to Zamiar, adding that I felt mother should be X-rayed and examined by a doctor in the hospital. If I was wrong then she could punish me. Zamiar promptly agreed to this proposition, no doubt quite sure that she knew best, although thereafter she was forced to recognise my intuitive ability. Typically, after this incident she put my intuitive powers to good use during the healing sessions. My intuitive sensing often enabled me to pinpoint what was wrong with patients who came for healing, thus I had been chosen as one of the principal healers to help Zamiar with diagnosis.

Father and I took mother to St Mary Abbot Hospital where she was X-rayed and kept in for observation. It turned out that I was right about her broken bone. My mother remained a patient in St Mary Abbot Hospital for six weeks. The doctor wanted to place a pin in her hip, but I refused to permit them to do so on my mother's behalf. The doctor made me sign a paper to that effect, which I did. A friend of mother's who had had a pin in her hip had always suffered pain and discomfort thereafter, which had made my mother very nervous about having it done. She was allowed her strict vegetarian diet and to everybody's surprise her leg soon mended under expert nursing care. The ward maids were laying bets with each other as to whether mother would walk out of hospital without a stick; and this is exactly what she did. She had lost so much weight that she was very agile, and after coming out of hospital she worked as hard as ever washing and ironing for the Guest House.

There were always occasions when I was full of doubts about the School, and always in the background was the pain at losing my children. I wanted reassurance as to why I was in this School. I longed for a sign from the 'Voice' I had heard in the circle that night of my mystical experience. However, nothing ever came to me. What kept me going was the ever-present hope that the 'Voice' might someday come back to me again. It never did, but I worked on tirelessly, ever hoping.

I was thankful that I never lost my sense of humour. When any member in the group was out of favour with Zamiar, I used the phrase I had coined: 'I see you have the 'initiate look'!' More often than not it drew a thin smile from around the corners of the mouth of the latest victim, as they gave me a furtive passing look as if to say, 'Be careful, it might be your turn next'—and invariably that was only too true.

Unexpectedly one day, John, Zamiar's son and his wife, Margaret, left the School and never came back. They had never shown any indication that they were unhappy or were thinking of leaving so it came as a complete surprise to us all. Margaret was Zamiar's personal secretary and typed all the scrolls for the Sunday lectures. There was great consternation, and Zamiar was by turns furious and very upset. James tried through his connections with the police to trace them, but he never did find out where they had gone. This caused us all to feel very vulnerable and sad. For my part, it was like parting with a sister and brother, but many in the group were resentful because we all had extra work to do. Diana, with secretarial experience took Margaret's place, while I helped with the letters for the School. Edward took over John's jobs and eventually life went on as usual.

After working hard at the Guest House for several years, we found much to our delight that we were making a good profit for the School. Just about this time another family joined the School, a mother, father and daughter. The daughter was a gifted artist and musician. She was their only child and her mother and father worshipped her. Zamiar felt a celibate marriage must be arranged immediately between Edward and their daughter Marian, a name she had been given by Zamiar. Another celibate marriage was therefore conducted, after both Marian's parents and Marian agreed.

Marian was only nineteen years old and she made a lovely bride, she was so sweetly innocent and shy. We all attended the wedding service in the Temple room. They registered their marriage in the Kensington registry office. Marion's parents gave their car to the School and after selling their home they handed over ten thousand pounds towards the School's expenses, since it was a stipulation when joining the School that no member of the group was allowed to keep any personal money or property.

Their generous gift enabled Zamiar to launch a magazine. After due consultation with James and the group she decided the magazine should be called the *Occult Gazette*. Marian designed the heading of the *Occult Gazette*, and it was published four times a year. It brought in much more activity and correspondence to the School doubled. I was therefore brought back to the Temple to deal with the office workload and all that it entailed. I was glad to return to my bedroom with Sekuntala. I was placed in charge of answering all mail to do with the *Occult Gazette*. I could touch-type, as I had been trained at St. James Secretarial College in London after leaving school when I was about seventeen years old, before I started my nursing career.

Marian, having designed the title page of the *Occult Gazette* helped Edward to lay out the pages and place the advertisements into position. The total number of pages came to about twelve—three double-spread sheets before they were folded over together. Marian was marvellously creative and worked untiringly. She was very young and had the most beautiful golden and gingery curly hair. Her eyes were a rich brown that had a way of screwing up delightfully when she laughed. She was very shy and did not speak very much. I remember she was always very fussy about washing all the fruit before she ate it and taking care of herself. She worked well with Edward, who was recalled from his job to manage the *Occult Gazette*.

The *Occult Gazette* was printed in Bury St. Edmunds every third month. My brothers and I would take it in turns to drive up to the printers to collect the magazines. The group worked very hard addressing labels and folding the magazines into wrappers. We purchased from agencies lists of names and addresses of cults, sects, religious organisations and societies. There were thousands of them, I recall. I suggested to Zamiar that we should search in our files for names and addresses of people who had contacted the School over the years, and she agreed. We also sent free samples of the magazines to visitors who had once attended a Sunday service or had written to the School. In this way we renewed our acquaintance with many people in many parts of the world. We also advertised the *Occult Gazette* in the magazine published by *The Spiritualist Association*.

About a year after the *Occult Gazette* was established, some of the members of the group, myself being one, took the magazine to special religious meetings that were held in nearby halls. I have to say that we were not always well received by people at these different meeting halls! We would stand outside the entrance, where we tried to sell the magazine. Sometimes we were chased away, but this did not deter us. We would also take the *Occult Gazette* to societies where we would leave introductory copies. Any spare copies of the magazine were distributed randomly to people's houses. A party from the School would travel by car to a selected district and place copies through letterboxes. I found this exercise very interesting. I began to infer what people were like from their front gardens, their polished or unpolished brass knobs, or their clean or dirty front steps.

One night I was working late in the office when the telephone rang. The voice at the other end sounded strange and agitated and barely discernible. I prayed the telephone call had not awakened Zamiar, whose bedroom was directly above the office. The voice was rough and the caller urgently asked to speak to me. I was a little hesitant, wondering who on earth could be ringing me at that time of night. He was very insistent that he would only speak to me. I told him it was indeed Elisabeth speaking. He said that my brother James had asked him to call me as he had been in a bad accident just outside Bury St. Edmunds. My heart missed a beat. I knew my mother had been with James when they set off to collect the magazines that night from the printers in Bury St. Edmunds. After ascertaining where the accident was and a few more details, I thanked him. He said our mother had been taken to hospital and that James appeared to be all right, adding that he would wait near the car to look after James and be there to meet me. I was most agitated and wondered in much trepidation whether mother was all right.

I crept upstairs past Zamiar's room onto the next landing to my brother Edward's bedroom on the floor above. I noiselessly woke him, warning him of the situation, and begged him to dress quickly, as we would have to set off immediately to rescue our brother and mother. I whispered that mother was in hospital. Edward dressed quickly and we crept downstairs past Zamiar's bedroom, frightened that she might wake up. In silence, Edward organised a thermos of hot water and some fruit, while I gathered rugs, cushions, and hot water bottles. We did not know what we were about to encounter. We crept out of the house soundlessly by the back door and packed the car. It was about 12.30 a.m. We pushed the car away from the Temple until it was out of earshot from Zamiar, then I started up the engine. We made our way quickly out of London. We felt in a nervous, agitated state, wondering if mother was still alive and whether James was all right.

We scarcely spoke as I drove as fast as I dared. As we came nearer to Bury St. Edmunds, we soon spotted the car that James had been driving. To our horror it was lying upside down on the verge of the road, near a sharp bend. Most of the magazines were strewn all over the verge, where the car had finally come to rest. The scene was awful. The lorry and driver were on the other side of the road. James was by the car. One glance at James told me he was suffering from shock and needed medical treatment at once. James said mother had been taken by ambulance to a nearby hospital. I guided James into the front seat of my car and wrapped him in rugs putting the hot water bottles at his feet, for he was in a very shocked condition. Edward gave him some hot water to drink from our flask. I looked around everywhere to see if there was anything I could find to help explain the cause of the accident to cover up for James. To my concern I found my mother's false teeth, which I knew the hospital staff would be glad to receive. The lorry driver said he would wait until we returned from the hospital; I thanked him profusely for telephoning me, and Edward gave him some hot water to drink and some fruit. Edward gathered up as many magazines as he could, and I helped him stack them by the car, covering them with some plastic sheeting, which the lorry driver had kindly given us. The lorry driver promised to remain there to report to the police and look after the magazines until we returned to collect them.

Fortunately, it was a hot summer night with no rain or mist. We drove straight to the hospital. I asked the nursing Sister to give my brother James a bed to rest on, as he was very badly shocked. At first she refused, but I was insistent. Still she refused. However, when I asked for the duty Doctor, she relented and put James into a side ward and gave him a sedative. I handed the Sister my mother's false teeth, which I could see relieved her very much, for she smiled her gratitude and it seemed to change her attitude. I found my mother severely concussed, her eyes were closed but bulging, and her face was all swollen. She was unconscious. The doctors wanted to give her a lumbar puncture, but I refused to allow it, until my mother came round to speak for herself. We stayed with her for about an hour. I could see that I could do nothing more for mother and that she was in good hands. I knew the doctor or sister would not like being told by me not to give my mother a lumbar puncture, but the sister acquiesced when I agreed to sign a paper for the doctor.

When the police came they could not talk to my mother or brother, as they were both unable to speak, mother being unconscious and James being sedated. We gave the police our address and telephone number. We could give no evidence. But we gathered that the lorry driver had told the police that he thought my brother had taken the bend in the road too sharply, and with such a heavy load of magazines, the weight had turned the car over. No other cars were involved. The lorry driver said he was coming behind James and reported that James was driving with due care and attention and not at all fast. The lorry driver was badly shaken as he pulled over the road to avoid hitting James's car. Fortunately for him nothing was coming.

After being sure mother was all right, the sister gave my brother Edward and me a cup of tea while we waited for James to awaken. When James finally awoke and finished his tea we left to collect the magazines. Eventually all papers were packed into my car and to our delight most of the magazines were undamaged. The upside down car was taken to the garage for insurance purposes by a breakdown lorry called by the police. It was quite obviously a write-off. Edward and I shared the driving back to the Temple. We quietly helped poor James into bed as soon as we arrived back; he was very upset and very frightened of what Zamiar might say to him. We made him take a hot drink and told him to stay where he was until we came to him in the morning.

Then we reported to Zamiar, who for once could not say very much, as we had taken the initiative out of her hands and everything was already accomplished. She was not very pleased that we had not informed her before we left to pick up James, and she did not take kindly to the fact that the police were involved and that we had dealt with the situation without her direction. She asked me where James was and I told her we had put him to bed as he was in a bad way. Then Edward and I unloaded the magazines from the car. We were putting them into the office when Zamiar came downstairs. She seemed pleased that only a few of the magazines were spoilt, and took one of them with her on her way upstairs to her room. We stacked them onto a long trestle table ready for the group as soon as they came down at 5.30 a.m. to put them into wrappers.

Edward and I worked all morning and most of the afternoon assisting the group. Once all the wrapped magazines were finally placed into boxes, we all helped Edward carry the boxes into the car ready for posting. Then Edward and I drove to the Postal Sorting Office Headquarters, behind St Paul's Cathedral, which kept open throughout the night. This was the usual drill that we followed when the new *Occult Gazette* was ready for dispatching every three months. After about six weeks mother recovered and returned to the School, without having had a lumbar puncture.

Some time later, after several editions of the *Occult Gazette* had been distributed I found the task of answering the many letters that poured into the office from all parts of the world very time-consuming. My accumulated experience of group life in the School, reinforced by my involvement with the magazine, opened my eyes to many new aspects of life, and this greater awareness gave me a different and wider outlook.

The group was always busy; we had very little time to ourselves. But no one seemed to mind. Generally speaking we all got on very well together, and I cannot remember any serious altercations. The only real disturbance came from Zamiar, when she had one of her intuitive feelings that a member of the group was not pulling their weight or had been on a binge. Zamiar held the School under a strictly religious atmosphere, and most of us were mesmerised into believing that whatever we were told to do was for the benefit of The Masters.

Chapter Eight

Awakening

This above all: to thine own self be true,
And it must follow, as the night the day,
Thou canst not then be false to any man.

William Shakespeare
Hamlet Act 1 Scene 3
From Polonius' speech to Laertes

IN MY EARLY DAYS at the School I was forced to recognise just how unaware I was with regard to the way I behaved. However, at this stage in my life I rapidly discovered that learning what not to do was more beneficial to me than learning what to do. I noticed that some of the group were 'taking the mickey' out of me in various different ways, constantly imitating mannerisms of which I was totally unaware. Not only was it very revealing to me, but very surprising and at times quite shattering. For example, their mimes revealed what a self-opinionated person I was. As I thought about this, I realised that the quicker I became aware of my personality and mannerisms, the sooner would my agony end. I realised, too, that I needed to change quickly if I was to fit in with group life. It was definitely learning what not to do rather than learning what to do.

Another of my idiosyncrasies, which they decided must end rapidly, was my snobbish attitude. The group took it in turns to mime this image, which they did so realistically that I was left in no doubt that I was a snob. Another thing they did was to mime the inconsiderate way that I left the door open behind me when entering the communal room, where we all had our meals and sometimes watched television. At the same time, they portrayed my standoffish attitude by revealing how patronisingly I treated some members of the group, particularly those who did the more menial tasks.

Other members of the group imitated other behavioural traits in my personality with such precision that I was left in no doubt as to my behaviour. The way I walked, the way I talked, my artificial poses and the tilt of my head, the expressions on my face and the look in my eyes were not lost on any of them. Zamiar was my greatest teacher, for her flamboyant cockney background and her no nonsense approach soon rubbed off any points in my make-up that the group had missed. I was only too thankful for my sense of humour, for it guided me away from being too hurt or too offended. It certainly brought to my attention my superficial behaviour and awakened me to the effect that I was having on the other members of the group.

What was interesting to me was that I was not left with any unpleasant memories of these 'what not to do's', since I dealt with them immediately I recognised them. Should I be too stupid not to understand at once what the mimes meant, I was soon very sharply enlightened.

During those early days at the School, the group and Zamiar revealed that for most of my life I had been unconsciously copying habits and behaviour patterns from other people; which brought my attention to my lack of self-awareness. I soon realised that I had formed a pseudo-cloak of habits around myself that must have started in my younger days when I copied my parents, especially my mother. This process of copying other people unconsciously happens all the time, but mostly in such a way that we do not even notice. I could not help wondering if parental example, so necessary in our younger days, might cause us to form habits of continual copying. If this was so, then I felt I had certainly acted out most of my life rather like a copy machine. When I seriously considered this, I was quite shocked. I saw that these habits that we all glean from one another become the root cause of many of the complex behaviour patterns that are formed within ourselves and eventually make up our personality. For example, we unconsciously copy fashion trends, film stars, people in the public eye and so on, or we copy other people's habits or expressions or behaviour.

However, my very presence at the School kept forcing me back on to myself, and I knew that if I wanted to survive spiritually, I had to recognise that the treatment I was receiving was the very means of helping me to become more aware of myself. Whether I liked it or not, I had to accept that the group were my teachers and were really doing me a great favour.

Nevertheless, during the time I was at the School I got to know the group very well, and in spite of Zamiar's process of 'divide and rule' we learned to pull together. Zamiar had an engaging personality and a lovable side, as well as the bluntness to call a spade a spade. She was small in stature, and although she had an open face she was by no means beautiful. She had a masterful capability to use her psychological skills to cajole us into following her dictates, no matter how outrageous. There was no doubt that she had her struggles, but she covered them up by being the voice of The Masters, which often disguised her real feelings. It was difficult to assess the difference between her natural character and her assumed character. More often than not Zamiar acted rather like a dictator, although behind this façade—for I suspected it was a façade—I could see there was a very sensitive side to her nature.

My interactions within group life were changing my whole approach to life. It reminded me of the vivid dream I had some weeks before I left my home. I dreamed I was confined with my family and many people in a place where it seemed that we were doomed to remain. In my dream I felt that nobody had any idea that it was possible to get out of that place. But I suddenly knew that there was a way out and that I could find it. At the same time, I knew that I would have to leave everybody behind that I loved, since I could see that nobody else would want to move away; for if they had any inkling to do so, they would not want to risk leaving behind what they considered to be their security and calling. In my dream everyone told me not to try to escape. But I felt such an overpowering desire to follow my convictions, that in spite of my family and friends, I was determined to find a way out. In my dream it seemed as if I was being told that by finding a way out there would be hope for others. I found in my dream that I was being sucked away into a different world. I knew that I could never return to all those that I was leaving behind. Yet I knew I had to let go of the world that I knew, if I was to understand the world that I did not know. All I could think about was the family and friends that I was leaving behind; although I wanted very much for them to come with me, I knew they never would. My dream revealed that even if I managed to return to tell them all about the wonders of such a different world, no one would ever believe me.

Whenever I recall this dream and its possible significance, I realise that my involvement in the School had made a drastic change to my life, which the dream appeared to have foreshadowed, so that in the cold light of day I saw the impossibility of ever returning to my former ways. I felt certain that absolutely nobody I knew would really be interested in what I was discovering, and maybe I never would be able to see them all again.

Still not being fully aware of the effects that the drastic change in my lifestyle was having on me, I found myself very restless, in spite of being forced to let go of the old life and its habits. I recognised that my new way of life filled me sometimes with apprehension and dread. Nevertheless, I had a deepened desire to learn about myself, which I had never experienced before. Although in the beginning I found my new life was both horrific and traumatic, nevertheless it remains vividly imprinted on my mind as an extraordinarily enlightening personal experience. Soon I became aware that all that I had once known was beginning to crumble beneath my feet.

Unknown to myself at that time, through my unaware-ness, I had not realised that such a catastrophic move away from my family had shocked me 'out of myself'. I believe that many, if not most situations that are catastrophic and horrific, provide an opportunity for radical and beneficial change—just as the Second World War, terrible as it was, resulted in a better way of life for many, many thousands of people world-wide. Hence, I learned that from any catas-trophe there is always a beneficial lesson to be learned.

I wondered, too, if my move into the School could be linked with my dream of entering another new world. I asked myself: would I ever be able to make another move? Or was my move into the School the only move I would ever make? But I was too caught up in my involvement with and commitment to Zamiar and the Group to think seriously of leaving the School. Besides, where would I go and what would I do?

There were times when Zamiar would bring me down to earth and take me under her wing. She would ask me to drive her to see people she felt would be interested in the

School. On the way she would tell me about her early life and how she had had singing lessons to train her voice. She said that the singing master had told her that she had an unusually deep voice and that he had trained her voice to reach across the heads of the audience. As she was telling me this, I could not help thinking of our Sunday services and Ra-Men-Ra's deep booming voice.

Much later, on one particular Sunday in the middle of her trance lecture, I remember that Zamiar suddenly left the Temple room. I followed her to find she was vomiting. Now, as I watched her carefully, I found it difficult to believe she was still in trance whilst she was being sick, or indeed even directly afterwards. She took the towel I gave to her to wipe her face and then drank some water from the glass I offered her. She had been very sick and I was concerned for her. But without a word to me, she returned to the Temple room. I followed closely behind her, noticing how very pale she looked. I was just in time to hear Ra-Men-Ra's booming voice call for extra power from the audience. He explained that he had to withdraw the Instrument from the room, as the group were not giving his instrument enough power for the Spirit world to maintain their flow.

Zamiar may very well have been quite genuine and have had the ability to slip in and out of trance more readily than she appeared to do at the beginning of Ra-Men-Ra's talks; but in order to be sick, I felt certain she would have to be out of trance. Now that my suspicions had been roused, I felt certain that she was aware of how I felt. But she had such a curious character that it was almost impossible for me to make any judgment on her credibility. I could not help but admire the way she handled the situation, it certainly showed pluck to continue, as if she had never vomited moments before.

The next day Zamiar called James from the group study session. We waited in anticipation feeling sure that because of what had happened the day before at the lecture in the Temple we were all in for another turbulent frenzy. However, James returned to say that Zamiar wanted me. My heart missed a beat. Zamiar told me that she had been reminded by Chang-Fu that an old lady had written a letter some time ago to say she was leaving money to the School. She asked me to search through the files until I found it. Eventually I returned to Zamiar's room with two letters from the old lady. James was called into Zamiar's room again to ask if, in his legal opinion, the contents of the letters facilitated sufficient proof in law to justify making contact with the old lady to ask for the money she had promised. After some consideration James said the letters would appear to be binding in law and constituted a legitimate promise of money, in spite of the letters being dated a year previously. James made an investigation into the old lady's whereabouts and discovered that she had recently been found wandering, and had been picked up by the police and taken into an asylum. Nothing daunted, Zamiar decided to go immediately to the asylum and bring her back to the Temple.

I was ordered to drive James and Zamiar to the asylum, some thirty to forty miles out of London. I felt very apprehensive. I was given strict instructions by Zamiar to drive through the main gates of the asylum as soon as James cleared our entry with the porter. Eventually, after the porter had unlocked the huge iron gates to allow us to pass through, and being told to keep them open until we returned, I drove slowly through a long tree-lined driveway to the rambling red brick building beyond, which felt and indeed looked very frightening to me. I was told to drive as close to the front door as possible and turn the car round in readiness for a quick departure. Then Zamiar gave me strict instructions not to move away on any account until she returned and then to do exactly what I was told. James and Zamiar walked calmly through the main entrance door into the asylum to find the old lady, whilst I waited in trepidation outside at the wheel of the car.

Parkland surrounded the old red brick mansion. I assumed that a vegetable garden lay behind the house, as I could see the tops of what looked like large greenhouses close to the side of the building nearest to me. I caught glimpses of people working in the greenhouses and kitchen gardens. They were in all kinds of states of dysfunction, both mentally and physically. As I waited I could hear unnatural laughter and horrible screams coming every now and then from the hospital. I shuddered. After about three quarters of an hour, the main doors suddenly swung open and James and Zamiar came hurrying out clutching the old lady by her arms between them. As they bundled her into the back of the car, I started up the engine and was told to "Drive off!" Worried, I called to Zamiar, "What about you?" She banged on the car door screaming, "Drive!" I just managed to whizz through the front gates as they started to close behind me. I drove in a roundabout way to escape detection, finally ending up at the spot where I had been told to wait for Zamiar and James. At last they came. In the meantime the old lady and I had made friends.

That night the old lady, who was rechristened Sariah by Zamiar, was detailed to sleep with me in a twin-bedded room in the basement of the Guest House. The room overlooked the garden, and had two French windows that led out onto a small patio area leading into the back garden. After Sariah had her supper, I suggested to her that as she had had a rather upsetting day she might like to retire early. I helped her have a bath and tucked her into bed.

When I came to bed a couple of hours later she was sound asleep. I quickly undressed and got into bed. I found it more than a little disconcerting to be sleeping in a bed beside someone whom we had snatched out of an asylum just a few hours earlier. I had had such a long-standing fear of insanity.

This fear started when my sister Marguerite and I were alone in our parent's home when I was scarcely seventeen years old. My sister had had a very virulent form of influenza, which had left her in a highly nervous state. The doctor had advised mother to keep her in bed for a few more days until her temperature became normal. On this particular day mother and father had left for London to listen to a lecture by Kathleen Barkel and to seek her advice regarding my sister's health. Mother had told me to humour Marguerite and on no account to upset her. I was to be there for her just in case she needed me. Marguerite was a beautiful young girl, who had been studying in a Rudolph Steiner College in Birmingham to become a teacher. She was just eighteen and had caught this 'flu' germ whilst she was on holiday. We were completely alone in the house.

I was sitting quietly with her when she suddenly decided to wash her hair. She got out of bed and went along the corridor to the bathroom. I followed her to the large bathroom and started to run the hot tap in the hand basin, in which Marguerite would be washing her hair. I offered to help her, but she was in rather a troubled mood and would not let me, so I just stood by her. After she had washed her hair she allowed me to rinse it for her. I could see that she had been weakened by her illness, but I noticed that she had a certain unnatural strength about her. She insisted on squeezing her hair to get all the water out and began pulling her hair so fiercely that I thought she would pull it out of her head. I tried to distract her attention by giving her a warm towel to cover her hair, telling her that I would dry it for her. Finally she glared at me, and then suddenly let me help her as she sat down on the bathroom stool. I gently rubbed her hair and cuddled her close to me, for I loved my sister dearly. Gradually I thought I had calmed her down, so I suggested that perhaps she needed a rest. I received no response, but suddenly she got up and walked rapidly to our bedroom. I followed her quickly.

We shared a large room together, with twin beds and a basin. She had not wanted to wash her hair there because of the shelf over the basin. There was a lovely large window through which we could see the magnificent Mountain Hemlock tree dominating our back garden. There was also a smaller window on the left side of the room that overlooked an enclosed courtyard below, where we hung the washing to dry or where the gardener washed the car. Marguerite walked quickly toward this small side window, which she suddenly flung wide open, saying that she was going to throw herself out. I froze, quite unable to think or move as I watched her closely. I remained totally still, frightened to attract her attention in case she carried out her threat.

Thankfully, all my instincts came to my rescue, and before I realised it I managed to say as calmly as I could muster: "You'll make an awful mess of yourself if you throw yourself out there. It's quite a long way down." My sister began leaning further out of the window as if to taunt me. I held my breath. I did not know what to do and was very afraid she would throw herself out. I edged slowly nearer to her. She stayed in that position for what seemed like hours to me. Then quite suddenly she lifted her head slowly and turned her face towards me with a funny, unnatural smile. She slowly walked towards her bed, as I quickly closed the window. I put my arm around her and helped her into bed and gave her hair a final rub to make sure it was as dry as possible. Then I combed and brushed her long hair, she became as meek and mild as a little baby, doing exactly what I asked her to do without a word. I knew that Marguerite was very poorly, but I felt that she at least trusted me, and as I tucked her into bed, she kissed me good night. I hugged her gently, and helped her back onto her pillows, smoothing her damp hair. I lit a night-light, which I placed on the dressing table by the bay window, and turned the main light off. Marguerite was nearly asleep as I sat down on my bed and stretched over to hold her hand. I stayed close to her until I knew she had drifted off. Tears were running down my cheeks, as I felt so helpless and found my sister's pathetic state so difficult to bear.

The next day Marguerite's condition deteriorated. The doctor gave her a sedative and said that she would have to be taken into care, which meant an asylum. My father flatly refused to allow this, as he knew that a mental hospital would certify my sister as soon as she was admitted. Father asked the doctor for an alternative. He suggested that my parents should engage a day and night nurse, but after trying this for a few days it became obvious that Marguerite needed more specialised treatment than could be provided for her at home.

My father found a nursing home about thirty-five miles away that catered for the wealthy who did not want their relatives to be certified in an asylum. The nursing home was in a secluded area in the country on a large enclosed estate surrounded by trees. It was here that my sister received treatment by a competent doctor and his staff. The mansion house was enclosed by a large walled garden surrounded by parkland. I remember the whole immensely tragic situation very well. It nearly crippled my father financially. But my parents felt my sister must have the very best possible care available outside of an asylum, for in those days the stigma of the asylum was a far greater consideration than the cost. Had my sister been certified and sent to an asylum she would have carried that stigma for the rest of her life. It was a very disturbing time for the family, especially as at that time very little was known about how to treat such cases resulting from influenza and other stresses.

My sister slowly recovered after receiving the shock treatment that was mostly used in those days. I visited her often whilst she was in this expensive nursing home. Despite her complete recovery and her return to normality, I was left with an intense fear of insanity. Thus when I was asked to look after Sariah, all my fears resurfaced again. Now I realised that this fear was being forced out into the open and I was compelled to face it.

In the middle of the night I awoke with an uncanny feeling of apprehension to find Sariah close beside my bed. Her long dark grey hair flowed wildly down her back and her eyes glared at me with what appeared to me to be a maniacal grin on her face. Her bony hands were shakily outstretched as they reached toward my neck. I lay perfectly still, then quite suddenly all my fear of insanity left me. In a flash I realised that there was no such thing as the insanity as I had imagined it to be. All my fears of such a state melted away in my acute realisation that insanity was really only a very disturbed state of mind. I said very quietly without making any movement, "Sariah, you will get your death of cold if you stand there much longer." Slowly her bony hands dropped to her sides as she turned toward her bed, her long white nightgown accentuating the dark grey hair down her back. As I helped her into bed, she put her long arms round my neck and kissed me. I tucked her up and kissed her good night. She stared at me for a moment or two, and then quite suddenly she gave me a perfectly normal smile. For the next six weeks I did not have any more trouble with her, although I did burn a night-light whenever I came to bed. I felt I had taken another step by overcoming my long-held dread and horror of insanity.

After James had managed to sort the money out that Sariah had donated to the School, Zamiar waited until the money was banked, then to my utter astonishment, she calmly ordered me to call an ambulance to take Sariah back to the asylum. At first I could not believe her, but she soon made me.

As far as I can remember that is how it rested. No one really knew the final outcome, except of course James and Zamiar. I duly helped Sariah into the ambulance, the poor darling was crying, as she did not want to leave me. I was truly sorry, as I had grown quite fond of her. However, she was perhaps going to the only place available for her condition, but when I thought of the asylum, it made me shudder and I could not help feeling that I was glad, oh so glad, that it was not me that was being taken away in the ambulance.

Another time Zamiar was involved with an irate lady whose husband had left several packets of hundreds of pounds on the altar in the Temple room. The lady came to the School crying that she had no money to feed her children, and asked for the money back that her husband had left on the altar. She said that he had left her penniless. Zamiar was unmoved and said the money had been placed on the Master's altar in good faith by the lady's husband, and she dare not remove it. I knew she had kept all my jewellery, and the money that the Court awarded me each week before my case was terminated. I was quite sure the money could have been returned to the poor woman, but that was not Zamiar's way. As far as I know we never heard what happened to the poor lady and her distraught husband, nor did we ever know how much money she had left to the Temple, though I feel it must have been considerable. I was definitely not very happy about the way that Zamiar had treated old Sariah, or the irate lady, which increased my doubts about her.

Sometimes it seems strange to me that we all obeyed Zamiar without question. I assumed it was because of the fear that she engendered within us. She placed a cloak of authority around herself in the name of The Masters, so none of the group ever thought of questioning her. It seemed, too, that Zamiar's word was law and that we automatically obeyed without question what we were asked to do, just as if we were automatons. I cannot help thinking that religious bodies who hide behind cloaks of righteousness, reveal their hypocrisy in their endeavours to accomplish their ideals of what they think is God's will. The effect of such 'religious authority' produces absolute obedience, which makes followers acquiesce to almost anything.

History shows that during the Middle Ages dreadful atrocities happened as a result of the acts of the Puritanical Christians, who imposed their beliefs over people regardless. I am convinced that acts of this nature by any religious organisation produce underlying conditions of fear, even though most human beings may not be aware of it. Even today, religious persuasions of any kind still hold very similar underlying powerful and emotional puritanical control.

These thoughts had begun to germinate unconsciously within me concerning all kinds of religious ideas. But when I started to realise the depth of my deep-seated religious beliefs, I understood that I had to be careful of my own reactions to the events in my life at the School. In spite of beginning to question the School's activities, I was compelled to obey Zamiar out of fear of The Masters, whom Zamiar kept emphasising were those to whose service she had devoted her life.

As I have said, Zamiar engineered her group through a process of psychological upheavals based on the old system of 'divide and rule', which prevented any real friendship amongst us, causing us to be secretive, divided and isolated. I think that is why I found it such a relief to find a friend in Geoffrey Watkins of Watkins Book Shop, off London's Charing Cross Road, where Zamiar bought so many of her books, which I was asked to collect.

Geoffrey's father, John Watkins, established this bookshop in 1894. It was his close and personal association with Madame Blavatsky, the founder of *The Theosophical Society* that gave John Watkins the opportunity to publish all their books and eventually to open his own bookshop. Many years prior to my joining *The School of Philosophy*, John Watkins had become a friend of my parents. His bookshop attracted many thinkers of that period, and as its reputation grew, it eventually became known affectionately as *The Meeting House for seekers of Truth*.

Geoffrey Watkins offered me much valuable advice and fatherly comfort during my most difficult years. I recall sitting in the snug little room at the back of his shop, where he used to keep all his valuable books, and having a cup of coffee with him as we entered into deep discussions about life, religions and the School. Although I always found that what Geoffrey had to say incorporated wisdom of a practical kind, he also knew just how to plant those little seeds of doubt in my head to make me think. I felt I owed him much, for he gave me a connection with the 'outside world' that strangely enough brought to me a feeling of security that I was so lacking.

He recognised that I was not happy. He said to me, "The lady protesteth too much!" when I supported Zamiar too vigorously. He passed hints to me that life held much more than just being cooped up in a religious community, and that I should explore other channels. I did not say that I was far too frightened to do so. Nonetheless, he comforted me by saying that I must never let anything deter me from searching into Truth and that I should always be true to myself.

With this encouragement I started to search into philosophical truths far beyond anything that the School offered. I learned much from Geoffrey and when I questioned him about Gurdjieff, whose works I had been studying before and after coming to the School, he told me that Gurdjieff used to buy books from the shop, and that Ouspensky also came sometimes. He warned me that I needed to become self-responsible and said to me with a kindly smile, "Have you not had enough of being told what to do? Don't you think it is time to think things out for yourself? None of us are left alone without help, you know. It is just a question of finding the courage to search deeply within yourself to find what you are looking for." Impulsively I hugged him and rushed out of the shop.

Geoffrey Watkins guided me as to what books to study and lent me quite a number on such subjects as esoteric mysticism, Eastern and Indian philosophy, which he felt would help me. I kept my friendship with Geoffrey Watkins a secret from the School. I felt very much indebted to him and read the books he lent me whenever I could. It was, however, Ouspensky's book *In Search of the Miraculous* and Gurdjieff's esoteric teachings that still held my interest the most. But reading the other books broadened my mind and outlook on life. I began to recognise that conditioning can be harmful if it becomes a fixed doctrine such as Zamiar was imposing on the group.

I gradually became aware that Zamiar's teachings were based on a false premise. She was still held by basic religious conditioning, as most people are, which coloured all her actions and her teachings, in spite of the fact that she proclaimed the uniqueness of her teachings that came through Ra-Man-Ra. In our ignorance, we in the group were enticed to believe that the teaching Zamiar brought when in trance came directly from the higher realms of the Great Universal Brotherhood of The Masters—the same Masters proclaimed by Madame Blavatsky in her books *Isis Unveiled* and *The Secret Doctrine*. I began to wonder if I would ever reach a point when I would feel strong enough to manage my own life; I felt so unsure of myself. The very thought of leaving and coming back into the world again, put me into an immediate panic. Zamiar had such a subtle, psychological control over all of us that it seemed unthinkable for me to leave the School. In spite of myself, I was depending on her.

When I tried to sell the *Occult Gazette* through second-hand bookshops, I often spent time browsing amongst the bookshelves. If I came across an interesting book, I would buy it; that is, if I had saved up enough money. After we sent out circulars about the *Occult Gazette* with news about the School, we received endless enquiries and many telephone calls and letters. Some letters needed further investigation, which I undertook when I had time. My work on the magazine gave me the opportunity for a certain amount of independence from the strict discipline of living in the School. I never told anyone at the School what I was doing or where I was going. I found it interesting to meet people in different associations and other religious organisations. I once met an interesting Sufi who played the flute rather well, I remember. He offered to take me to Spain with him, so that he could introduce me to a renowned Sufi Master whom he knew personally, and he said would help me. Although I thought of going, I was much too frightened.

Once a very young man of another religious inclination, who came to the service on Sundays, said he had a connection with a monastic order in Southern France, where the Fathers taught ancient secret teachings. He said he would be glad to take me there. Although I was intrigued, I was not interested enough in the Roman Catholic teachings, since I felt that it was impossible to tell how genuine these people were, and although I was sometimes tempted to investigate further, my instincts held me back. Another time an elderly, distinguished-looking gentleman, who came regularly to the lectures, suggested one day out of the blue, that he would like to take care of me. I was very surprised. He offered to marry me and provide me with a luxurious lifestyle. I never knew who he really was, but I had absolutely no interest in taking up such an offer.

My involvement in the *Occult Gazette* magazine caused me to question some of the activities of the School more strongly. I think it must have been my contact with so many other religious organisations that made such a difference to my way of thinking.

My brother Edward was responsible for the production of the magazine and my brother James had editorial management over the content, while Zamiar had supreme and final control. The material came mostly from Ra-Men-Ra's lectures, along with additional information describing the role that the group played in the School. Interesting quotes and asides were provided by Edward, plus the advertisements that Marian controlled.

My involvement with the correspondence occupied a great deal of my time. I answered hundreds of letters and enquiries both about the School and the *Occult Gazette.* Sometimes I met very intelligent people who dropped hints about philosophical ideas that I had never heard of before. It made me want to investigate further, which in due course I did. But whenever I got a chance, I called on my friend Geoffrey at his bookshop to ask his advice. He accepted the *Occult Gazette* for sale and if he was not too busy, I took the opportunity of asking his opinion on the magazine. He invariably avoided answering my direct questions by drawing my attention to something else, such as an interesting book that he thought Zamiar would like, or one that I should read. I was always comfortable in his presence and I was grateful for the cup of coffee or tea he offered. He impressed on me the importance of expanding my mind away from myself and searching into other philosophies and truths. He said that the School Zamiar had created gave him the impression of being more like a secluded cult than a School of Philosophy.

When I asked Geoffrey what he meant by a cult, I remember so well his words as he replied: "A cult is usually characterised by a leader who claims divinity or a special mission delegated to him or her by God. These cult leaders demand absolute and unquestionable obedience of their followers and are the sole judge of their pupil's faith and commitment." When these words sank in, I could not help but realise how exactly they fitted Zamiar. I knew that Geoffrey had seen the look of surprise on my face, because as he finished speaking, he put his arm around my shoulders in his fatherly way. Then, when he said goodbye, he added how glad he was to see that I was beginning to wake up a little to a greater awareness, which in itself, he said, was good.

Sometimes when I collected the books that James had ordered for Zamiar from Watkins Bookshop, I would browse through them before handing them over to Zamiar, and I confess I found them very interesting. As I recollected Geoffrey's definition of a cult, I could not help wondering if it was really sensible for me to hide away in this secluded cult. I was sure that what Geoffrey said was true and that he was a very genuine person, and that he had no reason to deceive me. After all, I said to myself, his father had been a close friend of my parents.

During the following Sunday's lecture my attention was riveted to some words on the overhead projector that Ra-Men-Ra was reading. They were an exact copy of a passage from one of the books, which I distinctly remembered having read before handing the book to Zamiar. Now real serious doubts shot through my mind about Zamiar, which I was again reluctant to face. When a few days later she declared to the group, in one of her early morning sessions in her bedroom, that she had been told by The Masters that 'she was the ear unto God', it felt definitely wrong to me. I immediately thought again of the words that Geoffrey had said about the School being more like a cult.

I was at a loss to know what to believe or how to act. I was very concerned, but it had confirmed my resolution to leave the School as soon as I could find enough courage to do so. I was consciously aware that I felt more suspicious than ever of the reality of Zamiar's connection to the 'Masters', especially now that she had declared herself to be the 'ear unto God'. I thought to myself, 'If she can plagiarise a passage from a book and treat it as if it were

Ra-Men-Ra's teachings, and for Ra-Men-Ra to read it out as if the words were his, how genuinely authentic were the rest of the teachings?' I even wondered if there actually was a Ra-Men-Ra.

My doubts increased even more as I remembered some of the things that Zamiar had done since I came to the School; things that I had for a long time suppressed by refusing to look at them dispassionately. The cruel way she had behaved toward my children and the blatant way she had removed Sariah from the mental institution to obtain her money haunted me. In particular, the way she used James's legal knowledge for her own ends made me feel very disturbed. I hated seeing the way she upset my brothers, especially James.

Nevertheless, I still did not feel ready to make the move away from the School all on my own with nowhere to go, no money, and no one to help me; besides, I was still afraid of the power that Zamiar held over us, which she reinforced by using The Masters' words to back everything she said and did. When I turned in prayer to Jesus, I remembered his words: 'Seek ye first the Kingdom of Heaven, and then all else shall be added unto you' (Luke chapter 12 verse 31). But Jesus did not say anything about there being a need for a mediator, and I was not at all sure that the way Zamiar behaved was ethical.

During all this time, whilst I was in the midst of my everyday work at the School, my mind was often too busy to comprehend or even be aware of the way in which I was being forced to behave. But I did feel a growing awareness of how easily I could fall into modes of automatic behaviour patterns. Yet things nearly always happened so quickly that I would be taken off my guard. Once I realised what I was doing, I put an end to my personal responses, but most of the time my pride and my hurts, my sorrows and my resistances swallowed up my good intentions.

Another experience that highlighted my dilemma over whether or not Zamiar was a vehicle of The Masters occurred as a result of Zamiar receiving a letter from someone in Wales. I cannot recall their name, but they had written on their headed notepaper asking for Zamiar's advice. The headed notepaper indicated that they lived in a castle. This no doubt intrigued Zamiar, since she asked me to reply to them saying that she never left the 'Temple' to see anyone and that they would have to make an appointment to see her. A week or so went by, but without receiving a reply. Zamiar then asked me to type a second letter saying that she had received a message from The Masters instructing her to make an exception on this particular occasion and to visit the couple. Zamiar further stated that if the couple met all her expenses, she would be willing to make the journey. Thus arrangements were made for Zamiar and me to stay overnight within their castle.

We drove to Wales a few days later. To my knowledge Zamiar had never made a journey to see anyone before, and I could not help wondering what motivated this trip to the castle in Wales, even though I knew that she had said that The Masters had instructed her to go. When we arrived at the castle we were treated like royalty.

In the evening, when we were sitting in the palatial drawing room before dinner, Zamiar suddenly and unexpectedly, with no warning, went into trance. Without a second thought, I followed the usual group procedure, and went over to where Zamiar sat and stood close beside her as a means of support. By this time her guide Chang-Fu had taken over. I listened to his messages, expressing the importance of Zamiar's work to the world, emphasising how fortunate and privileged the couple were to be chosen to hear these messages directly from 'The Masters'. As I watched the couple I could tell, by the way they were responding, that they were deeply impressed by the messages. Further personal messages followed, then Chang-Fu indicated to the couple that Zamiar needed all the love and support that she could get, pointing out to them the sacrifice Zamiar made in giving so much of her life to support The Masters' work. This profoundly affected the religious emotions of the couple, who were listening avidly to all that was being said.

I suddenly felt disturbed as I realised that the words that Chang-Fu had just used were almost exactly the same words that Zamiar had said to me, soon after I had come to the School. It was during the time that I was in a predicament over my baby's feeding problems, and my deeply emotional religious verve was very much to the fore. I remembered, too, that after not hearing from my husband these words had stimulated me. But there was one big difference. They had been said to me when Zamiar was not in trance. Now I observed these similar words were having the same effect on the couple as they had had on me, but this time Zamiar was 'in trance'. I experienced a nagging doubt that perhaps I had been trapped into the School by Zamiar's manipulative designs. Especially as I had heard from a member of the group that when I came down for the christening of my son with my husband, Zamiar had been heard to say that I was just the person she would like to have in her group.

Now observing the whole scene, in this exquisitely furnished drawing room, I witnessed the couple's sincerity as they thanked Zamiar for the messages they had received. They were both very near to tears as they promised to support Zamiar's work. Zamiar said that the words did not come from her personally and that she was 'not present when her guides came through'. As Zamiar wiped her face over and over again on the handkerchief that I handed to her, I felt my doubts receding. I was relieved that dinner was announced just then. Later when a large sum of money was handed to me for Zamiar's work, in addition to the expenses I had already received, my distrust in Zamiar returned.

The next day we made our way home and Zamiar, who was by now in very good spirits, could not have been kinder to me—which made me feel guilty about my mistrust in her. I thought that she must have enjoyed the compliments she had received from the couple, but I did not say anything—for I could not cast off my doubts. However, I did examine myself to see if I was being unnecessarily judgmental toward Zamiar.

Driving off with Zamiar sitting quietly beside me, I soon noticed that she was beginning to nod off, and thought that perhaps the droning of the engine was making her sleepy. It was then that my thoughts wandered back to the evening before in the castle, when the couple had been listening to Chang-Fu's words. I recalled that not only had the words been similar to those said to me when Zamiar was not in trance, but that the intonation had been almost exactly the same. I therefore could not help wondering if she really had been in trance in the castle. I kept asking myself was it my resistance that was the cause of my mistrust of Zamiar, or was Zamiar trying to coerce money from the couple in much the same way as it now appeared to me that she had trapped me into the School? I was unable to answer these questions. But it did occur to me that now that I was so much more aware of myself through searching into self-knowledge, I was not so blinded by Zamiar's manipulative powers, and consequently I was more alert to what was actually happening.

As I continued driving through the country across the mountains of Wales, Zamiar was still quietly dozing. I suddenly recalled a vivid dream that I had, just after I came to the School. I dreamt that I was watching a mummy that I knew was myself. I was attacking it with all my might with an axe, trying to break it open. The axe boomeranged off the mummy and hit my head. In the dream I ran away in fright. As I ruminated on my dream I began to connect the mummy with my resistant attitudes. It occurred to me that such attitudes were blinding me, and as I considered this I could see that 'thoughts' arising from beliefs could interfere and distort any understanding that I might glean of what was really happening. Then I wondered if the axe boomeranging off the mummy to hurt my head was an indication or a warning of something, an attempt to awaken me to the resistance of which I was gradually becoming more aware. Even with this realisation, I was still unable to decide whether my resistance or my doubts about Zamiar were really justified. I could not help wondering if my mind was playing tricks with me.

Many miles further on Zamiar awoke from her sleep, and while admiring the beautiful countryside she commented on how pleased she had been with our visit. I was glad to see she was in a happy mood. Later we stopped in a lovely spot by a mountain stream, for a picnic which had been prepared for us by the kitchen staff in the castle. It was a real treat to relax in the fresh open countryside and breathe in the invigorating air. It felt so good to be away from the smog of London and the noise of city life. Spreading a rug on the ground, I helped Zamiar out of the car. It was such a magnificent day, and the mountain air filled my heart with well being. We both enjoyed our picnic and very soon were on our way again. It was not long before Zamiar began to doze again. So my mind returned to my dream. I tried to make a further honest appraisal of it. Then I was aware that my mummified resistances stemmed from trying to protect myself. My heart warned me that I must be very honest or I would never be able to release myself from my conditioned self-centred states.

As I was pondering, it occurred to me that true self-knowledge was not a corrective discipline, nor was it a blame campaign. Rather, it was being aware of my reactions as they actually occurred, without any authority or judgements being imposed or directed toward my behaviour, neither telling me what to do or how to think. I could see, too, that self-knowledge was an on-going discovery, which each day brought a new opportunity to learn more about myself. Further, I realised that self-knowledge was not a question of accumulating intellectual knowledge, but more like a discarding of worn-out clothes that no longer fitted. It became clear to me that without self-knowledge I could not distinguish between illusion and reality.

I thought Zamiar had enjoyed her break in Wales, but I should have realised that she could never quite retain the same mood for very long. We had scarcely returned to the School when she suddenly called a meeting to voice her displeasure at the group's lack of support. She said The Masters needed more power and loyalty from the group, accusing us all of being slack and selfish. She pointed out to us that we were a special group selected by The Masters to do The Masters' bidding. In a high state of frustration she suddenly swept out of the room, demanding that James followed her. We all felt awful and quickly realised more reprimand was bound to follow. None of us knew what to do so we all waited. We did not have long to wait before James returned. He wanted to know if any of us had been 'off our strict vegan diet'. We did not say anything. He then said that one of The Masters had come through Zamiar as soon as she had returned to her room to say that some of the group were 'clogged up' and were therefore responsible for spoiling conditions for the rest of the group. James said we had better be careful of our behaviour, as it was a very, very serious matter to upset The Masters. He pointed out that the next day was Sunday, so we must all give of our best or the work of The Masters would be seriously affected. We often had these 'pep' talks from James.

James dismissed the meeting and asked me to remain. He requested the money that had been donated to the School by the couple in Wales, which I handed to him in the sealed envelope that had been given to me. He then added that I must go to Zamiar immediately as she wanted me to type a special letter to thank the couple in Wales for their hospitality and donation. Although I could not be sure of knowing if I was out of favour or not, I made my way in some trepidation to Zamiar's bedroom. As I knocked at her door and waited before entering her room, I realised that James was close behind me. According to the usual procedure we took off our shoes as we entered Zamiar's room. Zamiar gave me dictation for the letter I was to type. She stared at me in a penetrating way and said that The Masters were unhappy with my behaviour. I knew at once that her clairvoyant powers had enabled her to pick up the contradictory feelings of distrust and doubt that had crept over me during our recent visit. I wondered why she had not said anything when we were coming home from Wales. She said The Masters told her that they were worried about my loyalty. I did not know what to say, and in my fear and confusion, I began to cry. Zamiar shouted at me to get out of her sight and bring back the letter as quickly as I could. Trembling with fear, I left the room.

Reflecting back as I went to the office to type out the letter, I could not help thinking that my emotion of fear was a reaction that was blinding me, making me imagine all kinds of things that were probably not true. I could so easily be made to feel afraid of Zamiar, producing within myself many uncertainties and contradictions that immediately interfered with my awareness of what was actually happening to me. I knew so well the feelings that were emerging within me. For after a spell of being in good favour, an out of favour period was bound to follow. Slowly it dawned on me that the repetition of the 'in and out of favour' cycle occurred only when Zamiar was personally able to throw me off my balance, either by her rebukes or by helping me embark on an ego trip. I began to realise that it was my fear that enabled Zamiar to manipulate me as she was doing, immediately sending me out of favour. I was unaware of how I was being personally affected by her remarks, and that enabled Zamiar to force me into a corner of myself where my fears got the better of me.

However, as I was typing out the letter, I realised that crying when Zamiar rebuked me showed her that I was personally affected by her words and actions. In consequence, I had opened myself up for Zamiar's ability to manipulate me, and this explained how she was able to push me out of favour so easily. Whereas, were I to observe myself honestly without being so personally caught up by what Zamiar said to me, the outcome might be very different. By crying, I showed Zamiar how susceptible I was to what she said. I wondered whether I was ever going to change myself under such circumstances.

Some weeks later, when things were back to normal—or as normal as they would ever be—I became aware that Zamiar was once again using my strong emotional and religious desires, translating and moulding them into a form of worship directed toward herself. My emotional religious desires were blinding me and leading me into doing things that my conscience rejected. Finally, I perceived that Zamiar was using my religious desire of wanting to become more perfect in the sight of God to enable her to entice me into doing whatever she wanted, even though I was intuitively aware of being manipulated. By responding to her in that fashion, I became a perfect 'initiate' seeking perfection out of an ascetic, religious fervour. In other words I had once again become a victim to Zamiar's manipulation, and I realised that I was acting rather like an automaton.

As I tried to incorporate my own ideas and insights into my daily life I was often stopped in my tracks. I discovered that this gave me an awareness that helped me from rushing to respond to events and circumstances that might have led me to regret my actions afterwards. However, sometimes when I found Zamiar's behaviour unethical and against my instinctive principles, I knew I could not escape from being involved whilst I remained at the School. I had to face the fact that while I was living in the School I was forced to support Zamiar, and so I continued to serve and support her in all that she did. But the fears of what might happen if I abandoned my commitment to Zamiar and The Masters was a very different experience, and a real threat that created tremendous feelings of disloyalty and guilt within me, especially when I thought of leaving.

However, I made up my mind to stop running away from my problems, as I had done previously before I came to the School. I knew that my behaviour and attitudes were undergoing fundamental changes since I had left my home and family. Yet, in spite of feeling disorientated, I realised that the reason was that I only had a very limited understanding of myself and that I still did not have a proper realisation of what self-knowledge really meant. This insight spurred me on to recognise that self-knowledge was more accurately expressed when in conjunction with self-awareness. My need for more complete understanding of myself made me aware that I had to be absolutely honest. So I watched myself ever more carefully. I began to perceive that by trying to improve I was still seeking self-perfection, and therefore suffocating any attempts on my part to awaken to self-awareness.

This was how I came to recognise that my search for Truth through the teachings of Kathleen Barkel and various other religions came from an intellectual approach to Truth. I realised that these religious teachings in themselves did not, and could not, help me to become aware of myself, any more than the teachings of the School could. But I realised that in recognising the thick walls of resistance that I had built around myself, I could begin to expose those deep-rooted conditioned states that lay beneath my consciousness.

Thus I was forced to recognise that it was the experience of living in the School under the perpetual strain of Zamiar's masterful control that had awakened me to my system of self-defences and resistances. I asked myself; "did I need to look for a much deeper, more effective approach to life or if I did was I not coming from the same conditioned state?" I could see that I was still not in command of my life; it made me question myself more closely so that I became aware of the many unanswered questions that had repeatedly presented themselves to me over the years. It made me ask again: 'Who am I?' and 'What am I doing here on the earth?' and 'Why am I always turning to someone else to solve my problems?'

In my uncertainty, despite all the ups and downs, I continued to search for something or someone who could lead me to some form of salvation or deliverance. I wondered why I did this. I was not able to define what I meant by salvation or deliverance. Nonetheless, each time I thought I was closer to finding a better understanding, I was forced to look deeper. The irony was that in spite of not being able to break free from my past and become more aware of myself, I found that it was still those self-centred activities that so often brought me to a state of isolation within myself. I asked myself 'What should I do now?'. At least one thing became clear to me: I knew I was responsible for being where I now found myself, and that searching and seeking outside of myself for answers to my problems did not, and could not, help me either.

Chapter Nine

Awareness

Awhile, as won't may be,
self I did claim:
true Self I did not see,
but heard its name.
I, being self-confined
Self did not merit,
till, leaving self behind,
did Self inherit.

Jalal al Din Rumi
Man's Religious Quest

I NOTICED THAT ZAMIAR was not the only one who made use of the realms of The Masters, attributing to them the power to manage the evolutionary progress of the world. Madame H. P. Blavatsky, in her books *Isis Unveiled* and *The Secret Doctrine* also claimed that she was in close contact with The Masters of the Brotherhood of Humanity, or the Great White Brotherhood. In 1875 she established the *Worldwide Theosophical Society* and became an international figure of enormous influence. She claimed, too, that when people had dominion over themselves, secrets and unexplained laws pertaining to mankind's inherent powers would eventually be uncovered. These secrets, Madame Blavatsky explained, were not really secrets, but rather hidden only in so far as they cannot be divulged to those who have not awakened to full self-awareness; that is, only to human beings who have recognised the very roots of self-awareness and are ready to perceive the secret laws that govern mankind. I do not think it is simply a question of progressing to a state of readiness so that you can gain secrets.

My own investigation into self-knowledge had started before I left home through the teachings of G.I. Gurdjieff and R.P. Ouspensky[4]. It took me a long time to realise how important self-knowing was for all human beings and for me too; and especially to realise that so long as we are engaged in observing the imperfections of others—as if their imperfections were not the same as our own—we deprived ourselves of opportunities of learning about ourselves. What I realised was that it was my habit of allocating blame that prevented me from being aware that I was continually caught up in criticism. I also recognised that it was imperative to understand that so long as I was unaware, I was totally unconscious of what I was really doing to myself. This seemed to indicate to me that for most of my life I had been living in a dream world, isolating myself away from the rest of humanity by my insular behaviour. In reality, however, I could not deny that I was an intrinsic part of humanity and that I affected others as much as they affected me. Whether I faced this fact or not—realistically—I could not avoid coming under the same cosmic laws and materialistic influences as all other human beings.

Reading the books given to me by Geoffrey Watkins helped me to gain a much wider concept of Spirituality from other points of view. I wanted not only to understand and resolve my own difficulties, but also to find the root cause of the many problems and predicaments that I was meeting everyday in the School. I was, in particular, looking at the roots of my own behaviour to discover what had caused my predicament and dilemma in the first

[4] See Gurdjieff's book *Meetings with Remarkable Men* and P. D. Ouspensky's *In Search of the Miraculous.*

place. By reliving my traumas again and again in memory, I began to realise that if I could take a larger view, I might see that my predicament and dilemma were actually small in comparison to the rest of humanity's problems. Even so, that did not seem to be an answer as to why we human beings are here on earth or why we have problems or why in our ignorance we always seems to view our problems so divisively. I asked myself: "is the fundamental cause of our conflicts and problems rooted and grounded in our conditioning and ignorance? Or is it ignorance of our inner reality that is the cause of our problems? I wondered whether it was at all possible to open my eyes to a freedom that would lead to true self-awareness?"

But deep within, I felt that if I was to take charge of my life, I had to face myself completely and honestly. The steps that I had taken to hold on to my inner aspirations had compelled me to be true to myself. In my prayers I had begged for help from Jesus, but I never envisaged in my wildest dreams that I would actually have to be parted from my children. Therefore, when the time came that my marriage broke down—to say that I deliberately left my children was not true, though the fact that I did cannot be denied. To say that I chose to go away from them was also not true, though I cannot deny that the School gave me refuge, after it became impossible for me to return home through my fear of being sent to an asylum. My anguish was that at the time there was no other way. I do feel that to make judgments or to apportion blame cannot remove the facts or alleviate the pain of parting for any of us, but I knew I had to face the situation in its entirety.

However, during my time at the School when I was trying to understand myself, what alarmed me was to discover that my dilemma seemed to be strengthened by the repetitiveness of all the shoulds and the should not's, the hurts and the self-blames, the sorrows and the fears, the losses and the horrors that accompanied those memories. The events of the past kept repeating themselves in my mind as memory. Thus I realised that my thoughts were seeking for an explanation, and I became aware that my thoughts continually wanted to alter and shape what had been into what I felt should or could have been. This gave me no rest psychologically nor did it take the pain away.

Eventually, I observed that continual rehearsal of my traumas from memory was an endless process of no value and did not help me. In fact, I could see that my sorrows were being kept alive through my identification with the memory of them and through my misuse of personal thoughts. Therefore my sorrows were being tossed about endlessly in my mind in a form of thought dialogue. I saw that every time I identified myself with the past I was adding misery to what had already happened, which I could not change. When I realised that, I could see that I was keeping my sorrow alive, reinforcing it by repeatedly allowing my mind to churn my thoughts over and over in my head. I suddenly recognised that such behaviour prevented me from gaining any self-awareness. I had to be very watchful and very honest if I was to understand the root cause of my sorrow. At the same time, I recognised that there was no one to whom I could turn to for help but myself.

I noticed too, as I closely watched the movement of my thoughts, that my memory was resurrecting my sorrow away from myself, constituting it as an objectified image. It was as if my sorrow was no longer a part of myself any more, since I had purposely distanced myself from it, not being able to face it. At last, I understood that by doing this I would never be able to face my sorrow. Allowing my thoughts to run wild stopped me from being attentively aware of the conflicts that my present thought processes were causing. Slowly, as I remained with this discovery, it became very clear to me that my personal thoughts were only pushing me toward believing that the situation could have been different—no, would have been different—if only I had known better or circumstances had been different. Thus I saw by thinking this way I was keeping my sorrow alive in a close-fitting groove through thoughts, at the same time building a wall around myself, beyond which I did not allow anyone to enter; oddly enough, not even myself.

Then, I recognised that in order to understand my trauma in a rational way, I had to look at it exactly as it was, not as I thought it was, nor as I thought it should have been. Now I could no longer ignore what this negative personal thinking had been doing to my emotions through thoughts, which by this behaviour I could see nothing would ever change. When my thoughts ceased to interfere or push my sorrow away, I noticed that it was no longer just my sorrow, but sorrow per se. I realised that I had been isolating myself away from the very sorrow itself, living personally continually in the effects. At last I recognised that while I kept my sorrow alive in my memory through my thoughts churning it over and over, without seeing it as it really was in all its stark reality and staying with it, I could never understand my sorrow nor could I release myself from my thoughts concerning it.

Thus when my sorrow surfaced again I was no longer frightened of it. Further, I found that I could face it with no regret for the circumstances that had arisen to cause such a predicament and dilemma. I realised that by using thought in a personalised way I had kept those memories of sorrow alive. But when thought was quiet, when there was no space in which thought could move, I perceived that there was no space between myself and my sorrow; they shared but one identity. I recognised my sorrow as purely an intellectual projection, which I had not found the right way to deal with it in an impersonal way, so that it remained with me still.

After many years at the School I was thankful to find that I had begun to grow a new sense of awareness. Nevertheless, I was still very unsure of myself. But it was my firm conviction that first I needed to be totally committed to minute by minute of self-awareness, so that I could approach the Divinity within myself in a practical and sane way, without my religious emotions taking over. I knew it was almost impossible to be aware all the time—but I discovered that being aware of my unawareness worked well for me. I felt that the initial starting point was at least to know that I needed to be aware if I really wanted to know myself. A great many thinkers have pointed to 'Man know thyself.'

Life in the School's relationships offered no shortage of lessons to be learned about myself, and I certainly was aware of the fact that my mind and my thinking were very limited when I tried to deal with myself in the presence of Zamiar. Even the self-knowledge I had learned caused me to feel at times that I had blinkers over my eyes. I knew that a very important factor in helping myself to change was the degree of awareness and attention that I could develop toward my everyday tasks and encounters, such as the care that I took when making my bed or cleaning my room or doing my jobs, or listening to another member of the group; and in particular being conscious of my behaviour in the presence of Zamiar, particularly my fear of her. All these deeper considerations emerged as I widened my vision by the insights I received from working on myself and in my relationship with others.

I knew that before I had come to the School, I had put my faith in the religious indoctrination that had been instilled as I had grown up. Later I had put my faith in Grannie Barkel's Teachings. Now I recognised that even by putting my faith and security in Zamiar and the School, the situation within myself had not changed. In fact, I recognised that I was in much the same position as I had been before I came to the School; only I was now within a very different environment from any I had ever known before. It slowly dawned on me that there could be no security or happiness where there was any form of authoritative conditioning. This shocked me into the realisation that I was following Zamiar as if my life depended on her, if not totally, then certainly as long as I remained in the School.

As I turned my full attention to the life that we were leading within the group, I discovered that there was little or no real love generated amongst us, there was only the predominant emotion of fear. Yet in spite of Zamiar's 'divide and rule' strategy, which created that fear, there were unmistakable moments of kindness with her, when she drew us together, just at the right moment to bring a balance to our feelings of insecurity. She was using a side of herself that was loveable and endearing to manipulate us into responding to her every whim.

Much later, after I had been at the School some years, I questioned myself whether it had been necessary to obey Zamiar without question. In my doubting, I came to recognise that I had been responding to Zamiar and her use of the Master's powers in much the same way that I had responded to the powers of the Church, which upheld God. I remembered that in my childhood we, as a family, often discussed God and Jesus. Therefore I had naturally assumed that religion was the mediator between God and myself. I suppose, being very conditioned when I joined the School, I did not think to question Zamiar's authority any more than I had questioned my parents' or the Church's authority. I had no real ability to judge Zamiar's genuineness, but I found that neither my parents, nor the Church, nor Zamiar helped me to know myself or helped me to become self-aware. In fact, I had to face the fact that both Zamiar and the Church were openly encouraging their followers to lean on them—quite the opposite to the self-responsibility that I was beginning to understand was the essence of self-awareness.

Pursuing my new understanding sharpened a further awakening to self-awareness. It became clear to me that by supporting Zamiar and her School of Philosophy, I had been seeking spiritual self-gain. This was quite a shock to me as I pondered over such a consideration.

Thus with every increase in awareness, the strength of my desire to leave the School grew, but I was still unable to find the courage to do so. I was torn between my feelings of disloyalty to Zamiar and The Masters, and the insecurity I felt within myself of facing life alone. Nonetheless, I knew deep within me that I wanted to find a meaningful awareness of the Essence of all life. Although, I realised, I did not understand the Wholeness of all Life or the Connectedness of our lives to the Universe; but I did have an inner desire to find a relationship with those Unseen Powers of Divinity of which I was beginning to feel I was a part. I recognised, too, that the Essence of Life was the God Consciousness or His Essence that is within all human beings. It seemed to me at the time that I could never find this kind of Consciousness. I knew that this realisation had a tremendous effect on me as I became more aware of its implications.

I recognised that without awareness I could never find the reality of what it meant to be a human being or understand the meaning of the Essence of All Life. Yet I could not help but feel that it is open to all of us to awaken to that Spirit Essence, which is within us. For I felt that my present narrow outlook of a 'tunnel vision' only gave scope for a limited understanding that kept me within the confines of the School. Not that I thought the 'outside' world could help me, but I felt the need to be away from the total restrictions that Zamiar so authoritatively placed over the group; so that I could have the courage to be self-sufficient.

I began to question whether it was possible to rectify this predicament, which we all seemed to be in. At once I realised that the only possible way was to be aware through and through; that is, totally aware of the illusions that we had slipped into and were unconsciously creating for ourselves by following Zamiar. I could see that acting out our lives in this illusory way was very restricting, with no real recognition of the 'True Self I did not see', though I may have 'heard its name'.

I knew that the prime move in my life was to let go of the predominance of my self-centred activities, which arose through my identification with everything that the self undertook. Once I became aware that it was only my blindness and ignorance that prevented me from recognising the innate abilities that we all have to discover as our heritage—our God consciousness—I felt on surer and safer ground to stand on my own two feet. The very fact that all human beings have the same opportunity to make radical changes to their lives filled me with a feeling of hope. I visualised the way forward was resting on a clear perception of the heritage at the heart of our very being. As I struggled, it seemed to me that self-awareness was a key factor and absolutely essential if I was to appreciate what it meant to live a truly spiritual life. But I was only in the early stages of this awareness and so I had to tread very softly, like one walking on thin ice.

The question I asked myself was: 'What is the *self* that *self-responsibility* refers to?' I could see that the true essence was not my self-centredness with its conditioning, indoctrination and identification. In my heart, I questioned why I was divided from my true essence. If it was True—real—then why was I divided from it? Or was it my unawareness that had created this division within myself? Nonetheless, I was drawn to recognise that there must be a True Essence. It seemed to me that self-awareness embraced both—the male and the female, the Yin and the Yang that the Chinese portray, which is what the fairy tale *The Sleeping Beauty* illustrates.

In the story, the sleeping Princess is unable to play her part as the Essence until she has been kissed awake—recognised—by the prince. The prince is the active part of ourselves that needs to 'turn around', away from looking outwardly—objectively and self-centredly toward the materialistic world in the quest for Truth, and instead turn inwards to find the sleeping Princess—the True Essence that lies within. The Princess awakens the prince to the recognition of the God Consciousness within, which she portrays, which is the very source of our True Being. By the union of Prince and Princess, there is an immediate interaction between the opposite forces of male and female within us, so that these counterparts are no longer disconnected, are working in harmony together. An entirely different energy is therefore generated. The God Consciousness—the Princess—is the Light within that no one can extinguish. Jesus said: '*Let your light so shine before all men, that they may see your good works, and glorify your Father who is in heaven.*' (Matthew 5 verse 16).

I made one more discovery about myself before my days came to an end at the School. I discovered that I had always tried to fit Zamiar into the role that my mind imagined she should occupy. In reality I never saw the real Zamiar, only the image I had projected in my logical mind. I thought that her high ideals matched my own; but I had to learn that by following Zamiar I was chasing after fantasies of what I *imagined* perfection to be, a perfection that was built only on illusions of my own fabrication, and which could thus never be true. I felt Zamiar believed that her ideals would become realities if she took cover behind The Masters, in the same way that I was taking cover behind my own idealistic illusion by following what I thought she represented.

Then it suddenly occurred to me that I had done exactly the same thing when I married the father of my children. I had taken cover behind images of what I thought was my ideal husband. I had to learn the hard way that ideals were not realities. It was then that I recognised that I knew neither myself, nor my husband, nor Zamiar as each of us really are. I had tried to fit each of us into the imagined pattern in my mind. No wonder my life was so complicated and fragmented. It slowly dawned on me what illusions I had created for myself. Now as I carefully watched others, I perceived that this realisation applied to the way most of us unconsciously live our lives.

Furthermore, I saw that what I had been wanting and expecting of Zamiar and the group was that they should fit in with my mental preconceptions of what I thought they represented; which, I now realised, was exactly what I had wanted with regard to my marriage. I had created an image of myself of a perfect wife and mother, at the same time as projecting my husband as an image of a perfect partner, along with all that went with such imagined relationships.

And what is more I had been constantly refuelling such a notion to keep it alive. Now I realised that such concepts had no reality in fact, so that it became a case of two people living together as images, and neither ever understanding the illusionary world in which they lived until a crisis arose. There was, then, no solid foundation to their relationship to enable them to ride the storm. This realisation forced me to face the impossible situation that I had created for myself. No wonder such image making causes so many problems and conflicts. Basically, it seemed that I did not understand the power of the misuse of thought. I saw that image making inevitably produced a cause, followed by an effect, due to the embodiment of my thoughts into self-created images of what I thought I was or others were. My awareness at last opened my eyes to the way such stereotypical thinking was leading me astray. I saw that this was why I was unable to understand my actions, since I was always living in the projected illusion of those images.

Thus I realised that I was compelling myself to meet unnatural situations that I had created in my imagination. Although I was still not quite sure how to respond to this immensely interesting and fundamentally new understanding within myself, I nevertheless tried with all my heart to respond to its significance. As I carefully watched myself and others living in their own little worlds of image making I could see we were all responding to our own separate and unreal worlds. This realisation forced me to 'turn around' my whole approach to life. It was now that I knew for certain that I no longer wanted to remain at the School. Yet, to start a new life and earn a livelihood presented me with a huge problem that I did not know how to overcome. I could not help comparing my situation with The Nun's Story, as follows:

Kathryne Hulme, its author, gave a graphic description of what a nun has to do to relinquish her vows to God and the convent when she feels she can no longer remain a nun. This story engendered within me great sympathy towards the nun. I was struck by the similarities that we were both facing. Since neither of us could any longer accept the behaviour expected of us without feeling hypocritical, we had come to the end of being confined under the authority of a religious order. But for a nun to be able to leave, the Mother Superior of her convent had to make contact with the Pope to gain his permission. As soon as permission was granted, the Mother Superior would explain to the nun the release procedures that she was expected to follow. At the same time the convent would return all the money that her father had given to the convent for her dowry. The nun would be given a complete set of second-hand clothes in exchange for her nun's habit. She was then free to leave the convent and return to her family or do whatever she liked. These procedures had to be strictly adhered to, according to official Roman Catholic rules and regulations. One can only imagine what a shock this was for the nun.

By comparison, I had no release procedure, nor would any of the money or jewellery or the car that I had given to the School be returned to me; and since I had cut myself off from my family I did not feel very happy about returning to them either. These thoughts made me feel very uneasy and unsure of my path ahead. Kathryne Hulme's book made a big impression on me, and the nun's courage filled me with admiration.

In spite of reading the story of her return to ordinary life, I recognised that my present lack of confidence was deeply rooted in material insecurity. I wondered if there was such a thing as real security? Or was I placing my confidence in things that were not secure, and thereby creating resistance that blocked my understanding of self-recovery, self-responsibility and self-awareness. This new realisation made me aware that I still did not have enough faith in the Essence of All Life to feel secure enough to stand on my own feet.

Chapter Ten

Conditioning and Indoctrination

Those who know others are intelligent;
Those who know themselves have insight.
Those who master others have force;
Those who master themselves have strength.

Tao Te Ching
Translated by R.L.Wing

AS 1960 DREW TO A CLOSE I realised I had been at the School for nearly five years. Despite finding a certain sense of security from living in a group, l recognised with a feeling of uneasiness that my life was slipping away and I was becoming very isolated by dwelling in such a secluded environment. Zamiar claimed our whole attention and motivated us to do what she called 'the Master's work'. Her overbearing demands were kept alive by the School's general religious atmosphere. The lectures we had each Sunday spread a sense of euphoria amongst us that encouraged a devotion to serve.

In our daily activities Zamiar exercised her demands over us by continually emphasising the unseen powers of The Masters and the work we were committed to do. This subtle method of control prevented us from being conscious of her manipulative influence. However, we soon learned to justify any fears or uncertainties by obeying, without question, what we were asked to do in support of the work of The Masters.

The many shocks of rigid discipline that I received in my early and later years at the School always seemed to take me completely by surprise. Zamiar's acute clairvoyant powers enabled her to hold the group together under her total command. Her undeniable psychological skills enabled her to keep a masterful watch over most of the activities of the group. In many ways I cannot help but feel that the measures she took were justified, in the sense that without her constant discipline we could not have recognised the negative roles we might have played if left to our own devices.

Another important factor was that before I came to the School I had never really understood the effect that my previous religious involvements had had on me, either from an orthodox or an unorthodox point of view. However, I was aware through my own intuitive powers that there was something greater than myself urging me ever onward to find an answer to my immediate dilemma of trying to understand myself. My suppressed emotional feelings would often take the form of bouts of depression, or resistance in the form of habitual states of conditioned psychological processes that surfaced more strongly during my interactions with the group—and especially when I was with Zamiar. She was acutely aware of my unbalanced emotional behaviour, which she never allowed me to hide below the surface; I am sure that was why I was so often in trouble. This became even clearer to me as I watched the thoughts moving about in my head. I noticed that they were nearly always repetitive, especially with regard to my sorrow over the parting from my children. To my astonishment, as I became more conscious of my behaviour, I found that these thoughts would go on for hours if not for days, popping in and out of my head. I observed just how destructive and chaotic some of them were at times.

Before the *Occult Gazette* was published and while I was working in the Guest House, I remember, one particular lady regularly used to knock at our front door. One day I answered the door to her. She stood silently watching me and then suddenly blurted out, "I don't know what to do!" and she kept on repeating these words over and over again, wringing her hands in anguish. I tried to comfort her by telling her that I often did not know what to do either. But I soon discovered that she was beyond my help. She came so regularly to the door after this that we would say, 'Here comes Mrs I-don't-know-what-to-do!' She would come up the steps like one in a trance, and as soon as we opened the door she would suddenly stop muttering and glare at us, and then start saying over and over again: "I don't know what to do!" Then quite suddenly she would swiftly turn and descend the steps muttering all the while, "I don't know what to do…" This, of course, is an extreme example of how the mind becomes fixed in a repetitive psychological loop. It is as if the mind is grooved like a needle on a gramophone record caught on a defect, causing a continual repetition of the same piece of music over and over again.

However, I found that these thought dialogues only happened to me when I personally identified myself with a past situation. It was only when I managed to 'catch' myself in the very act of this personal identification enigma that I discovered the effect it was having on me and doubtless on the group. Then I realised that my thoughts were in a perpetual state of motion, and were never at rest or silent. I noticed, too, that I was unaware of the conditioned and indoctrinated influences that lay within my conscious and unconscious mind, automatically affecting my behaviour. But through watching myself carefully and being very honest, I became conscious of the rigidity of the conditioned thinking processes that kept confronting me in the guise of a certain automatic behavioural response, which I had never noticed when I was with my family.

After a while, I noticed that my conditioned behaviour had become so habitual that at times it was difficult to detect, since my responses were often so automatic. I was unable to understand why I behaved in this manner or how conditioned I was. I began to realise that my conditioning could lock me into a state of fear, which exactly describes the suffocating position I often found myself in when I was afraid of Zamiar and The Masters' power.

In hindsight, I could see that in order to hold complete control over the group, Zamiar had to use every means in her power to cajole the group to obey her slightest wish. Unfortunately, when we are swayed in such a fashion, we are unaware at the time of the implications arising from the weaknesses within ourselves that have made it possible for us to become easy prey to this deceptive form of authority. As I observed a gradual decline in Zamiar's behaviour, an increase in her egoism became more apparent, bordering on a form of megalomania. By ruminating on my new understanding, it occurred to me how similar this was to being ruled by potentates like Stalin, Hitler, Mao, Saddam Hussein and other dictators.

Pondering more deeply over my unconscious behaviour, I found that it was very necessary to distinguish between harmful conditioning, in the context of which our personalised thinking develops, and the necessary conditioning required in training and self-discipline within our work. Technological and scientific skills, for example, require a training and discipline that is a form of indoctrination, but which is essential preparation for work in schools, universities, engineering, military services, medical and nursing professions.

Zamiar was very efficient at administering such disciplined order, which is fundamental to the running of any

type of organisation where constraints are highly necessary. For without a disciplined order, relationships cannot
be reasonably maintained, either in the world at large or
in any establishment. Law and order, or the recognition
of human ethical interaction is absolutely necessary to a
democratic society.

Few of us perceive the lasting effects that harmful
conditioning can have on our minds, particularly when
authoritative beliefs have been introduced into our
minds in a particularly subtle manipulating way, as is
accomplished by dictators of any kind.

Harmful conditioning is highly interwoven with necessary conditioning, which makes it even more difficult
for us to detect; especially as harmful conditioning affects
our emotional selves, as I soon found out by being in the
School.

I became more and more conversant with the measures
that Zamiar used to keep us under her control, as I struggled
within to understand why I reacted in the ways that I did
to Zamiar's authority. For example, when Zamiar used her
authority over me, it produced an abject fear in my very
blood—as I have said before. But when she oozed kindness
to back her authority, she trapped my ego into obeying
her. She could not have done this to me if I had been
completely aware of my conditioning and indoctrination.
I noticed, too, that she would often insidiously use The
Masters' unseen authority to support her powers over me.
I felt she was behaving no differently to those Christian
leaders who use God to back their authority.

In the same way, a dictator gradually and skilfully
imposes his beliefs onto the minds of men, building fear
within them. When I recognised this, it caused me to keep
a closer watchfulness over Zamiar's methods of leadership,
spurred on by the realisation that my conditioning under

her was making me act more like an automaton than a human being, smothering all my ethical principles.

In my misguided effort to develop into a responsible human being, I often found myself deceived into believing that Zamiar's approach to a given situation was ethical, when all the time my deeper, hidden feelings told me that it was not. Had I squarely faced the fact that she was manipulating me into believing that what she said and did was right, I think I would have had the courage to stand up to her. Despite my reservations, my higher aspirations spurred me on to recognise the importance of watching myself in her presence. I realised that if I blamed her for her behaviour I would not only be defeating any chance I may have of understanding my own behaviour, but I would certainly draw to myself the worst aspect of Zamiar's discipline.

I often felt if only I could do a volte-face and be brave enough to leave the School, then perhaps all my difficulties would disappear. Yet I felt deep down within me that perhaps another set of difficulties might arise, with which I might find it just as difficult to cope. I was beginning to see that it was myself that was the trouble and not the School, even though the School felt more and more like a cult as described by Geoffrey Watkin. However, l recognised that being at the School was indeed a very unusual experience, where there was an opportunity to understand more about life, even if it was unrealistic to be sure of anything, especially one's self.

I remembered one example of conditioned behaviour, which showed me just how, caught up I could be. It happened one day when I was unexpectedly interviewing a very attractive man on behalf of the *Occult Gazette*. He had come to see me from another religious organisation, with the hope of putting his article into our magazine. I found myself attracted by his forceful character and the open-faced charm of his good looks. He was using manipulative, persuasive masculine power over me. I suddenly became aware that in turn I was subconsciously responding to him by using my feminine provocative charms. In a flash I saw that my responses to him and his to me proceeded from states of conditioned feminine and masculine behavioural patterns.

Immediately I recognised that my responses were conditioned, it put an end to the feminine behaviour that I was exhibiting. It all happened in a very short space of time, but in those few seconds of awareness I knew that my responses to the opposite sex were based on ignorance of my conditioned feminine behaviour. It felt strange to me that I had never been aware of this before, but I had never before acknowledged it or seen it in operation. Now, my awareness had given me a sharp insight, but I was to discover that this one incident did not entirely dissolve my conditioned behaviour regarding sex.

I needed much more awareness of the roots of this behaviour before I could say I fully recognised the conditioned influences that lurked deep within. My understanding was still very superficial, especially where magnetic sexual attraction was concerned. Nevertheless, this insight gave me encouragement to continue to take self-knowledge and self-awareness ever more seriously, and to realise that self-study required an unbiased scientific approach, free from negative emotional intervention.

It was not until I had been at the School for at least seven years that I had real doubts as to what the group's function really was under Zamiar's leadership. It often appeared to me that the role she was playing in the School was really motivated towards boosting her own self-esteem, despite her constant claim to serve The Masters. To be fair to

Zamiar, I do not think that it was all a deliberate act on her part, especially in her earlier days. But I think her authoritarian attitude grew with the passing years.

I noticed, for instance, that she took advantage of every opportunity to use our fervent desire to serve God as a means of manipulating us into serving her own ends, even though we were mostly unaware of this. She used our defensively self-righteous reactions to further her own ambitions. Thus, by persuasively controlling us, or alternatively castigating us into submission, she was able to draw energy from us to back all that she wanted to achieve.

When I realised that my desire for self-knowledge arose, in fact, out of a state of self-righteousness, I saw that I was creating a huge barrier to self-learning. Again and again I fell into my own trap of subconscious—automatic—conditioned—reflex reactions. However, when I honestly observed my own self-righteousness, without fear of the consequences, I could see why Zamiar was able to cajole me into obeying her slightest whim. As I challenged these self-righteous states of mine, I realised how easy it was for Zamiar to manipulate me—which allowed me to see that the way I was behaving was preventing any real spiritual understanding. Also, I perceived that there was no such thing as perfection as Zamiar believed there to be. I noticed that when I was unaware of my behaviour patterns, my actions were bounded by conditioning and indoctrination. Surely, I would say to myself, spiritual awareness can only arise when we live in the immediate moment, consciously attentive to what we are doing and saying. Then we must understand that what we thought was spiritual awareness fades into nothingness.

The more punishments I received, the more I could see how careful I had to be, for my ignorance could so easily trick me into a grandiose feeling of getting nearer to God. Zamiar recognised this delusion, and used it—I am sure—to manipulate me for her own ends. But at the same time she made me see that my aspirations were distorted by an ignorant desire for self-esteem. Despite the gradual realisation I received, her influences still had the effect of making me succumb to her influences again and again, in spite of myself.

In time, I realised with surprise that Zamiar was following the self-same structured institutionalisation that has underpinned the basic concepts of most orthodox and unorthodox religiosity for centuries. As in all religions, for example, her assertion of authority blinded our perception of right thinking and blocked our inner cognisance of right action, preventing us from developing a clear understanding of what it meant to serve God or The Masters. The very fact that we allowed her to dominate us made it impossible to be true to oneself. I felt that she was, like us, under the influences of deeply religious conditioning and indoctrination, but I was sure that she was unaware of it just as we were. I realised that she was basing all her teachings on the very same concepts as all other religious interpreters, the same that had been the very foundation of the Christian Religion, as we know it— hence, Zamiar's ability to control us. Incidentally, Zamiar gave us all a picture of Jesus to hang in our bedrooms when we joined the group.

The one main difference in Zamiar's approach to religion was that she imparted her own ideas of what she thought the Christian teachings meant, and then backed them by claiming that they came to her directly from The Masters. I discovered that she was using various other teachings gleaned from many tomes, which she reconstituted as the 'Teaching of Ra-Men-Ra'. This deception was a form of plagiarism that may have helped her uphold the notion that she was the mouthpiece of The Masters; but it did not totally deceive me, for I always had my doubts. I felt that Zamiar was playing a similar role to many gurus and teachers of Christianity, who set themselves up as intermediaries between God and their followers.

Therefore, by trusting Zamiar in the same way that I had once trusted the Church, I had fallen victim to them both. At one time I had perceived nothing wrong in following the Church's precepts, being conditioned and indoctrinated to believe that the Biblical interpretations and teachings about Jesus came directly from God. Now, as I examined myself more closely, I could see that I had fallen victim to influences similar to those Zamiar promulgated through the conditioning that she imposed on the group. It took me seven years to become fully aware of this fact, and to realise that I was becoming more like a copy-machine than a sincere seeker after Truth.

Thereafter, I began to question myself as to whether God needed an intermediary. I wondered if my conceptions of what the Church or Zamiar said about God or Jesus were true, or simply based on their misinterpretations. As I pondered this, the need for any intermediary between God and myself, or indeed God and any other member of the human race, seemed irrational, when all that was required was inherent communication between God and man—Himself.

I seriously considered that the Christian Church—and even Zamiar—coveted power, using the name of Jesus as a means to impose their own ideas and interpretations above 'His Teachings'. I knew that the Church had added its own creeds and dogmas to justify its axioms and beliefs, while it accumulated all manner of wealth and power as the established religious authority. However, there are other religions, under different names and guises, which follow more or less the same pattern as Christianity, since not one of them can help but represent the same deity. It seemed odd to me that there should be so many different religions to worship One God.

After many years of being at the School, I recognised to my astonishment that Zamiar ran it on more or less the same lines as the Church has run its convents and monasteries for centuries. It was very noticeable to me that neither Zamiar nor the Church taught self-knowledge or self-awareness, and that their approach to religious matters was founded on a system of punishment and reward, divide and rule, praise and blame, that enforced complete obedience through fear.

Zamiar's approach to her teachings was based on the implicit belief that they were backed by the hidden Masters' powers, in the same way that most religions base their beliefs on the hidden powers of God or Allah or the Lord or the Absolute. It was after this important realisation that I began to get a clearer understanding of religious conditioning. But I also realised deep in my heart that a truly religious life could not be founded on following anybody, including Zamiar.

I remembered one day feeling that what I had expected from the School was turning out to be very different in reality. Gradually, I recognised it was the same feeling as when my expectations of married life had fallen short of my idealistic conceptions; my feeling then had been that there was no such thing as the romantic love that I had imagined. I did not recognise that in spite of being encased in my earthly body of desires, I had also been trapped by a longing for the purity of Spirit—which I did not understand, nor had I any way of finding out where such purity came from or could be found. I did not understand then the significance indoctrination of the dual nature within a human being—an earthly body with a self—and a Spiritual Essence.

I vividly recall that after a month of being at the school, I was so convinced that I could find a greater closeness to God that when it did not transpire and my prayers appeared to be of no avail, I tried an extreme ascetic approach by fasting. I fasted every alternate week on orange juice only or on water only, alternating the two regimes. Nothing else passed my lips. After more than two months I reduced my weight to just over five stone, (32 kilograms) from more than eight and a half stone (54 kilograms). But after eight weeks of this extreme ascetic fast, I was forced to admit that I had not found God and nor could I ever find God by such an extreme ascetic method. However, I held on to my faith in the mystical experience that I had received soon after I came to the School, and never gave up my search for Truth.

Years later, to my mortification, I realised that any such self-imposition under the guise of seeking after Truth was yet another form of the same self-centred activity of trying to 'become better than', arising again out of my desire for self-perfection. But then, only by being very honest with myself, I came to realise that however hard I tried, to search for truth outside myself could never amount to anything. This realisation was yet another movement in understanding myself. I recognised at last that my conditioning and indoctrination were far too deeply embedded within for me to gain any form of release in my present state of mind.

However, I did recognise that my present understanding was only in its early infancy. I had to reach a far greater depth of inner awareness before I could comprehend right thinking in a day-to-day living experience.

Life in the School required that I be loyal in every respect to Zamiar, no matter what I thought. Even though I felt like a hypocrite. Although at times I devoutly wished not to stay at the School, I recognised that I had no alternative but to remain where I was, making the best of the situation in which I found myself, without resistance or rebellion, until circumstances could in some way release me.

Being in the School, I was aware of just how very hard it was to face the reality of the dilemma in which I found myself. I seemed not to fit in anywhere. Empty of my past convictions, with nothing to hold on to any longer and no one to turn to; with nowhere to go and only the religious beliefs instigated by Zamiar to lean on, I found myself utterly alone and at a standstill, with many doubts filling my mind. This was a frightening time for me. I needed all my strength not to give way to my fears.

My instincts of dissatisfaction had always prompted me to aspire toward the Spirit or the Sacred. But to my chagrin I realised that what I understood 'The Sacred' to mean was constituted only from the confused concepts held in my conditioned mind. I learned that my aspirations, however noble, had been wholly shaped by a conditioned desire for self-perfection. Now, in my despair, I recognised that to aspire towards the Sacred I had to be very, very wary of self-centredness, its desires and all that that entailed. In fact, my mind had to be emptied of all that I knew. But it was beyond me to know the way to do this.

I reflected that it was no wonder that I had found myself in a predicament after I had left my home. Indeed I was at a crossroad in my life—but at that time I had only been able to think of escaping. Conditioned by orthodox religious concepts, I had been taught that if I put all my faith in Jesus or God and begged for my sins to be forgiven, Jesus or God would save me. But in the end I found that awareness meant understanding the reality of existence, which could only come by acknowledging that the answers to my problems lay within myself and not with some external, imagined deity.

I realised that by wishing to change or shape either my problems or myself, I was avoiding facing myself. Finally, I was forced to face the truth: that when I came to the School my imagined hunger and thirst after righteousness was governed entirely by the self-righteous quest after self-perfection. This realisation profoundly shocked me, but I had to be honest with myself and face it. I discovered, as I tore into the fragments of my own worn-out beliefs, that there was no turning back. I was committed to continue my search for Truth. I was reminded of a passage from the sacred writings of the ancient Indian sages, who proclaimed that the self is like an onion: as one peels away the skins one by one, there is finally nothing left. In the same way, I supposed, by peeling away the self-centred preconceived states of accumulated conditioning and indoctrination, I would remove all the pseudo-layers of myself. That meant facing the erroneous conception of my own self-importance that had dominated my life. It was frightening enough to discover all these facts about myself, without feeling helpless by not knowing what to do about them. So in my unhappiness I turned to Jesus for help and guidance, praying for Him to show me the way.

Being in the School, it seemed, was the means of bringing to me the realisation of the importance of learning about myself. I do not think I would ever have realised this had I not been at the School. Yet, even at my lowest ebb, I knew within me that the deep-seated 'driving force' to seek for Truth would always be there to uphold me through all the changes in my life. It would provide resilience enough, day after day, continually to face what lay before me, as I struggled to empty myself of myself.

In spite of the agony and stress of my early predicament and dilemma, the most important thing to me was not to give in to the sufferings and sorrows, fears and hurts, loves and hates, angers and unhappiness—and to learn that I was no different from the rest of humanity. How I cried when I fully realised I was not walking alone, in spite of taking the lone road!

Once I saw clearly that my resistances were a product of conditioning, it struck me that I had reached another crossroad in my life. It was similar to the junction I had reached when I first came to the School all those years ago, and had been forced to accept the position in which I then found myself. But from now on there was going to be one big difference: I was not going to resist what lay in front of me! I felt I had at last started to realise that manipulation, resistance and escape are all equally meaningless.

My whole heart and energy now supported and upheld my conviction that there could never be any place of escape or refuge, nor could there ever be anyone to lean on but myself. I knew in my heart that there must be something Sacred and Untouched to guide me, but equally I recognised that any situation in which I found myself, wherever or whatever it might be, was what I had drawn to myself in order to help me find the True Essence. I could never find the Essence of all Life by trying to seek outwardly what I already had within myself. Despite everything, I knew what was in front of me was where my opportunity lay. Further, the more I understood myself, the greater was the force of energy within me to meet any circumstance in front of me. Somehow I knew that the Energy of the Spirit would always be there to enable me awaken to the God within.

This brings me to a beautiful and true story that I remember about a ten year-old girl called Alice. Her parents were missionaries in China during the Boxer Wars. The revolutionary Boxer soldiers had killed them, along with her brothers and sisters. The little girl had somehow managed to escape by hiding herself at the back of a dark cupboard when the soldiers were not looking. She knew that there was a missionary orphanage close by, which she was sure the Boxer soldiers would not destroy, because the Matron of the home cared for all children, including Chinese orphans. In desperation Alice followed her intuition to seek out the matron who, so she had heard, was very kind. So believing she would not find refuge at the orphanage, Alice hurried there after the soldiers had gone. In a horrific state of shock she eventually arrived at the door. She knocked nervously. A little old lady opened the door—she was the matron. Overwhelmed by the horror of what she had just witnessed, Alice was unable to say a word. But the matron read the anguish on her tear-stained face as she gathered the little girl into her arms. Alice felt safe at last and sobbed out her story.

The orphanage was crowded with children, some only a few months old. Alice soon began to help the matron, calling her mother—as did all the other children. Slowly she let the horror of the past go as she busied herself looking after the other orphans under the direction of her new found mother. After nearly three years, Alice became indispensable to the matron, working long hours and loving her adopted mother, whose only other help was a Chinese Cook?

One night, just before Alice's fifteenth birthday, the Chinese cook urgently called her to the matron's bedside.

As she entered the bedroom, Alice immediately saw that something was seriously wrong. She knelt beside the bed, knowing that her adopted mother was very ill. She put her arms around the little old lady and began to cry softly. She calmed down, as soon as her adopted mother began speaking in a hushed whisper. "I have not very long, the dear Lord has called me, and I am sorry to tell you, my darling little girl, that I shall soon be leaving you. I am so sorry that I have nothing to give to you. The only thing, which helped me throughout my troubled life, is what my mother, the first matron of this orphanage, said to me before she died." With that, the old lady lovingly stroked the little girl's hair. "Keep these words in your heart and repeat them every time you meet a difficulty: 'Do the next thing that comes first.'" Her last words were, "Then the dear Lord will always be there to help you." To the little girl's horror the old lady fell back on her pillows taking her last breath. Alice hugged and kissed her mother sobbing in despair. Then, knowing that the entire orphanage now depended on her, she turned away to start doing the next task that came first.

These words have been my constant inspiration ever since I first read this true story. I have been surprised how many times I have needed to repeat those words to myself, but they have always brought me balance and composure and kept me living in the present moment, especially when facing what seemed to be insurmountable difficulties.

As I looked back from where I stood in those last years of my seclusion in the School, I saw that whenever I was stimulated by any event outside myself, it was still influenced by my background conditioned behaviour; especially when concealed images, concepts and ideas were brought into the light of day. I became aware that my responses also came from the same background of indoctrination.

During my secluded years in the School I had learnt a great deal. I did not wish to pass judgement on either the School or Zamiar, nor blame the circumstances that had brought me into the School, nor the circumstances that might take me away. For those years gave me a freedom to examine myself in a way that I would never have been able to do if I had remained at home.

To live under the duress of the School was often disconcerting. The insights that I perceived were like little flickers of light burning within my own inner darkness. The light flashed brighter every now and again making my perseverance seem worthwhile.

When Jesus' disciples asked what they could do after He had left them, His reply was simply: 'Watch and Pray'.

Chapter Eleven

Leaving the School

With Ignorance wage eternal war,
To know thy self for ever strain,
Thine ignorance of thine ignorance is
Thy fiercest foe, thy deadliest bane
That blunts thy sense, dulls thy taste;
That deafs thine ears, and blinds thine eyes;
Creates the thing that never was,
The Thing that ever is defies.

The Kasidah, of Haji Abdu El-Yezdi
Translated By Sir Richard Burton

IN LATE 1962 A NEW VISITOR, George Fraser, came to the
School. The first time he came to the lectures he smelt so
strongly of whisky that it was apparent to the entire group.
James told him that he was not welcome to come again if
he returned smelling of whisky, and suggested that he gave
this some consideration before returning. In spite of this
reprimand, this new visitor came every Sunday, but always
without the aroma of whisky.

Zamiar had noticed the stranger and asked James to
keep a chair for him next to her as she could sense his
powerful personality and felt his strength would help her
through the long trance during which Ra-Men-Ra was
giving his lectures. On the following Sunday Ra-Men-Ra
gave this new visitor his special name of 'Laddie'.

After several weeks Laddie asked James if he could have
his horoscope read. The following Sunday after the lecture
James was too busy with Zamiar to read the horoscope
for him, so I was asked to do so instead. I only remember

two details of his reading. One was that if Laddie did not do something quickly about his lifestyle he would end up having a stroke and be seriously ill. The second point was that in his latter life he would find himself in a position where no one could help him, if he did not adhere strictly to a reformed way of life. Years later my brother Edward, who was present at the reading of Laddie's horoscope, reminded me of the accuracy of the reading.

One Sunday some weeks later Laddie asked James if he could borrow a book from the library. He was given permission provided he signed for it, giving details of what he had borrowed. As the library was in my office, he came in to find his library book. After some time he found what he wanted so he duly signed for it. We began talking about the lecture we had just heard. Suddenly Laddie went down on one knee and said: "My dear, you need someone to take care of you, and I would like to do just that." I was totally dumbfounded and embarrassed. But in spite of myself, I suppose I felt pleased.

I said that I was going on a fast. For his part he promised to give up drinking and become a vegetarian. Thereafter, each week we would exchange notes on our progress, and sometimes he would ring me during the week to tell me how he was getting along.

The group remarked how much better Laddie was looking as the weeks went by. This encouraged him, and soon a couple of months had gone by during which time Laddie had kept faithfully to his promise. He was not exactly a conformer nor, for that matter, one who would easily be brainwashed or manipulated. He appeared to be afraid of nothing or no one. His Scottish accent complemented his general tough demeanour. He was an ex-army man, who had fought throughout the Second World War. After the war he had earned a Judo black belt.

A few months later, Laddie was thinking of joining the group. He asked me to toss a coin, saying nonchalantly: "Heads I come into the School, tails I don't." I tossed the coin and it came down heads. We went in search of Zamiar to ask her permission for Laddie to join us. It was agreed.

I was attracted by Laddie's strength and his apparent unconcern at having 'nothing to lose by joining the School and everything to gain'. But I saw that in no way could Zamiar dominate Laddie. He refused to give up milk in his tea, and he did not seem to be settling down very well amongst the group. I felt a little nervous of his behaviour as he wandered about the School with no definite aim of supporting the activities of the group.

Early one morning three months later, and unexpectedly, Zamiar called me to her bedroom telling me that she was not feeling happy about Laddie. She said he reminded her of a man who had joined the group many years ago; she said that the man had been behaving much the same as Laddie. After some months she had been forced to tell him to leave the School, but not before he had created absolute bedlam. This must have occurred before I came to the School, since I had no recollection of such a person being in the School. Zamiar began cross-questioning me, saying she thought that Laddie was not settling down, as he should. And then she pointedly asked me what I thought. I immediately felt this was a leading question. Having so often experienced how Zamiar managed to worm things out of me and then turn them back on me to my disadvantage, I hesitated. I did not know what to say without incurring Zamiar's further displeasure towards Laddie. Saying nothing, she rang her bell for Myrtle, who came at once, pleased to be asked for her help.

It did not take them very long to decide that it was my entire fault, and I soon realised that I was becoming the target of Zamiar's suppressed feelings about Laddie. Myrtle was asked to fetch James. When he arrived, Zamiar and Myrtle both reiterated the criticism levelled against me about my attitude, and James at once agreed with all they said. I was sent immediately to my room and told to remain there, and speak to no one until James came to tell me what had been decided. I left Zamiar's room feeling vaguely sick, wondering what my fate would be, my apprehension made me feel very taut and miserable.

I remember so well what happened next when James eventually came to my room. I felt intuitively that I would be sent to the Guest House away from the Temple, which was exactly where I was told to go. I felt annoyed and said that I did not deserve such punishment, adding that I did not think there was any love in the Temple and that I had done nothing to warrant such chastisement. James said I was using my sexual power to make up to Laddie. I emphatically denied this. James ordered me to go to the Guest House, while Myrtle helped me pack my things. In their haste to get me out of the house before Laddie appeared, I was unable to take all of my clothes with me, so I was forced to leave most of them behind in the room I shared with Sekuntala.

I remember taking a walk a few days later in a forlorn state of anxiety. To my surprise I found that I was close to where I knew my sister Marguerite sometimes worked. She had married her childhood sweetheart, and they had two beautiful daughters. They lived in Kensington, but in spite of their being close to the School, I had never contacted her until now. I walked into where I thought she would be working. It was a large food factory where I remembered that she had worked once before to gain some pocket money. She said that she liked jobs where she did not have to think.

I found her sitting on a stool at a conveyor belt, dressed in a white overall and a trim white hat. She was putting cherries on the top of pies with a rubber-gloved hand. I watched her silently for a while. Quite suddenly she raised her eyes to me and smiled in recognition. As I came nearer to her, she did not stop putting cherries on the top of pies, but said quietly: 'Your skirts are far too long my dear, I would shorten them if I were you, you look positively out of fashion.' This remark, so unexpected and so out of context with my situation at the School, immediately restored my balance. I smiled and told her I hoped to see her again soon. I left her putting cherries on the top of pies, which affected me in an extraordinary way and made me feel tremendously endeared to her.

Shortly after returning to the Guest House from seeing my sister, I had a premonition that something was about to happen. I could not subdue my feelings, nor would my nervousness go away. I felt very disoriented. That night, (which was to be, unknown to myself, my last night at the School) I thought I would have an early night, as I had worked late the night before at the Guest House. I felt very tired and strangely disconcerted. I had a hot bath, and as I climbed into bed. I felt an uneasy feeling creeping all over me. My restless sleep did nothing to restore my confidence. I wondered why I could not find any cohesion within myself or with the School anymore. All that day I had the same uneasy feeling, a horrible feeling of fear that I could not suppress. I was sure it was a premonition of something about to happen that would terrify me. I knew it was imminent although I could not fathom out what it could be.

Early that same evening my brother James came over to the Guest House to inform me that Zamiar wanted to see me at once over at the Temple. James was impatient to go, giving me barely enough time to put on my coat. Without a word he immediately escorted me over to the School. I thought it rather strange, until I suddenly realised that the uneasy premonition I had been experiencing was obviously of yet another 'disgrace scene' that lay before me.

As we approached the School, I became more and more nervous. James did not utter a word, and I was far too afraid to challenge my brother as I walked closely beside him, each step making me feel more and more anxious, until James eventually led me down the steps into the back door of the School. Then my fear dropped to the pit of my stomach and my mouth felt very dry—my heart raced. James pulled me up the spiral staircase, the one on which I had laid a covering so many years before when, I remembered, I had also been in disgrace. Now it seemed I was in serious trouble again.

We entered the main hall and James drew me sharply towards the office, where Zamiar and the group were waiting for me. I stood awkwardly in the doorway. All my defences were down. I felt terribly afraid. I shall always remember that scene. Even the date is firmly fixed in my mind—the 8th day of October 1963.

James pushed me into the middle of the room. I felt my fear blinding me as I actually stumbled, nearly falling over. It all happened so very quickly and so unexpectedly that I was completely taken off my guard. I could not think what I had done; the sick feeling in my stomach almost stopped my heart from beating. Zamiar suddenly walked swiftly across the room toward me shrieking. "You harlot! You bitch! You have designs on Laddie! I am going to mark your face forever, you wicked bitch!" And as she raised her arm, I could see glittering in the light a long pointed carving knife in her hand. Her face was distorted with rage. I stood rooted to the spot, everything went blank, and all I could do was stare into her face. There was a deathly silence in the room.

Suddenly, all my fear of Zamiar miraculously vanished. I remained perfectly still facing her, steadily looking into her eyes; and as I did so, she slowly dropped the knife from her trembling hand. I said very quietly, yet in a voice sounding so unlike my own that rang through the room. "I gave you my life, my love and my loyalty, and you have just killed the lot…" There was not a sound from any member of the group. With a feeling of unutterable desolation I turned on my heel and walked out of the room, out of the front door and onto the street. No one tried to stop me.

To my astonishment, as I turned the corner from the street where the Temple was, I met Laddie walking up the road clutching in his hand his pint of milk. He could see that I was very upset. He wanted to know immediately what had happened. When I tried to tell him he wanted to take me straight back to the Temple, but I begged him not to, until I had explained to him all the details of what had led up to the present situation. I was feeling very shaken. I was crying, and quite unable to think properly.

There was a side entrance to Holland Park quite near the School, and as we walked towards it I began to sob as I tried to tell Laddie all that had happened. He suddenly took my arm and steered me into the park. I did not look at his face as he asked me what 'they' had done to me, meaning the Group. In shaking sobs I blurted out the whole miserable story. Laddie never said a word, but guided me away from the park towards a nearby telephone box. He stopped to make a call. Then to my utter dismay he took my arm in a crippling Judo grip and marched me back to the School. I was very, very frightened and shocked by Laddie's response and quite terrified of what he meant to do with me. I did not want to go back to the School after

Zamiar's attack, but Laddie gently reassured me he would not let any of 'them' harm me.

We went in through the back door. James must have seen us coming for he tried to stop Laddie from entering the house. But Laddie, with a quick Judo movement with his other arm and hand, forcefully sent James sprawling across the corridor to the entrance of the stairs that went up into the main house from the basement. My brother Edward came forward to try and stop Laddie, who said, "Let me pass or you will receive much worse treatment than James." Edward backed away. All the time Laddie was still holding me in a firm Judo grip with his other hand and arm. We went towards the spiral staircase that would take us into the entrance hall of the School. We could hear a commotion as we climbed the stairs. James must have fetched Zamiar, for she was coming down the main staircase into the hall below as we arrived at the top of the spiral stairs from the basement.

The moment Zamiar saw me she started screaming at me. But Laddie stopped her abruptly, asserting very forcefully yet in a quiet restrained voice, "I have never hit a woman, but if you so much as touch Elisabeth, I will." Zamiar backed away, glaring at me. Everybody in the group except my father was present. There was a moment of awful silence, then all hell was let loose as Laddie suddenly turned on Zamiar and asked her what she had done to upset me. Everybody spoke at once in support of Zamiar, who shouted again that I was a bitch and had tried to entice him with my behaviour and that I was upsetting her Temple. Laddie said that this was not true, and that my behaviour had always been exemplary towards him and so had his been towards me.

He turned on Zamiar and the group again, asking for proof of their accusation. No one said a word. Then Laddie said, "Elisabeth and I are leaving. Who else wants to leave with us?" Suddenly the reality of leaving and being the focal point of a hostile confrontation with Zamiar and the group was all too much for me, especially as Laddie was still holding me in a tight Judo grip. All my thinking froze as my fear dropped into the pit of my stomach. The reality of leaving the School suddenly dawned on me as I agitatedly looked around the group. But I could not utter a word.

Laddie quickly picked out a few names from the group at random and challenged them to come out with us. He was shouted down immediately by those named, who proclaimed their loyalty to Zamiar. Jeannie, who had not been very long at the School, plucked up enough courage to say that she wanted to leave the School with us. But first, she said, she wanted her eight hundred pounds back, which she said she had given to the School on joining. Laddie powerfully upheld her demands, forcing Zamiar to comply by threatening exposure to the press. Laddie said he had telephoned the press office of the *Daily Mirror* and told them to stand by for his next call. If Jeannie's money were not brought to her immediately he would keep his promise to the press office. I could see Zamiar was frightened. She told James to fetch the money from upstairs, which was in a strong box underneath her bed. She handed him the key from the bunch that she always carried around her waist.

Giving all our possessions and salaries to the School was one of the main conditions each member agreed on joining. Laddie had nothing to give since he had been out of a job when he joined the School, and appeared to have been living from hand to mouth. The only thing he possessed was an 'old banger', which fortunately for us was still registered in his name. He had given his car to the

Temple and strangely enough he had that very morning collected it from the garage where it had been fully serviced at the expense of the School, with four new tyres and a tank full of petrol.

Laddie turned to me and asked if I had given anything to the School, but I was far too terrified to say anything about what I had given, unable to utter a word. All I could do was to shake my head, wishing that I was anywhere else but there, still held in a Judo grip by Laddie. I felt conditions were already explosive enough and in any case I had no idea how to respond to the situation. I felt my fears were choking me. Knowing I was about to quit the School in the middle of the night with Laddie, a virtual stranger to me, was bad enough; but leaving my two younger brothers and my parents was devastating.

After Jeannie had been given her money and counted it, there was a great deal more commotion. Laddie at last demanded that Jeannie and he be allowed to collect their clothes. All the while holding my arm firmly in his judo grip, he hurriedly pushed his way upstairs to his room to collect his belongings. He pushed them into two large army bags while members of the group looked on. Jeannie did not take very long packing her cases either. Then after more abusive words from Zamiar and the group we left the School by the front door, which James held open for us, looking very shaken by the events.

Laddie's car was outside in the street not far from the front door of the Temple. He made me sit in the front passenger seat and helped Jeannie into the back seat with all her belongings. After putting his bags securely into the boot, he drove off. I could see my mother at the window of the office together with other members of the group, but there was no sign of Zamiar or James. We drove down the road to the Guest House so that I could collect my things and say goodbye to my father. I remember running to him crying, telling him what had happened. I knelt beside him asking what I should do. He quoted from Shakespeare's Hamlet:

> *"This above all, to thine own self be true,*
> *And it must follow, as the night the day,*
> *Thou canst not then be false to any man."*

We hugged. He knew I was leaving. I bundled all that I could carry into Laddie's car, and he helped me with the rest of my belongings. Unfortunately, half of my clothes had been left in Sekuntala's room at the Temple, which I had been too afraid to mention to Laddie.

Laddie took Jeannie and I to his ex-girlfriend's flat, about 35 minutes away. By now it was well past midnight. He introduced us to Barbara. She was obviously very pleased to see Laddie, in spite of the hour and the fact that she had been roused from her bed. She was very kind to us and quickly found a bed for me with her friend in the next-door flat, who immediately came to join us. It was suggested that Jeannie slept on the sofa in Barbara's flat.

Over a cup of coffee Laddie told them our somewhat explosive news. They were astonished to hear what had happened, but I think they were quite unable to believe that such extraordinary behaviour could take place in the middle of the night, or for that matter appreciate that such a thing could happen in twentieth century London. We tried to explain as best we could as we drank our coffee. But I could see that it was impossible for them to understand, no matter how hard we tried to explain. Laddie and Jeannie were made comfortable in the flat with Barbara, whilst Barbara's friend took me over to her flat for the night.

It was to be my first night of freedom after almost eight years away from the 'outside world'. As I got into bed I felt drained of all my strength. I tried to pray, but everything felt so unreal and I had such mixed emotions that I could not collect myself into a reasonable state of mind to pray. As I endeavoured to try and sleep the reality slowly dawned on me that I was now out of the School, with no money, no job and nowhere permanently to stay. I shivered—drawing the bedclothes up to my chin. I could never have imagined that I would find myself in such a predicament. Despite having wished many times to be away from the School, the actuality was quite terrifying. I dared not think of tomorrow. I could hardly sleep as I tossed and turned in this strange bed. A feeling of terrible apprehension suddenly came over me as I shuddered in utter disbelief that this could possibly be happening to me. I trembled to think what I had done, and when I tried to consider what would happen to me—I found myself in a blind panic. All my pent-up feelings broke as the stark reality of my position flooded over me. I told myself I must not think about it—that I would deal with it tomorrow, when my mind was less confused.

I awoke early the next morning to the trauma of the night before as it came flooding back. I was feeling more shattered and nervous than I had ever felt before in my life. I dressed in a daze, my stomach churning over and over in fear and foreboding. I made up my mind to buy a paper so that I could apply for a job as soon as possible. It was still very early when I let myself out of the flat. I left the front door on the latch, as I did not want to disturb my newfound friend, who had given me a bed at a moment's notice. I made my way to the newsagent's shop that I had noticed last night as we drove past the corner of the street. It was quite near to Barbara's flat. I needed to find a job quickly, for without steady money I was in a very precarious position. I had only enough 'pocket money' left to buy one paper, so I hoped I would find plenty of jobs advertised.

It was one of those unforgettable mornings, when the fresh morning air filled my lungs with a new spirit of hope. The friendly sun was just bringing in the new day as I walked slowly to the shop. There was a certain wonder at being out in the 'outside world' again after being cut off from it for so long. I was experiencing an inexplicable sense of freedom, accompanied by a sense of openness and joy that I hardly dared express or feel. But beneath this first touch of freedom lurked the ever-present feeling of uncertainty, guilt and insecurity. I could not make myself feel the reality of my position and I dared not think about what was going to happen next.

The comparative freedom from the confines of restricted life at the School felt strange to me as I waited in a queue to buy my paper. I realised that the noise around me was making me shrink into myself. Strangely enough I felt out of place, totally disoriented, and unable to grasp the reality of being a free human being. I suddenly realised that I did not really know what it meant to be a free human being, especially now that I was away from the School. I suppose I unconsciously missed the institutionalised 'security' that I had become so accustomed to feeling. Everything felt mysteriously different now that I was released from the pressure and domination of Zamiar. Yet I kept looking over my shoulder, expecting James to grab me by the arm and pull me back. I gulped in the fresh air and tried not to think about anything, as my heart bounded with an inexplicable sense of freedom I hardly dared contemplate.

Nevertheless, I was extremely nervous and unsure of myself. It made me suddenly realise just how hard it must be for long-term prisoners when they are finally released from their prison cells. I had heard that many, being unable to take their freedom, committed petty offences just to get back into the security of familiar life behind prison walls. At that precise moment, as I waited to be served, my feelings were closely related to those of a liberated prisoner. Deep down, missing the security of the School, I knew I had feelings of guilt at deserting Zamiar and the group. I hastily pushed these thoughts to the back of my mind, for I knew that I would never ever think of returning. I felt dazed, in a kind of limbo, quite unable to accept the position I found myself in. I paid for my paper hardly realising what I was doing and somehow managed to leave the shop. Nothing felt real anymore. I felt I must have been dreaming what was actually taking place.

Hurrying back to the flat after buying my paper, I could not comprehend why I felt so lost and strange amongst people, supersensitive as I mixed amongst them. I thought I had to some extent overcome my sensitivity yet now here I was feeling anything but confident. However, the feelings of exposure both before and after I was in the School were of quite a different order to those of which I became aware now that I had actually just left the School, or Cult as Mr Walkins called it. In my shattered state people seemed to be pressing in on me; as I became aware of them hurrying to work around me. I found myself withdrawing—we seemed worlds apart. Long skirts had been in fashion when I left home; now, I noticed, short skirts were the vogue. I was discovering an entirely different kind of world, one with which I felt totally out of touch; a world with which I had not the remotest link after living so long in a School that had all the hallmarks of a cult. I was aware, very aware of my mixed feelings, and as I thought of my present position my nervousness and disorientation increased. The shock of finding myself in the 'outside world' again made me want to run away and hide somewhere. But I had nowhere to run and nowhere to hide. I did not dare think of Laddie. I had never consciously been aware of feeling this way before, although I observed that my fears of today were completely different to the ghastly fears of yesterday's life in the Temple.

When I got back to the flat, my temporary flat-mate was already up and dressed. She said she had not missed me—in fact she said she did not know I had even been out. We were taught to move silently in the School; it had become a habit, so I was unaware of the impression I was making on my newfound friend. We went next door to the other flat where Jeannie and Laddie were already having their breakfast with Barbara. They asked me where I had been. I showed them the paper, opened on the page for advertisements for jobs; I was quite unable to utter a word. My communication was received in dead silence. I stood nervously clutching my paper.

Then Laddie said: "Before you can go after any jobs, we have to look after Jeannie." I sat down; my stomach churned nauseously over and over. I could not eat any breakfast. Besides, I was not used to breakfast, but I had a cup of tea. A little later that morning, Laddie asked Jeannie if she could spare some money, saying I badly needed some new shoes. I looked down at my shoes, perhaps for the first time, and noticed that they were very shabby, in fact parting at the seams. But I was far too worried to think about shoes. Jeannie gave us both fifty pounds each, which was very generous of her. Laddie took Jeannie home to her parents and I was left on my own in the flat after Barbara and her friend had left for work. I washed up all the dishes, feeling very strange being away from the School. I scanned the advertisements, but they were mostly for jobs beyond my capabilities, although I did mark two or three. One was for a post as companion, and there were several jobs available looking after children. I did not think I could manage a secretarial post. It is hard to express the anxiety and unreality of how I felt. I was so highly nervous and unbelievably frightened. I felt as if I were dreaming. Later I realised I must have been in deep shock.

When Laddie returned he insisted on taking me to one of the Oxford Street shoe shops. He said my shoes were in a deplorable state and that I would never be able to find a job looking like that. I looked at my shoes again. They were indeed in a dreadful condition. Laddie added that I would also have to wait until I had an address before trying to think about a job. I realised that I had never thought about that either. In fact, Laddie more or less said I was in no condition at present to think about earning a living. I could not help wondering what he thought I was going to do to survive, but he thought only about the next thing to do; so off we went to find a shoe shop in Oxford Street.

In the shoe shop I found it difficult to select a pair of shoes to fit. The assistant was becoming a little flustered at the number of shoes I was trying on and so was I, for causing her so much trouble. To my horror Laddie suddenly turned to the assistant and said: "Please be patient with her, she has just come out." The assistant looked at me incredulously, and then a flicker of comprehension dawned across her face. She immediately told us that her brother, too, had just come out of prison, so she knew exactly how I was feeling. Then she gathered up all the shoes into their boxes and whispered that she had a few very comfortable pairs in soft leather—ones due for the sale—which she thought would be sure to fit me. I looked at Laddie wondering what he would say next, but he was quite unconcerned and just gave me a wink.

The assistant returned with two pairs of soft leather shoes. One pair fitted me perfectly. I was feeling enormously grateful to the assistant, and with tears in my eyes I thanked her for her kindness. She turned to me rather shyly asking me whether I would like her to put my old shoes into the waste bin. I smiled my agreement, thanking her once again for all her kindness. As we left the shoe shop I hoped that my luck had turned. My new shoes felt so comfortable. I was pleased that they had been reduced, as even at a lower price they seemed enormously expensive to me. But then, I realised, I had not been into a shop to buy myself anything since I had left my home almost eight years before. All I knew was that I felt very grateful for Jeannie's money.

That evening after we had had our meal with our two new friends, Laddie suddenly turned to me saying: "Well, I'm off to Scotland tonight. Would you like to come with me?" I was too surprised to speak. When the full realisation of what he had just said began to sink into my consciousness, I quickly responded: "Do you really mean it?" "Certainly I do!" he replied, without any hesitation. I replied spontaneously as I rose, "Please, give me fifteen minutes to pack." Not that I had very much to pack, but I needed a few moments to gather myself together. I simply refused to think about what I had just agreed to. I dare not contemplate what I was involving myself with, and at this time of night too. I had never ever contemplated going off to Scotland with a man I hardly knew, to where I did not know. I was totally unable to understand myself; but then, nothing seemed real any more. It was obvious I could not stay where I was, and I was mortally afraid of being on my own in London in case James found me and took me back to the School. I had to trust Laddie. We left about an hour later, having stacked everything we possessed into the back of his car. We waved goodbye to our friends, who were crying and wishing us good luck.

Gradually I became more consciously aware of what I had done as I sat nervously twisting my hands in my lap beside Laddie, whilst he concentrated on his driving. I could not bring myself to believe for real what was happening to me. Nevertheless, my sense of propriety gave me a sudden jolt when I realised it was well past midnight, and here I was actually driving along the A 1 beside a man who had rescued me from the cult. 'Am I really driving away from the religious life I had been confined to for so long?' I thought nervously. Thinking about my position, I realised that my upbringing would never have sanctioned driving beside a man I hardly knew to where I did not know! But then, I thought modestly, things were not exactly the same for me as they used to be.

I kept turning things over in my mind as I sat in silence beside Laddie, very conscious of his presence and his strength. I glanced at him furtively several times, but each time he appeared to be concentrating fully on his driving. I could not make out what he was thinking. Suddenly I felt very frightened. After all, Laddie was a virtual stranger to me, a man I hardly knew anything about; yet here we were sitting side by side, speeding along the A1 North bound for Scotland, every mile taking me further and further away from the School, which had been my refuge and security for almost eight years. I reviewed our position. We had left the School in a storm of horror, to spend our first night in comparative freedom with Laddie's ex-girlfriend. Now, here we were on our way to Scotland, practically penniless, in spite of my new shoes and Jeanne's money. Whatever lay ahead I dared not imagine; but I could not help feeling it would certainly be a very different life. Again I glanced at Laddie, wondering what he was thinking. As I nervously glanced once again at Laddie's powerful face, recollecting how he had handled Zamiar of whom the group and I were so afraid, I suddenly felt very apprehensive.

I kept thinking, as I gave Laddie yet another quick half-glance, that I would not like to be on the wrong side of him, especially after the way he had handled our departure from the School. I looked at him again feeling distinctly nervous of what I had let myself in for, especially as I had never had to work in my life and I had no idea how to set about earning my own living. I had no academic skills to fall back on or any experience in the business world, nothing beyond a willingness to work hard at anything I undertook. It was true that I had had secretarial training at St James College in London, but that was years ago; and I had also had some training as a nurse at King's College Hospital in London during the war years. But in the middle of my training, I married and was forced to resign, so the few skills I had would not be very advantageous when seeking a job.

After driving silently for a considerable distance Laddie pulled off the road into a lay-by. He said he needed to stretch his legs. When he got back into the car he told me he was going to rest for a while and try to get some sleep, and he advised me to do the same, as it was very late at night. I could see that there was no question of sharing the driving, so I never volunteered.

I do not know how long we had been dozing, when there was a sharp rap on the window. It was a policeman. Laddie quickly told me to leave everything to him. Then winding down the window he said, "Good evening, Officer, we were just having a nap." The Officer had a torch in his hand, which he shone directly on my face. After having a good look at me, he said to Laddie that he was worried in case there was something the matter or that we may need help. Being reassured by Laddie and seeing that I was all right, for I gave him a quick smile, he bade us good night and a safe journey. He got back into his police car and, after a few moments, left the lay-by. The policemen's presence worried me, knowing that my brother James, a criminal barrister, had once used his connections with the police to search for Zamiar's son and his wife after they had deserted the School. Also I knew that James had Laddie's car registration number.

Once more I realised just how nervous and unsure of myself I was. I knew I was very frightened of being left alone and was therefore very glad of Laddie's presence. He was so strong and powerful, yet I was so unsure of what he might do next. I just could not figure him out. His light brown hair was cropped very short in a crew cut—which was a pity, I thought, as it made him look very severe. His powerful face depicted strength of character that brooked no interference in what he felt was the right thing to do. He had a broad Scottish accent and a friendly manner. Then to my surprise I suddenly felt comfortable with him, as if I had known him for many years. We continued our journey North much refreshed.

Slowly we began to catch up with each other's past. I told him briefly about what had happened to me. He made only one comment: "It's good that you are out of that nut-house." It was too early for me to think about that, I was still far too upset over the whole affair. Withdrawal feelings had already started to seep into my consciousness, and because I did not recognise the full significance of what they meant, I did not know how to respond to them. Like Scarlet O'Hara meeting overwhelming difficulties in *Gone with the Wind*, I pushed the whole situation to the back of my mind, telling myself that I would think about it tomorrow when I was feeling less frightened.

Laddie told me he had two brothers and one sister, and that his mother and father were both dead. He said he joined the army at sixteen as it meant one less mouth for his mother to feed. The Big Depression in the thirties caused so much unemployment and poverty all over the British Isles that no questions were asked by the army about his age, especially as Laddie was tall and strong. He signed on for twenty-one years' service, but he left the army at the end of World War Two after only fifteen years' service, which meant that he had to forfeit his pension. On his discharge from the army he said he had been given a pittance as a 'thank you' from the War Office for being willing to give his life for his country. With no other training than to kill, he found himself, like thousands of other servicemen, fighting to survive in a world ravished by war. He said he had been wounded twice during the war, and I felt that he must have been badly shell-shocked because of the peculiar shaking of his left shoulder, sometimes more pronounced than at other times. He did not tell me much about his war experiences or his army life and I did not like to intrude.

Laddie told me that after the war he had joined a Judo Club in London where he was taught Martial Arts by a famous Japanese master. He obtained a black belt after several years and continued until he was a Fourth Dan. He said he learned other forms of Martial Art, including Aikido, which originated in Wakayama in Japan in 1959, the deeper understanding of which goes way back in Japanese history. Literally Aikido means *Ai*—harmony, *Ki*—spirit, and *do*—the way of. Laddie did not say very much about his training in Aikido beyond the fact that the founder's name was Ueshiba Morihei, and he had been born on 14 December 1883 in Tanabe, Kumano in Japan. Laddie said that Martial Arts originated as a Way of Life. I was immediately very interested and determined to spend more time investigating the subject.

I found Laddie's knowledge of Martial arts fascinating, so I asked him to tell me more. I learned that when the Chinese Taoist Masters and high ranking Japanese Masters first taught their understanding of the self and self-awareness, they realised there was a need for a practical form of non-combative Martial Art that could be demonstrated on the Judo mat as a form of practical self-knowledge. Hence, in time, these Martial Art movements, structured by the ancient Japanese Masters as a way of life, awaken pupils to self-awareness whilst performing these Martial Art movements with a partner on the Judo mat. Laddie pointed out to me that this form of learning about the self was not always clearly understood by all present-day Western teachers of the Martial Art Schools.

He added that because of the way that the Martial Art movements were originally structured, they never lost their purpose of teaching pupils self-awareness, however hidden it may initially be for the pupils. The movements were assimilated first by learning what not to do on the training mat. As a result of this knowledge, pupils were able to absorb lessons about inner self-awareness and discipline. Laddie emphasised to me that the process is a very subtle one, and anyone who has had experience of Martial Arts is aware that a great deal more is required than simply physical strength and discipline. He added that control of the mind and body were required, which eventually brought the pupil recognition of the Spirit or soul that led to self-awareness and emptiness of self-desires.

I very easily understood all that Laddie had described about the Martial Arts and I was extremely interested in hearing more about all the forms that had been taught as a means of studying oneself through Martial Arts. To realise Laddie was a deep thinker brought me much closer to him, as I felt we had a lot in common. It made me recognise why I had felt so drawn to him in the first place.

Later, when I knew him better, it was easy for me to see why Laddie had turned to Martial Arts after coming out of the army. He told me that he had been thoroughly disillusioned by the horrors of the Second World War. I concluded that he had been drawn to Martial Arts because of his dislike and revulsion at being obliged to kill other human beings on the battlefield. At the same time he was aware that the Martial Arts had equipped him with an inner strength to deal with civilian life after his traumatic experiences of the war years. It seemed that his war experiences were the underlying reason why he had left the army before his twenty-one years of service had expired, but I suspected that shell shock had something to do with it. I learned afterwards that servicemen generally considered shell shock to be commensurate with cowardice. Since no one wanted to be thought a coward, no one came forward to be treated for shell shock unless it had become very seriously incapacitating.

After leaving the army, Laddie had taken various jobs in London, which had not given him much satisfaction. I discovered that when he first came to the School he had very little money and that he had no home of his own and no army pension. He was in much the same position as myself: no job, no place to lay his head, except perhaps in his car. As for me, I began to feel less nervous. In spite of having just had such a traumatic send-off from the School, at least Laddie was still there—very much alive and close beside me—willing to help. Beyond that my mind refused to go. I was very grateful to him.

Time had passed very quickly for we had nearly reached the border between England and Scotland.

Then, all of a sudden, I remembered what Laddie had said that day in the office, when he had borrowed a book from the School library, which now seemed an age ago. I was all confused again and embarrassed as I recollected his words: "My dear, you need someone to take care of you, and I would like to do just that." Tentatively, I asked him where we were going in Scotland. He said to a friend of his, who lived in Peebles. He showed me where it was on the map. But my mind was still too shocked by all that had happened to take in road maps. I dared not think about the future. I tried to pray for guidance. I kept experiencing dreadful guilt feelings that I had deserted The Masters, especially when I recalled the mystical experience I had had during the first week at the School. I repeatedly told myself that I needed to be more conscious of my actions, that I needed to discover what it meant to be a responsible human being, and not to be swamped by others around me. But it was a little late to think about that now and I could hardly say I was being responsible driving along the main road north in the early hours of the morning with a virtual stranger!

But events had happened far too quickly for me to think about being self-responsible. So where was I at this present moment in relation to my responsibilities? I repeatedly asked myself: 'What am I doing in a car with a virtual stranger?' I had for so many years not been my own person, only a disciple to Zamiar's dictates. Now here I was with no one to guide me or help me. I thought for whom, or for what, was I to be responsible? Surely, it could only be to myself? I decided that I was far from being responsible, and that what I had thought was self-responsibility at the School was just my imagination. Nothing appeared to have any relationship to the position I now found myself.

I wondered if I would always feel like this when drastic changes came into my life.

Laddie and I travelled on through the night to Scotland. He decided to go through Glasgow, where I suggested buying some fruit. We arrived at a shopping area where Laddie stopped the car and said he would wait for me. When I came out of the shop, Laddie was nowhere to be seen. I was absolutely panic-stricken. Then I heard a car hooting several times. I looked around again and suddenly saw Laddie's car further down the road. I raced toward the car shaking all over. Later, Laddie told me he had been forced to move on by a policeman. I was overcome and started to cry. I realised I was far more frightened about being left alone than I had realised. Laddie promised he would never leave me. He offered me a handkerchief to wipe the tears that were streaming down my cheeks. Then he made a joke about our situation that restored my balance. Between my tears and our laughter we continued on our way, enjoying the fruit I had bought.

We eventually arrived in Peebles where his friend was. But Laddie found that his friend had gone away and that he was no longer with his girlfriend, whom he appeared to have deserted. We were in a difficult position. Laddie asked if she knew where his friend had gone, but she said she had no idea. However, she added that we were welcome to stay the night with her until we were able to find somewhere else to stay. We could see that she was trying to be helpful but she was really very upset. She said she had no money or food. Laddie told her that we would buy some food for her and come back straightaway with it. She did not seem to be a very tidy person and I could see that the house looked anything but clean. She may have been depressed at being let down by her boyfriend; or was she perhaps finding the responsibility of two small children just too much for her on her own?

After we returned with the food, Laddie felt that we had to stay the night. She showed us to our room. When I examined the bed, I was horrified to discover that the sheets were quite grey, despite being newly ironed. After stripping the double bed, I washed as much of it and the area around as I could, and placed newspaper all over the mattress. I asked Laddie to bring the rugs and cushions in from the car. That night we did not undress, and were away very early the next day. I wanted to get away as fast as I possibly could, as I did not feel happy with the arrangements. Laddie gave his friend's girl some money, which he hoped would tide her over until she could get some more from the social services. We thanked her for her kindness and wished her well.

We stopped on the way so that I could drape the rugs and cushions over some hedges to let the sun cleanse them, for I was frightened of lice. I was only too thankful that Laddie had respected my privacy and had not attempted to take advantage of me. I could see I need not have worried about him on the journey up; he was a perfect gentleman in every way. He was very kind and attentive, and always ready to help me.

We found some beautifully clean, cheap accommodation just outside the country town of Peebles. The next day Laddie registered at the employment agency and signed on the dole. Also, he wrote to his previous employers for holiday pay, which amounted to over one hundred and fifty pounds. He also applied for a return on his Income Tax, as he had not worked for several months. Thus he received another one hundred and fifty pounds in tax return.

Several weeks later, as we walked up into one of the beautiful woods that surround much of Peebleshire,

Laddie took my hand. He said kindly, "Now, the time has come when I know you need looking after. Please let me do this for you, so we can start life again together." He drew me nearer to him as he continued, "We are pretty even pegging, though I guess you can steel a march over me as far as looks are concerned." He gave my hand a squeeze as I awkwardly looked up into his face. He kept hold of my hand, and gently tugging at it he added, "I'll stay by your side until you are strong enough to find your feet again. We'll spend time walking and getting to know each other in this magnificent countryside. Well?" he questioned. I remained silent, staring across the Peebleshire countryside. I knew I needed someone to be by my side to give me protection, for I was very, very unsure of myself. "This is a proposal of marriage, you know!" laughed Laddie, guessing my sense of propriety. I smiled; he'd guessed! We ran down the hill hand in hand, happy in one another's company as we made for the marriage registry office to put up the banns announcing our marriage.

Once we were settled in our new digs, I gave my sister a telephone call to give her all our news and to invite her to our wedding. She asked me for my address, which I gave her. Some days before our wedding day, she sent me a reverse-sided mackintosh. I put my hands unthinkingly into the pockets as I tried it on, and to my utter joy and surprise I found a five-pound note in either pocket. Laddie said, "Quick, quick, turn it over to the other side." I did so, and put my hands again in the pockets and pulled out another five-pound note from each pocket. It was such a surprise that tears ran down my cheeks. I was choked. The money came just at the right moment to pay the first instalment on our road fund license for the car. The police had placed a ticket on the car the night we arrived at our new digs, giving us just two weeks to pay. We were down to our last pound and the date due for the renewal of Laddies' road fund license was for the very next day. We had been wondering how on earth we were going to manage to pay for it.

Another surprise came shortly afterwards. A member of the audience at the School, who used to come every Sunday to the lectures and had become friendly with me, had somehow found my address and sent me two hundred pounds. I was completely overcome by her kindness. Laddie insisted that we open a Post Office account in my name as he said he wasn't very good where money was concerned. We were rich and happy! I still have that account some forty years later.

The three weeks to the wedding went by very quickly. With Laddie I began to feel less shy of being in the 'outside world' again, although it is impossible to convey the extraordinary feeling of nervousness and unreality that this freedom away from the School gave me, nonetheless, I was deeply grateful for the sense of protection that Laddie provided. He was always so attentive and kind.

On the morning of my wedding day, at Laddie's suggestion, I went to the hairdresser in Peebles—for the first time in more than eight years. I was delighted by their kindness, for when they discovered it was my wedding day, they would not let me pay for their services. Tears sprang to my eyes. I was beginning to feel myself more responsive to others. My sister came all the way

from London to be at our wedding and I loved her dearly for coming. That evening we all went to the Theatre Royal in Edinburgh to hear Mozart's Opera, *The Magic Flute*. It was a beautiful performance. We saw my sister off on the late train for London and then made our way back to Peebles. It had been a very happy day. My sister was indeed a treasure to have treated me so kindly, never once condemning me over the departure from my children as others in my family had done.

That Sunday I was idly looking through *The Scotsman* when my eyes lit on a list of Spiritualist meetings in Edinburgh. I asked Laddie if he would mind if we went to a spiritualist meeting. He agreed immediately. I put my finger at random on a name on the list. I had no conscious understanding what was driving me, but I knew I had to go. I shall never forget what happened. We were sitting in about the middle row. After the usual formalities, the secretary introduced the medium to the audience. He was standing by her side. He was a fine-looking man with clear blue eyes and a serious attentive demeanour. He gave a short talk and then began to give messages to many people in the audience. Just before the end of his messages, he suddenly turned on me saying urgently, 'I want to come to you little lady!" pointing at me. I was startled as he continued, "You feel to me as if you have been torn to pieces, but I want to say to you, Jesus is closer to you than hands to feet and you will always be looked after. I can see you one day living abroad." Tears were in my eyes. I was deeply moved. I remember Laddie asking the medium if he could see him also living abroad, but the medium gave him no reply. We made our way back to Peebles.

The following week Laddie decided it would be nice for us to visit Arran, an island off the west coast of Scotland. One reaches this island by way of a ferry. We drove through

Glasgow to Greenock to catch the Caledonian McBryne's ferryboat to Arran, landing at Brodick Pier. After we disembarked, Laddie decided to drive to the other side of the island where he said it was less crowded and particularly beautiful. We set off happily. It was splendid weather, and while crossing the mountains to get to the other side of the island, I felt happier than I had done for many years.

We were not sure if we would be able to find bed and breakfast accommodation, as it was very late in the season. But if all else failed we could easily camp in the car for the night. The island was a dream to me, the scenery unlike anything I had seen before. It was a joy to drive through the mountains where the sheep grazed freely on the hillsides. We caught glimpses of deer and were entranced by the views. Eventually we arrived at the other side of the island, which was even more rugged, with a rocky coastline. We found a beautiful spot by a fast-running burn, and as we stretched our legs, we noticed some twigs crossed in a curious shape. Laddie said he thought that they must have been made by gypsies, as he remembered hearing they marked their territory with signs. We were just thinking of staying, when we noticed a nearby bungalow. A man was walking toward us. He said that if we were thinking of staying the night, might he suggest that we use his large hut at the back of his bungalow, for it was equipped for staying in, and we would be welcome to use it. He smiled at our surprise, hastily saying, "At no cost to you as the season is now finished. Anyway," he added smiling, "it's too cold to camp out!"

He seemed so friendly. He invited us over to his house to meet his wife. It was late November and quite chilly, so we were glad to accept his kind invitation. Apparently many house owners on this side of the Island had built huts at the back of their gardens so they could use them for themselves in the tourist season, whilst they let their own rooms in their bungalows to visitors. This helped to supplement their income. It was a wonderful way of using their own accommodation for holiday people to enjoy their beautiful island.

We followed him to the house, delighted to meet his wife. She looked so motherly and kind. To our utter astonishment she was totally blind. We had not noticed anything wrong since she moved about giving no indication of her condition. We were invited to join them at the meal she had just prepared. Being vegetarians we declined, but she insisted and soon made Laddie a large omelette and gave me some baked beans on toast. We were astonished at the expert way she had overcome her disability.

Over the meal she told us her story. She said that she had picked up an infection in her eyes nearly thirty years ago, which proved to be incurable. It had happened one day when she was out riding on her bicycle. She suddenly felt something fly into her eyes. She had gone to bed early feeling very unwell since her eyes were hurting her. The doctor was called, but by now her eyes were all red and inflamed. She did not go into too many details, but continued to say that she had gone to the mainland to visit an eye specialist in Glasgow, and was told that he would do all he could and would report to her doctor as to the treatment she must undergo.

After receiving instructions for the necessary treatment from the specialist, her doctor gave her a month to see whether the treatment would work. But by this time Cathy—for that was her name—was slowly going blind She was in bed, when the doctor called and now almost completely blind. The doctor sat on the edge of her bed, Cathy continued, and told her as kindly as he could that he was afraid that the treatment had failed and there was nothing more the medical profession could do to save her sight. She would eventually be completely blind.

After the doctor had gone Cathy said she cried and cried—and then said to herself, 'Cathy, you can either mope yourself into your grave or get up and let your hands be your eyes.' She told us how she did it. She used her hands to measure her way along the wall of the house to the coalhouse, and then she filled the coal-bucket and returned to the house to lay the fires. She said it took her some time to learn to use her hands in this way. She said that she found it a little more difficult when she applied the same method in her kitchen to cook the meals on her stove and wash the dishes. Yet, as her hands responded, so did she recover her well-being. Cathy said her hands were now so sensitive that they virtually took the place of her eyes. She said that the worst blow she received was when the house was given electricity. She said how awful it felt that she was no longer needed to light or clean the oil lamps so that others could see what she could not.

All through this period she was bringing up three children. Continuing her story, Cathy told us that one day a television company unexpectedly visited her. They had heard of her story and wanted to make a documentary about her courage. Cathy said that although she was unable to see the programme the company had produced, they had given her a tape recording of her story. The television programme brought hundreds of letters, which had greatly encouraged her.

Cathy's courage became a constant inspiration to me and she helped me more than anything else to change my attitude toward my future.

Whilst we were there, Laddie hired a boat so that we could go fishing. We wanted to bring back some fish for Cathy to fill her deep freeze. We had a lucky day, coming across a shoal of herrings, amongst other fish, so we were able to bring her back a large bucket and a half of fish. We might have managed two full buckets, had it not been for the sudden appearance of several large fins passing close to our boat above the water line. We learned later from Cathy's husband that the fins belonged to basking sharks—which were not dangerous as they only ate plankton. To us they looked pretty enormous and Laddie thought they were after our fish, so we returned at full speed, glad of the outboard motor. I helped Cathy gut the fish to put in her deep freeze. To every one I gutted, Cathy gutted three. Her movements were deft and sure and she never faltered once.

The night after we caught the fish I had a very vivid dream. I dreamt my brother James was being held up against a wall at gunpoint by some members of the group. It was so vivid a dream and I felt so terribly distressed that I immediately woke Laddie, as I just knew that something awful must have happened to James. It was about six o'clock in the morning. With characteristic nonchalance, Laddie jumped out of bed and said, "Then we'll just have to make our way straight back down to London to his rescue." Tears splashed from my eyes. I had for sometime felt Laddie was my hero, but now I knew he really was. We packed our things immediately and called at the bungalow to say goodbye to our newfound friends, hoping to catch the first ferry across to the mainland. I hugged Cathy and quickly told her of my dream. She agreed that we must go immediately. I felt they were sorry to see us go—we were.

As we were driving south it occurred to me that my life was filled with unexpected events now that I was married to Laddie. We had hardly settled down for a holiday in Arran when we were off to London. It felt so comforting that Laddie believed that my vivid dream had a real significance. I could not imagine that my first husband would do such a thing as to follow up a dream at the drop of a hat. I looked at Laddie in a new light, feeling he was certainly following an unusual approach to life. His spontaneous reactions were so completely contrary to most people.

When we arrived in London we learned from a person still attending services at the School that James was in St Mary Abbot Hospital. We immediately made our way there; it was close to the School. When we arrived a nurse told us to wait. James was in bed in the casualty ward. Eventually I was shown into the ward where James was, I was told not to upset him, as he was in a highly nervous condition. I walked slowly toward his bed and could see that the nurse was right. I stood by his bed quietly saying how glad I was to see him and asking if I could do anything for him. But James was very agitated and refused to speak to me. He called the nurse to ask her to take me away. His distraught state alarmed me. I felt he was too afraid to have anything to do with me and that he must have been very threatened and bullied by some members of the School.

When I returned to Laddie, he said we must instantly go to the School to find out what they had done to James. I was absolutely horrified. But Laddie said he had been making enquiries whilst I had been in the ward, and that he had discovered that two men from the group at the School had been threatening and bullying James. In fact, that very day they had been banned from seeing James by the duty doctor.

Laddie was highly incensed and drove straight away to the School telling me to do exactly what he said and leave everything to him. I knew better by now than to argue with him, although my heart was racing and I was acutely afraid. When we got to the School, Laddie ordered me to remain in the driving seat of the car. I felt sick with worry. As soon as the front door of the School was opened by one of the group, I saw Laddie forcing his way in as someone struggled to shut the door in his face. I was worried because I knew that when Zamiar stirred the group they became frenzied and caught by her power.

After what seemed an age the front door burst open and Laddie came out followed by several members of the group. They were all attacking Laddie ferociously. To protect himself, Laddie picked up some stones and threw them at the two men, whom I did not recognise. One was hurt by a direct hit. There were about four or five members of the group shouting and screaming at Laddie. My attention was so taken up with Laddie that I failed to notice Diana sneaking up to the car on my side. Unfortunately my window was open and Diana was able to grab hold of a handful of my hair. I screamed as I tried to release myself from her vice-like grip. Laddie shouted to me to drive away, but I could not move, as Diana would not let go of my hair. In any case, I did not want to leave without Laddie. Eventually he managed to disentangle himself from the frenzied members of the group and jumped into the car. Diana hung on to my hair and as I drove sharply away she pulled out a handful of my hair.

Laddie said, "Quick! Drive straight to the police station!" When I resisted, Laddie insisted that we must get to the police before the School got there so we could give our side of the story first—otherwise the police would be after us. I would never have thought of doing that, but I realised that Laddie was far more worldly-wise than I was. In spite of being at the School for only a few months, he seemed well aware of Zamiar's character and knew exactly how she would react. As it happened, we only just managed to arrive at the Police Station minutes before the School contacted them. On our arrival at the police station we were interviewed in separate rooms. As we both told our story, the police took down our statements. In the middle of my interview the police interrogator was interrupted and he left me in the care of another officer.

Returning several moments later, the police interrogator said that the School had reported that Laddie had forced his way into the School. I denied this emphatically and informed the police that some of my hair had been pulled out of my head. To illustrate the point, I showed them my bleeding scalp. They sent for someone to treat my injury. I added that my brother was in hospital after being attacked by members of the School. I told the police officer that James was in a dreadful state and that we were both very concerned for his safety. I told him that James had been attacked again and again whilst he was in hospital; consequently the doctor in charge had barred all members of the group. Furthermore, the reason we had gone to the School was to find out just what they had been doing to James and to try and stop it. The police checked my story with the hospital and discovered it was true.

The police told me to give them an address in London where they could contact us. I gave my sister's address, which was in Kensington. We were advised to go there immediately. We left the police station and ten minutes later we met my sister's husband Ivor, who answered our urgent knock on their front door. Ivor stared in astonishment at me, but seeing how upset I was he immediately invited us in, at the same time calling for my sister Marguerite.

She was very glad to see me. After greeting each other with hugs and kisses, we told them what had happened. Marguerite insisted first on giving me first aid treatment for my head, and then on making a meal for us. Ivor suggested we stay the night. They had a large terraced house with a basement and five floors in a select part of Kensington. Ivor was an antique dealer and came from a very wealthy family that lived near Trowbridge. The house was full of beautiful old antique furniture and many wonderful works of art.

We all went downstairs to the kitchen. When the meal was ready, we began to retell the whole story to Ivor and Marguerite as we ate our supper. Ivor said he had always known that I would leave the School when I was ready. Neither Ivor nor my sister ever judged me for what happened with my family but were very kind and supportive. Ivor asked Laddie if he had a proper name, since to Ivor, Laddie was not a Scottish name. Laddie explained Zamiar had given him his present name. Ivor asked Laddie what his Christian names were. Laddie told him he had always been called George, but his other name was Alexander. Immediately Ivor heard this, he said, "Alexander is the name for you!"

From that moment onward I never called Alexander by any other name. Ivor Mackay was a Scot, so he and Alexander got on very well together. Ivor suggested it would be advisable for us to leave very early the next day. We promptly agreed, as Alexander was well aware that the laws in Scotland were different to the Laws in England, and therefore that it would be more difficult for the School to trace us in Scotland—especially if we reached there before the police decided to act.

But we need not have worried. Very early the following morning the police telephoned to advice us to leave for Scotland immediately, and that they were not pressing any charges against Alexander. We left as quickly as possible after gathering our possessions together. We were both very sorry to leave Ivor and my sister, who was in tears.

They had both been very supportive and kind. When we got out of London we felt much safer.

We took the very same route back to Scotland that Alexander and I had taken several weeks before, except that this time we made directly for the Borders. The School had no idea where we had gone, and we knew that the police would not inform them. But as I had given our Peebles address to the Police, we decided to play safe by moving away from there, leaving no forwarding address. We moved to Edinburgh as we both realised that funds were getting rather low and it was time we looked for work. It would be far easier to find a job in a big city than in a country town. I was feeling a lot more positive.

We were very sorry that we had been unable to help my brother James. He was so sensitive and sincere, giving his life to seek after Truth. After serving in the Rifle Brigade during World War Two, he had returned to his Chambers where he showed all indications of becoming a brilliant criminal barrister. For several years before joining the School he had been a Buddhist. He soon became virtually second in command to Zamiar, and was very much respected by the group for his abilities, although at times somewhat feared. As the years went by I noticed that Zamiar exploited his sensitivity and sincerity to such an extent that it interfered with his career. Although her influence over James was more dominant than over me, I understood how he was feeling.

I remember one instance when I was at the School. Zamiar had worked James up into a highly nervous condition, when he was telling her that her demands were impossible for him to meet, begging her to realise his professional obligations. On this occasion James was crying and pleading to be left alone. In spite of his distraught state, Zamiar ordered two members of the group to remove him from the study room where we had all assembled and to take him into the bathroom next door to Zamiar's bedroom.

I heard him calling out; I couldn't endure it any longer and rushed into the bathroom to find out exactly what they were doing to him. He had been stripped and placed into a bath of freezing cold water. My poor brother James was being forcibly held down in the water, shivering and blue with cold, begging to be allowed out of the bath. I was absolutely horrified and tried to help him. Zamiar shrieked at me to 'Get out!' I refused to go and pleaded with her to stop persecuting my brother. Then some members of the group forced me out of the bathroom. I never knew what Zamiar's motives were for doing this to my brother, but to me she was quite out of order, although I had noticed for some reason or another that she appeared to be frightened and agitated.

As I recalled this incident, I wondered what they had done to James after I had left the School that had caused him to become hospitalised. I loved my brother and my heart ached for him. I knew that he must have been badly frightened; otherwise he would have let me talk with him when I arrived at his bedside in the hospital ward.

When we returned to Peebles, I found a letter with an address of a barrister friend of James. I wrote to him begging him to help James, and told him which hospital he was in. I tried to persuade him to tell James to come and stay with me. Several days later I had a telephone call from James' colleague to say that James was in no condition to be helped. He said that he had visited him in hospital, but that James would not let him help. He pointed out that nothing could be done to help James until he requested help. But he said he would still try his best to see what he could do. He said it was tragic that James had come under the influence of 'such a mad-woman'; as he was an exceptionally brilliant barrister and that she was destroying him. This news made me feel very sad.

Although we were forced to leave Peebles, it had been a wonderful experience and we had very much enjoyed living there, but in the end we found the move was to our advantage.

During our life together, Alexander taught me much more about myself than I thought possible. In intimate relationships, I discovered that our nearest and dearest fulfilled the role of a teacher more readily and easily than most. He helped me adapt to life once again, and his sense of humour always restored my balance. At the same time, my fear that he might leave me made me instantly obey him. After living in such a secluded group for so many years, it was like coming out of prison, and I was mortally afraid to face life alone. For nine months Alexander never left my side. I felt so grateful to him. His very presence protected me and enabled me to begin life all over again. In the years that followed we had an extraordinary life together. I learned to love and respect him, although I do not think I ever quite understood him, and in consequence I feel that I may not have done all that I might to help him.

Chapter Twelve

Life with Alexander

We think the future is our own to fashion as we please,
Tomorrow is a golden door to which we hold the keys.
We map our lives, we look ahead,
we think the road is straight but suddenly it bends
and we are face to face with fate.
We challenge it, we fight it, but it gets us in the end
coming sometimes as a foe, and sometimes as a friend.
Bringing us misfortune or some good and lucky chance,
Fate the unseen hand that guides
the trend of circumstance.
We talk of what we're going to do
and what we're going to be
Just as if we had control of human destiny.
To a point perhaps we have,
beyond that there's a power fashioning the shape
and substance of the unborn hour.
We plot and dream, we plan and scheme,
we count and calculate,
but come what may there comes a day
when we must bow to fate.

Kismet
Author unknown
(Alexander knew this poem by heart and would often recite it to me)

As soon as we arrived in Peebles, Alexander and I collected our things from our room and made straight for Edinburgh. Arriving on the outskirts, we looked for another place to stay. We found a large and pleasant room, which was let by a Polish woman. It was very clean and the price suited us. We moved in at once. Our room was across the landing at the top of the stairs. It had a large bay window overlooking a fairly quiet residential area of Edinburgh. We shared a kitchen and bathroom on our landing with another married couple whose bedroom was the other side of the shared kitchen and bathroom.

Alexander and I were just beginning to know each other and I soon found that he liked to be the boss and was very intolerant of anyone who attempted to treat him unjustly. We had only been at our new address about three weeks, when one day Alexander asked me why it was that whenever I planned to make supper I was always kept out of the kitchen by the couple in the other bedroom. It happened with such regularity that we were sure that the other couple were doing it on purpose. Whatever time I happened to open our door to enter the kitchen, the other couple always managed to get there first. I explained to Alexander that their bedroom was closer than ours to the kitchen.

That evening, the same scenario took place when I tried to reach the kitchen to make supper. Alexander went onto the landing and confronted the woman in the kitchen. Immediately, her husband came to the woman's rescue. Alexander leaned against the doorway with his hand on his hip. He looked the husband quietly up and down and nonchalantly asked him if they were his own teeth. Much to the man's surprise and mine, he replied that they were indeed his own teeth. Sharply Alexander replied: "Then if you don't move out of the kitchen immediately you'll be picking your teeth up off the floor." I was so surprised at his remark that I thought I had better add a few supporting words. So I told the man that Alexander was a Judo expert, and that he had better take heed of what had just been said to him. I was promptly told by Alexander not to interfere and he ordered me back into our bedroom. I obeyed, in spite of finding it quite a challenge to my pride to be addressed in such a fashion in front of the next-door couple.

It was a good opportunity to watch my hurt reactions, so that I could get to know myself that much better now that I was living as a married woman, under a totally different environment to the School. From our room I could hear everything that was being said in the corridor outside and felt extremely nervous that there might be a fight. A few moments later Alexander joined me and asked me to make supper. He told me that the kitchen was now all clear and that he had sorted them out. He appeared to have forgotten how abruptly he had spoken to me, and by now I had sorted out my hurt feelings, so I went into the kitchen to make the meal. All appeared peaceful in the next bedroom.

It struck me forcibly that having come out of the School, self-knowledge was somewhat harder to learn now that I was married again. Indeed, now that I was living under very different circumstances 'out in the world', I found it was quite a challenge to 'keep my head' and not be affected by what Alexander might say. But I realised, as I watched myself carefully, that what I had been learning of self-knowledge at the School must only have been based on a form of self-defence, rather than in-depth learning about myself. To my dismay, I could see as I watched myself more closely that I was still using a defensive attitude towards Alexander that could easily provoke an argument. It had been different with Zamiar and the group, with whom I would not have dared to argue.

Nevertheless, I had come to realise that my familiarity with Alexander as a marriage partner was causing me difficulties, especially when he was very assertive. I wondered whether Alexander was only using his assertiveness to dominate me, as I remembered he had told me that he had been a Sergeant Major at one time in his army career. Notwithstanding, there was no doubt that one of the main masculine characteristics was an assumed right to be the boss. From observing other married couples' relationships, I noticed that most women have husband trouble every now and then. So I had to begin all over again to learn patiently and steadfastly what self-knowledge really meant. But in order to take advantage of my new environment, I needed to be aware that I was coming up against an immovable object, especially when I saw that feminine manipulation had not the slightest hope of working with Alexander!

The very next day after the episode with our floor neighbours, we were up early and just about to leave for a shopping session when there was a knock on our door. Alexander said "Come in!" and to our complete surprise our landlady entered. She was a very big woman and was puffing and blowing, since she had just climbed three flights of stairs from the basement. Alexander immediately offered her a chair. After she had sat down and caught her breath, she looked at Alexander steadily and said, "Please tell me how you did it!" "Did what?" asked Alexander mystified. "Well," said our landlady, "your next-door room-mates have just left for good." She had regained her breath by now as she continued: "I heard about the scuffle last night and guessed he must have been doing to you what he has been doing for the past two years to anybody to whom I let your room." She went on to tell Alexander how grateful and pleased she was for what he had done, emphasising how glad she was that Alexander's superior strength had forced them to leave her house. She was tremendously appreciative, telling Alexander how pleased she was to have us as her guests.

This incident filled me with respect for Alexander's unconventional way of handling such an awkward situation. I was discovering that Alexander had no time for anyone who attempted to stand in his way or appear to be uncaring towards others. I was beginning to see another side of life, which my conventional upbringing had kept well hidden from me. Most important of all, a deeper self-realisation began to emerge, and I made a surge forward in learning about myself so that I allowed things to happen, instead of expecting things to work out, as I wanted them to.

We were just leaving our room a day or so later when another visitor called to see us. I was absolutely astonished to see Zamiar's son John standing in the doorway. Alexander did not know him, since John had left the School before Alexander joined. John immediately gave me fifty pounds 'to help us out' as he put it. When he discovered that we were married he seemed very surprised. He said any time I needed help I must contact him. He vaguely said that he had heard from a visitor to the School that we had come to Scotland. We never discovered how he managed to find our address or what he had done since leaving the School. All in all he was somewhat equivocal and did not stay very long. Alexander was not at all keen to hold a conversation with him, and told me not to keep in touch with him after he had gone—although I did write at once to thank him for his generous gift. Shortly after John came to see us we moved and left no forwarding address. We were very sorry to leave our comfortable guesthouse and our friendly landlady. But soon after John's visit we had an offer that we could not refuse.

It all happened so unexpectedly one day as we were coming past the corner of Lothian Road and Prince's Street. To my utter astonishment we bumped into Lady Mayo, who used to be a frequent visitor to the School. She was as surprised to see us, as we were to see her. When she heard all our news she immediately invited us to stay with her as her guests. She told us that she had a large two-storied flat in Prince's Street. She refused to accept any payment and suggested we moved in straight away. We accepted her kind offer, although we felt rather discomfited at moving away from our comfortable digs. Lady Mayo offered us one of the rooms within her self-contained apartment on the floor above her own flat. We shared the upstairs facilities with the people to whom she let the other two rooms. However, we lived mostly within Lady Mayo's flat and had all our meals with her. It overlooked the Caledonian Hotel, and was situated directly above the American Express Office. On her window were the words 'Learn to think aright' printed in bold gold letters. They could easily be read by passers-by in the street who cared to raise their eyes. Thus we began an entirely different style of life, for Lady Mayo was an extraordinary character.

After we moved in I got to know Lady Mayo very well. She was always kind to me. She had rather an aristocratic personality with a voice to match, which always sounded to me as if she had either mixed with high society or had successfully cultivated that tone of voice. I never saw her dress in anything other than purple. She sometimes reminded me a little of my own grandmother on my father's side, although I do remember that my grandmother never used any make-up—she did not need to, for she was indeed a very beautiful woman. Lady Mayo, on the other hand, always used make-up, and sometimes applied it a little askew. But she never seemed aware of it and I would never have dreamt of pointing it out to her. I found Lady Mayo's personality completely different to anyone I had ever known; but she was no match for Alexander, although I very much doubt that she really appreciated that fact!

When Lady Mayo tried to put a wedge between us by saying that Alexander did not come from the same background as myself, she made absolutely no impression on me, since I had long since learned from being at the School that any form of class distinction was a form of hypocrisy and degradation. Even so, I detected that in a subtle way she used her title to hold position and rank over us. It was obvious to me that she was using Zamiar's methods of divide and rule between Alexander and myself. I suspected she had sensed that Alexander had a much stronger character than myself, especially when she suggested that I come to live in America with her where, she claimed, she owned a beautiful flat in New York City. I would not have dreamt of doing such a thing and quietly told her so, adding that I was very happy with Alexander. Even so, it was obvious to me that had I complied with her promises of riches, I would have ended up as her slave, in more or less the same way as I had served under Zamiar—but I guess—in a somewhat different capacity. Nonetheless, I realised I must have changed a little to be one step ahead of Lady Mayo. But I am confident that I would not have been feeling so sure of myself had it not been for Alexander at my side.

It certainly was a 'settling-in' period for me. At times, living with Lady Mayo was quite bizarre, at other times highly irregular, and at most times—to put it mildly— rather unusual. Lady Mayo liked dressing in purple; she told me she had done so ever since 1948, when she had lived in the Himalayas studying under a yogi lama who, she said, had advocated wearing the colour purple as it was a colour that represented spiritual status for women. It must have been for the same reason, I suddenly realised, that Zamiar had always worn purple.

To our surprise, it did not take Lady Mayo very long before she had commandeered us both as her unpaid servants. I suppose she felt that as we were not paying for our accommodation she was entitled to use us to do her bidding. Not that we minded helping her, as we felt very indebted to her for the free accommodation. But we discovered that such an arrangement is never very satisfactory, since we both found much of our freedom had been taken away. I did all her shopping and cleaning and Alexander became her chauffeur, using his own car to take her on excursions. On several occasions she failed to notice that the car needed petrol, which had to be paid for. Alexander would jokingly remind her before we started off on any trip to make sure that she had some money with her. Under such circumstances, Alexander was very tolerant with her, but I could sense once or twice that Lady Mayo was pushing him to his limits. One day, for example, she laid some silver on the table in front of him and asked him to clean it for her. I could tell by Alexander's attitude that it would be the very last time he ever cleaned it, and I rather think Lady Mayo felt she had come up against someone whom she could not easily manipulate, for she never asked Alexander to do any menial jobs again.

It really was an unbelievable experience living with Lady Mayo. I soon found that I was relegated to the kitchen to do all the cooking, which Lady Mayo pointed out was difficult for her to do as she was only used to cooking for herself. So before I knew where I was, I found myself not only responsible for all the catering and cooking, but for paying for it all as well. Again and again Lady Mayo conveniently seemed to forget that food had to be paid for, until I was forced to remind her that she needed to contribute towards the food bills. Then, with sweeping apologies and her sweetest smile, she would explain that she never carried money on her person and would I be a dear and trot off to the bank for her so that she could give me some remuneration.

At meal times, Lady Mayo would sit down at the top of the table, wedged into an almost inaccessible space that was difficult to move into or out of. So when she needed anything, all she had to do was to say in her most elegantly aristocratic voice: 'Could you kindly stretch a long arm for the butter, my dear?'—And always with the same intonation for whatever else she wanted. If she required me to run any errands for her, she would say: 'Dear, if it would not be too, too much trouble to post these letters…' I soon discovered to my dismay that she did not seem to be aware that letters required stamps. She would say, 'It would be so terribly kind of you, dear child, if you could buy some stamps, and tomorrow run to the bank for me as I need some finance.' Slowly it became obvious to me that Lady Mayo covered her own personality with carefully projected pseudo-mannerisms with a voice to match, which I felt that she must have copied from certain aristocrats and practised at some length.

Lady Mayo had philosophical 'meetings' every Sunday in which we were obliged to take part. She operated a rickety old gramophone in the corner of the room on which she played the Balalaika. She would then talk about her experiences in the Himalayas, referring to them as her 'ecumenical accomplishments'. Only a very few friends attended these meetings—five or six persons at the most. After the meeting, we withdrew into Lady Mayo's 'boudoir' for coffee. Lady Mayo liked to call her drawing room her boudoir, I never could understand why, but she told me it sounded more in keeping with her title. Alexander and I, of course, were enrolled to serve the coffee, biscuits and sandwiches, which I had prepared. Lady Mayo would gushingly say in a pseudo-surprised voice as she saw the attractively laid trolley: 'Oh, what a lovely surprise, my dear child, you have been too, too kind! Doesn't it look appetising!' She would then gaze around the room appealing for approval. Then she would positively lure Alexander into helping me by saying to him as she sat down in her usual chair: 'Will you be so kind, my dear, as to pass the guests some food, whilst Elisabeth attends to the coffee?' Being put on the spot, Alexander dutifully made everybody happy by passing round the biscuits, sandwiches and coffee, with an occasional humorous aside that made everybody laugh.

One day, Lady Mayo asked Alexander if he would be so kind as to help her, because she was having trouble with her swollen ankles. We looked at each other wondering what was coming next. She pointed out that she had been told that by raising the legs of her bed it would help to lessen the swelling of her ankles. She wanted Alexander to saw off about an inch or so from the legs at the head of her bed, to provide a gentle upward slope. Well, to begin with, I had discovered very early on in our married life that Alexander could in no way be described as a handyman! But to do him credit, he undertook the task manfully.

After his first attempt, Lady Mayo lay stretched out on the bed, resting her head on the pillow. She found to her horror that the slope was too high. Sounding perturbed, she suggested very tactfully and in a very subdued voice that Alexander should take a little off the bottom legs of the bed, as the slope was too steep. In anticipation, Lady Mayo and I watched Alexander saw a little off the bottom legs of the bed without measuring, which I thought was a mistake; but I hardly dared to say so, remembering the episode in the guesthouse. When Alexander had finished sawing he put the bed down on all its legs and suggested

Lady Mayo see if it was to her satisfaction. To her total consternation, the slope in her bed had disappeared Undismayed, Alexander suggested that if he took a little off the legs at the top of the bed it would introduce a slope once more.

As I watched, I could see there would soon be no legs left at all if I didn't quickly find a tape measure. So telling Alexander to wait until I returned before he sawed any more off the legs, I hastily searched for one. When I returned, I carefully measured the legs at the top end of the bed and marked the lengths to be cut. Alexander sawed a little more off the top legs, and although when he had finished he had sawn the legs off in a somewhat uneven way, Lady Mayo and I thought he had best stop, before the bed lost its legs altogether!

I never could make out whether Alexander had purposely made such a hash of the job in order to stop Lady Mayo using him any more, or whether he was just not cut out to be a handyman. By now I did not know what to believe. Lady Mayo was certainly a little constrained before asking Alexander to do anything else around the flat, until we discovered that the flat was over-run by mice.

We showed Lady Mayo the telltale droppings and suggested that something had to be done. She asked Alexander to be so kind as to set some traps. The first effort revealed a mother mouse and her three little babies, all caught in one trap in the kitchen. I was certain there must be more. So Lady Mayo and I suggested that Alexander set further traps around the rest of the flat. To our dismay, we had caught a mouse in every trap by the next day. This was getting a little too much for Alexander, but he persevered and set the traps once again. To our horror we found more mice in all the traps. This was when Alexander took the initiative and decided to take stronger measures.

Before resetting each trap, he went round the entire flat warning the little mice that their residence was about to be sabotaged. After resetting all the traps he took Lady Mayo and me round as he talked kindly to the mice, warning them of disaster should they be so indiscreet as to touch the traps. I wondered if Alexander had put something on the bread to entice the mice? If he had, he kept the information to himself. To Lady Mayo's astonishment and mine, we never found another mouse invading our territory. Alexander, to his dismay, found himself back in favour once again with Lady Mayo.

It was quite uncanny the way in which Lady Mayo knew exactly how to take advantage of Alexander and myself. She would make use of us whenever she could. She would persuade us to take her out in Alexander's car, often with questionable motives. Once she left us to pay for the tea at Gleneagles Hotel, another time she took us to see a new store that had just been built in Edinburgh with the same result. But when she took us to a large house in several acres of ground, which she told us she had once lived in, we became very uncertain about taking her out on any more excursions.

It transpired that the present occupier of her old home was a rather timid lady whom Lady Mayo took immediate advantage of, and before the poor lady knew where she was, Lady Mayo was showing us around her old home as if she still lived there. With a kind of sweeping gaiety, she informed us of all the alterations that she had instigated, much to the incredulity of the owner, who had no chance of saying a word. Indeed, Lady Mayo was so effusive and took so long in her excursion round the house and gardens that the new owner felt obliged to ask us if we would like to take tea with her—which Lady Mayo promptly and gushingly accepted!

After this episode, we were very wary of going anywhere with Lady Mayo, especially after she told me how she came across her title. Apparently, she had sent a telegram to a shipping line, asking them to reserve a passage for a lady in her name of 'Wilson' immediately following the word 'lady', with no separation. She told us that when she arrived at the ship, she was addressed as Lady Wilson, and was treated with so much respect that she was determined after this episode to obtain a title.

To my surprise, Lady Mayo then told us how she had gained her title. She said that once, long ago, she had met Lord Mayo in Ireland and was determined to meet up with him again. She did not say when or where or if she had engineered the meeting, but after a while they did indeed meet, and became acquainted again. Soon their relationship blossomed until they were on very good terms. With much prompting from Lady Mayo, Lord Mayo eventually popped the question. Soon a marriage was arranged, and after the wedding ceremony—which Lord Mayo naturally attended—he thought he would naturally be invited to share Lady Mayo's London mansion. The newly titled Lady Mayo had other ideas! Quietly but firmly, she informed her newly wedded husband that this was her house and not his. Then, to Lord Mayo's utter astonishment, she apparently shut the door in his face, immediately terminating any idea of a proper marriage as far as Lady Mayo was concerned.

Lady Mayo told me that from that moment onwards she spent much time cultivating a special intonation in her voice that imitated aristocratic speech exactly; and I must say she made a very good job of it! How true this story was I never did find out, for I discovered that Lady Mayo liked what she called 'a good story'.

We stayed with Lady Mayo for another six months, during which time Alexander obtained a job with a printing company selling offset-litho machines, while I was offered a job by Phonetas selling a service for cleaning telephones. Alexander encouraged me to take the job. Being very naïve, I had at first turned it down, thinking twenty-five per cent commission on each sale far too little. Alexander was horrified and sent me straight back to say I would accept the situation. It was the very first job that I had ever had and to my astonishment I started to earn what I thought was quite a lot of money. This was the very first time I realised I had selling capabilities. Soon I had sold the service to so many companies that Phonetas had to employ three more cleaning ladies, and I managed to save some money. We were beginning to feel that it was time to become more independent, so we searched for a place of our own. Besides, Alexander did not feel very happy living with Lady Mayo, although I must admit I was rather fond of her and did not mind her strange ways.

Soon we were lucky enough to find what is known in Scotland as a 'single end'. It is composed of a kitchen and an adjoining bed-cum-sitting-room area. Usually there were no bathrooms or loos within a 'single end' enclosure, but there was a shared loo just outside our front door. The main entrance to the 'single ends' came straight off the street. The design of these 'single ends' was more or less the same on each landing. Our 'single end' was on the ground floor, while the other 'single ends' were approached by a central staircase. They had no bathrooms, but that was not a problem for us for we had been sharing one for many months. We had a sink in the kitchen where we could strip wash. Also we used the swimming pool where there were hot showers. The rent was very cheap and it became our first home, giving us back our independence. We were both out working during the day, and at weekends we were free to go swimming or take a walk in Holyrood Park or climb

Arthur's Seat. Sometimes we visited some of Alexander's relatives. We found plenty to do and were nearly always happy together.

We had not been very long in the 'single-end' when Alexander said he wanted to introduce me to one of his customers, who happened to be from *The Scotsman Publications*. Alexander had just sold them one of the offset-litho printing machines, and it so happened that he had been boasting of my prowess as a saleswoman to his customer, who immediately became interested in meeting me. Following my introduction, I was asked to come for an interview at *The Scotsman*. That is how I obtained my first real professional selling position. After an initial period of training with the tele-ads department, I became the first woman ever to be employed as a classified advertising sales representative with *The Scotsman Publications*. The job also came with a car, which was very convenient.

Some weeks after this, Alexander told me that he had been made redundant. I suggested to him that the kitchen needed freshening up, adding that perhaps it would be an opportunity for him to apply a coat of paint while he

was waiting for another job. He seemed all for it, so we obtained two tins of emulsion paint for the walls, some gloss paint for the woodwork, and some brushes. I helped him to prepare the kitchen ready for painting. Before I went to bed I had washed and cleaned the woodwork, which included a large cupboard fixed to the wall above a shelf between the front door and the kitchen sink. Then Alexander and I covered

Elisabeth when working at *The Scotsman*, 1966–71.

everywhere with thick sheets of newspaper. The ceiling was much higher than normal, but Alexander thought he could stand on the shelves or borrow some steps to reach the inaccessible parts.

I shall never forget the scene that met my eyes when I came home that night and opened our front door leading into the kitchen. The walled cupboard was on the floor, part of the wall where the cupboard should have been had cracked plaster and large holes, and I could see the cupboard fixtures hanging, still half attached to the wall. On a shelf nearby was an open tin of emulsion paint, with the paintbrush lying across the top. I stared in horror, wondering how we were going to tell the landlady of the misfortune that her cupboard had encountered.

Just then Alexander appeared in the doorway of the kitchen from the bed-sitting room. "Whatever's happened?" I gasped. "However did you manage to pull the cupboard down?" Looking at Alexander, I was in time to realise I had said too much. He glared at me and said, "I fell down off the shelf and the cupboard came with me!" "Whatever shall we tell the owner?" I gasped—quickly adding, "I hope you didn't hurt yourself!" But I was far too late. Before I knew where I was, Alexander had swiped the tin of paint off the shelf towards the sink, its contents spilling all over the shelves and floor as he stalked past me out of the front door, slamming it shut as he went.

Stupefied, I gazed at the mess. Then hastily changing my clothes, I returned to the kitchen in search of the electric kettle, desperate for a cup of tea. I spotted it on a shelf, crushed and flattened, quite unusable. I supposed it must have taken the full brunt of the fallen cupboard and Alexander as well. It was fortunate that we had placed so much newspaper all over the floor and shelves the night before; I was able to gather up most of the spilt paint before it reached the floor surface. When Alexander came home some hours later the kitchen was all tidy again and I was busy painting the walls that I had filled with plaster. I dared not look at Alexander, who never said a word. He walked into the bedroom, undressed and got into bed. This was the first time that I had seen him behave in this way and I was deeply shocked.

I decided to finish the kitchen and worked on all night until it was completed. When I came home the next night, the cupboard was gone and the kitchen was all tidy. A new electric kettle was resting on the shelf and all traces of the disaster had vanished. Four large onions were sliced on plates. Alexander, somewhat subdued, told me that onions took away the smell of paint. The floor had been washed and supper was ready. How could I think of mentioning the unmentionable ever again? Painting in future became my chore, which I was relieved to accept. The subject was never mentioned again, nor was the cupboard. I must admit I hesitated ever to suggest any such job again to Alexander!

An ancient extinct volcano known as Arthur's Seat dominated the whole area where we were living. From the top there is a fantastic panoramic view over Edinburgh. We loved climbing Arthur's Seat, and often did so at weekends or on a summer evening after supper. Edinburgh is such a beautiful ancient city, with so many distinguishing landmarks. The city was built on seven hills and has a tremendously interesting historical background.

At the back of the block where we lived there was a main-line railway running north and south. The trains took a long time to shuttle past, and the noise echoed through the night—especially when the London-bound express thundered by—followed by a goods train an hour or so later that made a completely different noise. It came just when we were nearly asleep again, and seemed to take an age as it rumbled by.

One day we had a surprise telephone call from my brother Edward. We thought no one knew our new address. He told us that he had left the School shortly after Marion and her parents had left. Apparently, it took Edward a long time to find where Marion and her parents were living. As soon as he found her, Marion and her parents agreed between them that the choice should be hers to decide whether or not she wished to uphold the marriage that she and Edward had made whilst at the School. Both wanted to stay married, and they agreed to start their life together with a honeymoon in Spain. Unfortunately, to Edward's great anguish, they met with a very bad accident as they drove through France toward Spain. They had hired a car at Cherbourg and were travelling through the night when the accident happened near Bordeaux. Marion never regained consciousness and died of brain damage. Edward was devastated and in terrible shock. He brought Marion's body back to England and told me that he conducted a simple crematorium service for her, which her parent's attended. I felt that it was such a ghastly thing to have happened, particularly as she was so young and gifted. Her parents were unable to resign themselves to the tragedy and grieved for their only daughter until they both died several years later.

About four to five months after the accident, Edward married a lovely young girl from London, and we went down to the wedding. Edward had obtained another software development job near Liverpool as a direct result of the experience he had gained while working with a London Company that pioneered computer support for business operations. After their marriage Edward and his wife bought a house and started a family. Later, Edward was able to invite mother and father to live with them after they, too, had unexpectedly left the School at the end of 1966. Mother had caught her hand in the washing machine mangle and had been taken to hospital. This was the trigger that prompted them to leave. While mother was getting better, she told father that she did not want to return to the School, no matter what he might decide to do. I understood that father was only too pleased to hear mother say this, and made immediate arrangements to pack all his and mother's clothes and remove them from the School. When mother was better, Edward drove down to London to take them back to his home.

After a while, father and mother were able to find a flat of their own in Wales. They had found Edward's two small children rather difficult to cope with, especially as Edward also had a large St Bernard dog and two cats. It transpired that father wanted to be near the paint manufacturing company he once owned. After they had settled into their new flat I drove down to Wales to see them and found them well enough. We heard all their news and how they had managed to escape from the School. Father had the pension that he had received from his business, plus a state pension and an insurance policy, the premium for which had been automatically paid by his war pension. This helped them to afford a comfortably furnished flat, where they seemed happy enough together. On our way home we stayed a couple of nights with Edward and his wife in their new home near Liverpool.

Some months later, when we again visited my parents, I could see a big change in mother and felt deeply concerned. I recognised all the telltale signs of senile dementia, but I did not say anything to father in case it worried him. However, about three weeks after we had returned from visiting them, I received a telephone call from father asking me to come back, as he was feeling concerned. We hurried down to Wales that weekend. The reality of what I had suspected was now all too obvious. It seemed mother remained sitting in her chair all the time, leaving all the normal household chores to father, who was trying his best to cope, but was totally unable to understand what was the matter with mother.

We were all very distressed to see mother so incapacitated. I called in the local doctor to see her, who soon confirmed my suspicions. He said there was no alternative but to place both my parents into a home for old people. I could not bear the thought of this and made up my mind there and then that they should come and live with us. I was determined one—way or another—to find a way of taking care of them.

After the doctor had gone I had a serious talk with father. I told him I had managed to save £250, and said I would like to take care of them and that Alexander totally agreed. I continued, 'If I manage to find a house, would you be prepared to share expenses with me?' Father agreed at once. He volunteered that with their pensions and his insurance policy they could afford to contribute towards the upkeep of a shared house. To my joy father was prepared to borrow on his insurance policy, so that we would have ready funds to cover the purchase of furniture and the legal costs of buying a house. I told him not to worry and that we would soon find a home big enough for all of us, and that he should forget what the doctor had said about going into an old people's home. Father was very relieved and shook Alexander's hand heartily before we left, thanking him for agreeing to the plans.

For some time we had been finding the 'single-end' cramped, especially after the painting episode, so we were glad to start looking for somewhere else to live. Eventually one day, after looking at hundreds of different houses, flats and cottages within our price range in and around Edinburgh, I saw a cottage advertised in *The Scotsman* that looked promising. Alexander offered to take me to look at it in my lunch hour. It was a large detached cottage in an extremely neglected condition. A recent storm had taken off most of the coping on the top of the roof, and some windows at the back of the cottage were smashed. The garden was in a dreadful mess and the inside and outside of the cottage looked as if it had had nothing done to it for more than a century. There were at least five or six layers of wallpaper stuck one over the other in the living room as well as the hall and the bedrooms. There were four or five layers of linoleum on most of the floors. The outside woodwork inside the stone window frames was rotten, and all the windows needed attention. No paint had been applied for years either on the outside or the inside of the cottage, and all the garden walls were in need of pointing.

My friend from *The Scotsman* commented, when she came to look at the cottage, "If you take this on, you have a bigger heart than I have!"

But I was desperate for the sake of my parents, and I could already see possible immediate changes so that we would all be comfortable. If I painted the interior myself I felt sure I would save on the expense that this would entail. It felt perfect to me, although Alexander was not nearly as confident as I was. One blessing was that there was plenty of room, and because of the state of the cottage the price was right. When I left the cottage the following day after giving it a thorough check, I placed an imaginary sign of St Andrew's cross on the front door with my finger to keep it for me, whilst I began an immediate search for the owners.

The property agent would not tell me who the owners were or where they lived. So I began a systematic search for them myself. First I telephoned the local Police station and they suggested the local church might be of assistance. I was in luck, as the minister of the church knew the owner's brother, and gave me his telephone number. The brother told me that the owners of the cottage now lived in a tied cottage on an estate some twelve miles south of Edinburgh[5]. He gave me their telephone number. I immediately telephoned them and they told me that they would be glad to see me that night. It was nearly 9 p.m. when we reached them. Alexander objected, thinking I was mad. Nevertheless, when we eventually found the owners of the cottage we were somewhat shaken when we heard that the 'single end' where Alexander and I lived was owned by a great friend of theirs. None of us could believe it, and to further our surprise we discovered that we banked at the same bank, and belonged to the same building society; and—strange but true—the owner used to work for *The Scotsman*! The coincidences were too many; we were all astonished. They did not hesitate any longer in entering into negotiation as we all felt the sale to be guided by the hand of fate. Their cottage had been on the market for more than eighteen months and they were beginning to feel they would never sell it. I told them the figure I could afford to pay, and we agreed on a price somewhat under their asking price.

The very next day I approached the building society, and because of my good salary with *The Scotsman* they agreed to give me a mortgage. It was very unusual in those days for a woman to be allowed a mortgage, especially if she was married. Needless to say, I had to press for it. But

[5] A tied cottage belongs to and is owned by an estate. The occupier is an employee of the estate and his living accommodation is a part of his wage.

the building society only agreed if my husband took out an extra insurance policy on his life to cover the mortgage substantially. Alexander agreed to do this and the insurance policy was made out in his name. As the owners already had a mortgage with the same building society there was no need for a surveyor.

In 1967 the building society agreed to advance me a further sum on the mortgage, so that we could install gas central heating, a new hot water system, rewire the whole cottage, and replace all the old gas piping. This work began as soon as I could arrange it. We managed to have the coping on the roof and the smashed windows repaired through the previous owners' insurance policy. We soon took possession. I had purchased the cottage in my name since the deal was really going to be financed by my father and myself and I would be paying for the mortgage out of my own salary. This arrangement made my parents feel more secure. Alexander made no objection, for I agreed to finance the insurance policy, which we had taken out to cover the mortgage. It would be redeemable in 15 years and when it matured would be far in excess of the value of the cottage at that time, so Alexander was happy. As a double protection, my mortgage also included a sliding insurance policy, the premium of which lessened as the balance owing on the mortgage diminished, so we were well covered for any eventuality.

My father was delighted when I told him about the purchase, and said he would obtain all the necessary paint from his old paint manufacturing company at no charge to me. Meanwhile the electrician had begun to rewire the cottage, while Alexander and I lifted the several layers of linoleum from the spacious Georgian hall. To our delight we found that there were real stone flags laid on sand throughout the whole of the hall area. The front door had a fan-shaped Georgian window above it, badly in need of painting and repair.

Before the paint arrived we started to strip off all the wallpaper from the walls. We lifted several layers of wallpaper from each of the rooms and placed them in the garden, and generally cleaned the cottage. The Georgian part of the cottage consisted of four large main rooms with a spacious bathroom and an additional very small room, which we planned to turn into a cloakroom. This part of the house had been built on to the front of an original early 17th century cottage, and some very old and worn stone steps, which led up into the Georgian extension, formed part of the hall. There was a noticeable difference in the heights of the ceilings in both parts: the Georgian architecture favoured higher ceilings, lending a more spacious appearance to the rooms. The deeds of the cottage were very old with F's for S's and interestingly enough they contained an original nautical license. Everything seemed very promising.

According to the deeds, the first time the cottage had been sold, was in 1820, which made me feel the Georgian extension was built in the later half of the 1700s. The deeds apparently stated that the old 17th century cottage was the only building situated on the dunes at that time and looked out across the Firth of Forth. The Nautical license had at one time made it obligatory for a light to be shown at night as a marker to guide the ships that used the shipping lanes in the Firth of Forth. In the old cottage there is a little windowed alcove facing out to sea where a lighted lantern use to sit at night. I could not find any information to tell me whether the original cottage was specially built for the purpose, but it seems to me it might well have been[6].

[6] In the 17th Century a Nautical license required the owner of a property to show a light to guide ships passing along the Shipping lanes. The Shipping lanes for this cottage were through the Firth of Forth.

The Gas Company installed the central heating boiler in a small room that led out of the only large room of the old cottage. When we bought the cottage this small room had a structured framework of wood fixed on to three of the walls. This alcove, I learned, used to hold a straw double bed. Apparently in those earlier years this type of bed was quite common in old cottages in 15th, 16th and 17th century Scotland.

There was a tiny window in that room too, which unfortunately we had to remove as we found traces of dry rot. This window was composed of four very small glass panes framed in lead, and one of the four panes could be opened independently. I had never seen anything like this before and was very sorry to part with it, but we could not risk retaining it because of the dry rot. The room was still big enough to be used as a small single bedroom in spite of the central heating boiler, which had been installed there.

The back door was so low in the old cottage that Alexander had to bend his head to get through. We discovered the old cottage still had its own separate roof, with a skylight that leaked. The very small kitchen, converted from an old washhouse, led to a lean-to sun porch, which had collapsed onto its dirt floor. After making the main cottage habitable, we took the dilapidated sun porch down and turned the area into an enclosed sunroom. We thought my parents would appreciate such a room as it overlooked the garden and faced almost due south. After Alexander had dug the foundation, we upgraded it into a very pleasant room, which we called the sun-parlour.

The front wall of the Georgian part of the cottage was directly connected to an old stonewall that totally surrounded the cottage and enclosed the back garden. An attached back door led through an alleyway between the Georgian cottage and the old stone garden wall, which opened out onto the back garden and served as a back entrance to the old cottage. The alleyway had been covered at one time and turned into a lean-to shed, but it was far too dilapidated to remain. The lovely old walled garden at the back of the cottage had obvious potential, but unfortunately the garden seemed never to have had any compost on it since the house had been built. The soil surrounding the grass in the front and back of the cottage was very dry, and looked and felt like grey sand. It badly needed manure and fertiliser. The cottage had been neglected for such a long time that all the outside walls of the cottage required re-pointing and re-painting. Also all the garden walls badly needed pointing. The roofs of the cottages, although basically sound, needed many slates replacing.

After I had finished painting and wallpapering, and the rest of the renovations were completed, I hunted for some second-hand furniture. Through my advertising contacts with *The Scotsman*, I knew all the second hand shops, pawnbrokers and auction markets, thus I had no difficulty in obtaining the furniture and carpets we needed. From the pawnbrokers I bought all our linen—unredeemed pledges—at a third of the cost, and they were all 'as new'. Father advanced me five hundred pounds to help pay for the conveyancing costs and the furniture.

Shortly after completing the painting of the cottage I received a letter from the council informing me that our cottage was now a 'listed class B building'. This considerably increased the value of the cottage, but at the same time restricted us as to what alterations we could make. We could not change any part of the structure of the buildings without permission from the Historic Buildings Council, a part of the City of Edinburgh Council. Much to my relief, all our alterations had already been completed before we received this letter.

Alexander and I were delighted to have, at long last, a real home of our own for the first time since leaving the School nearly four years before. Edward brought our parents up to Scotland from Wales one weekend and I managed to take a few days off from my work at *The Scotsman*. Father and mother were happy to be with us and loved the bedroom we had prepared for them, overlooking a part of the garden at the back of the cottage. Edward brought up some pieces of furniture as he had decided to emigrate. It was a thrilling start to a new life together with my aged parents, in our own home. It was late in 1967 when we were all settled in.

Elisabeth and her brother, Edward.

I can remember that when we were first married I was very unsure of myself after so many years of being in an enclosed religious cult-like School and I had hardly any confidence at all, relying very much on Alexander. But now I was gradually becoming more confident in my own abilities. Initially, Lady Mayo had helped me to find a more stable way to adapt to life, which helped me to shed the influence of the School. And my selling experience with Phonetas had given me the necessary boost of confidence that equipped me to join *The Scotsman Publications*, where I learned to sell professionally through an excellent training system.

An incident that happened very early on in my eight years with *The Scotsman* finally enabled me to overcome my shyness. It was during my first week on my own, after I had been given a territory with lists of customers to call on. In trepidation I made my first big call. As I advanced to the huge reception desk and stared at all the girls behind the counter, all I could think of saying was, "Please could you help me?" Before I knew where I was several young girls came forward eagerly replying, "How may I help you?" their bright smiles showing such warmth and friendliness that I quite forget about being so shy. For the rest of my selling career of more than thirty odd years I always used the same approach.

Throughout all the time I was learning to sell, Alexander was totally supportive of my efforts, constantly encouraging my endeavours. While I was gaining confidence, Alexander kept jogging along in his same old way, the way he had always been used to, a process of constantly changing jobs. He seemed quite happy to do this, and in spite of not providing any income he managed to hold his own, and I was happy as he contributed in so many other ways.

We had not long moved into our new home when Mary Wolstenholme—a friend of mine and a person of considerable talent—moved in with us. Her professional nursing experience was of long standing. In addition she was an expert masseuse and a Naturopath, and in later life she became a qualified Radionics practitioner. I had met her through the manager of my classified advertising department at *The Scotsman*. The manager recommended her to me after I told him about my sore back, which had developed after horse riding with Alexander. I was a far less experienced rider than he, an ex-cavalryman. He had taken me out one weekend, and as I had not ridden for a very long time I was very, very stiff and sore. Alexander had judged me by his own years of army training and I was quite unable to meet his expectations. My manager had been one of Mary's patients, who had helped him considerably by her massage skills. I, too, found after some weeks that Mary's expert massage took away the soreness in my back. I felt so much better, and we soon became close friends.

Mary offered to help me with my parents and was very capable. She had worked at the Kingston Clinic under James C. Thomson, a pioneer of Nature Cure and at that time President of *The Society of British Naturopaths*. Mary was a trained nurse, a vegetarian, well versed in natural foods, and she fitted in perfectly with us. She moved into our spare bedroom the very next week, a nice sunny room at the back of the Georgian part of the cottage. I gave her the front room exclusively for her massage practice. She provided exactly the help I so badly needed for my parents. I did not want her to contribute anything, but she insisted on paying towards her keep. With her she brought furniture, books, linen, pictures and other items, and since we had bought only the bare necessities for the cottage, it did not overcrowd us in the least but made her feel so much more at home.

In our new life together with my parents, we were all facing changes. It was no longer simply Alexander and I, for now that Mary and my parents had joined us we were quite a family. Our chief concern was to see that my parents were happy and comfortable. We were, after all, sharing a home together despite my parent's failing health. We did not want them to feel that they had lost their independence. Alexander was very patient with them too, always willing to help whenever he could. For my part, I concentrated on managing the household and providing all necessary care for my parents. My job with *The Scotsman* kept me busy. It was a happy time for all of us.

I found it hard to believe that a few years ago I had been part of a religious School/cult, and now I was established in a career with a home of my own. At times I could not believe that my life had changed so much. What was very important to me was that I had at last met up with all my children. Words are impossible to describe my feelings as I met them one by one. The boys had all grown into responsible young men and my daughter into a beautiful young woman. I am very proud of them all. To express our feelings when we met would be to intrude on very private reunions that to my delight brought us together once again.

Chapter Thirteen

A New Life Opens Up

All things, by immortal power
Near or Far
Hiddenly
To each other linked are
That thou canst not stir a flower
Without troubling a star.

Francis Thompson

Now that Alexander and I, my parents and Mary Wolstenholme were living together under one roof, a new life was opening up for us all. Although, I certainly never expected to encounter the many different situations that were about to arise now that we had changed our environment.

What I found interesting to observe was that when five people live together many different behavioural responses become apparent. At times there was a strength derived from our unified relationship, but at other times circumstances forced the hidden weaknesses in our characters to surface, which made it difficult to recognise what was happening or indeed to understand the implications.

I was often unaware of the effect that my behaviour had on the others, especially when I unthinkingly created discord with Alexander. I recognised, too, that on a day-to-day basis we all behaved differently according to circumstances or the way we felt. Particularly was this so, since the new environment required us to make many adjustments in our behaviour patterns, and that often dramatically altered events and circumstances to a remarkable degree.

It came to pass, therefore, that sometimes the interaction between us was good and at other times it could be quite strained. I realised, too, that by allowing whatever took place in front of me to remain so without trying to alter, change or shape it, my attention fell back onto myself and I became more aware of my own behaviour toward others.

During that summer Alexander applied for an agency with an Australian Saddlery Company based in London. His experience with horses through being in the cavalry stood him in good stead. We both felt that he would easily qualify for the agency appointment. After he had been accepted to cover the North of England and the whole of Scotland, he sold his car and put the money on a down pay-ment for a second-hand van. Part of the Agency agreement was that Alexander was to pick up a supply of leather goods and samples to show his customers. Our problem was where to store them.

I had been most anxious to help Alexander, and strange-ly enough I had a dream that showed me a stairway up into the roof where there was sufficient space to make a room for Alexander's leather goods. On talking this over with Alexander, we were sure that my dream indicated there would be space enough in the roof area to make a proper attic. So we went ahead with our plans for conversion, which turned out to be very successful. When it was completed, Alexander went down to London to collect the many samples of leather goods he required from the Saddlery Company. He was supplied with order forms and a list of customers, plus a further list of potential customers to call on. He seemed happy enough in spite of the large territory he had to cover. He was also able to sleep in his van, which enabled him to call more frequently on his customers and at the same time save over-night expenses. I bought him a present of a sleeping bag and a rolled up mattress, and a few other items such as a stove and kettle for his home comforts.

Everything seemed to be going along very nicely for several months, and we all had high hopes that Alexander had at last found a job that he liked and could manage. But, sadly, after only a few more months had passed, Alexander's business sense, including his paperwork, did not meet with the company's expectations or approval. The company required details of all his activities with their customers, but Alexander seemed altogether too casual to comply. The company therefore withheld Alexander's commission on the sales that he had made, until they received the proper backing of paper work; which was not the best way to handle the situation as far as Alexander was concerned. He immediately became totally uncooperative. I could not help but feel that the company had miscalculated the situation with regard to Alexander's mentality. Having no money, Alexander began to sell off his samples for cash, which he explained to me was only because the company had refused to pay his rightful commission, and his expenses had to be met. I understood how he was feeling, but did not like to make any suggestions as to how I thought he should manage the situation in case I made the position worse.

However, I was not surprised to hear some weeks later that the company had terminated his agency, requesting the return of all their leather goods and samples. But Alexander ignored their request. This infuriated the company, who in return sent a writ for the recovery of their leather goods, which they assessed at £2000.

Alexander was well aware that he did not have the total consignment of leather goods left to return. He could not possibly say that he had not received the samples, so he asked his solicitor to contest the case on the grounds that he had the right to sell off the samples in lieu of his withheld commission. As I watched with mounting fear, I realised Alexander was putting himself into an awkward situation, and I was very nervous as to how the law would respond, especially as I did not think Alexander had the right kind of solicitor to handle his case.

After two sessions in court it appeared as if Alexander would be sued for the total return of the goods or the equivalent of £2000. I was intensely glad that the house was in my name, for if the case went in the Saddler's favour, I knew that the Court would enforce costs or the return of the leather goods. I was also at my wits' end to know just how I could possibly help Alexander deal with the situation, in the light of his somewhat unconventional behaviour.

I felt deeply concerned as the day approached for the Small Court to assemble for the third time. Alexander was due to appear in the morning. I walked up and down the hall of our cottage wracking my brain to think of a way to help Alexander. It is never very easy when one is forced before the Law courts, especially as Alexander did not seem to realise the seriousness of the situation that he was confronting.

Suddenly, it occurred to me that perhaps Alexander had not received any invoice for the samples that he had collected from the firm, knowing the somewhat carefree way in which he dealt with business affairs. When I asked him if this was so, he replied that he had never received one single invoice from the Saddlery Company with regard to the goods and samples he had collected from the warehouse. I repeated my question to make quite sure that he understood me correctly. He insisted that he had never received any invoices, either when he collected the goods and samples or thereafter. Then it came to me suddenly as

I stood quite still in the centre of the hall: if Alexander did not have an invoice to state what leather goods or samples he was supposed to have uplifted, how could the company place a price on the goods? Moreover, what proof did they have with regard to any goods and samples Alexander may have taken from the warehouse, in the absence of any invoice to substantiate their claims? How could they possibly assess the value of the samples in their court order to be £2000 without an invoice to back their claim, even supposing all the goods that had been uplifted were new?

I typed all this out most carefully and asked Alexander to hand the letter to his solicitor as soon as he arrived in Court. A few days later I heard that the case had been thrown out of Court, because there was no supporting evidence from the Saddler's Company to justify their claims. The case was dismissed, although Alexander had to pay his own legal expenses. However, he was allowed to keep the rest of the goods and samples in lieu of any commission owing. It was a tremendous relief to have the case behind us.

After this episode, I must admit that I became somewhat wary of trusting Alexander's future undertakings. His attitude appeared to be so extremely casual, that at times I was hard pressed to understand the raison d'être for his behaviour. I could see in hindsight that his inexperience in the business world was due to the fact that he had joined the army at a very young age and that he had no experience other than army life. The army environment and battlefield training had not prepared him for civilian life. I am sure that drifting from job to job, made Alexander feel inadequate, but he never said anything to suggest this. It was especially difficult for him as I am certain that he was suffering from shell shock as a direct result of his war experiences. Retrospectively, I feel I might have been able to understand his problem better had I more knowledge of what shell-shock did to soldiers, for I knew in my heart he was a good man. Thus it was that we drifted along together, struggling in our own different ways. At that time I did not realise that shell shock was judged by military personnel to be commensurate with cowardice; or I would have known better how to handle the situation for Alexander was certainly no coward. But at the end of the Second World War very little was known about the damage that war does to the minds of servicemen or the horrendous long-term effects such destruction and loss of life can have on them.

I recall that within six months of settling into our own home with my parents, I had a telephone call from my brother James, begging me to reconsider my position and return to the School to do the Master's work as he was doing. I did my best to inform him why I had left the School, indicating that I would never return. I told him that mother and father were now living with me. I told him I loved him and that we all wanted to help him. I begged him to come and stay with us, but he put the down the telephone receiver. I was crying, so were my parents. We had a pretty good idea that poor James was in trouble with Zamiar and I knew he was afraid and required my support, but what could I do? I informed the Police, but they said it was a civil matter and that they could not interfere unless violence or frauds were committed.

Another six months was to pass before I had a letter from the School to say that James had died in the School and that he had left all his estate to them—which I knew could only be the Insurance Policy that he had taken out when he had begun his law practice. The letter threatened me, saying that the School would take me to Court if I tried to contest my brother's will. But we were not interested in what James had left as a legacy. I felt the letter was in very poor taste, as did my parents. But it influenced me to write to the Police in Kensington to ask them to make enquiries about my brother's death. I sent them a copy of the letter that I had received from the School and asked for their help.

After some considerable time, I received a letter back from the Police, in which they said they had no reason to suspect that any foul play had occurred at the School to cause James's death, and added that they had seen James's will, which they found to be in order. As James had died, there was no point in pursuing the matter.

A very interesting and strange psychic warning had come to me six months before my brother's death, and later before the deaths of both my father and my mother. The first warning occurred in the cottage very early one morning. We were all sound asleep, when suddenly we were awakened by two loud thumps. Alexander and I jumped out of bed to find two pictures had fallen off their hooks on the same wall in the lounge. The hooks were still intact on the walls and the cords holding them were both unbroken. The pictures had crashed on to the floor, without any damage to either frames or glass. As I reflected on this, it seemed to me to be an omen. It felt like a warning, although at the time I could not understand what it meant, or why pictures should fall off walls for no apparent reason. I was most mystified, particularly as these two pictures had fallen off the same wall at the same time. Strangely enough, I recollected that about six months before my predicament and dilemma, a picture in my home had fallen off the wall without sustaining any damage, and whose cord was intact. I remember being very much affected by the phenomenon at the time.

Six months before my mother died another strange psychic experience happened. It occurred under even stranger circumstances. At the time, I was working in Scotland for a publishing company and Alexander was helping me by driving. We had left home that morning only to find at the end of the day that nearly all the books I had for sale in the caravanette had been sold. In consequence, I felt it would not be worth travelling further north into the Highlands without replenishing my stock. So we returned home that night.

The next morning, in the early hours, there was a crash, which awakened us both with a start. We hurriedly jumped out of bed to find a picture had fallen off the wall onto the floor in our bedroom, close to my side of the bed. Again, it was undamaged and the cord was intact. It was particularly extraordinary, as it seemed that I had to return home to receive the warning. I could only think the incident must refer to my mother, who was by now in a nursing home. Indeed, as with the other warnings, before six months had passed, my mother died. All the deaths were as sudden as my departure had been from my home.

I wondered if psychic ability is handed down through the genes. It so happened that both sides of my family had psychic powers. My mother was very clairvoyant and so was my aunt on my mother's side. She often knew of deaths of relatives long before their deaths occurred. Both parents on my father's side had second sight. I am sure that it is not peculiar to my family, because I know many, many people, who have had numerous extraordinary psychic experiences. I know I have had many myself during my lifetime.

Down through the ages, ever since mankind came to the earth, many different forms of psychic and esoteric phenomena have been reported. I do not hesitate to say that religion has been instrumental in conditioning us to fear our own innate, inherent sixth sense. Witches in the Middle Ages were burnt at the stake by the Church's command, when in reality they were only expressing their own natural psychic abilities. It is no wonder, therefore, that by denying these precious gifts, the Church has been responsible for conditioning us to suppress our own psychic powers. Many of us are therefore inhibited from using them, while others decry them or make mockery, when in ages past such gifts were accepted and valued as a part of living. Indeed, Shamans, medicine men and women of the Native North American tribes and other indigenous peoples of our earth have upheld such powers from time immemorial. Some scientists are beginning, very begrudgingly, to realise that 'there is a power fashioning the shape and substance of the unborn hour.' (Taken from Kismet, see chapter 11.)

To return to my story: I was very glad of the presence of my parents. I loved them dearly and was sorry to see that they were so frail and in such poor health, especially father who was so bothered with the sore on his hand that had been diagnosed as skin cancer. As his sore looked so ominous, I put honey on it every night until it began to disappear. The reason I used honey was because I discovered that in days gone by, when Scottish soldiers went into battle, honey was considered an indispensable part of their equipment. Not only did it heal their wounds, it was also an effective antiseptic. The sore on father's hand gradually disappeared, but the lump under his arm grew larger. Even so, it did not appear to bother him overmuch in the beginning.

During the following year the lump under father's arm increased in size and he had much pain. The doctor suggested he be treated as an outpatient in a nearby hospital.

The first treatment for the cancer under his arm made him feel so nauseous that he refused to go back to the hospital again. Unfortunately, the treatment caused the lump under his arm to become an open wound, which thereafter constantly required attention. I was unhappy for him and began to investigate alternative medicine. Father was by now over 80 years of age. In the end it was Alexander who successfully searched the health stores to find an alternative remedy for father's cancer.

We were all sitting in the Sun Parlour one sunny day when suddenly Alexander appeared. He looked very pleased with himself as he announced that he had picked up a book in a health shop. He showed me *The Grape Cure* by Johanna Brandt, published in New York[7]. He said he felt sure that it would help father. The author was a South African doctor, who claimed she had discovered a cure for cancer. She asserted that by fasting and eating only grapes she had cured herself of a large cancerous tumour in her stomach, which had been with her for more than twenty years. The cure required drinking plenty of pure water and eating plenty of grapes. A complete change of diet away from meat and dairy produce, with no smoking or drinking of alcohol, tea, coffee or taking of drugs, was what Dr Johanna Brandt recommended. She emphasised that as we are all so different, nobody should try the grape cure if there was any doubt in their minds as to the seriousness of their illness, and that they should always consult a specialist. She also recommended that in all cases the services of a qualified physician should always be available. To this advice we faithfully kept.

---

[7] In 1927 Johanna Brandt travelled the length and breadth of the USA to tell others of her own cure from cancer with grapes. Having little success, she wrote her book *The Grape Cure*, which was published by Ehret Literature Publishing Co. Inc., Yonkers N.Y. 10701-2714 some months later.

Dr Johanna Brandt was born in 1876 in the heart of South Africa. Her ancestors had been heavy meat eaters and practically lived on game. She wondered if that had anything to do with the fact that cancer had become the greatest scourge in her country. Recognising her stomach cancer, she had for years tried every kind of remedy she could find in the medical world, but nothing had cured her. By experimenting on herself over nine years she discovered that cancer 'thrived on every form of animal food—the more impure—the better'. She graphically described her long fasts and her longing for meat, especially red meat. She disclosed that the cancer was pushing its way through her diaphragm towards her heart and left lung. After several bouts of fasting she claimed that no sign of the growth appeared to remain, though she was still in pain.

Further experimentation with fasting followed. But it was only when she followed the fast for another seven days consuming nothing but grapes that she at last discovered the food she had been looking for to complement the regime. The grape food she believed effectively destroyed the cancerous growth, and was instrumental in building up new tissue. She also found that the grapes were capable of eliminating the toxins from her system. She concluded the account of her recovery by stating that the cure led to 'the miraculous effect of healing me completely within six weeks after a period of initial fasting.'

She felt strongly that taking the grape cure every now and then provided a way to prevent cancer reoccurring, and what is more, to prevent other disease. She lived until she was 85 years old, and right up to the end of her life she could be seen helping her patients in her clinic, using herself as a living example of the grape cure.

In 1969, after reading the book very carefully and feeling much encouraged, we all went on the grape cure to help father cure his cancer. In so doing we ultimately helped ourselves. I took particular note of all the necessary stages we had to go through. I went to the fruit market to buy the grapes by the box and bought a variety of different colours and kinds. Apparently, the seedless grapes are particularly beneficial. We followed exactly the suggested methods prescribed by Dr Johanna Brandt.

Just before we started on the diet it so happened that mother had fallen, breaking her shoulder bone, and had been taken to hospital. When she returned we did not think it advisable for her to fast so we left the decision up to her as to whether she took the grape cure with us. She decided to join in so that she could assist father. The sister at the hospital had warned me that it would probably take about three to six months before mother would be able to dress herself. To our immense surprise, after just two weeks on only grapes and water, I entered mother's bedroom one day to find that she was dressing herself without even realising what she was doing. She was actually lifting her arms above her head to pull on her clothes! As I watched her, she smiled at me. She could easily pull on her stockings and put on her shoes, something she had found difficult to do even before going to hospital. We were all delighted, and it was this that encouraged father to remain on his grape diet. It took him a few days longer on only grapes to bring about his healing crisis.

In her book, Dr Brandt mentioned that a crisis could possibly take place during the cure. She referred to it as a healing crisis, and in father's case it took the form of a bad haemorrhage. Fortunately, I was by his side at the time it happened. I quickly plugged the hole under his arm with gauze and cotton wool, which stopped the bleeding, and

I immediately helped him to bed, propping him up on plenty of pillows. To my surprise, that night when I dressed his wound, the awful smell of the cancer had disappeared. He no longer had any pain and seemed to be at peace. The doctor, who came later, was quite impressed after he had examined the hole under father's armpit and said that it looked remarkably clean. However, he still insisted on leaving pain-relieving pills. We all immediately went on the second stage of *The Grape Cure*.

About two months after father had completed all the stages of the grape cure, he seemed to be slowly recovering. When I came home from work I usually found him sitting in his chair in his dressing gown by the window overlooking the garden. Mary had wrapped him in rugs. My friend Mary was always there to help mother and father while I was at work.

About three weeks later, a colleague at *The Scotsman* asked me to exchange an allocated local holiday with him. I at once agreed. I clearly remember that on the day I took my swopped holiday, I dressed father's wound under his arm, which was still quite clean. The doctor had just left the cottage and told me that father looked a little tired and it would perhaps be as well if he stayed in bed. Before the doctor went he left me more pain tablets in case father found sleeping difficult. About an hour later I was in his room tidying, when suddenly I saw father trying to attract mother's attention. When I pointed this out to mother, she immediately went over to his bedside. Father asked mother to kiss him and hold his hand, and then he turned to me, begging me to take care of her. I promised to do so, suspecting nothing. Suddenly mother urgently pointed to father. I looked quickly toward him.

Mother and I watched as a shadow emerged from the area of father's navel and slowly move up over his heart, eventually passing over his head until we could see it no more. Putting my finger on his pulse I felt it slow down appreciably until it stopped altogether. Father had passed over so peacefully and in no pain, with a smile on his face, just before his 82nd birthday. I had never before observed a shadow move away from any person I had witnessed dying. It was quite extraordinary to watch such a wonderfully peaceful passing. I could not help feeling that fate had stepped in when my colleague had exchanged the local holiday with me.

I called Mary, who hurriedly entered, and seeing our faces immediately guessed what had happened. She felt father's pulse and confirmed that he had passed over. When I told her about the shadow, she said that she had never seen anything like that happen to any patient that she had been with when they died, and she had been at the bedside of hundreds who had taken their last breath.

I felt that the grape cure had in fact brought a great change within him that allowed him consciously to pass peacefully. All the destructive cancer had left his body. All the nasty odours had been dispelled from the house and the sore under his arm was now clean.

The doctor gave me father's death certificate and the district nurse came to make him ready for the undertaker to place him into his coffin. We carried the coffin into the front room, where Mary used to meet with her patients during the day. I gathered flowers from the garden and decorated the room with them, placing flowers all round father's coffin. He lay there for three days with the coffin lid off. I have always had strong feelings that the greatest care should be taken to give the departing soul the necessary space, so that the soul makes the transition between life and death as peacefully as possible. That is why to me the horrors of war or violent deaths have a far greater unseen effect on departing souls than is realised. But the power of Love overcomes all.

On the morning of the funeral I said a prayer before my eldest brother, Charles and Alexander helped the undertakers to carry the flower-decked coffin shoulder-high from the cottage. I noticed my neighbours had pulled their curtains as a sign of respect. All the while the Neubeucher Slave Song by Verdi was being played loudly on the gramophone. My mother was not in a fit state to go to the Crematorium, so I stayed at home with her. My father had been a life-long Mason, so in accordance with his wishes his ashes were scattered to the four winds on the turn of the first high tide.

To carry out father's wishes, Alexander, mother and I drove along the North Berwick coast road to find a suitable spot to scatter his ashes. On seeing a dirt road winding down toward the seashore we decided to follow it. It wound its way to a small car park. We parked the car and walked the rest of the way to the rocky beach with mother. As we approached the beach, we saw to our great surprise a huge cross, erected beyond the shallow water out to sea. The water was at high tide and was swirling all around the massive rock that supported the huge cross. Due to the high tide the cross appeared to be further out to sea than it actually was. Even so, it blended ideally with the surrounding coastline. We decided that this was the very spot to scatter father's ashes.

Alexander, who was also a Mason, climbed some rocks in order to find a better area beyond the waves to scatter father's remains. He said a beautiful prayer as he dispersed the ashes to the four winds. As we watched, we could clearly see the sea carrying away the ashes toward the cross perched on the rock.

I think mother only vaguely understood what was going on, and it proved difficult to talk to her about father's death, as she was now not very communicative. So in order to help her over this difficult period we took her on a sea trip to the Western Isles. While we were away, Mary reorganised the room she had shared with father, and had it redecorated. The sea voyage, although short, helped mother to readjust and come to terms with father's death.

I continued my job at *The Scotsman Publications*. I felt that I was doing quite well, being the only woman on the team of advertising representatives with whom I worked. In the late 1960s, there were very few women representing firms in the field. A few days after my return after father's death, a special competition was arranged by the manager of the classified advertising department, for which there were to be two prizes, one for the tele-ads girls and one for sales representatives. A date had been fixed and we were all conscious of the extra effort and excitement that this competition engendered. There were about nine of us on our team and about twice as many on the tele-ads team. My figures showed that within my team I was in the lead by a considerable margin.

For various different reasons undisclosed to us all, it was unexpectedly decided a few weeks later to judge the whole of the classified advertising department as a whole, which meant at such a late stage the only fair way was to have a draw. So we were all asked to write our names on a piece of paper, fold it into four and place it into an enclosed, sealed container. The draw was arranged for 4.00 p.m. the following Friday night, when everybody in the whole of the classified advertising department were asked to gather together, so that the lucky winner could be picked. A senior member of the management of *The Scotsman* was asked to preside to draw one of the pieces of paper from the container to see who the lucky winner would be. We all waited in anticipation.

After the container had been given a good shake, amidst much laughter, a sudden deathly silence descended whilst the senior manager broke the seal of the container and put his hand in to take out one of the pieces of paper. As he shuffled them about the tension in the room mounted to fever pitch. At last he removed one piece of folded paper and slowly began to unfold it. Without a word he passed it on to the classified manager, who likewise looked at the name on the piece of paper, passing it on without a word to the field sales manager. Not a sound could be heard throughout the department. All faces were riveted on the unfolded piece of paper. There was a confused silence. I, and many others around me, noticed the astonishment on the faces of the managerial staff, and one of the representatives whispered in my ear that it must be my name that was on the piece of paper. Secretly I had wondered if it might be so. After a further silence that amounted to an anti-climax, they eventually called out my name as the winner. I had won a four-day holiday for two in Holland, to visit the famous bulb show!

After my free holiday in Holland with Alexander, I returned to *The Scotsman* to continue my work. To my surprise I found a pretty young girl had taken over my territory, and in my absence I had been given another.

I remained with *The Scotsman* for a further six months. However, I found it difficult to get on with my job as I felt that the management was making my position difficult. So to protect myself, I joined the Advertising Representative's Union. To my consternation the Union could not help me and within six months *The Scotsman* terminated my agreement.

When I recall my days at *The Scotsman*, I have fond memories of all the years I spent there, especially of the unexpected bonus I received. It happened in a strange way. Like many others I had the opportunity whilst I was there to buy shares in the parent Company, The Thomson Organisation. We were all allowed to buy the shares out of our salaries and take a year over the payment. Once the shares were fully paid, we were able to obtain our share certificates and thereafter any dividends the shares had accumulated. Only two offers were made whilst I was with *The Scotsman*, which I took immediate advantage of, particularly when I realised that the Thomson Organisation had just acquired large oil fields in Scottish waters. I never regretted buying those shares or my years at *The Scotsman*.

After I left, I forgot all about the shares, but I remember that I always took every opportunity the Thomson Organisation offered to increase the number I held. In my later years when I needed a new car, I remembered them. I was absolutely dumb-founded when I realised the value of each share. After well over 35 years, I had accumulated more than 1,596 shares. I still have more than half those shares left after 'buying' my new Honda Aerodeck. They were the very first shares I had bought. I cannot help but feel again that my guardian angel was watching over me.

In the course of the eighteen months after I left *The Scotsman*, I worked freelance, selling for an advertising firm, during which time I met up with a Publishing Company, which eventually offered me an Agency for their Northern Territory of Scotland. I accepted, and Alexander, who was still not in a job, asked if he might come round with me to help with the driving. I was very pleased, as I thought it better for him to be with me rather than move from job to job. We bought a caravanette in which we were able to sleep, which helped our finances considerably. My mother was still being cared for by Mary whilst I was away, which was a considerable help.

Scotland is a most magnificent country to travel around

in, and no matter how many times we covered the same territory, we always managed to find yet another delightful spot to park our cara-vanette for the night. It was the atmosphere of the Scottish Highlands and the Isles of Scotland that I found so entranc-ing. Nowhere in the world have I savoured such enjoy-ment from the very air and the very feel of this extraordi-nary land.

On one occasion, we were making for the Western Isles by way of the Isle of Skye. I remember it well, because we had taken Alexander's niece Carol with us, still only a young girl at school. At Kyle of Lochalsh we waited in a queue to cross over to Skye on the ferryboat. There was no bridge in those days. Waiting in the long queue made us later than we had wanted to be. I was driving at the time, as Alexander had driven all the way from Edinburgh and I was giving him a break. Once on Skye, it would be a matter of only an hour's journey through to Uig where the Caledonian McBrayne's Ferry would take us over to the Western Isles. I remember thinking to myself, 'If we are lucky enough to catch the Ferry at Uig, I will have to go a mile a minute through Skye to catch the Ferry!'

Alexander sang old Scottish songs to help us on our way, and Carol joined in. I remember one of the songs was *The Massacre of Glencoe* and another was *Isle of*

Innisfree, which begins with the words: 'Come with me to a land—where fancy is free, and the cares of tomorrow must wait until this day is done!'—Alexander had a good strong voice, and between them, they made it a happy and memorable occasion. At last we arrived at the top of the hill overlooking Uig Harbour. We could see the Uig Ferry still waiting far below ready to leave for the Western Isles. Alexander said, "Quick! Quick! Flash your lights!" I did so at once—several times—as we raced for the ferry. We reached it in time. They had waited for us! One of the crewmen, who recognised me, said, "Well, we might have known it would be you!" Amidst smiles all round I drove the caravanette on board and thanked them for waiting.

In the early part of 1974 I was sad to find that my mother required more attention than Mary and I were able to provide. Not only had she become more senile, but also one day I found that she was quite unwell with a slight haemorrhage from her womb. I called in the doctor, who was amazed that I had managed to look after her for so long. But I could not have done so without Mary, who had always been such a great help. Mother was also incontinent and could not dress or undress herself. She sat in a chair most of the day unable to do much to help herself. The Doctor immediately felt arrangements should be made for her to be placed into a home. He found a very comfortable one in the country only half an hour away from our cottage. Mother did not seem to mind; it was I who cried. I had not wanted this to happen as I had promised father I would always look after her, but there seemed to be no other way, as she was beginning to require twenty-four hour care. The nurses were very kind to mother and that was a great comfort. I visited her as often as I could and took her out in a wheelchair nearly every weekend. Mother stayed there for more than a year, slowly getting more senile.

One day I urgently felt I needed to see my mother, although I had only seen her a few days before. Alexander was with me at the time and did not want me to go because we had just picked up my daughter from the station, who was visiting me for the first time. But I persuaded him to take me and at last he acquiesced. When we reached the nursing home, I found mother in great distress. I gathered she had been given drugs to quieten her. She was trying desperately hard to say something to me as I kissed and hugged her. I could not understand why she seemed so agitated as she clung to me. I was torn in two directions, wanting to stay with her, yet having to leave her lying in bed looking so unwell. I wondered if it was the drugs she had been given, but the nursing staff did not feel that there was anything to be seriously concerned about. As she was totally incoherent and I did not realise just what it was that was distressing her so, I had to leave her.

The next morning at six o'clock, the nursing home rang to say I had better come over at once as they thought my mother's condition was rapidly deteriorating. I was just about to leave home when the telephone rang again from the nursing home to say that they were very sorry to have to inform me that my mother had passed quietly away. Alexander and I were both shocked, so was my daughter. I felt very sad that I had not been sensitive enough to realise that my mother was trying to warn me of her coming death. How glad I was that I had obeyed my intuitive instinct to see her. I left the cottage to be with my mother and say goodbye and to make the necessary arrangements with the nursing home with regard to the funeral. My mother looked so peaceful. I held her hand and said a few prayers, laying some roses from our garden onto her breast. I was grateful that I had been able to look after my parents and share a home with them before they both died. Alexander and I took mother's ashes to the same place where we had scattered father's ashes, a few years earlier.

Alexander, to cheer me up, reminded me of the story of the master who was dying. The monks were all gathered around him, weeping at the thought of their master leaving them. Suddenly, the master arose from his deathbed and said: "What are you all weeping for?"

"Master! Master!" cried the monks in much distress, "We don't want you to go!"

"What!" exclaimed the master? "You don't mean to say there is somewhere to go?" So saying he lay back on his pillows, drawing his last breath.

Chapter Fourteen

Challenging Changes

For in and out, above, about below,
'Tis nothing but a magic shadow-show,
Play'd in a Box whose Candle is the Sun,
Round which we Phantom Figures come and go.

The Rubáiyát of Omar Khayyám stanza 46,
Translated by Edward Fitzgerald (1809–93)

AFTER THE PASSING OF MY MOTHER in 1976, Mary decided to move to a flat of her own, leaving Alexander and me in a new environment in which there were new challenges that gave us both an opportunity of learning further about ourselves.

My busy life as an agent for the publishing company was all consuming, particularly as I had accepted an increase in my territory, which meant that I was now responsible for the whole of Scotland. I was glad that Alexander agreed to continue to help me as I now estimated that we would be driving between 30,000 to 40,000 miles a year.

The increased territory involved being away from home on and off during the whole year. I bought a larger caravanette, which gave us a little more space and allowed us to carry more books and maps. Looking back on those early days it was in many ways a positive period for us both. We had time to discuss the things that mattered to us, which we were learning from attending the Krishnamurti gatherings at Brockwood Park during our holidays, which I describe fully in a later chapter.

We both enjoyed the opportunity to discover the Lowlands of Scotland, very different to the Scottish Highlands that I loved. Alexander was far more familiar with my new territory in the Lowlands of Scotland than I was, but I soon discovered the Lowlands were easier to manage than the Highlands. In spite of cities such as Glasgow, Edinburgh, Dundee, etc. being very time consuming and parking always a problem.

However, the beauty of the more remote areas of the Lowlands came as quite a surprise to me. I noticed there was a vast contrast between Highlands and Lowlands; even the atmosphere seemed different to me, and so indeed were the people. The coastal scenery around Southern Scotland appeared hardly to have changed over the passing centuries. But further inland in the border regions, between Scotland and England, there were more changes in that roads had improved and there were better services. In particular the area around the Solway Firth, with its inland Nature and Forestry reserves, was quite a contrast. But I still felt more at home in the Western Highlands, for the rugged scenery and extensive mountain ranges were always so awe-inspiring.

The area around the lowland hills, known as Sir Walter Scott country, and the more hilly areas around Moffat and St Mary's Loch were really beautiful. In the Border area I visited some of the large country estates, now open to the public, in which so much history has been enacted. Also, the tourism for which my Agencies catered was definitely increasing, and there were many more overseas visitors.

We were quite fussy where we parked the caravanette for the night, and soon became familiar with the best places to stop. We would take food and water with us when we were away all week. I loved my job, and if the weather was good we sometimes went for long walks in the evening.

The months passed. On one particular occasion that I shall never forget, when we had finished the week's work in the Dumfries and Galloway district and were on our way home, I could not help but notice that Alexander seemed much happier than usual. After having sorted out the caravanette so that it was ready for the coming week, we were relaxing in the lounge that overlooked the street, when suddenly I saw to my utter astonishment—a boat on a trailer drawing up in front of the cottage. I looked at Alexander, but he was already on his way to the front door, with what I thought was a rather restrained look on his face. I followed him onto the street, to discover that Alexander had completely neglected to tell me that he had negotiated the purchase of a boat during our visit that very week in the Dumfries area. I was quite dumbstruck! It is true it was only a small boat as boats go, but being much larger than our caravanette, it looked positively enormous outside our front door. I could not think what had possessed Alexander or how he could have managed to negotiate the purchase of a comparatively small boat without my knowledge. But then, Alexander was definitely unpredictable. Apparently he had bought this small sailing yacht, for that was what it was, through a hire purchase agreement from the man who was now delivering it to our doorstep. I was utterly speechless!

By now, I had learned that it was absolutely no use saying a single word to countermand Alexander's decisions. I expect he felt that had he asked me I would flatly have refused to buy a yacht. No doubt he was right! At this moment, I certainly did not want a scene on the front doorstep, so I gulped down my surprise and in trepidation quietly listened to the man now delivering the yacht. It looked well over 18 feet, and was called Kiss. By now I was certain that the cost would soon be laid at my door, for doubtless there would be expenses to meet in many ways with regard to owning a yacht. Not only that, but with our busy schedule I could not imagine how we were going to fit such a project into our lifestyle, particularly with the heavy workload to which I was already committed. I must confess I have never been so surprised; but strangely enough, despite myself, I was beginning to rather like the idea of yachting, as I love the sea.

I cannot say as the months went by that I did not thoroughly enjoy Alexander's latest acquisition, but as I had no sailing experience and Alexander—had very little I soon discovered—it turned out to be an extraordinary and exciting adventure that lasted several years. Since we could hardly leave the yacht on our front doorstep, we had to join a Yachting Club in Mussleburgh in order to obtain a suitable anchorage in the harbour. Naturally the monthly instalments had to be met by someone, which Alexander nonchalantly passed over to me, counting it as his reward for helping me to drive all the miles that we had been covering in Scotland, which amounted to quite a few! How could I possibly refuse?

One thing I was beginning to recognise was that Alexander was definitely my teacher in more ways than one. Unfortunately, the familiarity of married life often got in the way of total submission to the lessons he was teaching

me. Perhaps, it would have been all right had I managed to count up to ten before saying anything, but that discipline I was still to learn. Most of the time I was far too slow to respond to his wishes, and far too quick to resist what I felt was unreasonable. I was always taken aback when all hell was let loose, wondering what I had done to upset him. I realised I had so much still to learn about myself.

Thereafter, every weekend without fail for the next few years we spent down at the harbour or out on the yacht, weather permitting—and at other times when it definitely was not! Although I was a trifle nervous, I trusted Alexander completely and naturally treated him as the skipper. With hindsight, I this may have been why he subconsciously decided to buy the yacht, for this was his golden opportunity to be sole boss, knowing perfectly well there could not be two skippers on a boat. Proudly and with delight he took sole responsibility for the yacht, expecting me to obey his slightest command. I did not mind doing this in the least and was pleased to see he had found something he was interested in doing. I realised that Alexander needed this enjoyable outlet to balance his long hours of

driving. However, it was not all plain sailing—I remember not being quick enough to obey a command from Alexander after he had decided to change course—to find my head got in the way of the boom!

We began taking our leisure hours very earnestly. It was fun sailing along the Firth of Forth, exploring the area and learning new yachting skills. The yacht had a small cabin, and after I had given her a good clean and equipped her with some cushions and various other commodities, she was much more presentable, although never exactly comfortable. At times I felt we risked much by going out in rough weather, but I did not want to spoil Alexander's pleasure. I could not help noticing, though, that there were very few other members of our fraternity chancing the rough seas. I found it better to leave it all to Alexander and just do exactly as I was told. Besides, it gave him space to learn more quickly the art of sailing.

After several years of the excitement of sailing most weekends in good weather, Alexander and I met another yachtsman and his wife one stormy day down by the harbour. Both men were apparently planning to sail, but the weather looked very uncertain; neither the yachtsman's wife nor I felt it was safe to go out. However, the men decided to risk the 'high seas' and chance the rough weather. To my horror it was decided that they would take Alexander's yacht, which only had a small outboard motor to help us out of trouble. The yachtsman's wife and her five children remained behind, but I felt I had to go with Alexander if only for moral support, as there were no other yachts out at sea. To my utter dismay, Alexander allowed the 'yachtsman' to take control of the helm, in the mistaken belief that he was a far more experienced yachtsman than himself. I remember thinking that this was definitely an unwise move, but did not dare say a word. They had planned to go to Inch Keith Island, it was off shore some two sea miles away from Mussleburgh in the Firth of Forth, towards the Fife coast. I got gingerly on board, feeling anything but happy, and I remember as we set sail the anxious look on the faces of those waving us goodbye.

After being out at sea for an hour or so, the weather rapidly deteriorated. I clutched the side rail hoping my luck of being born with a 'caul' would keep us out of trouble. A heavy swell was now visible all around us. Black clouds had gathered and we were being swiftly taken out to sea. It was obvious to me that the outboard motor would be less than useless in those heavy seas. The yacht was bobbing up and down like a Jack-in-the-box. She looked no bigger than a toy yacht in comparison with the huge white-capped waves. By now the wind had increased, causing the inflated sails to billow alarmingly. We were skimming along the water and the yacht was leaning more and more over to one side as it negotiated the huge waves, at what I thought was an extremely dangerous angle. After a while, I timidly suggested that perhaps we had better take down some of the sails, although I did not feel strong enough to help under such conditions, in fact I might have made matters worse had I tried. Without any comment, Alexander began to gather in most of the sails, using his extraordinary strength; nevertheless, he was by now looking very pale. After the sails had been taken down, I felt a little more comfortable, and thankfully the men decided to return to the harbour.

By now I suspected our new skipper knew far less than Alexander about sailing, for he was fast losing the battle in trying to start the outboard motor. When he was at last successful he was unable to control it. Every time there was a huge wave the outboard motor rose out of the water so that our progress was almost static. I felt that we were really in a dangerous position, having no proper life-saving equipment other than our lifejackets and a very small dingy. By now I realised that neither man had any experience of rough weather, and I was beginning to be distinctly nervous. Looking helplessly around at the increasingly rough seas, I knew that we were in serious trouble. I think Alexander suspected this too, for he was as white as a sheet.

Suddenly, I spotted a fishing craft making its way toward us from the shore. To my utter astonishment, the clown at the helm of our boat refused the line that they threw to us. To my utmost dismay, the fishing craft turned back once the line had been refused. In a reflex action of disbelief I stood up waving frantically. Had a member of the crew not spotted me, a woman, standing up in the yacht frantically waving, we would certainly have been left to the mercy of the sea. I remember standing clutching the rail, ready to catch the line when it came, as the fishing-boat turned to help us once again. I hesitated no longer to remain under the command of the clown at the helm. I grabbed the line, tying it to the rail, feeling relieved when I felt Alexander helping me to secure the line with a proper sailor's knot. Being towed to the harbour in this manner, with never a word said, was as surreal as anything I can ever remember.

There was no doubt that we would have been swept rapidly out to sea, had we not accepted the line. The yacht was already taking in water at an alarming rate and the outboard motor proved to be totally useless in such high seas. We were all scooping up water from inside the yacht as vast as we could. I learned later that there had been about a force nine gale blowing and that it had been the wife of the yachtsman who had raised the alarm. On guessing our dilemma she had begged her fishermen friends to rescue us, no doubt having visions of her five children bereft of their father. Much to our relief the Captain of the fishing boat never asked us for any salvage dues. However, the episode had unfortunately affected Alexander's pride, which was hardly to be wondered at.

Thereafter, Alexander did not like to be seen in the harbour any more or in the Yachting Club. After dropping the yachtsman off and securing our yacht in the harbour, he decided in future to moor our boat out at sea—at the end of our road that went down to the sea. I knew this was not permissible. However, the very next day, as the weather had abated, we moored Kiss as close to the beach as possible. Alexander had found a very strong anchor from somewhere, and after making sure all hatches were down, we came ashore in the dinghy. I may add that shortly after this we took the yacht up to Loch Katrine in The Trossachs, where Alexander's brother lived alongside the loch. Mercifully he found a buyer for our little yacht. I was sorry that our yachting days had ended in the way they had, since we both enjoyed this period in our lives and missed the general excitement that it entailed.

One day, whilst we were driving toward the Forth Road Bridge on one of our long journeys north, I realised too late that my argumentative resistance was beginning to upset Alexander. I stopped in despair, thinking that I would never learn. Then, as I sat very quietly beside him wondering how to face the dilemma of the cross-purpose that I had managed to lock us into, I suddenly felt as if all thoughts had ceased. As I sat in silence, there came unexpectedly to me the following words, which gave me a huge jolt. They were: *"The greatest gift man has in life is to see everything as it is and to allow it to remain so."* I repeated the words to Alexander, who said, "Quick, quick! Write them down before you forget them!" I quickly wrote the words down and soon all our altercation was forgotten, as we both began to realise the potency of those words.

Alexander thought it no coincidence that the sentence amounted to twenty-one words. One and two (twenty) made three, an esoteric number, which when multiplied by three, adds up to the whole number of nine. I felt profoundly moved on hearing these words, knowing that some power within myself was able to respond since my usual self had gone quiet. I realised that the moment my argumentative, limited, self-centred self had stopped responding and remained absolutely quiet and silent, with no thoughts running around in my head, then the other part of myself would respond in an immediate and unexpected way. It was as if a part of myself, totally unknown, had surfaced without any effort or volition on my part. It was an unforgettable moment of silent bliss that left me filled with inexpressible awe and wonder.

I think those words helped me more than anything else I have ever known. I immediately understood the necessity of remaining absolutely quiet, when all around seems chaotic. But I realised that there could be no volitional movement of any kind to bring this state into being. It was like the stillness within the eye of the hurricane and it brought home to me that argumentative behaviour provokes conflict more quickly than anything else.

I realised that I resisted Alexander's control over me more often than I had realised. The words 'The greatest gift man has in life' revealed to us that all mankind is endowed with this innate gift, which is a part of his or her structural heritage. If we pause for a moment to review the words, we can see that '*the greatest gift*' could only refer to the means we have within us to take care of whatever is in front of us; the 'what is' that Krishnamurti so often described in his talks. If we allow whatever is in front of us to remain so, then that other part of ourselves that is within us all will act spontaneously. But it can never be a volitional movement when we are not totally silent. Perhaps this is the only real action of any importance that there is; that is, simply to '*allow everything to remain so*'. When I followed those words through very carefully, I could see that I had no need ever to argue my point.

I found that I did not have to experience any of those accustomed methods, which I had always followed, through habit rather than design: such as arguing, being upset and hurt and heavens knows what else. It was an entirely different approach and required a new kind of discipline that I knew I needed, in order that the greatest gift could work. I wished I could say that I was always attentive enough for it to manifest, before the crucial moment had slipped by! My habit of arguing was too embedded to come to an end by just hearing those words.

I remembered something that Krishnamurti had said, which had made a deep impression on me: 'Understanding comes swiftly, unknowingly, when the effort is passive. Only when the maker of the effort is silent does the wave of understanding come.' These words made me realise that when I had heard 'The greatest gift man has in life is to see everything as it is and to allow it to remain so', I had been very silent. I had given up—not knowing how to respond to Alexander.

I felt that what lay behind the words I had heard had tremendous significance. They precipitated a formidable realisation: I had to give complete attention to—the 'what is' directly in front of me—as Krishnamurti expressed it— to remain exactly as it is, without trying to alter, change, or shape, or even escape from what lay in front of me through thought, then 'the greatest gift' worked.

I realised, too, that I did not need to move away from myself and become identified with another person's troubles or violence or words, or to justify their behavioural responses. If I did not try to do anything about what was happening in front of me, I could be sure that 'the greatest gift,' would spontaneously act. But if I interfered by any of my thoughts in any way whatsoever, I would be back at square one again—engaged in conflict and argument. I proved over and over again that these words really worked. It was not a question of remembering to put these words into action; rather it was seeing the significance of the words that gave me a totally changed attitude of mind that made it possible for spontaneous action to take place. If I tried in any way to put these words into action I was again coming from an interfering 'me' that made silence impossible. I realised that a silent mind can only be passive—as I had been when I gave up arguing—by seeing the futility of my actions, which had stopped me—thus the movement of thought came to an end—and I was able to hear those words: 'The Greatest Gift man has in Life is to see everything as it is and allow it to remain so.' But for them to come into action, I had to work hard, very hard on myself through awareness of my actions and reactions; then 'The Greatest Gift' was there.

Alexander continued to drive the caravanette for me, but he had become very restless and would demand that we returned home on Thursday nights instead of Fridays. This made it much more difficult for me to organise my weekly journeys, as it inevitably curtailed the time that I could spend with my customers. Therefore, instead of enjoying my job, I began to feel an unbearable pressure forcing me to work more rapidly to get the calls done. By acquiescing I kept the peace. I think I was too occupied with my work to notice that Alexander was finding the continual driving irksome. To some extent, I suppose I had taken it for granted that he would have to fit in with what my job entailed, since it had been his own choice to come round Scotland to help me with the driving.

At the end of the 1979/80, Alexander once again became interested in Martial Arts and joined a local club, which he visited during the weekends. I was pleased when he joined the Judo club, for his interest in Martial Arts had always fascinated him. We both felt that there was much wisdom to be learned through studying an art that had been developed for thousands of years by Japanese and Chinese Masters. I bought myself a Martial Arts outfit at Alexander's suggestion and at weekends would join him and his friends for Ki lessons in Martial Arts. Alexander became friends with a German doctor who taught Ki in particular. Alexander made several trips to Germany and in return the doctor came over to Scotland. We had many learning efforts on the Judo Mat.

As time went by Alexander wanted me to spend more time with him in Martial Arts than just at the weekends, but I had to consider the company I was working for as my first priority. It was, after all, our only means of livelihood, but Alexander simply did not seem to understand what

earning a livelihood entailed. I felt it was an enormous bonus in any job to travel round such a beautiful country as Scotland. True, Scotland was a very large territory to cover; yet the many diversions of the countryside were far from boring.

In spite of our expensive holidays abroad at Christmas time, Alexander remained in an unsettled state until he finally demanded that I work at a slower pace, I simply could not do so without neglecting my job, and this I was not prepared to do. Several things were bothering me, not the least of which was our pension. I had started very late in life to save for a pension for us both, which made me feel I had no option other than to continue working. As time went by Alexander became more persistent in his demands, and when that did not work he turned his attention to demanding that I place his name on the deeds of the cottage. This I would gladly have done had Alexander not proved himself to be so erratic and impractical. In fact, it would have been irresponsible of me to agree, since I operated my business from the cottage, and I was never quite sure of what he might do next.

When I bought the cottage for my parents, I had purchased a fifteen-year insurance policy for Alexander in order to balance our future assets. At that time, it appeared as if Alexander would be much better off than I would by owning the cottage. Also it had been my responsibility to pay for both the mortgage on the cottage and the premiums on his insurance policy. This arrangement had met with Alexander's full approval. But now he appeared to have forgotten these arrangements, especially now that he was mixing more and more with his Ki friends and making new acquaintances. I noticed that he was beginning to change his lifestyle and his way of thinking. I could feel we were drifting apart.

From my point of view I was worried that Alexander was not strong enough to withstand the temptation of drinking when out with his friends. I knew that if he reverted to taking even one glass of alcohol again, he would soon find one drink was not enough and would return to the former alcoholic habits, which he had given up when he had married me. It is well known that if an alcoholic who has given up drinking starts again after a considerable space of time, the gap seems to have the effect of making the renewed drinking get out of hand more quickly. Whilst we were working together, we were too busy to be involved with socialising, so the problem of his past drinking habits had not arisen. I was always very afraid they might, as I felt that Alexander could easily be influenced where drink was concerned. I did not feel inclined to interfere by explaining my fears to his various friends and acquaintances, for they would be quite unaware of his past alcoholic problems. I tried to tell one of his friends in an indirect way, but it did not work, since the friend had misunderstood my concern, and reported my feelings back to Alexander. So I had to persevere alone, hoping against hope that Alexander had learned the dangers of alcohol.

I tried to enlist help from the German Doctor who was teaching Alexander the martial art form of Ki, and he responded by giving him acupuncture treatment in both of his ears and talking to him about the dangers of alcoholic consumption. However, the doctor, who never drank any alcohol, recognised that such treatment needed serious commitment on Alexander's part, if he was to overcome his alcoholic inclination. Again, as with most of Alexander's undertakings, he co-operated with the doctor for a while; however, the return of his drinking habits overcame his good intention. He simply could not take just one drink, so things became worse for him and me.

I had observed over the years that Alexander was a very sensitive person, and being sensitive myself, I found this a challenge, although I never became used to his sudden temperamental outbursts. The two extremes in his make-up, I am sure, made it difficult for him to keep a balanced control of himself, especially as he also had a very quick temper. When he wanted me to stop working he never considered where the money would come from to meet all our commitments, especially the pension fund, the mortgage and the insurance policies.

It was after Alexander had been driving with me for about five years that I realised he was showing signs of real unrest, and this worried me. At times I felt a crisis looming, and although I was at a loss to know what to do, I tried my best to accommodate his inability to settle, even suggesting that he stop coming round with me, despite finding him to be such a tremendous help and companion. I wondered if the loss of the yacht had unsettled him. The days went by, and since I was very busy with my job I did not have time to be too involved with anything else, except our weekends at Ki.

However, at the end of January 1981, Alexander suddenly flatly refused to come around with me any more. In spite of my suggestion that he should do so, his decision came as a tremendous shock. I was so afraid of his drinking problem. I knew that he was due for his state pension in a few months' time, which, I suppose, had influenced him. As time passed, Alexander drifted further away from me, preferring the company of his friends. He had by now joined a shooting club and had made many more friends. I realised that now we were spending so much time apart, our lives together had taken a very different turn. I kept wishing things had remained as they were, little realising that I was not accepting Alexander's new life-style. I was still clinging on to what I thought should really be happening—a big mistake on my part. Then I remembered the words I had heard that had changed my whole attitude: 'The greatest gift man has in life is to see everything as it is and allow it to remain so.'

Nevertheless, I was horrified one day when out of the blue I received a letter from Alexander's solicitor demanding settlement from me for half the value of the cottage, or for me to place his name on the deeds of the cottage—together with mine. Also, I was informed that I owed Alexander wages and that I had not paid him for all the years he had been driving for me. I felt this to be totally unreasonable, as I had paid for all our living expenses, his insurance premium, the expensive holidays abroad every year, besides the airfares he needed to see his doctor friend in Germany. And Alexander had had everything he asked for in the way of clothes etc. as well as any money he needed. And it was not my suggestion in the beginning that he came round with me.

After my father's death I had paid off the mortgage on the cottage with the money that my father had left to my mother. Mother felt that this would give her greater security; provided I kept my promise to her that I would keep my name solely on the deeds of the cottage. Now that my mother was dead, Alexander knew this no longer applied.

I was really terrified of what Alexander might do. He threatened to cut the house in half and burn it down if I did not comply with his demands. I was unable to believe he could act in such a manner and felt the root cause of his changed behaviour and threats must be his drinking. Since he had joined the gun club he had bought several guns, which he kept locked up in a safe under the stairs. This did not make me feel very secure. Eventually, through my solicitor, I gave him ten thousand pounds as a settlement, which seemed to make him happy. His life insurance policy was soon due to mature, and he now had his state pension.

In spite of the extra money, after a while Alexander began to repeat his demands all over again for his name to be placed on the deeds of the cottage. More solicitors' letters followed. I refused to be drawn into his unreasonable demands and pressed ahead with my work despite being concerned about leaving him alone in the house, as I never knew what he might be planning or who he was inviting to the house from the pubs.

What made me particularly unhappy was that we were still going down to Brockwood Park to listen to the Krishnamurti talks. Under such circumstances, I felt it was unreasonable that we could not settle our differences. Alexander had been so good to me when we left the School, I could not believe that he had changed so much, and kept wondering if it was my entire fault. But I did not know how to resolve the situation without giving in to his unreasonable demands, so I followed the words I had heard: 'The greatest gift man has in life is to see everything as it is and to allow it to remain so.'

I realised that my beliefs or conditioning had made me feel that the male partner was the protector and provider, which made me unconsciously dependent on Alexander. Although I acknowledged at last that I had to work things out for myself, it was quite another matter to try to do so. It took me some time before the full awareness of the situation between Alexander and myself dawned on me. Even so I found his threats easier to deal with than the hurts and fears that arose in me from his attitude.

It became obvious to me that my fears were rooted in my inability to deal with my own uncertainties, my emotions, my unhappiness; and above all my inability to stand on my own two feet. Indeed, I discovered it was the very word fear that I was most afraid of, and by naming the 'what is' as fear, I had empowered it. Every time I thought of the word, I was caught up with it. Dreadful feelings of fear began to arise in the pit of my stomach making my mouth feel dry. I felt so lost and alone. Yet when I managed to stay with these fears and stop escaping from them any more, the division between my fear and myself ended. Thought, I found, created the images and illusions of my fears, and my attitude made it impossible for me to face those images and illusions. But by objectifying fear through personalised thinking as something distinct from myself I was still identifying myself with those fears. This understanding gave me a totally different perspective. I had come across the following words from the book *Jesus Untouched by the Church* by Hugh McGregor Ross, from the Coptic text of *The Gospel of Thomas*:

> *Jesus said:*
> *In the days you see your resemblance,*
> *you rejoice.*
> *But when you will see your images*
> *that in the beginning were in you*
> *which neither die nor are manifest,*
> *oh! how will you bear the revelation!*

These words showed me how Jesus knew mankind's need to understand how personal thoughts create images, which are the instigators of emotional feelings of fear and sorrow, as well as countless other self-inflicted emotional feelings of hurt etc. These lines of Jesus enabled me to understand fear and what it was doing to me. I was therefore more able to adjust to being out on my own without Alexander's help with the driving.

In December 1981 I bought a new Volkswagen van, a VW 28 LT with a high rooftop and no side windows. I had it converted to my own design to suit my needs at a boat-building yard in Troon. It was bigger to drive, and although it did not have a diesel engine or power assisted steering, it was equipped with all I required to live and work while I continued my job.

I had two bunks installed. I slept in the top bunk while the bottom one held lots of books, for which there was plenty of room. I incorporated a wardrobe, and as there were no windows around the sides of the van, I had a large skylight fitted in the roof. I also had curtains placed around the front of the van between the driver's seat and the interior. The lights inside the van ran off an extra battery, which I placed in the wardrobe behind the driver's seat. For heating the inside of the van I utilised space beneath the bottom bunk to contain a heating unit that ran off diesel oil.

Besides two batteries, I had two large containers for water and a cooking oven and hob supplied by two Calor gas bottles, which also supplied a shower and the hot water system. The hot water for the shower ran off a special heating contraption attached to the calor gas bottle. I had to be very careful to turn the calor gas off before going to bed and especially when the van was running. I was always a little nervous about the calor gas, particularly after an accident that happened to two young policewomen on holiday in Glencoe in their dormobile, whose gas bottle had exploded, killing them both. I had passed the dormobile lying on its side in a ditch, and I shuddered to think of their horrific deaths. I made a mental note to be extremely careful to make sure my Calor gas bottles were always turned off before travelling and before going to sleep.

Meanwhile, back at home; Alexander was managing to find plenty to do. He was asked to speak at *The Theosophical Society*. One of his shooting friends had introduced him, which led Alexander to invite a group of people to the cottage for discussions. I could not join in with them as I was always away working, but I was glad he was doing this and hoped it would solve our problems.

Everything seemed to be going all right for a while. He was well thought of by *The Theosophical Society*, where he spoke of Wei Wu Wei, author of several books, amongst others—*Open Secret, All Else Is Bondage, Posthumous Pieces, Unworldly Wise* and *The Tenth Man*—Wei Wu Wei's style of philosophy was very much Alexander's, as there was a certain satirical humour in his teachings which appealed to him; he had an excellent memory and could recite long passages from these books. Alexander also spoke about Buddhism, Krishnamurti and many other philosophical figures and subjects, besides demonstrating his skills at Martial Arts. He was in his element. His ability to quote passages from the poems of Robert Burns, Alexander Pope and Shakespeare made him very popular with his friends. He had a very real talent for getting a message across to his audience—he was a wonderful speaker.

However, at the same time Alexander never ceased pressurising me to place his name on the deeds of the cottage and I never ceased by refusing. I could not understand why he was so insistent. But the very fact that he so persistently pressurised me to gain equal rights over the property my father had left me made me suspicious of his motives. I reasoned that it could not be that he was short of money as he now had his insurance policy and his pension, which he kept to himself, besides the ten thousand he had earned by driving me around Scotland. We appeared to be drifting even further apart as Alexander continued to pursue his own disciplines at Martial Arts and the shooting club, with short spells abroad in Germany with his doctor friend or over in Greece seeing his Greeks friends.

I did accompany him once or twice to Greece as I was fond of his Grecian friends and enjoyed cruising in the Mediterranean, and I still continued to participate in his Martial Art classes. But by 1985, when the talks at Brockwood Park came to an end due to the death of Krishnamurti in Ojai on 17th February 1986, Alexander and I ceased to take any more holidays together.

Whilst at the cult, I remembered seeing a wonderful film, which to me illustrated Alexander's character, and there is no doubt that it applied to me as well as to most other people. The story was called The Mask. It was only a short film, but it aptly illustrated how we produce images of ourselves rather as actors do, concealing who we really are by covering our faces with masks. The film was all about a man who wore masks; he always moved about in a constant state of 'masked' agitation. He was a jovial fellow with bright sparkling eyes, a mop of black curly hair and a snub nose, and when he did not wear a mask he seemed a reasonable enough fellow. The film begins by showing him about to get into bed with his wife. He can be seen looking at the masks that lay on his bedside table. Before getting into bed he feels them and then fiddles with them to reassure himself that they are really there, lifting them up one by one. He looks mystified, as his face shifts into peculiar grimaces. By now his long-suffering wife begs him to turn out the light and climb into bed, saying impatiently, 'I'm tired!' and in an exasperated voice, 'For heaven's sake put out the light!' He climbs into bed and as he does so quickly switches off the light.

The next morning his wife goes downstairs to prepare breakfast for him. He searches on the table beside him for his 'mask to greet the day'. As he finds it, he fixes his mood into the mask. Today he feels great as he jumps out of bed, hastily grabbing his shaving mask. After he has shaved, he takes off the shaving mask and examines his face in the mirror. Satisfied, he runs down to breakfast, hastily taking from his pocket the mask he always puts on for being with his wife. As he greets his wife, his mask positively purrs like a large overgrown kitten. After breakfast he waves goodbye to his wife. Once in his car he replaces his wife's mask with his driving mask. He then becomes quite a different person as he drives to work in his usual hurry, cursing other motorists that are slow. Often forcing his car at speed, he moves in and out of the traffic, counting every manoeuvred success a victory. Then he moves rapidly toward the lights managing to squeeze in front of another car just in time before the lights turn red. Seconds later he is cursing another motorist, who squeezes in front of his car, doing exactly what he has done a few seconds earlier to another car. Eventually he arrives at the office and thankfully removes his driving mask. He hurries up the stairs to his office, and as he slides through the door, he readjusts his office mask.

He repeats the switching of masks throughout the day, until he is no longer even conscious of what he is doing. It has become such a habit to keep changing his masks while at the office, that he has become very adept. No one ever sees who he really is, since the changing of the masks hides his real self behind every changing 'masked' mood.

At last he goes home. Now he has to meet his children, which requires the mask that shows a loving parent. But he soon loses his patience and hastily has to replace the parent mask with his strict father's mask. By night time he was utterly exhausted and laying down the last mask he is wearing he climbs thankfully into bed with his wife.

Suddenly in the middle of the night he awakens in a sweat, dreaming that he has lost his masks. He searches around on the table near his bed. No masks. On the floor—no masks to be seen. On his bed still no masks. He is dumbfounded, scratching his head in disbelief. He begins to wonder whether his dream about losing his masks has been real or whether in fact he had ever had any masks to either dream about or to lose. Or was his life just one continual dream? He jumps out of bed, terribly agitated. The film ends with a mystified look creeping all over his face as he looks around saying: 'Perhaps I have been dreaming the whole business of the masks, losing them and putting them on—or is my whole life nothing but a perpetual dream?'

This film was actually discovered by me whilst I was at the cult. I had borrowed it from a film company, so it could be shown to the group—with Zamiar's permission, of course. The only trouble was that the group failed to remember or even recognise that mask swopping was a common practice amongst us all. I wondered whether this mythical mask swopping had become a complaisant habit amongst all humanity and that we either deliberately ignored it, or it had furtively become an accepted part of our behaviour?

The film in turn reminded me of the story of two monks who were making their way to a ford. The elder monk reached the ford first and noticed a young woman in much distress waiting to cross the ford. The water was too deep for her and she was obviously frightened, so the elder monk spontaneously lifted the young woman and carried her across the ford. When the younger monk eventually caught up with the elder, he turned to him saying, 'Brother, we are monks and are therefore not supposed to touch women; yet I watched you carry that young woman across the ford. Why did you disobey our rules?' 'Ah!' observed the elder monk, unconcernedly continuing his walk. 'Why should you be so troubled? I put her down at the ford, but I notice that you are still carrying her.'

By now, unfortunately, Alexander's drinking habits were beginning to become an obvious problem, although I was aware that he was trying to hide them both from himself and me; but his behaviour as a consequence deteriorated. Unable to obtain his own way over the deeds of the house, he became more aggressive and even resorted to physical violence. I still did not want to put an end to my relationship with Alexander, as I could see his addiction to drink was a real problem, but it is a well known fact that unless the person concerned wants to stop their drinking habits, nothing can be done to help them. So I let things drift, escaping more than ever into my work. At the same time, I was becoming aware of particularly unpleasant odours seeping into the cottage from Alexander's clothes. I suspected that he must have been spending more time than I realised at the local pubs whilst I was away. I was afraid that he might inadvertently become prey to any criminally minded person whom he might meet there, for I was sure that he would be in no condition to realise what was happening.

One day he returned to the cottage very drunk. I shall never forget the occasion as I learned a great lesson. I was in the dining room, the room that had two steps going down into it from the hall of the Georgian part of the cottage. As he stood on the steps before coming down into the dining room he leaned against the open doorway. I stood looking up at him thinking, 'If you could only see yourself as you are now, you would never be drunk again.' As quick as lightening another thought flashed through my mind: 'And if you (meaning myself) were not thinking those thoughts, you would not be encouraging him to drink!' At once I thought, 'Oh, my God, how interesting! Oh, my God, how very interesting!' My whole attitude changed instantly. Now I only wanted to help him. So I asked him if he would like some soup. He sat down on a chair in a daze and said he would. After he had his soup he allowed me to help him into bed. I now realised that he obviously had got a very serious problem, and from that moment onward I changed.

Years ago when I had first met Alexander in London, he had a very severe alcoholic problem which, I must admit, I had always been very afraid would return again. After this episode I no longer objected to his drinking and never tried to stop him, and I was no longer afraid of his outbursts. By 1991 his drink intake had increased. But I am sure most of his friends did not realise the serious nature of his addiction, since he still continued to meet with his group at *The Theosophical Society* or the gun clubs or at his Martial Arts sessions, and he continued to hold a group at home.

How he managed to conceal his alcoholic problems from his friends I never knew. One night when I had come home a day early from my travels—it must have been about two in the morning—I was in bed nearly asleep when there was a loud knock on the door. In trepidation I called. 'Who is there?' I was answered by the voice of a police officer at the door. I unfastened the door but kept the chain on. Being very nervous, I asked for ID, which the two policemen produced. They were bringing Alexander back drunk, explaining to me that they were actually being kind to him by returning him home, rather than taking him to the cells. Unfortunately, Alexander was 'fighting drunk', and when the police brought him in, as soon as he saw me he became abusive. The police officers tried to contain him, but he suddenly hit one of the officers. He was then instantly charged, handcuffed, and taken back into the police van that was still waiting outside my door, with lights flashing. I was totally horrified and very upset. He was charged to appear before the Magistrate the next day. I learned later that he had been bound over and released. He returned home. I dreaded his return, but after he had a shower he went straight to bed. I left him some food and departed to do my work, glad to escape. He had apparently been handcuffed all night to another drunkard, much to his disgust.

Several months later, Alexander again brought up his demands for half the house. Unable to get his own way, he became angry and threatened me. He raised his strong arm as if to strike me. I sat down on a stool feeling utterly defeated. I stopped resisting him any longer and waited for what would happen. I could not cope with his tantrums any more or my own inability to know how to manage the situation. Suddenly, as he forcefully brought his arm down to strike me, he caught his hand on a nail in the wall that held a small ornament. Instead of striking me he pulled a nerve out of the edge of his hand. Turning deathly white, he immediately blamed me. I said I thought I had better take him to hospital, but he demanded that I fetch some scissors to cut off the dangling nerve. I did as he bid, for I knew very well, having been a nurse, that I only had to put the scissors within a foot or so of the dangling nerve for him instantly to pull his hand away—which, of course, is exactly what he did. After I had bandaged his hand as best I could, he finally submitted to being taken to hospital. He kept on insisting he wanted to drive, but I took no notice, and helped him into the front passenger seat of the car and drove him to the hospital.

We had to wait for some time to see the doctor in the outpatient's department. The doctor eventually saw Alexander and said that as he required surgery he would have to be kept in overnight. I fetched his overnight clothes etc. But I had to leave to do my work before he returned home. Apparently, I heard later that he was very, very lucky, as the surgeon was able to stitch the nerve in place again. That was the last time Alexander ever tried to strike me. I realised that I had unconsciously allowed 'the greatest gift' to take care of the situation, and the thought reduced me to tears.

Things came to a head one day in 1992, as I felt all along that they assuredly must if Alexander did not change. Once I had stopped resisting his behaviour and tried to help him, I knew that he would have to change or leave. Things had gone too far and I was powerless to change the situation. Alexander came to me one day insisting he wanted 'out' unless I met his demands and placed his name on the deeds. Once again I refused. He had so many times threatened to leave me that now I felt I could do nothing to stop him. I told him that I was sorry that he felt the way he did, and that if he really meant what he said then I would not try to stop him from going. I suggested that he had better put down on paper what he wanted. I said I would discuss the letter with my solicitor in order to accommodate his demands.

So it was agreed between our two solicitors that I would help him find a place in which to live. I would buy the property for him, but the property had to be in my name so that I could pay the mortgage and the upkeep of the cottage inside and out for his lifetime, as well as pay his community charge. In this way I would be sure that he had a roof over his head. I furnished the cottage from home and gave him all he asked for, including a very large sum of money, and a car, and stocked larder.

Thereafter, Alexander said he did not want any more solicitors' bills and asked me to use my solicitor to do all the arrangements for the Separation Agreement. I felt we were on a more realistic and friendly footing than we had been for a long time. Unfortunately, his cottage was just in England, which entailed having two solicitors, due to the fact that Scottish Law is different from English Law. I agreed that Alexander could take anything he wanted from my cottage to help him to settle into his own cottage, and did what I could to help him move. I think he began to feel he did not want what he had got, now that he had got what he wanted, for he seemed to take very little interest in moving into his cottage.

When the day finally came for our parting, he was crying. I was too. I felt at a loss to know how to understand him and found myself blaming myself for being unable to help him or to see his point of view or indeed to realise what he really wanted. His moods were so extreme. Had he asked to remain, I know I would have agreed without question. I was just as upset as he was to see him leave. I felt in the deepest of despair, hardly knowing what I was doing or saying.

During the years following Alexander's move, we met most weekends at a halfway restaurant. In 1994, I decided to make improvements to my cottage, which was badly needed. This took four months. I put in two dormer windows that transformed the attic into a large proper bedroom with a new staircase. Then I organised a modern kitchen, which was a great challenge. But in the end, the improvements meant that my cottage was at last a saleable proposition. So all the tremendous upheaval was well worthwhile. I suppose I was so busy coping with the alterations and at the same time continuing to work that I did not have much time to think about Alexander, so we ceased to meet as often, although we would telephone each other quite frequently. But when I became involved in writing a history book of Scotland in 1995, I no longer had time to meet him at weekends.

Thus it was to my utmost astonishment and complete horror that in late 1995, with the help of two of his friends, Alexander lodged a Writ in the High Court in Edinburgh for a divorce with demands for half the matrimonial assets and pensions. I was totally shocked and unable to believe he could do such a thing to me after I had complied with all his wishes and very much more besides through our legal Separation Agreement.

Regarding the Court Case, which I was now forced to defend, suffice to say that after two and half years, Alexander was forced to bring the case to a closure because his own solicitors would not act for him any more. In late 1997 Alexander telephoned me begging me not to put down the receiver on him, saying he wanted to end the case. I said that of course I would not do any such thing as to put down the receiver. I felt Alexander was ill, no doubt due to his excessive drinking and the worry over the Court Case.

Once Alexander had agreed to the divorce and the court had upheld the Separation Agreement, I telephoned him to ask if he needed any money. I found Alexander was penniless. What he had done with the very large sum of money I had given him in 1992, his own insurance money of over fifteen thousand pounds sterling, to say nothing of the previous ten thousand pounds sterling that I had given him, I could not imagine; although I had circumstantial evidence that he had given a large sum away to a woman friend for safe keeping, so that he could apply for legal aid.

Needless to say, that was the last he ever saw of it. However, as he was obviously not well and needed money, I sent him some cash immediately by registered mail, followed by a further sum that I suggested he place in his Post Office Bank, which he did.

As the days went by after the divorce, Alexander telephoned me every day at all hours. I could feel he was losing his ability to hold himself together through the alcohol that he had been and still was consuming. I told him that if he stopped drinking I would pull out every stop to help him. He said he would. He did so by the help and encouragement of two very loyal friends, who lived in the same village where Alexander lived, and were tireless in their efforts to help and guide him.

I set into motion a plan of action at once to help Alexander. I wrote three letters, one to the social services, one to his doctor and one to the army. The net result was that he was admitted to hospital in Berwick-on-Tweed so that he could 'dry out'. Unfortunately he became unmanageable and was soon transferred to a psychiatric hospital in Morpeth. Eventually I managed to obtain a place for him in a nursing home in Edinburgh. He only lasted a month, but he was at least able to retain some sort of dignity before he died. I visited him every day and stayed by his bedside as long as I could each day after he had moved to Edinburgh. I said to him one day, "I think you know I am here, you old dog." My reward was a thin little smile that arose from the corner of his mouth. Just before he sank into unconsciousness, he called out aloud, "Mother! Mother!" and after two to three days he passed over peacefully. I arranged his funeral and took his ashes to the same place that we had taken my mother's and my father's ashes. The cross was still there.

He had been very kind and helpful to me after I had left the cult, from which he had rescued me all those years ago. His further help and encouragement was freely given during the time that I needed it most. I was very upset over the whole affair and wanted very much to know if he was at last at peace. In my heart I knew that Alexander was a good man. There is no doubt in my mind that the main difficulty between us was the psychological damage he received from shell shock during the Second World War. It had been behind many of his behavioural difficulties. War is so dreadful, particularly for those who fought and survived its horrors by being maimed both physically and mentally.

I had unfortunately not fully recognised or understood the extent of the damage he had received from his war years fighting in so many different places as a regular soldier and if I had to some degree, I do not know how I could have coped with his resultant behaviour. I am naturally a strong character, and because I was the only one earning a livelihood for us both, I think Alexander found my growing independence difficult to tolerate. Being unable to rectify the situation, for whatever reason, his self-image was wounded. He probably misguidedly believed I no longer needed him as I had in the early days of our marriage. I was sure that the diabolical traumas of the Second World War had had such an effect on Alexander that he was unable to settle to civilian life.

Way back in the 1930s in Scotland jobs were difficult to obtain, and the military services seemed the only alternative for those families who could not afford a higher education. Alexander was barely seventeen when he appled on his own volition to join the army. It must have been very hard for him to settle down to the reality of army life, being so young and immature, especially as the main training was to learn to kill, and Alexander was so sensitive.

When the Second World War came, he was forced to put his training to kill into action. His resultant wounds and shell shock caused him nothing but frustration, obvious to me by the frequent movements of his right shoulder. Perhaps his pride would not let him seek any help or maybe he did not even know he needed it. The terrible effects of the war years had no doubt disillusioned him, and like so many serving men, he had turned to heavy drinking to cope with civilian life.

For over sixteen years after Alexander married me, to my knowledge he never touched any alcohol. In spite of his restlessness he had always helped me to the best of his ability. It made me feel very, very sad when he turned to drink again. Perhaps I had expected more from Alexander than he was able to give, not realising anything was deeply troubling him since I thought he was so much stronger than myself. In hindsight it is so easy to explain away the faults in oneself or others. Nevertheless, I have very happy memories of our life together, albeit some sad ones too.

I remember Alexander telling me a truly moving story of something that happened to him in his youth, which clearly illustrated his sensitivity and warm-hearted nature.

When he was about fourteen, he found a white ball of fluff outside the front door of his home. It was a wee tawny owl that must have fallen out of its nest. It was scarcely big enough for Alexander to pick up, for his hands were large and expressive. He took the wee bird inside and fed it through a fountain pen until it could fend for itself. The owl and Alexander formed an unbelievable friendship. He called the little morsel Snowy; they became inseparable. It would perch on Alexander's hand or shoulder, and when it was old enough, would roost on a branch of a tree just outside their front door. Wherever Alexander went Snowy went too. When he left home for school on his bicycle, Snowy would perch on his shoulder. When school was over Snowy would be there to greet him. They were real friends.

The relationship was perfect until the owl was fully grown. It was then that Snowy became more and more protective of Alexander.

One day an important visitor came to see his father, a stranger to Snowy, who swooped down suddenly upon the poor man's bald head. Alexander felt that Snowy had mistaken the bald patch on the man's head for a plate—the plate on which Alexander would place the many tip-bits he gathered for Snowy, such as a succulent mouse, a collection of beetles and worms or various other tasty scraps rescued from his dinner. But Alexander was unable to explain to the visitor that the owl meant him no harm. Alexander's father, however, took a different view, and pointed out later to Alexander that his relationship could not continue with Snowy. He said that his employers would never tolerate the owl's behaviour. He therefore advised Alexander to take Snowy on a long journey into the country and say goodbye to him.

Much affected by this, Alexander took his little friend some five to six miles distant on his bicycle and told Snowy that they must now part company. Alexander peddled home, full of sorrow at having parted with Snowy. When he arrived home his father asked him if he had sent the owl away. Alexander said he had. 'Then what is that up there on that branch?' asked his father. Alexander looked up to see his little friend on his usual perch in the tree. Immediately the owl flew onto Alexander's shoulder.

The very next day Alexander had to take Snowy on a much, much longer ride. He rode away on his bicycle with Snowy perched on his shoulder. He peddled some fifteen miles away, until he found a wood where he felt Snowy would be happy. He took his little friend onto his wrist, where the owl perched happily, then after stroking his back and whispering his farewell, Alexander lifted his arm up high, which was a signal for Snowy to leave. But Snowy did not immediately fly away. The owl made three graceful circles above and around Alexander's head as it climbed higher and higher and then disappeared from sight into the wood. Alexander knew he would never see his little friend again. But he said he would never forget the extraordinary feeling that Snowy had generated within him, as that beautiful bird performed its spectacular farewell.

I realised that Alexander's passing had affected me very deeply, in a way that I found hard to explain. Some weeks later, I begged him in my mind to reveal to me that all was well with him. That night I had an extraordinary dream. I saw Alexander sitting up in his coffin looking the same way as I knew him when I had first met him; happy and relaxed. His coffin was being carried along on a conveyer belt and he was waving goodbye with a humorous smile at the corner of his mouth, just as if to say 'even in death we have little or no choice'. I am sure that he was telling me he was being looked after.

Meanwhile, I had terminated my agreement with the publishing company, as I was shortly to have my first hip replacement operation. After my hip replacement operation I returned home to Scotland to find that in the meanwhile Alexander's cottage had been sold. So another chapter in my life closed.

Chapter Fifteen

My Scottish Experiences

Enough to think that Truth can be:
Come sit we where the roses glow;
Indeed he knows not how to know
Who knows not also how to unknow.

The Kasidah of Haji Abdu El-Ye, Book Six
Translated by Sir Richard Burton, his friend & pupil

AN ESSENTIAL THEME underlying our life's journey seems to me to be the opportunity to use our daily experiences as a means whereby we may attain self-awareness. My story would hence be incomplete without bringing to the fore some of my more provoking experiences, as well as the utterly enjoyable ones that I encountered during the thirty years that I earned my living travelling around Scotland as an agent for a large publishing company. My greatest delight was that it brought me close to Nature, with all its wonders.

I cannot tell you how many times I have been around Scotland, nor the mileage that I have covered, but I can tell you that Scotland is where my heart is. I have travelled extensively abroad, but I have always returned home glad to be back to my adopted land. It holds a kind of magic for me when I breathe in the air and savour the beauty of its nature. The history of this land is fascinating, and its traditions and culture have a certain romance that fills my heart with expectation. Yes, I know that the climate is not what today's average human might desire, but I have learned to blend with the changes that autumn, winter, spring and summer provide. There is a beauty in accepting what is, even if it is raining and blowing a gale.

My job took me all around Scotland year after year. In order to save expenses I bought a caravanette, which gave me my independence. Indeed, in my wanderings I virtually turned into a gypsy. Stopping where my work took me and loving every moment, I nearly always managed to find a convenient spot that looked safe. Alexander drove me around for the first five years or so then after January 1981 I was on my own until January 1999, when I said goodbye to my working life and started to write this my autobiography.

From 1965, for more than six years I worked with *The Scotsman Publications*, changing to work for a larger publishing company on an agency basis. Later I added another publishing company to my Agency, supplying maps, which complemented the tourist books, calendars, and postcards that I was selling. Over the years, the map company increased its products. Finding it was getting too much for me to manage, I resigned. But I remained with the publishing company with whom I had started.

In 1973 I had only the Scottish Highlands as my territory, which included most of the Islands, In 1976 I was given the whole of Scotland to cover. I learned to appreciate nature, but at the same time to be wary of its sudden changes. Alexander and I travelled in all weathers—driving rain, snow, hail, storms, icy conditions, fog—and, of course, beautifully sunny days. We slept in the caravanette through all seasons of the year, rather like vagrants.

After Alexander decided not to come with me any more, in January 1981 I bought a VW LT 28 van, and converted her into a working-cum-delivery-cum-sleeping home on wheels, which I have described in Chapter 14, *Challenging Changes*. I was away from Monday to Friday, often leaving my cottage on a Sunday so that I would be near my first customer early on Monday morning. When I needed to visit some of the remoter Isles I would stay away for two weeks at a time.

To my chagrin, I twice managed to run out of petrol, both times in remote areas in the Highlands of Scotland. Both times I was lucky to find help, once from a kindly man who took pity on me and drove me to a petrol station about ten miles away—and brought me all the way back with a gallon of petrol to get me out of trouble. The other occasion happened on the Isle of Mull. I had arrived on the Island rather late and in my haste to catch the ferry I completely forgot about getting petrol. I was suddenly reminded when the engine began to splutter and grumble. Knowing I was about to run out of petrol, I reacted by running the van on to the verge. I was only just in time, as the engine stopped. I made a mental note never to be caught like that again. I climbed somewhat dejectedly onto the road. It was pitch black, but I could see a light in the distance, so I trotted off shrugging my shoulders, mortified by my stupidity.

After I had been walking hard for half a mile or so I could see the light more clearly. It was coming from a farmstead. Encouraged, I quickened my pace praying that the occupants had not gone to bed, for it was well past 10 p.m. Optimistically saying to myself: 'Most farmers have spare petrol, so I shall be all right I'm sure,' I trudged on, thankful it wasn't raining. I could see some deer but they didn't bother me. At last I reached the farmstead and gingerly knocked on the door. The farmer's wife opened the door. She stared at me in disbelief. Before I could open my mouth, she said, "Come in, dearie, out of the cold!" and turning to her husband said, "She's run out of petrol, I'll be bound!" They gave me a cup of tea saying: "You are lucky!

Five minutes more and we'd have been in bed and you'd have had to wait till the morning!"

The farmer went into the yard to find a gallon can of petrol. In no time he was organised and invited me to join him in the tractor. I climbed in beside him feeling very guilty at disturbing such kindly folk so late at night. He emptied his gallon can of petrol into my home on wheels and with a cheery, "Mind you don't do that again!" he left me. Knowing that there might be some dirt collected in the bottom of my tank, I prayed she would start. Thankfully there was no problem. Once she was purring again, I went in search of a parking place for the night. I was soon lucky enough to find a petrol pump where I knew I could get petrol in the morning. With a huge sigh of relief I climbed into my sleeping bag and so to sleep.

I had several other adventures when I started out on my own. I learned the hard way most of the time. For instance, I found it was awful when I had to change over the Calor gas bottles for the first time. The weather was freezing cold, and I only discovered that the gas bottles needed changing after I was parked up for the night. As I had omitted to get any diesel oil, I could not use the heating system under the bunks. Now I had a real problem on my hands. I had absolutely no idea how to change over, the gas bottles, as I had always left that to Alexander. Now I had no alternative but to change them myself or freeze. It took me a long time before I managed to find out how it worked. It took even longer to unscrew the connecting link between the bottles with my freezing hands, causing me much consternation, since the connecting links had been screwed on so tightly. With an extra effort and a damp towel, I at last managed, and fortunately, when the bottles had been changed over, I was able to boil a kettle for a hot drink.

During the same evening I suddenly recognised that I had parked my van facing away from the road so that I would have to back out. In this way I would not be ready to take off at the slightest hint of danger, so I made a quick turn about in the dark. The first thing I did when I was once again on the road was to buy a can of diesel oil. I had discovered just how vulnerable a woman is on her own when she parks for the night beside the road in a lay-by.

I vividly remember many other experiences that I had while travelling around Scotland, particularly when I was on my own. On one occasion on my way back to Stornoway after I had called on some customers by the Callendish Standing Stones on the Isle of Lewis in the Outer Hebrides, I took a corner too quickly. Down I went into a steep ditch. I was badly shaken and totally horrified. The van finally came to rest perched at a very steep angle just on the side of the road. I tried to get my bearings while still holding tightly to the steering wheel, unable to believe what I had done. The ditch was so steep and the corner so deceptively rounded that I could not think how I had been so unaware of my actions. Now as I sat in my new VW LT 28 high-topped working van—so recently converted into a home on wheels, I was thankful that my load of books on the lower bunk had saved me from toppling right over. I managed with great difficulty to open my door, which was quite a heavy one, but now it was unbelievably heavy to open as the van was leaning over at such a steep angle.

I kind of fell out of the van on to the verge of the road and gazed in horror at what I had done. The van appeared to have sunk very deeply into the ditch. I put my hands over my face in dismay wondering what on earth I should do next. Slowly I shut the heavy door, shrugging my shoulders in utter disbelief at the situation that now faced me. I began to walk towards a row of cottages close by. I had a major problem on my hands. I wondered what I had done to my livelihood, my night's lodgings, and my home on wheels. I drew in some deep breaths of Hebridean air, as I looked around me in utter dismay. Whatever could I do?

Suddenly in front of me there appeared a car, coming straight towards me. The driver pulled down his window as he stopped, saying with a smile, "You'd better jump in; we've all seen what happened! If it's any consolation to you, it's happened many times before!" On hearing this I privately wondered why something had not been done to make it a safer corner, but of course I did not say a word, being only too thankful to find my rescuer was so obliging. "We'll get a tractor and we'll have you out in no time!" he added cheerfully. I wasn't so sure of his optimistic approach, but I climbed thankfully in beside him, totally ashamed of myself. He was immensely kind. I could see that my van and I were going to be the talk of this tiny village for months to come.

We drove to a farm where a very obliging crofter came to my rescue by bringing his tractor to where I was ditched. In no time he had hitched his tractor to the front of my van. But my home on wheels was stubborn and would not budge. Then they hitched the tractor firmly to the back of my van, but it seemed to be so stuck in the ditch that this second attempt did not work either. By this time the villagers were watching in great excitement, all lined up alongside the road with their eyes glued to my van watching in anticipation. They were nodding their heads as they caught sight of me. I guessed what they must have been thinking, that it was typical of a woman driver! I gave them a sheepish grin. Soon it was a case of all hands on the van to push it, but still the van simply would not budge. Then my rescuer drove off to fetch another tractor. It took the power of two large tractors, to pull the van out of the ditch. I was never so grateful in all my life as it shuddered back onto the road.

The villagers greeted the success with a huge applause, little children joining in the excitement. I was so grateful that I could have cried—and very nearly did! I hardly knew how to thank them. Apart from being very muddy there was not a scratch on the poor thing. The engine started up straight away, and to waves and cheers from my kindly rescuers, I left in tears. I had never experienced such spontaneous kindness undertaken so willingly. I shall never forget that extraordinary day or the generosity so freely given to extract me from such a deep ditch. These experiences always had a great effect on me, and I learned that in spite of all the terrible things that go on in the world, there are good folk who care.

Often in the late summer I stopped to wander through the purple heather as I stretched my legs by the mountainside after being cramped in the driving seat for mile upon mile. Once, very early in the morning, I came across what I felt was one of nature's mysterious wonders. It happened one particularly early morn when I caught sight of a heron in the middle of the road. I immediately stopped and—wonders of wonders—I saw the heron creating a huge rumpus, screeching and flapping its huge wings. I could see it was very cross about something, and was trying to chase after whatever it was that I could not see. I sat quietly watching in amazement. Then, quite suddenly, I caught sight of what was troubling the heron: a beautiful golden eagle swooped, just above my caravanette, with what appeared to be a creature struggling in its strong talons. I watched the huge bird as it flew higher and higher toward the mountains, to be seen no more.

The heron meanwhile had remained in the middle of the road flapping its wings. Then slowly it made its way down the bank side from the road to the burn in the glen below. I watched it through my binoculars as it reached the water. It began 'high stepping' in the dignified way that herons do, first on one long leg and then on another, moving slowly along the burn. It continued on its way for a while like this, stopping every now and then, until finally it rested on one leg remaining absolutely motionless, like the silent immovable 'watcher' that it is, hardly perceptible to the rest of nature. It was fishing; and it suddenly occurred to me why the heron was so angry. The eagle must have stolen its catch!

Another time my journey took me along the isolated west coastline in the very far north of the Scottish Highlands. The breath-taking views held me spellbound. I stopped and slithered down from my home-on-wheels, walking close to the edge of the cliff where there was a waterfall, and there all around me I beheld a view that made me realise why Robert Burns, the great Scottish Bard, had written his famous Highland poem, during the time that he made his remarkable tour around the Highlands of Scotland:

My heart's in the Highlands, my heart's not here,
My heart's in the Highlands, a-chasing the deer,
A-chasing the wild deer, and following the roe—
My hearts in the Highlands, wherever I go!

On another occasion, I was lucky enough to park by the seashore on the Island of Arran. Very early in the morning I awoke to what sounded like munching coming from beside my home on wheels. I lay in my bunk very still, wondering what on earth it was. Carefully I lifted the blind, and there all around my van were dozens of deer happily munching seaweed. I could hardly believe my eyes.

Once when I was in the Highlands near Aberdeen, I had parked in the wilds of the Braemar Mountains. The night had brought heavy snow, and as I awoke the next day there was a sea of whiteness all around me. I watched the scene, accentuated by the early morning sun peeping through the trees. I was enraptured as I looked up at the mountains covered in snow and the heavily laden trees glistening in the early morning sunshine. I realised that if I jumped out of the van and walked onto that snow I would be intruding on its pristine beauty and spoiling it for ever. It felt just as if I dare not do so, or I would be trespassing on sacred ground.

I remember a terrifying night I had near Carrbridge, when I was travelling south one afternoon on the A9. The weather was horrendous. There was a driving blizzard and thick fog. The snow covered the windscreen making it difficult to see, the windscreen wipers couldn't cope as the snow was turning to ice. The terrible snowstorm had not abated, so I was going very slowly through the thick snow. It was before there were any snow gates to prevent traffic from continuing when the pass was blocked. I had just come through Carrbridge, making my way to Drumochter Pass (which reaches a height of 1,484 feet), when I noticed there was no moving traffic and none coming towards me. I had nearly reached the Pass in this dreadful blizzard. The wind was shrieking all around me and I could hardly see in front of me—but I was not over-concerned, as I had never before been stopped by snow on the road to Drumochter Pass, so I carried on regardless.

Suddenly, I became aware of a long line of lorries parked on my left hand side. The line looked very grim in the semi-darkness of the blizzard. I wondered if the road ahead was blocked by snow after all. Scarcely had the thought developed before I became aware of lights flashing behind me. In my mirror I perceived a police car. At once I realised that my guess was correct. I looked around for a place to stop, but unable to find one, I just stopped in the middle of the road. In a very short while a policeman stood by my window, which I hastily turned down. He was covered in snow and looked more like a ghost than a policeman. Abruptly he said without so much as a preamble: "And where do you think you are going, Miss?" Astonished, I said, "Home to Edinburgh." "Not tonight, Miss, at least, not on this road, it's blocked by snow." The time was only about 3.30 p.m. but it looked more like an evening hour. "Oh!" said I, rather worried. "Now, Miss, please will you turn around?" I looked around helplessly. Seeing my concern he added, "Do you want me to turn the van for you?" "No!" I said, rather breathlessly. He said: "Then do exactly what I tell you to do, and we'll have you turned around in no time." He added that he would give me an escort back to the turn-off at Carrbridge, where I would be able to get back to Edinburgh via Aberdeen and Dundee on the Huntly Road.

True to his word, he patiently directed my turn about in the thick snow and driving blizzard, which was very difficult to do, especially as I could not see the verge of the road. Following the policeman's instructions to the letter, I finally managed to turn around. The policeman indicated to me to follow his car, which I did most thankfully. I could not help but feel an odd disturbance in the pit of my stomach. It felt so strange being escorted by a police car with flashing lights in the middle of a blizzard. Anyone might have thought I was royalty!

When we eventually arrived at Carrbridge, we stopped. One of the policemen got out of the car, and coming up to me, he said: "I've been in touch with the Huntly police and they tell me you will be able to make it through to Aberdeen." I was very grateful to them for their help. I only just managed to make my way through via Huntly to Aberdeen before that road, too, was blocked. I heard this later, on the news. I finally arrived home at 3 a.m. the following day, having driven continuously through this frightening weather, practically non-stop, for twelve hours. I did not dare to stop, as the roads were very dangerous. Tired, but glad to be home in one piece, I made myself a cup of tea and after a hot shower climbed thankfully into bed.

On one of my journeys I was held up on the lsle of Islay, due to a temporary strike by the ferry service. When we eventually disembarked from the island it was quite late, nearly eight o'clock at night. I had to catch another ferry to cross over to Arran where I was aiming to park for the night. As I drove past Brodick Pier on Arran, I said to myself, 'That is one place I refuse to stop at!' and carried on driving. Eventually I saw a turning off from the main road. I wound my way down the hill towards what looked like a bay. In the half-light of the Moon it looked a perfect place to spend the night. After carefully parking facing outwards, I got out of the sliding door to stretch my legs and inspect the area. It was indeed very spectacular, at least what I could see of it. It must have been nearly 12 o'clock at night.

After I had carefully locked all the doors and pulled all the curtains and made sure the Calor gas was turned off, I hastily undressed and climbed into the top bunk and so to sleep, as I thought. Barely had I snuggled down into my sleeping bag when there was a sharp rat-a-tat on the sliding door. I froze. A man's voice called something that I could not hear. I wondered if it was a gypsy, as I knew there were some that parked on Arran. The sharp knock was repeated. By this time I was hurriedly dressing. Then a Glaswegian voice shouted, "You're on private property!"

Before I realised it, I indignantly shouted "Nonsense." Now I had given myself away! So I added hastily, "I'll set my husband on you if you don't go away!" Where I was going to find him I could not think! By this time I was fully dressed. The voice replied, "I only want a natter, please open the door." I had at that moment just managed to climb into the driver's seat and prayed to God that the engine would not let me down. I started it up. The engine purred. I pulled my window down a few inches or so, as I put my headlights full on, shouting, "You'd better move out of the b—way or I'll b—well run you down!" and I revved the engine to climb the hill. I had never felt more aware of my vulnerability—which spurred me onward. Had I stayed, the man might easily have cut into my tyres. As fate would have it I spent the rest of the night on Brodick Pier! After that I was much more careful where I parked for the night—though it was usually all right. In those days of the early '80s, I felt safe enough.

It was in the faraway, remoter areas of Scotland that I found the most enjoyment and interest in my travels. I loved the mountains and lochs, especially early in the morning when the sun was reflecting the mountains in the lochs below. It was a delight to feel the sheer beauty of the undisturbed mountains and lochs, particularly when I was near the mountain of Sullivan, which I felt to be the most sacred mountain in the Scottish Highlands. It looked so unbelievably lovely that I wanted to climb it. All around the mountain the country was most beautiful. Few people were about even in the tourist season. It felt like sharing a sacredness that one could not utter. I loved every blade of grass and every bird that called. When the heather was in full bloom I could feel its magic speaking to me as I sat listening to the occasional call of the grouse, and sometimes catching a glimpse of a golden eagle flying gracefully amongst the rugged splendour of that beautiful mountain.

I was never afraid in this part of the world; it was good to be amid nature. But I had work to do, so could not tarry long. Once a large dragonfly rested on my windscreen. I stopped the car as it fell off onto the road, the poor wee thing was hardly moving when I carefully picked it up. I felt I could not leave it on the road in that state. They are exquisitely fashioned, so delicate and original in their colourings, and quite large as insects go. Before I had time to start the engine I saw it fly away, to my delight.

I was not always so lucky on my travels. One night when I was coming home after a week's work it suddenly turned very foggy. Soon I could not see anything in front of me. I had just left Stirling and I suppose I was tired, though I have no recollection of feeling so. The fog became denser and denser so that I could hardly get my bearings; I seemed suddenly to be on a very narrow road. I felt hedged in. Then the fog lifted just enough to show me that I was lost. I could not believe that I had got where I was! It looked as if I was on a private road. I had no alternative but to keep driving, there was nowhere to turn my large van. The fog was now very patchy and I began to feel rather concerned. Then ahead I saw a car coming towards me. Fortunately I saw an open verge and pulled over, otherwise the car could not have passed. When it was alongside, the driver shouted that he could not stop but there was an area further up where I could turn. He said I was on a moorland road. I was thunderstruck. How on earth could I have managed that? I thought I knew my Scotland fairly well. Stupefied I continued, hoping that the man had not been deceiving me. My wheels were touching either verge so I had no way of turning. It seemed ages before I at last came across a wider part in the lane. There was an opening in a dipped part of the road where I thought I might turn, but it didn't look at all promising. But I tried, not wanting to go any further.

I don't know how I eventually made the turn. My van wasn't like a car to turn, and I had no power-assisted steering, but somehow I managed. I made my way back very slowly to the main road, where fortunately the fog had lifted somewhat. I felt very lucky to have met the car for I never saw anyone else on that mystery lane. Had I been dreaming, I wondered? I never did find out how I had inadvertently made such an error.

I remember an unfortunate accident that occurred when I was trying to take some pictures. I had recently bought a very good camera and I liked to take pictures for the calendars and post cards that the publishing company supplied for me to sell to my customers. Although I was not a professional photographer by any means, I sometimes managed to get a good shot. Of course, they had very good photographers on their staff, and they didn't really need me, but I often thought it was a pity to miss a good picture as I was frequently in the right place at the right time. One of the photographers had given me some good tips, which I tried to apply. One of those tips certainly did not include what happened next.

I'd parked my van in a lay-by and jumped down to take the picture. It was one of those days in which Loch Earn looked unusually spectacular. It was a perfect day for taking pictures and there were enough white clouds in the sky to give the picture an interesting background. Somehow, from where I stood I wasn't satisfied, so I began walking down the slope nearer to the loch to get a better view. I didn't pay enough attention to what I was doing, being too anxious to take the picture. As I looked for a better view I went on down the slope and did not notice that it was getting steeper and steeper, until suddenly I lost my balance and went tumbling down, turning over and over, quite unable to stop. There was absolutely nothing I could do, except let myself yield to the falling sensation. I remember feeling this must be what it feels like to a mountaineer when he falls. Before I knew where I was, I was at the bottom of the slope by the side of Loch Earn.

I was terribly shaken. I lay completely still. Slowly I collected myself together and found to my intense relief that I could stand up. As I looked up the steep slope, I shuddered in horror realising that I would have to climb it if I was ever to reach my van again. It was then that I became aware that I had dropped my camera during the fall. In utter dismay I began to feel conscious of my poor bruised body. But with a shrug I slowly began climbing breathlessly up the steep slope. I managed to find my camera, and finally I reached the van in a very sorry state. The first thought I had was for a cup of tea. This I made with shaking hands. I could not believe that I had been so distracted in taking a picture that I had been oblivious of the danger I was in. After several cups of tea, I felt able to drive home. It was indeed a very salutary lesson.

One of the most extraordinary experiences I ever had was mostly due to my psychic abilities. I had parked for the night on a particularly beautiful part of the West coast of the Scottish Lowlands. I remember being very tired, for I had driven a long way that day. It felt as if I had hardly been asleep when I was conscious of a voice in my head saying, "We are very worried for your safety." I heard it over and over again before I became consciously aware of the urgency of the voice. I shot up in my bunk, banging my head on the roof. As I began to feel the significance of those words I became very worried. Completely mystified I climbed wearily out of my sleeping bag and slipped to the floor of the van. I rapidly dressed, dumb-founded by what I had heard.

My first thought was to check the Calor gas. I had indeed turned it off. But I was not satisfied. I dared not turn on the gas to test anything, so I sat in the front seat of the van gazing across the loch, wondering whatever 'they' were worried about. As it so happened, I had parked the previous night in an area directly by a loch, close to shops. I knew there was a shop in the village that sold Calor gas, where I could seek help. I drove the van close to the shop on the dot of nine. The man who was serving happened to be the owner and very obligingly came out to test all the appliances that used Calor. Bravely I thought—still thinking of what had awakened me so urgently in the middle of the night—he began to test everything systematically. Mystified, he found no fault. Then he said, "I think I had better test the pipe that comes into the stove." That was in the cupboard below. On doing so he gasped, "My God! You have a leak that could have blown you and your van to smithereens had you put a match to any of your gas rings!" So saying, he quickly turned off the Calor gas tap. I was horrified, but didn't like to tell the owner what had transpired in the middle of the night. I thanked him profusely and asked him if he could mend it. Happily he could. I wished I were able to thank my 'kind friends' personally, whomever they were, who had certainly saved my life. The voice had said 'we' so there must have been more than one kind friend. I knew then that 'God works in mysterious ways, his wonders to perform.'

What I enjoyed very much was the general excitement of the activity that Caledonian McBraynes Ferries created, with the loading and unloading of the cars and lorries, to say nothing of the people. I had to use their service to reach the islands of the Inner and Outer Hebrides in order to see my customers dotted about on the Islands. I used to go from one island to another. I remember there was always a constant coming and going from the queues of cars waiting to drive off and onto the Ferry. The clatter of the car lifts and the shouts of the crew added to the general commotion. No one was allowed to remain with their cars once they were loaded in the hold, we had to climb the steep stairs to the main part of the ship, where you could get refreshments or laze about on deck. The cry of the seagulls and the general anticipation of a voyage engendered a feeling of inexplicable distance between those coming and those going. I loved the feel of the water lashing against the sides of the ship as I leaned over the railings, absorbed in the atmosphere created in the harbour by the departing ship. The best part of my travels was indeed the Ferry trips that I enjoyed so much, particularly as they gave me some respite from driving. I sold maps to the head office of the Caledonian McBraynes in Glasgow and always checked to see if there was a good supply. I could then relax and give my attention to the wonders of the scenery and feel the soothing movement of the ship over the water. Sometimes, of course, it was a bit choppy, but even that I enjoyed.

The small ferry to the Isle of Iona, in contrast with the larger Caledonian McBraynes Ferry from Oban to Mull, never really duplicated the bustle and general commotion one finds at any other jetty. In the holiday season coaches from the Mull would park at the Ferry terminal at Fionnphort, opposite to the Isle of Iona, where St. Columba founded Christianity in Scotland. The Cathedral and Abbey precincts, the focal point of the island, can plainly be seen from Fionnphort, where people wait to board the ferry to take them across to St. Ronan's Bay, Iona. Only the islanders and trades-people are allowed to take their cars over to the Island, only a short crossing away. Over the years I became friendly with the family who own a store and restaurant in St. Ronan's Bay, and they also have a boat in which they take people over to Staffa. The magic of Staffa is captured by the grandeur of Mendelssohn's Fingal's Cave Overture, envied by Brahms who said, 'I would sacrifice all my works to have been able to compose an overture like that!'

The spectacular wonders of the extraordinary formation of the basaltic columns on Staffa, must surely be unique in the world, and the inside of Fingal's Cave is just as spectacular, with its fifty-foot wide entrance and its 230-foot deep interior. Staffa is also famous for the naturalist Sir Joseph Banks, who in 1772 visited this unique isle on his way to Iceland. He declared: 'Compared to this, what are the cathedrals and palaces built by men? Mere models or playthings, imitations, as his works will always be when compared to those of nature.' Staffa is an island of about 70 acres and its highest point is 135 feet above sea level. Its extraordinary caves with their geological wonders intrigued me, but I could never spend the time to see all the other caves that I would have loved to explore.

I have walked all over Iona and once I nearly lost my way—unbelievably, since the isle is so small. In the lovely bay where Columba landed I gathered some green stones, for which the Island is famous. I found a peace in Iona where one can feel that there is something special. Here follows some interesting historical facts about St. Columba:

Born of royal blood in AD 521 in Ireland, or Scotia as it was then called, Columba was responsible for converting many to Christianity. In AD 563, Columba, with twelve monks, settled on Iona, off the coast of the Isle of Mull. Here he constructed his first Celtic Church, using clay and wood, and then established a monastic community. The reputation of the community was soon widespread and it came to be recognised in Europe as an outstanding missionary centre and place of learning. Consequently Iona became a sacred Isle where kings of Scotland and Norway were buried.[8]

Legend has it that St. Regulus (or Rule), who may also have been the Irish St. Riagail, a contemporary of St. Columba, brought the relics of St. Andrew from the East—possibly from Patras, where St. Andrew had been crucified on a *saltire,* or diagonal cross—to Muckross or Kilrimont in Scotland. Where Regulus landed. A vision of the Apostle was revealed to the King of the Picts, Angus MacFergus, promising him victory over his enemy. In gratitude Angus dedicated Kilrimont to the relics of St. Andrew, and the settlement took the name of St. Andrew. St. Andrew was later adopted as the patron saint of Scotland and his saltire has become the national symbol. His relics were possibly laid to rest in the church named after him, and the magnificent sarcophagus, which still survives in St. Andrew's Cathedral, was possibly fashioned for his body. A Celtic Caldee monastery, also established at St. Andrew, survived until the thirteenth century. Incidentally the name 'Caldee' is derived from the Gaelic *Cele Dei* meaning 'friends of God'.

[8] Taken from *Illustrated History of Scotland* by Elisabeth Fraser, designed and produced by Jarrold Publishing Norwich, 1997, reprinted 2000 (now out of print).

Chapter Sixteen

Meeting Krishnamurti

Can there be action unrelated to the past?
Can there be action without the burden of experience, the
knowledge of yesterday? As long as action is the outcome of
the past, action can never be free,
and only in freedom can you discover what is true.

J. Krishnamurti

MY INTRODUCTION TO KRISHNAMURTI came in 1969, when my friend Mary Wolstenhome brought with her a book entitled *Education and the Significance of Life* by Jiddu Krishnamurti. At the particular time that I encountered this book, I had been feeling rather despondent and in need of some kind of a jolt to move me away from the bothersome problems I was having with myself. I opened the book at random. The first paragraph I read stated that if one had a problem, the best way to tackle it was to take a long walk. After reading to the end of the chapter I remember doing just that.

The cottage I had bought was very near to the sea and close to a promenade that was more than a few miles long. I could easily reach it at the end of my street, so I strode off. The fresh sea air soon revived me, and the few paragraphs that I had read in Krishnamurti's book still remained fresh in my mind. I watched the waves roll over the shore as I pondered his words. Slowly my mind became quiet and my mood began to evaporate in a way that I had

often noticed before when I was close to nature. A beautiful wide-open beach stretched out for miles on either side of me. The tide was well out and there were numerous gulls and smaller birds busily pecking along the foreshore amidst the seaweed left by the tide. I wondered why I did not come down to the sea more often; it was so refreshingly beautiful. I crossed over the sands towards the sea, gazing at the great waters of the Firth of Forth extending before me. I was reminded of the fact that my cottage was at one time a lone building amongst the dunes. It was here, too, that long, long ago the Romans made their entry into the East of Scotland, and I suppose long after I am gone the tides will still be coming and going along this stretch of the beach.

The crisp air and the solitude of walking along the sands brought me back to the ground where I stood, the place where I needed to be to sort myself out. I went over my problems minutely, refusing to spare myself or move away into the 'could-have-beens' or 'should-have-beens.' As I penetrated below the surface of my tight-knit resistance against accepting Alexander for whom he was, I was able to open myself to myself, and then something gave. Looking across the Firth of Forth, an overwhelming awareness came over me as though I were interdependent with everything else in the Universe. I was quite alone on those sands close by the sea as I heard those words: 'Everything in nature depends on everything else, nature is not separate or alone, neither are you'. I stooped to pick up an intriguing-looking shell, and as I turned the shell over, I was fascinated by its unusual and unique design. This little shell had recently contained a living organism, now it was a shell of its former self. Quite suddenly, I knew all I wanted was to find Krishnamurti, the author of that book, whose words rang so true.

Refreshed by my walk, I made rapid strides for home, realising that my lifestyle had changed dramatically now that I was away from the Cult School. I had gained sufficient self-confidence and independence for my self-centredness to reassert itself and swamp me sometimes with unnecessary personal mind concepts. I found I was totally responsible for earning my own living with no financial help from Alexander. Not that I blamed him for that since, I knew that he could not help it, for he found holding down a job very difficult. However, the psychological support he gave me was far more valuable than any monetary contribution. But, as yet, I had not learned sufficient discipline to see 'everything as it is and allow it to remain so'.

With this quick about-turn of mood, I reached home. I knew I had found a teaching I could relate to. I realised I still needed guidance and to be with serious-minded people striving like myself to find greater meaning to Life. The first thing I did when I got home was to telephone *The Theosophical Society* to discover where I could find Krishnamurti. I was unable to receive any help from the person I spoke to. I vaguely remembered that my parents, who had been members of that Society, had mentioned that they knew Annie Besant had declared the coming of a World Teacher, giving his name as Jiddu Krishnamurti. But it was such a long time ago that I could not recall any more details. It must have been in the early 1930s when my parents were members of *The Theosophical Society*, because I remember attending a talk there with them in London.

Alexander came to my rescue by visiting *The Theosophical Society* in Edinburgh. He discovered that there was a Krishnamurti gathering at Brockwood Park in Hampshire that very weekend, but he could not find out any more details. Then to my joy Alexander found the telephone number of the *Krishnamurti Foundation* at Brockwood Park, so I telephoned at once and asked if we could attend. I was informed that there were some spaces within the grounds for camping and that we would be very welcome. Whoever I spoke to sounded as if she was in a hurry, as she quickly told me that thousands of people had already arrived and that she needed to attend to them. I immediately arranged with *The Scotsman* to take my summer holidays.

Alexander was always ready for a diversion and threw himself into the preparations. We made an early start the next day for our long drive South. We packed our tent and all the necessary articles for camping in the car and thankfully managed to arrive in plenty of time for the talks. As we drove into the spacious grounds, we could see many beautiful old trees around the parkland, beyond which we had a glimpse of a very large white Georgian building, which we discovered was the English Krishnamurti School. Moving on through the gates, where the grounds extended further, we began to feel the general excitement and expectation all around us.

There were a great number of people wandering about. A steward drew our attention to the camping area within the orchard, after telling us where we could park our car. We soon found a parking spot. Having unpacked our tent and assembled it in the orchard amongst the other tents, we approached the huge marquee, where the talks were being held. I realised just how true were the words spoken over the telephone about the thousands of people present. We went through a very large tent where there were several helpers and tables where coffee and tea were being served. Other tables were all around the wall of the tent and some people were sitting at long tables in the middle drinking coffee and earnestly chatting.

Another helper directed us through the tent to the adjoining entrance of an even larger marquee, which we could see was full of chairs. Nearly all the seats were taken. We asked an attendant at the entrance to that marquee if we had to pay and were quickly assured that Krishnamurti never ever charged any money for attending his talks. We were directed to two vacant seats at the back. The chairs were assembled in a semi-circle around a little raised platform, on which was placed a solitary hard-backed upright chair. There was a buzz of excited murmurs all around us.

We were very fortunate to find these two seats together as many people had to stand. We were just in time, for scarcely had we taken our seats before there was a sudden hush. A flap of the marquee by the raised platform was pulled aside to allow Krishnamurti to enter. His slight figure was held erect within an aura of humility and quietness. He carefully sat down on the wooden chair on the platform. He waited patiently while a staff member from the Krishnamurti School fixed a microphone on to his cardigan. Then carefully composing himself, he placed both of his slender hands under his thighs and slowly looked around very attentively at the assembled people. The expectant faces in front of him were silent and heedful. It took Krishnamurti some moments to observe the huge crowd of people present. His glance finally rested on the students directly in front of him, who were sitting on cushions. He acknowledged them with a smile, slowly looking at them with his large, expressive eyes. Then he made a few comments about the weather and the gathering, declaring that to him the talks were 'a very serious affair' and that he would be continuing his talks and dialogues during the coming weeks, and that they were being recorded.

It was an extraordinary gathering of various nationalities and different ages, all eagerly waiting for Krishnamurti to begin. More tent flaps were opened to allow those outside the marquee to hear him and to allow much-needed air into the marquee. It was a beautiful, hot sunny day. As far as I could guess there were between two to three thousand people present, maybe more.

During this very first talk that Alexander and I attended in 1969 at Brockwood Park, I had an unexpected inner flash of intuition. As I watched Krishnamurti closely, I first perceived him as a man, and in the very next moment as a woman. Thereafter, to me he represented a whole human being. It made me realise that I had been totally unaware of the true meaning and understanding of the opposite forces that I perceived Krishnamurti so vividly displaying by the unity of male and female aspects of himself.

Before he began to speak he almost closed his eyes, then a smile appeared on his beautiful face as he suddenly looked at everyone, and shyly asked whether we minded if he told us a joke that he had just heard. Without waiting for a reply he started to tell his joke, which brought a ripple of laughter throughout the marquee, thus relieving the tension of expectancy we had all been feeling. Then in earnest he began his talk. He did not talk 'at us' or 'tell us' what we should or should not do. I noticed he was fond of saying 'use the speaker as a mirror to see yourselves', but I don't think in those early days many of us knew what he was driving at. I certainly did not. He was always ready for any untimely interruption but never made anyone feel uncomfortable. Yet he did not encourage questions. As he pointed out, there would be two dialogues held during each week, where questions and answers would take place. However, he would always bring the question raised into the talk, if it was at all appropriate.

There was no doubt that he had a skilful way of holding the attention of the vast crowd, and that he kept a total command of his audience throughout the duration of the one to two-hour long talk. He did not lack humour, and in spite of his unassuming manner and quiet dignity he was an accomplished speaker. There was an air about him that drew respect and attention. He had no notes to refer to, and he never hesitated in what he had to say. His passion and sincerity for the truth of what he was bringing stirred the very soul of my being.

The talk was an inspiration to me, for I was hungry for what Krishnamurti was saying and I absorbed all he said, in my own way, with enthusiasm and gratitude. It had been nearly six years since I had left the cult/school and I realised just how deeply I needed to be amongst people who were also eagerly seeking into the deeper issues of life. So enthusiastic was I, that once the talks had finished and Krishnamurti had left the tent, I asked an attendant if I could approach him. Being told I could speak to him, I soon caught up with him as he was crossing the grounds toward the School.

I called my thanks to him for his talk and asked if I could arrange to have a talk with him. Krishnamurti turned round abruptly towards me; holding up his hands to stop me, he said he seldom gave private talks. I felt instantly rebuffed, which psychologically knocked me backwards.

It was not until I thought deeply on this that I realised just why Krishnamurti had made what seemed an involuntary movement. I felt it was because I was moving towards him in the persona of my usual pushy self. By rushing after him following such an inspirational talk, I had shown no respect. I had been thinking only about my own wants instead of attending to the substance of his talk. I realised that had I been more aware I would never have run after him as I did. It was a sharp lesson that stood me in good stead for the years that followed.

I never again asked Krishnamurti for a personal talk since I realised, in spite of being less aware then, that all I had to do was to give my full attention during his talks and I would receive and eventually absorb all the answers to my queries. I understood that no matter what may be presented by a teacher, no understanding would reach the closed mind of a listener whose own awareness is limited by self-centred personal states. In the final analysis, no teacher can ever teach anyone anything; each person must learn to understand him or herself through awareness. And then with sincerity, perseverance and courage, perhaps what the teacher is saying may awaken a glimpse of truth within. Like a seed falling on fertile ground, understanding may eventually grow.

After the talk we gathered in the adjacent food tent, where lunch was being served. The meals were vegetarian, inexpensive and absolutely delicious. After a while we could see that Krishnamurti had joined us all. The general buzz of conversation in the tent made me realise just how much everyone had been stimulated by his words. There were several long tables where we could sit and eat while holding discussions together. Or alternatively, as the weather was good, we could take our meals out into the sunshine and sit on the grass amongst others who had come to listen.

Inside the food tent was a stall where one could buy books, tapes and—in later years—videos. Over the years, I gradually became acquainted with the helpers and organisers of all the Krishnamurti Centres, as people from all over the world came to Krishnamurti talks at Brockwood Park. I could not help feeling glad that I had been made more aware of my self-centred behaviour whilst at the Cult School, in spite of the extraordinary methods that the Principal had used, but I had a long way to go.

I bought Krishnamurti's books and tapes to keep me in contact with his teachings throughout the year, until we were able to return to Brockwood Park the following year and be refreshed once again by his presence, his talks and dialogues.

From listening to Krishnamurti's talks and then listening several times to the videos and tapes, I learned a very different approach to Life. Never before or since have I read or experienced anything quite like those talks with Krishnamurti.

During the gathering we made friends with many people from a variety of backgrounds and countries, which led to fascinating cultural exchanges. We often took long walks around the country lanes of Hampshire with our newfound friends, especially on days when there were no talks or discussions. Everybody was friendly and the general atmosphere was one of getting together for a common purpose. We were requested not to invade the privacy of the School, although we could walk around the grounds. Also we were reminded to respect farmers' property if we took walks across the fields or woods around the by-lanes.

Near the School, across the field owned by Brockwood, was a small wood, which we were allowed to visit. There were some very fine mature trees to be found there, especially the Sequoia trees from America. I loved this little wood. The Principal of the School at that time, Dorothy Simmons, with whom I became friendly, told me the interesting and unusual story about how it became part of Brockwood Park and the *Krishnamurti Foundation Trust*. Apparently, when the estate had been purchased in 1968 for the purposes of establishing a Krishnamurti School, the wood had not been included in the purchase price. Krishnamurti asked Dorothy to investigate the possibility of acquiring the wood. It so happened that the purchased estate did include several large fields, one of which a farmer would have liked for grazing his sheep. Dorothy told me that she approached the farmer to whom it belonged. After a little discussion it was officially agreed that it was simply a case of swopping a field for a wood. Both parties were happy with this arrangement, thus no money was exchanged. Krishnamurti was delighted and called this beautiful little wood 'The Grove'. The trees are magnificent and I noticed there were several Scots Pines besides the huge stately Sequoia trees.

In those early years one might see Krishnamurti gathering up stray branches that had fallen on the natural grassy paths that wound their way through The Grove. To me, the wood always feels sanctified and it is a joy to sit on the wooden seats or wander among the huge variety of specially selected trees so carefully chosen by the former owners. To be in the wood is a close encounter with Nature, something that awakens the spirit within to learn from Her and the solitary silence of those magnificent trees.

On our way home at the end of the talks, Alexander gave a lift to another member of the audience. Alexander was very free with his opinions relating to the whole gathering, and made it quite clear it was something he did not particularly want to become involved with. I remember wondering why. But later, when it came around for the talks to take place again the following year, he made no objection to coming with me. I think he was far more cautious than I was. Perhaps, too, he was a little frightened that I might become too involved, remembering that he had not so long ago extricated me from another School of a very different kind. But he need not have worried; I was in an entirely different place within myself.

After our first experience at Brockwood Park, Alexander and I listened to the tapes and discussed endlessly what Krishnamurti had talked about. We learned, too, that talks had been held over a three week period in Saanen, Switzerland, every July since the early 1960s, and that Krishnamurti also talked in Bombay, Madras and Benares, and thereafter at Ojai, America. From 1969 onwards the talks and dialogues at Brockwood Park were held from the middle of August to the middle of September to an ever-increasing audience. All through the period covered in the previous two chapters, we came to Brockwood Park each year to listen to Krishnamurti talks, camping with hundreds of others. We looked forward immensely to this annual event.

Occasionally over the years, during Krishnamurti's lifetime, Alexander and I visited other Krishnamurti Centres

overseas. We went to Ojai in America several times to listen to Krishnamurti talks in the Oak Grove, where Mark Lee had organised another Krishnamurti School. We also visited India and attended private talks in Delhi, Madras and Bombay, beside the general talks, where at least 4,000 to 5,000 people attended each gathering. These talks and dialogues in India also lasted several weeks, and it was exciting to discover that there were so many people in every walk of life from all over the world who were deeply interested in what Krishnamurti was bringing. It is impossible to describe the feeling induced in most of us young and old alike, while we listened attentively to his talks.

In later years at Brockwood Park, we found to our joy that we were allowed to bring our caravanette into the open grounds alongside other caravanettes. The position chosen was directly opposite the Krishnamurti School, on the other side of a very large ditch. We were at some distance from the School, but nearer to some of the finest old trees in the park. One could hear the birds singing their songs of delight in the early morning and at eventide. Tents were erected all around us. Early in the morning there was an eerie atmosphere as we silently passed one another on our way to the toilets or to the washhouse to make our daily ablutions. Sometimes it was quite misty, which added to the general feeling of being somewhere special. Some of us, myself included, would very early take our place in a queue outside the tent, in order to reserve a place in the marquee as close to Krishnamurti as possible. On the days when there were no talks or dialogues we took a little longer to rise in the morning.

As the numbers of campers increased each year, so did it become obligatory for the *Krishnamurti Foundation Trust* to provide better and better facilities, eventually furnishing campers with more and more toilets and showers? We could also share a communal evening meal around a huge campfire.

At no time were we ever approached or coerced by anyone from the Krishnamurti School to follow Krishnamurti as a guru. On the contrary, we were all made thoroughly aware by Krishnamurti himself that he did not want followers, and that in no way did he consider himself a guru. He said he was there to set men unconditionally free. He repeated this year after year, pointing out the self-imposed absurdity of relying or leaning on anyone else to live one's life. To Krishnamurti it was the teachings that were important, not the speaker.

Krishnamurti founded schools in many countries, especially in India where schools were needed more than they were in Europe or America, although all the schools are run on completely different lines from ordinary state or private schools. Nevertheless, all pupils have the same opportunities to take the state examinations, and many students pursue further education at Universities. All Krishnamurti Schools foster a high standard of education designed to bring out pupils' innate intelligence from within so that they can absorb learning at their own pace, finding their own discipline without competition or comparison. Over the years I met with some of these pupils, and some came to stay with us once or twice during school holidays. I could definitely see the difference that the Krishnamurti School wrought in them. When pupils leave the schools they appear to have special self-knowledge that remains with them for the rest of their lives.

The huge marquee became larger and larger each year to accommodate ever-increasing crowds. As one listened each year to the Krishnamurti talks his sincerity came across. One could sense the passion and intensity he was generating within and among us all. I realised for a short space of time just how trivial were my self-centred states that obliterated my awareness of the spiritual realities of Truth. His famous words 'You are the World, and the World is you' and 'the observer is the observed' were puzzling to me at first. But I eventually understood when he pointed out that we are all responsible for making society

what it is today, and that we are no different from the society that we have created. He was pointing out, I felt, that
there was no division between what we are and what we
project ourselves to be—or for that matter—what we see
in others. Although what he was saying was not always
easy to follow in depth at first, the more his words sank in,
the more the Truth of what he was revealing made sense
to me.

Krishnamurti made me aware that our conditioning
is an enormous barrier both to understanding ourselves
and to embrace what he was trying to convey concerning
human nature and the truth about ourselves. Observing
myself, I saw that in interaction with others I automatically fell into conditioned habits of reflection, from whence
arose criticism and blame. Hitherto, I had been ignorant
of my own conditioned nature.

On page 82 of his Journal, Krishnamurti says:

*Only in relationship can you know yourself, not in
abstraction and certainly not in isolation. The movement
of behaviour is the sure guide to yourself. It's the mirror of
your consciousness: this mirror will reveal its content, the
images, the attachments, the fears, the loneliness, the joy
and the sorrow. Poverty lies in running away from this,
either in its sublimations or its identities.*

I noticed that Krishnamurti was always pointing out that
'the important thing is to understand what it is that creates conditioning.' He added: 'Your mind is conditioned
right through and through: there is no part of you, which
is unconditioned.' And again: 'All thinking is conditioned;
there is no such thing as free thinking.' I realised that I
had to be deeply concerned with the way that I operated

or I could never make changes. At the same time I had to realise I was part of the whole human family and that all my reactions affected others.

I observed that Krishnamurti fully understood and lived the teachings that he brought to us. He was alive with them, sparkling passionately with an intensity of energy and depth of feeling. I noticed, too, the difference between the impersonal energy he portrayed—which made him stand out—in contrast with the many thousands on thousands, including myself, who came to listen to his talks.

I felt that Krishnamurti lived as he really was, his interconnectedness with the impersonal Cosmic energies placed him, as it were, at the top of a mountain, while we were on the valley floor below. In contrast, I found it extraordinarily difficult actually to be myself, without my personality interfering. No doubt, it was that I was too absorbed in myself, so that I was unable to be properly aware of my actions and reactions. Krishnamurti seemed to be empowered by Forces beyond my understanding.

I think our deep-rooted, self-centred motives are hard to detect. Only through Krishnamurti's teachings was I able to perceive the many conditioned states that hitherto I had not noticed, such as conceptual thinking that always seemed to lead me astray. In the beginning it slowly dawned on me that the 'radical change within the nature of mankind' that Krishnamurti was addressing was way above my head. But I could understand the vital part we all play in forming our society into what it is today, although I found it very difficult to be sufficiently aware of either my thinking or my actions, before I had said and done what I regretted.

I felt that while Krishnamurti's teachings stressed the importance of self-responsibility, self-reliance and self-awareness, he was at the same time pointing out the significant role our conditioned minds play in preventing us from seeing the ignorance of our behaviour.

In the first year or so that we returned for the Krishnamurti talks, I often felt caught, I remember, by the campers' general feeling of separation from the intimacy of the School where Krishnamurti was staying. There was an inevitable sense of division, since one could not go to the School unless invited, and then one could only mix with those staying at the centre when they were attending the talks. I suppose it was because Krishnamurti was staying at the School that we felt the lack of contact with him that the privileged few enjoyed. Once I saw where my feelings were coming from, envy of those closer to Krishnamurti than I was—disappeared. It was a good lesson that taught me more about myself. Mistakenly, I had never thought I was envious until this situation revealed it to me.

Before listening to Krishnamurti at Brockwood, I realised, I had never experienced what it really meant just to listen; to listen without evaluating and assessing what was said in relation to the little I already knew. It took me a long time to fully realise that my former kind of listening was conditioned, and that it was blocking my understanding of what Krishnamurti was saying. I realised that I had not, in fact, been listening at all.

I recognised that my habits and conditioning were very deeply embedded beneath my consciousness, and that I was responding most of the time only to conceptual pictures that I had built in my mind, or to what my conditioning told me or my education had instigated. I was sure that listening in this way was preventing me from understanding Krishnamurti's teachings. I thought my mode of listening must have originated in academic learning—the accumulation of intellectual knowledge—whereas now, to me, listening to Krishnamurti there was not a question of listening in order to acquire knowledge, but to acquire an immediate awareness of myself. It meant letting go of all preconceived ideas and conditioning. I discovered I had been trying to grasp what he was saying in order to become 'better than I was', which of course I now see is an absurdity. It dawned on me that I was there at the talks to assimilate and respond inwardly to what Krishnamurti was saying by perceiving there and then what was false in myself even as I listened.

So I realised at last that all it required to listen was full attention—absolute awareness. But I knew that when caught in the trap of my conditioned self, I used thought to identify myself with what Krishnamurti was saying instead of paying complete attention. I remember at one talk, someone said: "Krishnamurti, we can't always be attentive, can we?" The prompt reply was, "Of course not. You don't want to be greedy, do you?"—which made everyone laugh.

I found to listen effectively to Krishnamurti's words and to embrace the meaning of what he was saying required total attention and complete honesty. I discovered that my habits of accumulating knowledge when I was listening ran very deep, so for several years I tried to listen to him as I thought I should, until I gave up trying—I just sat down and said to myself: 'That's it! I don't know how to listen to him properly, period, full stop'. And as I sat very still, I became so interested in what Krishnamurti was saying that I forgot all about myself. Suddenly, it dawned on me that I was, in fact, for the first time really listening, indeed; I actually effortlessly understood what he was saying.

During these years Alexander and I were fortunate to be invited to hear Krishnamurti converse with invited guests. These smaller groups of between twenty to forty people at Brockwood Park, or in India at Delhi, Bombay or Madras, helped me enormously to gain insight into the deeper meaning of what Krishnamurti was bringing. It left a great impression on me. My life changed again with yet another realisation.

It was at one of these smaller groups that Alexander and I attended in India, where I reached a deeper under-standing of why I had found it so difficult in the begin-ning to listen to Krishnamurti. As I watched myself, I was aware that I had been trying to grasp his words, losing the significance of what he was saying. His words had slipped through my fingers. Even when I struggled to remember what he said, I could not recall it. I realised that any move-ment of personalised thinking interrupted the flow of what he was saying so that my mind closed down. The force of this realisation helped me to be more aware. The next time I listened to his talks, I gained an even further under-standing of why I grasped for knowledge in the way that I did. I saw that I had been responding from a deep-rooted self-centred conditioning of wanting to grasp something as mine, wanting to know, wanting to gain, wanting to 'be-come better' than, wanting something with which to en-hance my ego. I discovered that the many layers encrusted around my self-centred states constantly created a cause, which inevitably was followed by an effect.

These little movements of awareness cemented my understanding that it was impossible to listen really at-tentively whilst I kept responding from conditioned self-centred states. I could see that I was trying to accumulate knowledge, to gather information for future reference. True listening brought me flashes of insight into the Truth of what he was saying. But now I knew just why it had taken me so long to understand what it meant to listen. My own conditioned limitations had been the cause of my incomprehension.

By such little movements of perseverance year after year I became more aware of what the Krishnamurti teachings really meant. It was the difference between being in a subconscious conditioned state and suddenly participating with an active awareness. I was spontaneously listening attentively. Spontaneity is aptly illustrated by this beautiful, true story recounted in a Scottish newspaper.

The report described the spontaneous attentive intelligence of a dog, which responded to the urgent need of the moment by following its in-built instinct. I was so struck by the story that after reading it I immediately tracked down the owner of the dog and spoke to him over the telephone. He confirmed the truth of the newspaper account in every respect.

The story stayed in my mind for a very long time. On a pleasant sunny day a father, his four-year old son and a huge Labrador dog were strolling along a pathway beside a burn—a Scottish stream. It eventually led to a weir. The burn was in full spate—actively rushing along, due to the snow melting on the mountains above. The dog was at the heel of his master whose leg, recently broken, was still encased in plaster. The little boy, walking closest to the burn, held his father's left hand while clutching his ball in his other hand. Suddenly the little boy cried out as he dropped his ball, which began to roll down toward the burn. The child quickly and unexpectedly pulled his left hand away from his father's hand and ran after it. In spite of his father's protests, the boy continued to chase the ball. Horrified, his father hobbled after him, only to find that his son had already fallen into the burn and was being swept away by the fast-moving waters towards the weir. The father was helpless. In agony he watched his son struggling in the water. Rooted to the spot, he realised there was absolutely nothing he could do to save his child.

Suddenly, the father caught a glimpse of the dog racing along the pathway towards the weir, soon disappearing out of sight. Hobbling along, he followed the dog as quickly as he could. No one could say what prompted the dog into action, and certainly it did not occur to the father at the time to wonder what power had propelled the dog along the path toward the weir. Was it an attentive, intelligent response born of his conditioning as a dog, one may ask, or was it his love of the child?

In no time at all the dog was waiting before the weir, standing precariously on a branch that lay out over the burn, ready to pick the boy out of the water as he passed beneath the branch. The father had limped along the path and could see all that was happening. At the precise moment that the boy floated beneath the branch the dog grabbed his coat and pants in his teeth and hauled the child from the water. Despite standing on a very narrow tree branch, this fully-grown Labrador still managed to keep his balance and bring the unconscious child to safety. He laid the boy down on his side on the grass by the path. Then standing close beside the boy, he barked furiously for his master. All this time the boy's father had been hobbling along the path toward the weir, terrified that his son would be dead. He could scarcely believe his eyes when he saw the child lying on his side where the dog had laid him. Soon the father was administering Cardio-pulmonary Resuscitation to his unconscious child. After what seemed a lifetime to the father, the child suddenly responded, coughing and spluttering up water as he regained consciousness.

In no time at all, the little boy was once again fully conscious and back on his feet—dripping wet—shivering and crying. The child flung his arms around the dog's neck, cuddling him, and crying in choking sobs as he thanked his friend for saving him. Meanwhile the dog was licking him all over his face, wagging his tail, whimpering in between sharp little barks. The father wondered: 'Who gave that dog the knowledge of what to do? How did he know that he had to wait at the weir? No one had told him what to do. Where did he get the ability to keep his balance?' The father confirmed that his son and his dog were now inseparable.

The story made me realise that the world we live in is a shared world, not a world over here just for human beings—with animals as objects over there—for their gratification.

I could see I had so much more to learn about life from the action of that animal. It seemed to me that the dog had responded totally to the need of the moment and perhaps an inner prompting out of love for his little friend; furthermore, all nature has the same innate spontaneity, born of Love.

I can only say, speaking for myself, that it took me a very long time to acknowledge my inherent gifts, and even now I find it difficult to be aware that I am mostly unaware. I needed to be constantly alert and continually watchful to learn what it really means to be attentive, so that I could respond spontaneously in the same way as the dog had. I realised there was no way that I could conjure up spontaneity; any attempt to do so on my part would introduce the process of thought, which would instantly result in reaction from the self—the me—the ego. There can only be spontaneous action, it seemed, when the self is passive.

At the Brockwood Park talks I would occasionally come across Krishnamurti by himself. I found him occupying a 'space' different from my own. His gentleness, humour and humility at those rare moments sparkled with an extraordinary power of intensity, which left me feeling that while he could 'touch' me, I was quite unable to reach him.

In his first public talk, given in Madras, India, on November 22 1959 Krishnamurti revealed:

"To me there is only one perception—to see something that is false or true immediately—.
This immediate perception of what is false and what is true is the essential factor—not the intellect, with it's reasoning based upon its cunning, its knowledge, and its commitments. It must sometime have happened to you that you have seen the truth of something immediately— such as the truth that you cannot belong to anything. That is perception."

I could relate to what Krishnamurti said, and I found that my experience in the Cult/School had helped me to realise the absurdity of following anyone. Indeed, I realised it was only through 'taking up my own bed' that I could walk away from the illusions I had accumulated around myself during the first part of my life, especially the cult.

One day I read from Krishnamurti's 3rd public talk in Rajahmundry, India. December 4th, 1949:

Understanding comes swiftly, unknowingly when the effort is passive; only when the maker of the effort is silent does the wave of understanding come.

I often felt as I listened to Krishnamurti that he was a natural poet. His words were chosen so carefully and expressed in such a way as to touch the very heart of the listener.

Again, I read another passage from the 5th Public Talk he gave in Benares, India February 20th. The intensity of his feeling shows in the words so carefully chosen:

There is a flash of understanding, that extraordinary rapidity of insight when the mind is very still, when the thought is absent, when the mind is not burdened with its own noise.

One can feel the vibrancy he emanated as he said these words. I learned much later to relate to what Krishnamurti said about the self:

We must be aware of the cunning and devious ways of the self, and in understanding them, virtue comes into being, but virtue is not an end in itself. Self-interest cannot cultivate virtue, it can only perpetrate it as self under the mask of virtue—under cover of virtue there is still the activity of self.

True awareness is the constant awareness of everyday life in itself: to be aware inwardly and outwardly every moment of every day. To be conscious of the 'what is' that is being presented before you, the mind must be clear of memories. This only happens when the mind is still. Often I was caught out, unaware of my actions and reactions, when thoughts raced round and round in my head. Then I would perceive the devious ways of the self that caused this unawareness. I hoped one day to awaken fully, so I persevered, never giving up.

My interest in Krishnamurti's teachings continued after his death in 1986. I learned about his purpose as a world teacher from the 'Pathless Land' talk, which Krishnamurti gave as a young man.

The Order of the Star in the East was founded in 1911 to proclaim the coming of the World Teacher. Krishnamurti was made the Head of the Order. On 3rd August 1929, the opening day of annual Star Camp at Omen, Holland, Krishnamurti dissolved the order before three thousand members. The full text of the talk he gave on that occasion is reproduced below, with grateful acknowledgement to *The Krishnamurti Foundation of America* and *The Krishnamurti Foundation Trust* for permission to reproduce it.[9]

We are going to discuss this morning the dissolution of the Order of the Star. Many people will be delighted, and others will be rather sad. It is a question neither for rejoicing nor for sadness because it is inevitable, as I am going to explain.

You may remember the story of how the devil and a friend of his were walking down the street, when they saw ahead of them a man stoop down and pick something from the ground, look at it, and put it away in his pocket. The friend said to the devil, 'What did that man pick up?' 'He picked up a piece of Truth,' said the devil. 'That is a very bad business for you, then,' said his friend. 'Oh, not at all,' the devil replied, 'I am going to let him organise it.'

I maintain that Truth is a pathless land, and you cannot approach it by any path whatsoever, by any religion, by any sect. That is my point of view, and I adhere to that absolutely and unconditionally. Truth being limitless, unconditioned, unapproachable by any path whatsoever, cannot be organised; nor should any organisation be formed to lead or coerce people along any particular path. If you first understand that, then you will see how impossible it is to organise a belief. A

---

[9] The full title is 'Truth is a Pathless Land', from the book *Total Freedom* by Krishnamurti.

belief is purely an individual matter, and you cannot and must not organise it. If you do, it becomes dead, crystallized; it becomes a creed, a sect, a religion, to be imposed on others. This is what everyone throughout the world is attempting to do. Truth is narrowed down and made a plaything for those who are weak, for those who are only momentarily discontented. Truth cannot be brought down; rather the individual must make the effort to ascend to it. You cannot bring the mountain-top to the valley. If you would attain to the mountain-top you must pass through the valley, climb the steeps, unafraid of the dangerous precipices. You must climb toward the Truth, it cannot be 'stepped down' or organized for you. Interest in ideas is mainly sustained by organisations, but organisations only awaken interest from without. Interest, which is not born out of love of Truth for its own sake, but aroused by an organisation, is of no value. The organisation becomes a framework into which its members can conveniently fit. They no longer strive after Truth or the mountain-top, but rather carve for themselves a convenient niche in which they put themselves, or let the organisation place them, and consider that the organisation will thereby lead them to Truth.

So that is the first reason, from my point of view, why the Order of the Star should be dissolved. In spite of this, you will probably form other Orders; you will continue to belong to other organisations searching for Truth. I do not want to belong to any organisations of a spiritual kind, please understand this. I would make use of an organisation, which would take me to London, for example; this is quite a different kind of organisation, merely mechanical, like the post or the telegraph. I would use a motorcar or a steamship to travel; these are only physical mechanisms, which have nothing whatever to do with spirituality. Again, I maintain that no organisation can lead man to spirituality.

If an organisation be created for this purpose, it becomes a crutch, a weakness, a bondage, and must cripple the individual, and prevent him from growing, from establishing his uniqueness, which lies in the discovery for himself of that absolute, unconditioned Truth. So that is another reason why I have decided, as I happen to be the Head of the Order, to dissolve it. No one has persuaded me to this decision.

This is no magnificent deed, because I do not want followers, and I mean this. The moment you follow someone you cease to follow Truth. I am not concerned whether you pay attention to what I say or not. I want to do a certain thing in the world and I am going to do it with unwavering concentration. I am concerning myself with only one essential thing: to set man free. I desire to free him from all cages, from all fears, and not to found religions, new sects, nor to establish new theories and new philosophies. Then you will naturally ask me why I go the world over, continually speaking. I will tell you for what reason I do this: not because I desire a following, not because I desire a special group of special disciples. (How men love to be different from their fellow-men, however ridiculous, absurd, and trivial their distinctions may be! I do not want to encourage that absurdity.) I have no disciples, no apostles, either on earth or in the realm of spirituality.

Nor is it the lure of money, nor the desire to live a comfortable life, which attracts me. If I wanted to lead a comfortable life I would not come to a Camp or live in a damp country! I am speaking frankly because I want this settled once and for all. I do not want these childish discussions year after year.

One newspaper reporter, who interviewed me, considered it a magnificent act to dissolve an organisation in which there were thousands and thousands of members. To him it was a great act because, he said: 'What will you do after-

wards, how will you live? You will have no following, peo-ple will no longer listen to you.' If there are only five people who will listen, who will live, who have their faces turned toward eternity, it will be sufficient. Of what use is it to have thousands who do not understand, who are fully embalmed in prejudice, who do not want the new, but would rather translate the new to suit their own sterile, stagnant selves? If I speak strongly, please do not misunderstand me; it is not through lack of compassion. If you go to a surgeon for an operation, is it not kindness on his part to operate even if he causes you pain? So, in like manner, if I speak straightly, it is not through lack of real affection, on the contrary.

As I have said, I have only one purpose: to make man free, to urge him toward freedom, to help him to break away from all limitations, for that alone will give him eternal hap-piness, will give him the unconditioned realisation of the self.

Because I am free, unconditioned, whole—not the part, not the relative, but the whole Truth that is eternal—I desire those who seek to understand me to be free; not to follow me, not to make out of me a cage which will become a religion, a sect. Rather should they be free from all fears—from the fear of religion, from the fear of salvation, from the fear of spir-ituality, from the fear of love, from the fear of death, from the fear of life itself. As an artist paints a picture because he takes delight in that painting, because it is his self-expres-sion, his glory, his well-being, so I do this and not because I want anything from anyone.

You are accustomed to authority, or to the atmosphere of authority, which you think will lead you to spirituality. You think and hope that another can, by his extraordinary powers—a miracle—transport you to this realm of eternal freedom, which is Happiness. Your whole outlook on life is based on that authority.

You have listened to me for three years now, without any change taking place except in the few. Now analyse what I am saying, be critical, so that you may understand thoroughly, fundamentally. When you look for an authority to lead you to spirituality, you are bound automatically to build an organisation around that authority. By the very creation of that organisation, which, you think, will help this authority to lead you to spirituality, you are held in a cage.

If I talk frankly, please remember that I do so, not out of harshness, not out of cruelty, not out of the enthusiasm of my purpose, but because I want you to understand what I am saying. That is the reason why you are here, and it would be a waste of time if I did not explain clearly, decisively, my point of view.

For eighteen years you have been preparing for this event, for the Coming of the World Teacher. For eighteen years you have organised, you have looked for someone who would give a new delight to your hearts and minds, who would transform your whole life, who would give you a new understanding; for someone who would raise you to a new plane of life, who would give you a new encouragement, who would set you free—and now look what is happening! Consider, reason with yourselves, and discover in what way that belief has made you different—not with the superficial difference of the wearing of the badge, which is trivial, absurd. In what manner has such a belief swept away all the unessential things of life? That is the only way to judge: In what way are you freer, greater, more dangerous to every Society, which is based on the false and the unessential? In what way have the members of this organisation of the Star become different?

As I said, you have been preparing for eighteen years for me. I do not care if you believe that I am the World Teacher or not. That is of very little importance. Since you belong to the organisation of the Order of the Star, you have given your sympathy, your energy, acknowledging that Krishnamurti is the World Teacher partially or wholly: wholly for those who are really seeking, only partially for those who are satisfied with their own half-truths.

You have been preparing for eighteen years, and look how many difficulties there are in the way of your understanding, how many complications and how many trivial things. Your prejudices, your fears, your authorities, your churches new and old—all these, I maintain, are a barrier to understanding. I cannot make myself clearer than this. I do not want you to agree with me. I do not want you to follow me. I want you to understand what I am saying.

This understanding is necessary because your belief has not transformed you but only complicated you, and because you are not willing to face things as they are. You want to have your own gods—new gods instead of the old, new religions instead of the old, new forms instead of the old—all equally valueless, all barriers, all limitations, all crutches. Instead of old spiritual distinctions you have new spiritual distinctions, instead of old worships you have new worships. You are all depending for your spirituality on someone else, for your happiness on someone else, for your enlightenment on someone else; and although you have been preparing for me for eighteen years, when I say all these things are unnecessary, when I say that you must put them all away and look within yourselves for the enlightenment, for the glory, for the purifications, and for the incorruptibility of the self, not one of you is willing to do it. There may be a few, but very, very few.

So why have an organisation?

Why have false, hypocritical people following me, the embodiment of Truth? Please remember that I am not saying something harsh or unkind, but we have reached a situation when you must face things as they are. I said last year that I would not compromise. Very few listened to me then.

This year I have made it absolutely clear. I do not know how many thousands throughout the world—members of the Order—have been preparing for me for eighteen years, and yet now they are not willing to listen unconditionally, wholly, to what I say.

So why have an organisation?

As I said before, my purpose is to make men unconditionally free, for I maintain that the only spirituality is the incorruptibility of the self, which is eternal, is the harmony between reason and love. This is the absolute, unconditioned Truth, which is Life itself. I want, therefore, to set man free, rejoicing as the bird in the clear sky, unburdened, independent, ecstatic in that freedom. And I, for whom you have been preparing for eighteen years, now say that you must be free of all these things, free from your complications, your entanglements. For this you need not have an organisation based on spiritual beliefs. Why have an organisation for five or ten people in the world who understand, who are struggling, who have put aside all trivial things? And for the weak people there can be no organisation to help them to find the Truth, because Truth is in everyone; it is not far, it is not near; it is eternally there.

Organisations cannot make you free. No man from outside can make you free; nor can organised worship, nor the immolation of yourselves for a cause, make you free; nor can forming yourselves into an organisation, nor throwing yourselves into works, make you free. You use a typewriter to write letters, but you do not put it on an altar and worship it. But that is what you are doing when organisations become your chief concern. 'How many members are there in it?' That is the first question I am asked by all newspaper reporters. 'How many followers have you? By their number we shall judge whether what you say is true or false.' I do not know how many there are. I am not concerned with that. As I said, if there were even one man who had been set free, that is enough.

Again, you have the idea that only certain people hold the key to the Kingdom of Happiness. No one holds it. No one has the authority to hold that key. That key is your own self, and in the development and the purification and in the incorruptibility of that self alone is the Kingdom of Eternity.

So you will see how absurd is the whole structure that you have built, looking for external help, depending on others for your comfort, for your happiness, for your strength. These can only be found within yourselves.

So why have an organisation?

You are accustomed to being told how far you have advanced, what is your spiritual status. How childish! Who but yourself can tell you if you are beautiful or ugly within? Who but yourself can tell you if you are incorruptible? You are not serious in these things.

So why have an organisation?

But those who really desire to understand, who are looking to find that which is eternal, without beginning and without an end, will walk together with a greater intensity, will be a danger to everything that is unessential, to unrealities, to shadows. And they will concentrate, they will become the flame, because they understand. Such a body we must create, and that is my purpose. Because of that real understanding there will be true friendship. Because of that true friendship—which you do not seem to know—there will be real co-operation on the part of each one. And this not because of authority, not because of salvation, not because of immolation for a cause, but because you really understand,

and hence are capable of living in the eternal. This is a greater thing than all pleasure, than all sacrifice.

So these are some of the reasons why, after careful consideration for two years, I have made this decision. It is not from a momentary impulse. I have not been persuaded to it by anyone. I am not persuaded in such things. For two years I have been thinking about this, slowly, carefully, patiently, and I have now decided to disband the Order, as I happen to be its Head. You can form other organisations and expect someone else. With that I am not concerned, nor with creating new cages, new decorations, for those cages. My only concern is to set men absolutely, unconditionally free.

This talk, given to the world in 1929, gave me a clear indication of Krishnamurti's committed dedication to Truth. I found it so enlightening. Every word fitted into my own experience of the cult/school in which I had found myself entrenched for nearly eight years. Questioning and awareness set me free from the cult/school and with the help and protection of Alexander I was able to come back into the world.

Krishnamurti's talks and dialogues gave me the profound realisation that there were hundreds and hundreds of people all over the world, like myself, seeking to discover a way to live without conflict, without authority and without conditioned restrictions. As I continue to study Krishnamurti's Teachings, I realise that I have never found anything in any books or teachings to hold a candle to his extraordinary perception of Truth and Living, nor anyone with such intense love and humility as that which always emanated from him.

In July 1985 I travelled to Saanen, Switzerland for the first time to attend the usual talks and dialogues. However, this transpired to be the last time the talks were held there.

Photograph of J. Krishnamurti by Edward Weston, which appeared in the book by Rom Landau, entitled *God is My Adventure*, published in 1935 by Ivor Nicholson and Watson Ltd, London.

Yet, in spite of being in poor health, Krishnamurti kept to his usual programme, spanning three weeks. He was now over 90 years old, yet his talks were as vibrant as ever, they held a special message as he said to us very seriously that it was up to each one of us radically to change. He urged us to be aware of the need for this radical change and to re-alise our responsibility toward humanity as a whole since we were humanity and humanity was us. He said it was up to each one of us to realise how we affected one another in our relationships. This was a huge gathering. On the last day Krishnamurti announced that there would be no more talks held in Saanen.

Sadly, Krishnamurti gave his last European talk at Bro-ckwood Park in August/September of 1985, followed by a few talks in India, before he left for Ojai in USA where, after a brief illness, he died at his Pine Cottage on the 17th February 1986.

I was sad when the talks ended. Then I was reminded of Krishnamurti's tireless and constant effort to engender freedom within us, to initiate spontaneity within, to free us from 'our petty little selves', by speaking as he constantly did on the same subject, which yet always seemed differ-ent to me. He travelled the world for sixty years, tirelessly talking to thousands of different people, always maintain-ing that it was the teachings that mattered, not the speak-er. I feel these words of his so well sum up the teachings to which we can all respond:

I speak from my heart. A truly intelligent mind can have no choice... in the way that the whole of the field of consciousness begins to unfold. And as it unfolds, you have to follow; and the following becomes extraordinary difficult—following in the sense to follow the movement of thought, of every feeling, of every secret desire. It becomes difficult the moment you resist, the moment that you say 'That's ugly! this is good, that is bad, this I will keep, that I will not keep'. So you begin with the outer and move inwardly. Then you will find, when you move inward that the inward and the outward are not two different things, that the outward awareness is not different from the inward awareness, and that they are both the same.[10]

After the death of Krishnamurti there followed for me many years of hard work on myself—putting his teachings into my daily life. In the next two chapters I relate in some detail the way in which these Teachings, helped by my insights, dawned upon me, as alone I sought to live the innermost depth of his vital Teachings.

At Brockwood Park.

[10] *Total Freedom, the Essential Krishnamurti* published by HarperSanFrancisco in 1996, pages 1–7.

Chapter Seventeen

Learning to Understand Who We Are

Jesus said:
The images are manifest to man
and the light that is amongst them is hidden.
In the image of the Light of the Father
the Light will reveal itself
And his image is hidden by his Light.

Taken from

Jesus, Untouched by the Church, His Teachings in the Gospel of Thomas,
by Hugh McGregor Ross, published by William Sessions Ltd York, 1998.

THESE WORDS HAD A DEEP EFFECT ON ME. I came to see that for most of my life my emotions had been caught up in the 'me's' and 'I's' that expressed conceptions of myself as images of my self-centred states. It was as if I was unaware of what the images were doing to my mind and body. I was unconscious of the fact that as the observer, I was separating and dividing myself from what I was observing. By doing this to myself, I was allowing my thoughts to identify myself with what I was observing, when in fact the very observation process itself could not separate me from what I was observing,

In Krishnamurti's dialogue with Dr Bohm and Dr Shainberg on the question of image-making and whether the observer is different from that which he is observing, is brought out very clearly in a passage taken from the book *The Wholeness of Life by Krishnamurti,* page 114, *Dialogue VI* (Victor Gollancz 1978): where Krishnamurti points out in the dialogue of that day—these profound words:

When thought stops, when there is no image-maker,
there is complete transformation in consciousness
because there is no anxiety, there is no fear, there is no
pursuit of pleasure—there are none of the things that
create turmoil and division. Then what comes into being,
what happens? Not as an experience because that is out.
What takes place? I have to find out, for you may be
leading me up the wrong path!

Clarity, however, did not come to me all at once, I read and re-read the whole of this dialogue and probed into myself from every angle before I realised that my questions started with the realisation that I was trapped by my own personalised wants, self-images and conditioned behaviours. I could see that I often felt in a confused state of anxiety and ignorance when I formed images of what I thought was the way to escape from my predicament. Perhaps the most deadly of these personalised wants was my self-righteous desire for spirituality. But, whichever way I turned, my desires kept blinding me. Oh, how imprisoned I felt!

Inevitably I came to a standstill. I ceased my internal dialogue. Then when I stopped trying to find a way out of my trapped condition, to my disbelief I found myself carried away yet again, with a sudden personal want regarding my health. This took the form of declaring that all my possessions were but chaff compared to my health. No sooner had this thought formed in my mind than a voice within me emphatically declared: "If you want your health you must earn it." In the next four years I was busy doing just that. I had three major operations—two hip replacements and a hysterectomy—this made me realise that perhaps I had challenged a Power that I did not know anything about.

After these experiences I was always afraid that my wants might unconsciously again challenge that Power that I knew so little about, but awareness of this phenomenon allowed me to see that *wanting* my wants to go away was still a want. And in much the same way I realised that until I stopped resisting where I found myself within my wants, they would always arise within me. Unless I stayed with the 'what is' I was held by the wants that were governed by my beliefs—so I could never be free of them. Unconsciously, my conditioning encouraged my wants, preventing my inner feelings from surfacing; and my ignorance stifled any new way forward. Blinkered by beliefs, I remained blind to my deeper conditioning; the two were firmly linked. Consequently, I perceived that the bonds of belief constrained me within a prison of conditioning. Plainly, one set of beliefs led to another.

But without being open to receive or willing to let go of all preconceived notions, I was held captive by my beliefs and to be a free human being, I had to be unhindered by past memories. So I said to myself, 'Surely, it is vital to meet the present moment with a freshness of uncontaminated yesterdays?'

Not knowing what to do and with no one to help me but myself—I at last turned within and acknowledged the 'Kingdom of Heaven'. Then I became conscious that my wants were coming from my desire for personal gain. Thus by seeing my limitations I began to really observe myself, perhaps for the first time, as I really was, with all my personal wants and mental demands. By no longer trying to be in control, I ceased struggling to find a way out of my predicaments.

I finally perceived that my struggling only required constant acute attention, plus vigilance and determination, to sustain an inner attentiveness; so that when any emotional energy arose from personal wants I would be able to give it my full attention, whereby there would be no resistance. It seemed to me that it is only when the personal self is quiet that there can be attention to the 'Kingdom of Heaven within,' as Jesus proclaimed.

The 'attention' referred to above is not the usual attention that the logical mind pays to our emotions of daily activities, which is when the mind is more concerned with intellectual or academical pursuits. The logical mind tends to make explanations through thought, which interfere with total attention. With real 'attention', there is no thought interfering or an 'I' standing apart acting attentively, there is just 'attention'—not an action of the conscious self expressing negative emotional energy, nor even an attempt at being impersonal. I realised that any effort made by personalised thinking to control emotional feelings created conflict. I also saw that any intervention from the usual self—where the psychological emotional energies of hurt, fear, anger, greed or jealousy occur—always originates out of personalised thinking.

Thus, in place of a subjective interfering 'I' standing apart, there is only observation from an impersonal stance, which produces an entirely different perspective to the way I feel when held by personalised feelings. Now that I no longer generated personal conflictive energy, the interfering 'I' evaporated as soon as I saw it arise. Then, in the absence of any division, conflict was no longer a problem. Now as I interact with others, my emotions respond quite differently. In the stillness and silence of attention there is no conflict—just a responding to the energy field that comes from being attentively impersonal.

I realised that an 'I' standing apart always interferes with our actions and reactions. To approach the 'what is' impersonally requires complete and undivided attention.

This is quite imperative, if we are not to be caught up in personal emotions all over again, by allowing distracting thoughts, derived from knowledge to interfere with our attention. By fixing complete attention on the Now of 'what is'—the 'self'—is no longer in control. Being present in the Now we meet each new event with fresh mind alertness without prejudice or criticism. This is what I feel it means to be impersonally attentive. Thus when provoked we are always in an orderly state of control over any situation we encounter. I further discovered that as a result of such unrestrained attention, the usual watcher that is the 'self'—the observer—is no longer active, it is replaced by total attention, which is so strong that all else within the Now is stilled. The observer is then the observed: there is a transformation in consciousness.

It is when we struggle to control our emotions as if they were outside of ourselves as an objectified, conceptual mind image from our logical minds through interfering thoughts, that there is neither the ability to rectify or avoid conflict.

I gradually became fully aware that an impersonal approach engenders a totally different attitude toward every circumstance. And by releasing the 'self' from the sum total of my 'me's' and 'I's', I yielded unconditionally to the 'what is' in front of me. This new understanding gave me an awareness of the destructive way my image making took control, especially when I had feelings of self-satisfaction. Consequently, I was able to detect any illusory emotion before it produced any conflict or unnecessary 'aggro'.

Being impersonal and totally attentive I could face hurtful remarks addressed to me without the usual response of identification. Hurtful remarks were noted, of course, revealing to me the way that I had been caught in the past by identifying myself through thought with such a remark.

By not responding to the hurtful remark, it allowed me to remain unattached with no movement of identification on my part whatsoever, which absolved me from conflict. By total attention to the 'what is' in front of me, my emotions and thoughts were not involved. In consequence, a totally different way of dealing with my emotions came into play, whereby there was no movement away from the 'what is'. In fact, I found myself unconsciously responding impersonally. I still felt emotions, of course, but now they arose out of empathy with others, and the whole current of life took on a totally different meaning. I found myself quiet within 'the what is' with no movement away by being caught up in knowledge from thoughts through lack of attention, thus by being exceedingly watchful, and at the same time allowing other people to be exactly who they were, whatever the circumstance, removed me from any conflict. I related this impersonal approach to what Sekkeii Harada says in his book *The Essence of Zen*:

'Zen koan', which is ultimate reality itself... is something that cannot be understood or not understood, defined, or given significance by means of human thought.

Further, on page 100, under the heading of *Reality Exists Prior to Thought*, he says:

Once thought has arisen, the reality has already disappeared. It is a mistake to think that you can reach what is real by thought or as a process of refining your thought.

Can personalised thinking lead to impersonal action?

To me, personalised thinking can never lead to impersonal actions—personal behaviour being controlled by our self-centred states, knowledge and thought. To be impersonal is to be unaffected by personalised behaviour inflicted upon us.

Personalised thinking is predominately found in family circles and personal relationships, but also most noticeably around personal agendas within politics, places of work, sporting activities, schools, and all types of institutions and government services. While there may be no direct answer to a particular problem, there is always room for an extended, impersonal mind perception to stand in place of personal wants, if conflict is to be avoided.

That is why it is inconceivable to me that a Universe, which operates with such balanced order and precision, could possibly exclude humanity from the same ordered balance as itself. Surely our civilisation depends on our recovery to that balanced order?

I feel it is so absurd to imagine that we can be perfect, when in reality we are born with the capacity to be perfectly in tune with the Infinite. It is only when we give ourselves license to behave like morons, running after perfection, that the 'now of living'—that moment in which we have the possibility of meeting the 'what is'—sanely and happily—passes us by. To think that we can be perfect is the same as imagining that our sins can be forgiven. How can anyone forgive what is past? To forgive another means we have been personally affected, so how then can we forgive or be forgiven? In being impersonal the question of forgiveness does not arise. Words have no meaning except in intellectual pursuits.

The great thing that matters is to be able to live with the reality of change, but not to be affected by it. We are more aware of the real significance of perpetual change in the Universe, in nature and around us, when we are unaware or unconscious of our own perpetual changes. The better we appreciate that fact, I feel, the sooner we remember those who have gone before us, who for generation after generation have played their part in contributing changes to our well-being as well as others playing a part in the degeneration of our society. I feel that it is important to recognise that we are in the stream of humanity and that we are all caught up in its combinations of negative and positive emotions—greed, cruelty, fear, hurt, as well as the positive emotions of giving, loving, being happy and so on. Nothing and no one can remove us from that stream until we comprehend that we are caught in it. Until we see our limitations and want freedom as much as we would want air when we are drowning, we will always fail to recognise what it means to be a human being—obliged to meet *life as it is and the 'what is' as it is presented before us.* This builds our ability to see ourselves as we really are— and not as we think we are—thus we are able to meet any circumstance without conflict—either within ourselves or within others.

We are each fashioned in the same way and each one of us has the same opportunity to discover the God within or whatever you call your Essence of Life, which is always there no matter what happens, for we are no-thing without it. It is only when we recognise and acknowledge It—that *It* finds *us.* Either we consciously understand that or we pass on oblivious to Its Presence.

Notwithstanding, It will make itself known to us the moment we are ready.

In times of disaster we all pull together. I remember so well how everyone worked unceasingly during World War Two to accomplish the needs of the war effort. In sharing our horrors we came nearer, closer together. When a telegram arrived by special delivery, I remember the sense of dread as I opened the orange envelope whose contents informed me of my husband's battle injury. As I looked up to thank the boy I suddenly noticed the deep concern on his face. I told him it was all right and that my husband was injured but not dead. We exchanged comforting smiles and he went on his way, no doubt glad not to be the bearer of devastating news.

Surely, it is more than possible in years of peace to exceed anything we ever did during the bitter struggle and loss of life of those horrific war years. By refraining from resorting to personal wants and demands, there can be no interfering 'I' standing apart, causing untold misery and conflict to others.

There is yet another aspect of dealing with unkind remarks before they arouse our emotions. (I used to count up to ten, but found I never got further than three before I had responded in my usual resistant, contentious way). I found another method that really works. If we go together, I will show you the way I discovered it.

Unkind remarks or actions cause us to react instantly in response to our personalised thoughts—as, indeed, we do when we meet kindness. When we feel hurt, careful attention reveals that in a matter of seconds we have objectified the hurt away from ourselves into a mind concept—through our thought, which are registered as memory in the brain. At the same time, our conditioned personalised thinking reacts, as it usually does and blames the other person for the hurt. However, when our total attention is turned on ourselves within the 'what is' no thoughts circulate in our heads—we are quiet and alert with no reaction to the hurt. But when we use personalised thinking we can never deal with the hurt; it is interesting to note why. When thought is used it is used in response to memory and knowledge, either to surface memory from a similar situation that has happened before or a deep-rooted memory within our subconscious mind registered in our brain. By using thought we revive our memory of hurts from another day or hurts from long ago and long forgotten. The deep-rooted memories of hurts are seldom associated with the present hurt or the fact that as a part of humanity we all partake of everyone's else's unconscious behaviour. By being usually oblivious to this, which is conditioning, we are unable to reflect clearly on what occurs, so we think such things as: 'How could he be so hurtful to me?' 'What have I done to deserve such an unkind remark?' By being sincere and honestly wanting to understand ourselves, within no time a recollection will come when you were hurt and through attention were able to resolve the hurt without using thought as memory. Try this next time you are hurt.

We do not understand that by identifying ourselves with the situation or the hurtful remark, we have objectified our feelings outside of ourselves. We have created a space between our subjective selves—where we really feel the hurt—and the objectified image of the hurt—where the hurt is not—it is in this deadly space that thought creates its mischief. In reality, the objectified image is non-existent, being a mere product of our imagination. But it is within this space that personalised thought moves in registration within our brain, activating mental antagonism against the author of the hurtful remark or action. Consequently, we meet the 'what is' by a form of resistance, instead of allowing the 'what is' to stand before us without contention or wishing to shape or change it to conform to our expectation or wants. By realising this, deeply there is no registration made in the brain since there is no thought being activated to be registered.

When we face the hurtful remark without resistance or blame, simply allowing it to be as it is, we cannot be in conflict—as I discovered to my joy. This is being impersonal, through self-learning and self-awareness.

We can never change what is happening or reverse what has been said through personalised thinking, which can only be divisive and contentious. If we try to do so, we only make matters far worse, as I am sure you will have noticed. But when we act impersonally we are in harmony with our Essence within, which acts for us. We either see this or we do not. No one can make us see it, as I came to realise.

If we persevere, our heads clear, the crippling burden of the 'self' carried for so long, drops away and we are at last released from the grip of personalised thinking and have become unmoved—impersonal. No doubt there will be times when, we unconsciously, out of habit, continue in one form or another to be affected by others. But we soon correct ourselves. I cannot begin to tell you how different I feel now that I have understood and implemented all I have conveyed above. So take courage and persevere as I have done—it will change your life and the lives of those around you, for it brings beauty into Love, Compassion into Being.

I have found that in allowing personalised thinking to run our lives, we fail to address the irritant of our dissatisfaction—common to us all—although we are not consciously aware of it for most of the time. Such dissatisfaction is an unconscious reminder that something is not in harmony. So unconsciously we begin to feel restless and unsure of ourselves. And instead of seeking the remedy for these feelings of dissatisfaction—by turning within—we turn away either to seek help from others, as I did, or to indulge in diversions such as drugs, over-eating, entertainment, pub-crawling or self-centred behaviour. Even if we seek to use diversionary pursuits and religious distractions or entertainments we are still avoiding dealing with those feelings of dissatisfaction. The sad part is that we are not even aware of the underlying cause of our behaviour; nor do we know why we feel dissatisfaction. So we never address the feelings of dissatisfaction that is trying to warn us to be wakefully aware of our behaviour—instead of turning inward—we escape.

It is only when we are absolutely attentive that we have our only opportunity of observing this interfering 'I'. Then we see what happens when we express our personal emotions of hurts, jealousies, fears, angers and so on. By really seeing the effect of taking everything we encounter within the 'what is' so personally we are suddenly brought to a halt, and in that stillness of mind we can effect the transition to impersonal behaviour. Through using an impersonal attentive awareness we see we are unconscious when an 'I' standing apart interferes with our emotional feelings arising from being hurt.

Under the influence of a quiet mind that neither responds personally to emotional feelings nor moves us away from them, we can allow the 'what is' to remain exactly where it is—directly in front of us—on the ground on which we stand. Then we discover that this is the only place where our experiences can be dealt with effectively. It is when personalised thinking moves us away from the 'what is' that the whole scenario of so-called 'normal' behaviour begins, thus we move from one entanglement of our own making to another, as it goes round and round in our heads.

By being impersonal we do not contend or resist or escape or try to control the 'what is' that lies before us. Rather, we become consciously aware of the present moment—the NOW—for then we are in the Reality of the present moment, alert, attentive and non-combative. Thus, we find through attention we are in the NOW, which cannot then be interfered with by personalised thinking. We are able to act spontaneously from the stillness of the mind where there is emptiness—no movement. Emptiness here means absence of the usual 'self'—the collective 'me's'.

By understanding the steps required to make this inner journey, we let go of personalised thinking with all the conflict, unrest and negativity that affects health and well-being, and we discover, as I did, that our whole life begins again to change. We find that it is only in relationships that we have this opportunity to understand ourselves.

Nonetheless, by keeping our attention on ourselves helps us to realise that we do not know what to do. For we feel as if we have arrived at a nothingness. This is perhaps the beginning of wisdom. It is a time to be silent, quiet and still, to observe what is taking place, allowing others to be who they are without trying to alter or shape them. Uninvolved with our emotional energies, we remain inter-blended with the 'what is' and the interdependency that it inevitably entrains. In this stillness we cease to be affected. The forces of negative and positive, Yin and Yang, meet up without conflict—thus we are responding from a Oneness of being in the Now—and in consequence in command of any situation.

We can never change or reverse what is past—what has been said or done—through personalised thinking, which is so often both divisive and contentious. But by unconsciously trying to do so, we only make matters worse; as I am sure you will have noticed. Then we are exhausted—inwardly and outwardly—through the argument that inevitably follows we feel desperate. This is the moment when we have let go, which is an impersonal act—we are in the stillness of the God Essence within, which spontaneously acts for us. But we cannot make ourselves become impersonal. We either see this or we do not. No one can make us see it, as I came to realise.

There is no doubt that we will continually meet difficult situations and hurts, but we have only to put attention on ourselves to bring impersonality back into being, for this changes our attitudes and motives, bringing us to a real sense of Love.

It is only in silence that love can exist. The quality of love is not born out of desire, conflict and all the rest of the ugliness and torture: it comes into being with the understanding of time, space, desire, pleasure; it is then that it is seen that love is not desire and pleasure. That 'innocent' mind can solve all the problems and all the challenges that it meets. It is completely aware of all the problems of man—and it becomes immeasurable. To such a mind there is no time and no death; to come across such a mind one has to end sorrow the ending of sorrow is the beginning of wisdom.[11]

Our dissatisfaction
Dissatisfaction compelled me to search through bookshops and libraries in my quest for answers to why I happen to be feeling dissatisfied! Often I felt dazed by the clutter of mistaken beliefs I had collected around me, so that I seemed to be swamped by other people's concepts and ideas and

[11] The full title is 'Truth is a Pathless Land', from the book *Total Freedom* by Krishnamurti.

further away than ever from my own inner connections. Was that why I was feeling dissatisfied—I wondered?

I feel, to be wakefully aware of our behaviour, our way of life, our habits, our conditioning and countless other behavioural patterns that have consciously or unconsciously crept into our lives, we have to respond to this dissatisfaction instead of escaping from it, through unawareness.

For most of my life I have been primarily unaware of my own true nature and the reasons for my inner feelings of dissatisfaction. But as soon as I became convinced that my dissatisfaction sprung from the depths of my inner being, calling me to awaken to the Reality of the Dynamic Energy force—and to shun religious conditioning and self-righteousness—I felt alive and vibrant, unsullied by deception and only conscious of the fact that this moment counts and can never be repeated, never be lost and never come again.

By using an impersonal, attentive, silent awareness we are able to be more conscious when an 'I' standing apart interferes with emotional feelings that arise from hurts. It is only when there is absolute attention to our dissatisfaction that we have our best opportunity to observe this interfering 'I'. By seeing the effect of taking everything we encounter so personally we are—at last—aware of what we are doing and this brings a stillness; and in that stillness of mind we have the best opportunity of motivating a transition to impersonal behaviour.

When I first became aware of the isolation that my behaviour caused, I could not believe how ignorant I was. But as I became more watchfully aware I was horrified into silence, and in this stillness I felt the fervent need to seek the 'The Kingdom of Heaven within'.

Jesus said:
He who seeks shall find,
and to him who knocks it shall be opened.[12]

Under the influence of a quiet mind that neither responds personally to emotional feelings nor moves us away from them, we can look into the deeper meaning of the 'what is' and why we have to keep meeting it day in and day out. As we observe the 'what is'—always directly in front of us on the ground on which we stand—without making any movement away with our personalised thinking, then we discover that being personal prevents us from seeing that the only key to dealing effectively with our problems is to be impersonal. It is when we move away from the 'what is' through personalised feelings of escape that the whole scenario of our so-called normal behaviour begins and we are then dysfunctional.

By being impersonal we feel less dissatisfied and more able to work with the 'what is' that lies before us—so that we can be consciously aware of the present moment—the now; for then we are part of the Living Universe. This feeling then dispels dissatisfaction. Thus, with our attention in the now, we naturally respond to the God within, which removes us from conflict and ourselves. Actions are then spontaneous, arising out of the stillness of the mind where there is emptiness—no movement. Emptiness here means absence of the usual 'self'—the collective 'me's' & 'I's'.

Our understanding of dissatisfaction guides us to make this inner journey on the 'pathless path', so that our whole life begins to 'turn around'. As Krishnamurti said: 'Where there is no conflict, there is something far greater than thought.'

[12] Taken from *Jesus, Untouched by the Church:*
   His teachings in the Gospel of Thomas by Hugh McGregor Ross.

Meeting up with my 'Me's' and my 'I's

When I first observed that my personality expressed my 'me's' & 'I's' through self-pictures and images, I wanted to find out why. I discovered—as history shows—that human beings have never ceased to operate in this degenerative way since The Fall. It made me feel more than ever that there must be a way out of the stream of humanity. By sharing, our relationships, we learn more about the way we affect each other, recognising that we are all caught in the stream of humanity. Then we open our hearts to what it means to be a human being, and since we are fundamentally all the same, whoever we are, or where ever we live—we learn that it is only in relationship that we uncover ourselves to ourselves.

As I kept observing myself, it became obvious that the persona I believed myself to be was composed of hundreds of different 'me's' & 'I's. Consequently, I kept acting from these images, like everyone else. After a while it no longer seemed important whether the 'me' or the 'I' was real or false, it was enough to be aware that my behaviour patterns were sometimes robotic, mechanical and nearly always personal. It was important to discover why these 'me's' and 'I's were operating in the way they did and why they seemed to be playing such a prominent part in my life.

I must confess, I could see that I was no different to the rest of humanity; for which ever way I turned I was still locked in by human action and reaction, just as everybody else was; we have inherited our genes from generation on generation. I was interested the other day to watch the television programme to celebrate The Pride of Britain Awards; I was surprised and immensely impressed to hear the scientist Sir John Sulston expressing thanks for his award in the following way:

I really think this world needs to feel 'one'. And this genome—these genes of ours—remind us, because we all share our genes: My genes are your genes—your genes are mine. And they belong to everybody else in the world, just the same. They can't be owned.
So let's remember that and be together.[13]

It felt good to hear a scientist speak such words so spontaneously and sincerely. Sir John Sulston's knowledge of the human genetics helped me to gain a much wider sense of what it really means to move away from the personal to the impersonal, to move away from the narrow personal outlook to the much broader impersonal view.

The more I hid away from myself the more I was caught up in my 'me's' & 'I's. To see my 'me's' & 'I's' exactly as they were was one of the most difficult things I had to do—being aware of the way they interacted in relationships—mostly copying others, or succumbing to their influences, or resisting them, or inflating my own ego, the process was endless while I succumbed to my 'me's' & 'I's.

I guess it takes serious commitment. Maybe we prefer to remain with our imperfections—it is easier—and doubtless we are more familiar with them! Often within a few seconds of watching myself, personalised thoughts intervened, putting an end to all my good resolutions. In fact, I noticed that it was difficult to be conscious of my actions or reactions as they actually occurred. Unconscious of the way that my various 'me's' and 'I's' took centre stage, I failed to observe the way they manipulated events. But on those occasions when I was conscious of my personal behaviour, it became clearer than ever that there was

---

[13] Quoted by permission of Don Powell, Press & P.R. Officer, and Cambridge. Sir John Sulston is a former director of the *Welcome Trust Sanger Institution* and leader of *The Human Project*.

no possible way of knowing myself except through self-knowledge and self-awareness, and that required constant watchfulness. Despite all my endeavours my 'me's' would change from one set of 'I's' to another. In fact, through my endeavours it became obvious that my behaviour continually resorted to personalised states—the 'I's' and 'me's' popping up so quickly—leading me into thinking I knew—when obviously I did not.

By patiently enumerating the many self-images that created the 'me's' and the 'I's' and watching them in action, I discovered literally hundreds. And they were all acting and reacting from different self-centred states.

These 'me's' or 'I's' in the field of the ego arose from time to time as a defence mechanism, based on ignorance or aggression or justification or resistance or pride or all manner of other familiar behaviour patterns, no doubt common to us all. But when regarding my 'me's' and 'I's' dispassionately and honestly, it was obvious that most of them either resisted everything they did not like, or accepted everything they liked. It was as if these 'me's' and 'I's' were in continual strife with one another, fighting for prime position. I read an interesting paragraph in Krishnamurti's book, *Education and the Significance of Life*:

> *The self is a bundle of many entities, each opposed to the others. It is a battlefield of conflicting desires, a centre of constant struggle between the 'mine' and the 'not mine'; and as long as we give importance to the self, to the 'me'; and the 'mine' there will be increasing conflict within ourselves and in the world.*

Gradually I realised that whereas some 'me's' were frightened, the 'I's' knew everything and could be told nothing. Some 'me's' were constantly judging or criticising, while other 'me's' never admitted to having created the conditions where they found themselves. Most 'I's' were afraid of being honest and consequently told lies. Then there were the patronising 'I's—almost insufferable—as they always wanted to be right. To my consternation there was positively no end to the length the 'me's' & 'I's' would go to justify themselves by blaming others. In fact it was easy to be lost within any of my 'me's' or 'I's', for personalised thinking activated them so powerfully.

Repeatedly it was clear that my hidden 'me's' were lethargic, and that they were often provoked by something or someone. Then the 'I's' would pop up at an alarming rate, particularly the resisting or argumentative ones—and each time in a different guise—which made it difficult for the 'me's' to see them clearly. In fact, to my consternation, the 'me's' seldom noticed the 'I's' trying to outwit them as they were too busy initiating their own wants. Their continual subversion seemed to be taking over my entire life.

If by any chance you do not believe in 'me's' or 'I's' and you do not think as you read this that they trouble you, or you think it is normal for them to behave as they do, then consider for a moment whether your behaviour is ever out of control, or pompous, or self-righteous, or arrogant, or full of pride, or jealous, or resistant, or angry, or fearful. Should these emotions never trouble you, maybe you can recollect a time when something or someone annoyed or hurt you—or maybe you find it easier to notice someone else's out of hand emotions! You may perhaps in a moment of being 'absence', notice that your self-images are being aroused and suddenly exposed before you by an emergent 'me' or 'I'. Or will you still blame another for putting you into that position?

Despite constant endeavour to monitor my 'me's' & 'I's', there were times when they emerged regardless—in fact an unruly 'me' is there before the 'I's' are even aware of it. In my confusion, these 'me's' and 'I's' appeared to be real; or were they monsters of my imagination? There appears no easy way around such a phenomena, but there is one consolation they can only manifest when awareness is null and void.

It felt as if I was a 'nobody' swollen with 'me's' and 'I's'! "Surely not!" the 'self' thought defensively. Or were the 'me's' and 'I's' just fighting each other for positions of power? The only way to find out was to pay close attention to these troublesome 'me's' & 'I's'—something I found most difficult to do.

In looking outwardly, away from the ground on which I stood, there could be no coming to terms with these unruly 'me's' or 'I's'. Without continual watchful attention, one of these rampaging 'me's' or 'I's' could easily gain a controlling position of power, hoodwinking the others into believing they were something they definitely were not! Should the presumed entity move so much as a centimetre; there is no hope of becoming familiar with the persona that appears as the 'self'. One of the usurping 'me's' can escape detection, for these 'me's' are so manipulative, devious and elusive.

Under close scrutiny, unable to qualify their positions, the 'me's' and the 'I's' can be brought to a standstill. As awareness grew that the 'me's' and 'I's' had no substance, being mere conceptualisations of self-images related only to what they thought they were, the 'me's' and 'I's began to show signs of defeat. At this stage of my awakening, alertness and honesty were essential. Otherwise self-images might easily turn everything upside down again.

Is religious conditioning inhibiting our development?

Virtually all human beings are exposed to one form of religious conditioning or another that claims to address basic human needs and questions concerning philosophical/ spiritual issues about life. Presently, the world is more or less controlled by conditioning and the 'me's' & 'I's' indulging in personalised thinking. Our human emotions and image making are reflected from memory through our thoughts. The fact is that our 'me's' & 'I's' and images want to be as certain as they can of surviving today, tomorrow, and forever, particularly when we think about the underlying fear of death. Or is it just our conditioning that wants this certainty? Only a truly impersonal mind is unconcerned with survival.

There are many, many people in the world today dissatisfied with their lives and the happenings around them. They seek to escape into diversions of all kinds, such as entertainment and sports, particularly religious pursuits. But there are other very serious and committed souls who have realised that it is up to them to change, if they want to change their world.

Experience eventually brought me to realise that philosophising and knowledge simply confines us to intellectual thinking. We go round and round in circles, grasping and gaining, in order to know more and to become 'better than'. I found myself locked into rationalising and justifying who I thought I was or should be.

Ever since I read Eugene Marais' book *The Soul of the Ape* and *The Soul of the White Ant*, I have been fascinated by the structure, function and extraordinary power of the insect world, which to my way of thinking relates in some way to the function of ourselves and our brains. Briefly, Marais points out the function of the Queen of the White

Ant colony, who is in control of her termitary since she is the brain of the community, sealed off as she is in her cell—the palace cavity. Interestingly enough, the queen's body lies orientated with her head pointing to the west. She eventually grows too large to move herself and consequently relies completely on the King Ant and the worker ants, which come and go. Some feed her, while others carry away her eggs or clean her body. The more eggs the queen lays the stronger is the community. When the queen dies the colony dies. She is like the brain of a human, and controls the colony in the same way that the human brain controls the cells and all functions of the body. In fact, to handle her is almost like touching a human brain! But there is a great mystery in that the anthill operates in unity, directed by the queen who is constantly fed by the mysterious nectar that sustains her and her colony—very much like the unseen mysterious activities of the human brain—which is fed by hormones, and manifests the spirit of the life force within our bodies that relates to the Order of the Universe.

Disease and mental illness result from lack of harmony between brain and mind-spirit, in just the same way that disconnection from the Source of All Being manifests in breakdowns in human relationships that occur constantly all around the world.

It is interesting to observe, incidentally, that the insect kingdom was one of the earliest to inhabit the earth as moving beings, some millions of years ago. Further, the algorithm that brought insects into being has not altered, as the later species inhabited the earth. All follow more or less the same structural design, though we may not recognise this at first. Take white ants, for example: the structure of their colony, encased in a hardened mud exterior, parallels that of our human bodies. The Queen is the brain, and the King the heart of the colony. Counterparts of all our internal organs can be discovered within the anthill, as Eugene Marais observed over many years of diligent investigation.

The ants are divided into many different classes, in the same way that we have different cells in our bodies. Some ants industriously move hundreds of tons of earth to ensure that their colony is provided with water. The root of the anthill strikes deep into the earth as its feet. There are chambers within the anthill where food is digested and waste processed before disposal. If the anthill is attacked, hundreds of soldier ants immediately repair the damage to their outer mud wall, just as our white cells repair broken skin. Special ants tend to the Queen ant—the brain of the colony. Should she die the colony dies, even as a human being becomes dysfunctional or dies if the brain is damaged?[14]

I feel that we do not treat our brains with enough decorum, which is perhaps why there are so many homes for the sick and aged. It is only when our brain is attacked by disease that we notice its lack of function. We use our brain for personal gain rather than in an impersonal capacity thus we actually misuse it, frequently creating ideas that do not assist us to live responsibly and sanely. Our brain can generate infinite opportunities for us to open ourselves to a much more powerful and productive way to live, if only we understood the wholeness of all our interdependent functions and the proper use of our thoughts.

It is evident that our brain has enormous capacity, and according to medical science it only operates at a third of its potential, yet when challenged there is no end to its ingenuity. Only when our brain is not recording dysfunc-

[14] The Insectia DVD set, by IMA Vision, is recommended; better still read Eugene Marais' book!

tionally through personal emotional states can it be totally efficient. When an impersonal state is in operation, the brain is more attuned to the wholeness of the spirit, mind and body functions, then the male and female part of ourselves interblend in alchemical union, producing pure ineffable love—the very mystery of the Last Supper. Thus, one could say that the proper function of the brain is to be a free channel for the pure mind to be fulfilled.

Judging by the technological advancement over the last seventy to a hundred years, there is a pressing need to find a balance between our materialistic selves and those immense, interrelated Forces of Energy that bind us all together within Creation. It seems to me that while we remain personal the enormous potential of the brain evades us. I am convinced that whilst we take our body for granted and do not recognise its extraordinary potential; the brain cannot be totally operative. Nevertheless, it is obvious that when we *use the true capacity* of our brains nothing is withheld from us. We have only to be aware of the inventive power of mankind, which has revolutionised our present world, to realise that there are no limits to man's ingenuity when he uses his brain power for the benefit of humanity. Thus I feel there is more opportunity now than ever before to find a balance between the personal and the impersonal.

Today we have everything going for us. The Age of Aquarius offers a mind-boggling opportunity to progress toward a Unity. No longer are we misled so much by outmoded religious authority and conditioning, but rather we move with a spirit of non-personal integrity toward one another. Those who are earnest and sincere can, in their immediate individual way, bring Love and Compassion to their fellow beings. This example helps others to learn to use the power of their minds and brains impersonally for the benefit of all humanity.

As I see it, we all have the potential to 'unfold', as both Jesus and the Buddha did, and as all the ancient masters have done. From far back in antiquity, sages made their way alone, praying and fasting, revealing and loving, meditating and teaching, healing and blessing; but never once did they neglect Love and Compassion as the nucleus of their Teachings, which they drew out from the very Essence within. They all taught the need for humans to learn about themselves. These holy men and women never failed to recognise and speak of the Sacredness of all life, of which humanity is a part. But they can only impart what mankind is able to receive. Now if we can go further, beyond the personal into the impersonal, then we are open to receive a truly Sacred Mystery.

I have begun to understand that all I need to do is to be conscious of the mind-clutter that I have collected around myself and by seeing and being aware of this clutter, it the ending of it. I realise that to follow any sort of training or belief system to become 'better than', or perfect, or transported into some supposed meditative enlightenment tantamount to a personal endeavour. Initially, I was too confused and ignorant to realise that all I needed to achieve radical change was already within my power, being part of my original God given nature. But so bound have I been by false conceptions of religious beliefs and systems of authority that Truth has evaded me. I needed something dynamic to shatter the conditioning that entrenched me: hence my time in the cult. Conditioning has robbed mankind of their self-responsibility to take charge of their own lives and be warriors of power working from their hearts toward Truth. Once 'turned about' it became clear that everything we can think of depends on something else, and that ultimately everything comes from the same Source—the same Oneness—the same Force of Dynamic Energy. And that Oneness is in continual flux—with an inbuilt capacity to adjust.

We have surely lost our way by believing in an outside agency of human contrivance. In the same way we have set ourselves up in the form of a personalised pseudo-self. We have been mesmerised into worshipping deities created in the image of a God, which bears no relationship whatsoever to fact. Yet we believe firmly that we need only pray to such and such a deity and all will be well. How absurd that is!

Chapter Eighteen

Penetrating Self-Awareness of The Now

Regard the Void and it is empty. In emptiness there is no emptiness. In emptiness there is nothing. In the nothingness there is nothing. Since there is nothing in nothingness, there is always stillness. In absolute stillness how can desire arrive? When craving does not arise this is true stillness.

Taken from the book *Cultivating Stillness,* a Taoist manual for transforming body and mind. With a commentary by Shui-ch'ing Tzu. Translated with an introduction by Eva Wong. Published by Shambhala of Boston & London, 1929. Illustrations by un-yen Tzu.

To be fully present in the now, means that it is not possible to 'know' such an experience, nor is it possible to understand why there is 'no knowing' of this experience. It is just that one sees it is so, and in that seeing there is no yesterday, today or tomorrow. It is like seeing one's anger or fear, and then there is the ending of that negative emotion. All division has gone.

One could say it is like seeing with 'sound.' One first listens to music, but strangely enough we do not fully hear the sound. For example, the body unconsciously resists if one does not like the music, so all movement of hearing ceases. When the body is completely relaxed neither accepting nor rejecting: what sound is heard? The mind is empty of its internal dialogue, free to be engaged with the sound. To give you an example of what I mean: I fell down one day recently and felt the shock and the hurts all over my body. I immediately lay on my bed and put on the music that was in my recorder. My body relaxed totally. To my astonishment I felt a tingling in the era of my head where I had knocked it rather badly during the fall. My body continued to relax. Soon the tingling moved to my back, where I had also been hurt. Meanwhile I was seeing that the music was bringing a tingling around my body where I had felt shock. Presently, I must have dozed off, for the next moment it seemed as if I was wide-awake finding myself spontaneously getting off the bed. I had no sensations of shock or hurt anymore.

I had watched a doctor from the medical world, some days previous, experimenting with music and singing to aid an extreme case of human immobility. Slowly the patient responded although he was blind and extremely incapacitated, both mentally and physically. He began to be conscious of the singing from the doctor and the sound of the music—in spite of being blind and incapable mentally and physically of making any sense of his body—yet there was a responsive movement from the patient. It was marvellous to see him aware of the sound of the music and singing—albeit only somewhat vaguely.

My continual search into self-awareness over the years has furnished me with penetrating insights both into others and myself. I learned that:

- Whilst I remain ignorant of myself I am unaware not only of being irresponsible, but of the way my irresponsibility reflects back onto society, helping to make it what it is today.
- It is only through self-knowledge and self-awareness that I can perceive how my personal behaviour blocks me from learning about who I am and my God Given purpose here on this marvellous earth.
- I realise that opportunities are always at hand every moment of the day to help me observe myself.

- Adversities, I found are the best way in which to learn about ourselves and once embraced as such, they cease to be adversities.
- I learnt that my real security lies in innate instinctive awareness.
- I found that relationship with others provide an excellent way of seeing ourselves as we really are; it gives us the best opportunity of learning through another, through reflection, what we are like, particularly if we are honest.
- The self-images formed from childhood onwards—shapes the background behaviour that remains with us for the rest of our lives—unless we discard it through self-knowledge.
- When I identify myself with what others say or do—I am a follower—and thereby miss the opportunity of developing my inner potentials.
- My conflicts and traumas can never be resolved from the images that I build of others or myself.
- Experience comes from my own behaviour and no one else's, and when I blame others, I blame myself and I keep repeating my experiences.
- I can never know myself completely or the way that I behave, when I hold beliefs.
- It is only in learning about myself that I learnt to behave impersonally.
- Nothing is permanent, neither the world in which we live nor our self-imposed dreamlike imaginations, but life is very precious.
- Our way ahead is a lone 'pathless path'; but through courage and perseverance we can face the 'what is' in our daily life without imposing conflict on others.
- I learnt that no one can help you but yourself, and that Truth is only found in your own heart.

- The most important thing of all is to recognise that your background behaviour forms patterns that we are unaware of, hence the importance of learning self-knowledge and self-awareness.
- We remain ignorant of our problems while we follow another.
- Above all we need to recognise and acknowledge the Supreme Energy of the All- pervading Absolute Power of the Unseen Energy and of the Forces of the Absolute. Then we can realise who we are and our purpose here on earth.

None of these realisations were easy to come by, but I knew that they would be of little use as only words, the importance was to incorporate them in my daily life, and as no one could do this for me, it seemed to me imperative that I became aware of this fact. But first I needed to realise that I was unaware of myself—that was the way that I began. Secondly, I persevered by making changes to my wilderness, perceiving that it was only in my relationships that I could learn from others about my emotional and psychological behaviours. In fact, I am sure the root cause of most of my trouble was unawareness of the way I expressed my emotions through my ignorance. I think it is a mistake to believe that we can achieve self-awareness without a lot of hard work on ourselves. But I do believe that by keeping constantly vigilant it is possible to find the self-awareness so necessary for radically changing our way of life. Most importantly there needs to be attention to our observations and realise that our thoughts are dangerous unless we become familiar with the way in which they operate.

We are taught to rely on doctors, therapists, psychologists and para-psychologists to preserve our health, and rely on religion of every kind for our spiritual well being.

So to hard work on ourselves is seldom appreciated as a necessary part of our development, thus we offload our troubles on other people's shoulders. Mostly we tend to view life from an intellectual standpoint, but intellectuality does not take us to the root of our problems, it barely brushes the surface. Only through a greater self-awareness can we learn self-responsibility for our own health and wellbeing. It is a pity that self-knowledge and self-awareness are seldom seen to be a necessary part of education. Sadly, such a lack is, I am sure, the basic cause of many of the problems we face in the world today, particularly at present with our young.

Indeed, personalised thinking often blocks intelligent perception of our inherent birthright. Perhaps that is why so many of us feel a continual undercurrent of dissatisfaction unconsciously intruding on our lives, causing us to be restless, so that all too often we are drawn into situations we would much rather not be in. Perhaps that is why these feelings of dissatisfaction sometimes seem to resemble a 'prick of conscience'; while at other times they act as an irritant waiting to be acknowledged. Nevertheless, I was happier to accept my feelings of dissatisfaction when I likened them to the irritant that causes an oyster to produce a pearl! I shall always be grateful for the years that I spent listening to Krishnamurti's talks at Brockwood Park and elsewhere in the world, since they had a profound effect on my life, easing my dissatisfaction considerably by an increased awareness.

Also, I found that I had a special place in my heart for Ringu Tulku Rinpoche, a Tibetan Buddhist who had a wealth of understanding of what human beings really need to transform their lives. His fluent English enables him to convey to the Western World the deep inner teachings of Tibetan Buddhism of the East. I found that Ringu

Tulku imparted a 'giving' such, as all true masters are able to do. It is not a giving of himself, but the giving of the Truth that shines through his face as he shares with us what it is to discover the essence of the Enlightened Mind. He points out through his teachings that this Essence of the Enlightened Mind resides within each one of us and has always been there waiting for us to uncover it when we know what it is to be 'empty' of the wilderness of the conceptual mind.

Through Ringu Tulku I also listened several times to talks given by His Holiness the Dalia Lama and found that his understanding and humility enabled me to feel that in spite of the Chinese invasion of his country, he was not afraid to face life and meet the 'what is' as it came in front of him. He will always be there for his people albeit in exile. And in a strange way too, I could not help but feel that the rest of the world has greatly benefited from his enforced exile. He would not have been able to share his understanding of Tibetan Buddhism with so many people from different parts of the world, had he remained in Tibet. Nor would the world have benefited from so many Tibetan Teachers or been able to gain the advantage of Tibetan medicine. Samye Ling, in Scotland was the first Tibetan Monastery to be erected outside Tibet, a huge complex that is now nearly complete and I am sure that there will be many more around the world.

It is very difficult sometimes to understand the ways the Almighty works, especially when we are suffering, but I strongly feel now is the time for humanity to realise the pressing need for Unity. The world has arrived at a very critical period in its history, in more ways than one, whereby we all stand to loose the benefits of our precious earth. Now there is a greater need than ever before to recognise that personal states deplete the Dynamic Energy that is ours to share, so it is urgent to be open to an impersonal understanding of ourselves. It does not take many of us, who are ready, to start putting this into action in our daily lives with an earnest heart to work together for Peace and Goodwill toward each other. We need to start a revolution within ourselves by putting into action an example of all that we do and say. So together let us unite in an endeavour to bring an end to war and strife, so that we can build a foundation of trust and unity amongst us all, no matter who we are or what we may have done. But we can only do this through a sincere impersonal Love and Compassion toward all men, including ourselves. It is only our *ignorance* that leads us into the *blindness* of our own conflicting actions, so we have 'to start very near to go very far' as Krishnamurti often says. Remember that one word of disharmony from our lips sends waves of unrest to the rest of the world—but one word of harmony from our lips brings peace to all, even if we cannot perceive it.

The interdependency of all things
In our busy materialistic world we rarely ponder the interdependency of all things around us. Certainly we seldom consider nature or the extraordinary interrelationship within a colony of white ants, for example. Even less, do we consider the interdependency within ourselves, or the unity between the organs of our bodies? Yet we could not live without this interdependency, nor could the rest of the Universe exist.

The inference is that all is derived from the same Source. I love the thought that we humans, the planets, even the furthest star are all constituted from the same stardust, and that everything we know of belong to, and is connected with, everything else.

As I observe the world about me, I marvel that we live in only a three-dimensional cocoon, unable to comprehend the awesome enormity of these immense Forces of The God Given Energy around and about us. For instance, we have little conception of the principle of resonance that continually operates within cosmic law—not just in music—but also in art, architecture, or the mathematically ordered whorls and spirals in nature—of which the ancient philosophers such as Plato were well aware.

However, I feel our individual task is surely to discover how to attune ourselves with this immense Order of inter-dependency by establishing harmony within our own immediate environment and with the rest of humanity. This we can do by allowing the 'what is' to be as it is, instead of resisting events encountered day by day, which surely manifest as a part of the interdependency of all things, if only we could see it.

On considering the Truth of Reality within and about us, it became clear to me that there is no path to Truth. No one can find Truth; it finds us. Truth is in our hearts and our sincerity and hard work is all it takes to open the door.

How could it be up to us for example to change any-thing, when we cannot change ourselves? In any case, we can have no real comprehension of what lies beyond this earth and the mystery entrained. No one can help us find Truth. Truth is too immense, too numinous to comprehend until we are ready to receive it. As Krishnamurti says:

Please let us be clear on this point, that you cannot by any process, through any disciplines, through any form of meditation, go to truth, God, or whatever name you like to give it. It is much too vast, it cannot possibly be conceived of, no description will cover it; no book can hold it nor through any guru go to it. You must await, it will come to you, and you cannot go to it. This is the first fundamental thing one has to understand, that not through any trick of the mind, not through any control, through any virtue, any compulsion, any form of suppression, can the mind possibly go to truth. All that the mind can do is to be quiet—but not with the intention of receiving it. And that is one of the most difficult things of all because we think that truth can be experienced right away through doing certain things. Truth is not to be bought any more than Love can be bought.[15]

Again consider the mother, seeing her child caught under the wheel of a car, instantly capable of lifting the vehicle to release her child—something she could never have done normally, but this was a truth. Her action showed that she forgot herself entirely, so that in a split second she was blended with the interdependency of The All, in total communion with the Great Unseen God Given Energy Force, which is always active when we forget ourselves, especially in the service of another. Was it her spontaneity that was so significant?

We demonstrate the opposite of attunement with the Power of the Universe when we use our own limited energy to the detriment of others. Consider the school bully, reported in the local news, who intimidated children to join his gang. Using his superior physical strength to hold power over other schoolmates, he caused untold misery. Once a child joined the gang he was forced to conform to the rules. When he did not, he too would be bullied. One child was so frightened that he committed suicide. So it seems that we are part of this Power, and when we use it

[15] J. Krishnamurti extract from *The Collected Work*, volume DK page 20

for our own ends we are dissipating it into a limited personal energy—to the detriment both of ourselves and of others.

Consider our planet's continual interdependency with the sun. I am enthralled by the unusual appearance of sunbeams behind black clouds. It is breathtaking to see that Life on this planet depends on those awesome rays of energy constantly streaming from our sun. We also take for granted the Moon's energies; my grandfather, like many a farmer of his day, always planted and harvested his crops according to the phases of the moon, for he recognised the dependency between organic growth and lunar energy. When we come to think about it, it is just as incredible to think that our tides also depend on the gravitational pulls of the sun and moon.

Is there a pathway to Enlightenment?

Now that I am continually aware of my background behaviour that influenced my life, I see the world and humanity very differently and wonder if there is a pathway to enlightenment. I perceive humanity to be like an immense shoal of fish, or a flock of birds, directed and driven by a far greater Force of Light than we can possibly conceive or imagine from our limited three-dimensional viewpoint.

So to me, each of us has a very definite purpose in life as part of this Living Universe—as indeed does the very Life Force Itself that emanates through us. Then, I asked myself, do we need other people to be our mentors or show us the way to enlightenment? Yes, we need others to help us focus on our inner potentials so that we can awaken. But let's face it: transforming ourselves will go a long way toward helping us do just that—especially if we acknowledge our limitations, by realising that we know nothing; nothing in the sense of opening ourselves up to the unknown

God Given Forces within us. For example, to rely on an outside guru or teacher tantamounts to handing control of ourselves over to someone else, as I did in the cult. I now feel inside me that we have each been born with all the potential to challenge the *status quo*. Most importantly, the Supreme Energy Force has always been there within and around us, waiting to be acknowledged.

I discovered this when I was aware of the self-opinionated thoughts that arose from my background behaviour and their associated personalised thinking. This inevitably inhibited me from being my natural inborn self. As I let go of some of these misconceptions, I caught a glimpse of a different world no longer encased only in matter. I perceived that I was connected in some way with the interdependence within myself, urging me to awaken to my potentials.

As I probed, I sensed that all that we require to assist us to awaken to our potentials is to work hard on ourselves, watching what we do to others and aware of the need to share. Such a realisation is consistent with both Buddha's and Jesus' teachings of an awakened approach to the interdependency of All Life. They both deeply understood our purpose here on earth. Perhaps it is only the misguided interpretations of a pseudo-religious nature that has obscured the deeper truths from us. It was both natural and practical for them to pass on to all humanity what they had discovered and learned as unshakeable Truth.

In his book[16], Hugh McGregor Ross presents his painstaking studies over a period of twenty years of the teachings of Jesus in *The Gospel of Thomas*, found amongst the Dead Sea Scrolls in 1945. McGregor Ross took the text from *The Nag Hammadi Library*, published in English in

---

[16] *Jesus, Untouched by the Church: His teachings in the Gospel of Thomas.*

1978. *The Gospel of Thomas* was the only Scroll to be made available before Roman Catholic Priests took charge of them to translate them from the Coptic Text. This particular document used by McGregor Ross escaped their close scrutiny and was known as *The Acts of Thomas*, *The Hymn of the Pearl*, and *The Book of Thomas*. It is considered that it was written during the period 150 to 350 A.D and almost certainly in Syriac.

Mistranslations passed by unnoticed; one of which I feel has tremendous significance. McGegor Ross points out that the original Syriac word meaning 'live', 'life' and 'life-giver' was translated in the Greek version by '*sozo*', whose meaning relates to 'save', 'salvation' and 'saviour'. The original Syriac translator referred to Jesus as 'the Life Giver in the here and now'; The truth being so different from the saviour and only Son of God worshipped by Western Christianity.

Thus we see that just one word can be mistranslated to give two completely different meanings. In fact, I am sure that this one mistranslated Greek word 'sozo' has put a totally different complexion both on Jesus the man, and his teachings.[17]

The New Testament of Western Christianity came into being as an orthodoxy under the auspices of the Roman Catholic Church, very different from that of Eastern Christianity, which leans more towards Taoism and Buddhism. Incidentally, Martin Palmer expresses this so well in his book *The Jesus Sutra, rediscovering the lost religion of Taoist Christianity.*

What I found particularly interesting was a whole new vista of facts about Christianity. Martin Palmer found the

---

[17] Taken from the book *The Nag Hammadi Library,* copyright 1978, 1988 by E.J. Brill, Leidon, The Netherlands, from the Coptic text published by HarperCollins Publishers, New York, paperback 1990.

Jesus sutras in the *Da Qin Pagoda*, which dates back to the seventh century A.D. Here, near to the Pagoda, and in this remote part of northwestern China are the ruins of an early Christian monastery, known locally to have been associated with Jesus and his teachings. The scrolls of the Jesus sutra refer to these teachings as 'the religion of Light'. After reading this most intriguing and enlightening book, I could not help but feel that Eastern Christianity portrayed a far more authentic understanding of the teachings of Jesus—so astonishingly dissimilar to that of Western Christianity.

The true wisdom that this holy man Jesus imparted can only be accurately perceived, I feel, through the guidance of the inner Truth, within us all. When we cannot accept our conditioning, then we are held in thrall by the misinterpretation of Western Christianity. No wonder, in this new Age of Aquarius, more and more thinking people are questioning the authenticity of the Western Christian religion.

The life of holy men such as Jesus and the Buddha demonstrates the total commitment required of each to give forth what they knew as Truth. They walked alone, as Givers of Life, guided by the signposts that other holy men had erected before them. So what we extrapolate by the process of rational interpretation can only be a catalyst to facilitate access to the real meaning of Jesus' teachings. This, to me, is achieving enlightenment.

As the above example suggests, adopting and accepting as Truth from others' interpretations of the teachings imparted by these holy men, has perpetuated misconceptions about their teachings, which originally required human beings to be committed to find their own *light* within. The only Truth that can be of any real significance is that which we learn as we try, test and live it out in our own daily lives, as the holy men taught us to do: and particularly by being continually conscious that the Truth we receive cannot adequately be expressed in words. This is why Jesus and other Masters used parables.

We remember the Old Testament account of 'manna' miraculously supplied to the Israelites in their journey through the wilderness of themselves: they were instructed to eat it only today and not thereafter. All we human beings need is to find self-awareness, so that we are ready for the Truth that will come to awaken us as we tread our individual paths through the wilderness of ourselves, so that our Light may be kindled and shine forth. Our station in life—whether that of king or beggar—matters not one iota. What matters most is our ability to live the Truth that we perceive within ourselves during our particular life, and to go where it leads as we awaken to our interdependency with the Source of All Life. Then we become a living testimony to Truth.

I learned that our worldly situation, our job, is not what really matters. It is the way that we conduct ourselves as we go about our work that is of the utmost significance in the scheme of things—being led by our mentor within. And in following the 'pathless path' through our wildernesses we find that everything changes. Changes came about for me that I would never have thought possible. Above all, I have discovered a Love within my heart that nothing and no one can shake or destroy.

Through new eyes, what I once saw as a rose no longer seems the same; though actually it is no different from the flower it has always been. Now my changed vision sees it as a rose in all its glory. It is my attitudes, my intentions, my joy in living that make the rose seem so different. What blooms before my eyes is my new perception of the rose, the 'what is'—the manifestation immediately before me; or to put it another way, that which comes next in the course of the 'what is.'

To see the reality of my 'self' in action requires much courage, and the courage that I continually discovered was very needful as I journeyed ever onwards. I am sure that it is like this for most of us. Sometimes I am still caught in difficult situations and conditions that need fortitude, but we all have our crosses to bear and no one can be really sure which way that they will deal with their cross until it is right in front of them.

I feel it is unfortunate that instead of standing on our own two feet, we turn to consultants. Psychologists try to explain how we tick: then we lean on them. We have to remember that some of these therapists may be unaware—as most of us are—of the limiting influence of their own background behaviour, to the exclusion of all else.

Interestingly enough, elitism of any kind is corruptive, divisive and detrimental to the harmony and well being of any society, as the exclusivity of numerous religious bodies clearly demonstrates. By definition, the word 'exclusive' immediately characterises separation between others and ourselves—as, for example, between the modern world and the so-called Third World. The parable of the Good Samaritan illustrates the point. In fact, I feel that exclusivity is so highly ingrained in society, that we can almost say it is a prime cause of constant war, criminality, disease, and so much corruption. I think we must realise that exclusivity, at any level, leads to separation and isolation, constituting a main barrier to world harmony. In this knowledge, I suppose at best, we can all be listening posts lending each other much-needed support, empathy, and love.

To learn about myself I had to be unafraid to expose my 'self' to myself and to others. Then I found it possible to accept 'what I am' and walk alone with that understanding.

Once able to access the door of my inner being, I could see how I really ticked. Such understanding is for me an ongoing journey through the wilderness of the 'self'. Then it is no one but myself—I—who am holding the key that opens the door to my inner mentor or God within, and no one else can do it for me. That is why Jesus was the 'Giver of Light in the here and now', and why his life's actions on earth are a catalyst that perpetuated a fired-energy, enabling mankind to avoid self-destruction.

Jesus said:
I have cast fire upon the world
and behold, I guard it
until it is ablaze.[18]

In the shamanic tradition, Fire is synonymous with Truth, representing a refining rebirth. In shattering past delusions, Truth—itself indestructible and incontrovertible—regenerates. Sometimes we use attention-seeking techniques to invoke power over others, consciously or unconsciously—for example, in the way the cult's Principal exercised power over me. Such behaviour is universally rife, in governments, institutions and religious organisations, as well as within personal relationships. Always these methods are derived from conditioned background behaviours. When we realise what is happening, we cannot be affected by such power play.

Once we discover the power of our conditioned background behaviour to restrict, we are ready to move away from these personal restrictions, and begin to act as an integral part of the Whole manifestation of the Divine Absolute. It was through responding to my endeavours that I

---

[18] Taken from *Jesus, Untouched by the Church: His teachings in the Gospel of Thomas* by Hugh McGregor Ross.

felt able to stand on my own two feet and open up to the power of the God within. A joyful awakening to the reality of meeting the 'what is'—whenever it appeared. Especially when I could sense the Oneness of humanity and everything else in the Universe.

I found that my 'wilderness' required a great deal of careful and patient attention, and serious watchfulness—in which there is no 'self' doing the watching; and then a sincere earnestness and honesty of purpose comes into being. It is my experience that it is attention, and attention alone, that allows us to turn inwardly to where the Spirit Essence of God is, that is there to guide us, which I believe to be the only real guidance. Jesus called it our Heaven within.

It is a very different kind of conformity to that which we learn as a vulnerable child of six or seven, but indeed no different from that with which we were clothed when we came to earth as an innocent babe—before we became enmeshed by conditioning. Our real background behaviour—that of the innocent babe—is indeed the only one that is of any value to us. Perhaps it is to this understanding that our dissatisfaction has for so long been trying to awaken us. In our growing years we have become smothered, by our parents, our education, our livelihood, our indoctrination, our conditioning, our religion and our society. This has happened to us all, in one form or another, so we have all the same opportunity of amending our lives to face 'what is' together in a new way of living our lives without conflict as an example for the next generation.

Can life be as a Childlike Joyousness?

All who have trodden the way of self-knowledge have found that the resultant self-awareness does not remove us from daily living with all its natural beauty; indeed, we discover—as I have—that it is exactly the reverse. A new understanding awakens within—self-awareness opens up a whole new world—we see the world through the eyes of a little child, knowing and trusting. Life is very precious. We learn that each moment counts. As we devote our lives to responding to the 'what is' without question or resistance, we acknowledge nature in a totally different fashion, having respect and love for all things and all creatures. My own experience confirms that self-awareness breaks open the cage in which we have imprisoned ourselves, liberating us from the restrictions so long imposed.

As soon as I began to shed my mistaken beliefs and ego-driven misconceptions, I started to understand the teachings of the ancient Hindu sages and other Holy men who trod the earth so long ago. They described their growing awareness like an onion in which they peeled away layer after layer until nothing was left.

Each little step enabled me to let go of the ego-driven, self-centred states that persuaded me to believe I was a separate entity—unlike anyone else—when in reality humanity is all ONE, as indeed is all of Creation. Hence I discarded numerous layers of ignorance, conditioning and self-centred states that I had accumulated. Paradoxically I still appear as an individual—but with a difference—I no longer aspire to act as such.

I feel strongly that gaining true self-awareness is a daily learning process that has nothing to do with academic study or accumulating or grasping information to hoard in our memory. Self-awareness allows everyone to be brought together, to be part of one united human family; for we all need each other. None of us is in a position to judge another, whatever that individual may have done. We do not have that 'exclusive' right.

Self-awareness enables us to experience the truth behind the beauty, joy, and love that is ours to share as we live our lives in the NOW of Truth. The alternative is to hold on to intellectual knowledge, vices, sufferings, pain, cruelties, injustices, hatreds, fears, hurts, jealousies, ambitions, crimes, wars, self-wants and attachments and exclusivity of every kind, all of which have come out of Pandora's Box.

It was only in being truly vulnerable—like a little flower—that I had any perception of what real humility meant. The delicate little flower braves insects, animals, people, storms, and endless changes in the weather. After the storm this same little flower is seen to welcome another day. Surely, I said to myself, I can follow such a simple example and walk tall and steady on my own ground, unafraid to walk alone—unafraid to live to the best of my ability by the Spirit of God within instead of living in spiritual poverty, alienated from Divinity. James Rhoades expressed it so well in his beautiful little verse:

Again that Voice, that on my listening ears
Falls like star music filtering through the spheres
Know this, O man, sole root of sin in thee
Is not to know thine own Divinity!

Are we aware of our Nothingness and Emptiness?
It is understanding who is 'the controller' that I found to be so essential when I examined what it meant to be empty, and thus aware of my nothingness. I noticed that the notion of 'self' or 'me' interferes with our natural flowering. This seemed to indicate that the controller originated from the self-images I had formed, so that at times I was overtaken by unpleasant negative emotional influences that arose from believing these self-pictures to be real. It

was as though these images drew me into experiences, and dragged me into unreal situations, so that I had no idea of what was really happening until too late. I had to admit that my endeavours to cope with ensuing predicaments arose from self-images. I was compelled to ask: 'Who is the controller of my life?'

I found an interesting passage by Krishnamurti, which answered my query:

Is it possible to live without control? Because what is control? And who is the controller? The controller is the controlled. When I say I must control my thoughts, the controller is the creation of the thought. It has no meaning. One fragment controls another fragment, and they therefore remain fragments. So I say is there a way of living without control? That is without conflict or opposites? Nor one desire against another desire, one thought opposed to another thought, one achievement opposed to another achievement? So, no control? Is that possible? Because I must find out. You follow, sir? It's not just asking a question, then leaving it alone. I've got energy now because I am not carrying their burden anymore. Nor am I carrying my own burden, because their burden is my burden. When I have discarded that I have discarded this. So I have got energy when I say: 'Is it possible to live without control'? And it is a tremendous thing, I must find out. Because the people who have control, have said through control you arrive at Nirvana, heaven—to me that's wrong totally absurd. So I say, 'Can I live a life of meditation in which there is no control?'[19]

---

[19] Krishnamurti in dialogue with Professor Alan Anderson, taken from *A wholly Different Way of Living* published by Victor Gollancz Ltd, 1991.

Even so, these false self-images—controllers, I supposed, that I had erroneously believed to be real—turned out to be mere projections of who I believed myself to be. Nevertheless, they were instrumental in bringing to the fore both my ignorance and susceptibility to a conditioned way of life. Above all, I was aware that I needed a constant reminder—a pointer—to guide me away from my memories and misconceptions. The Zen Buddhist Masters describe it thus in their teachings:

...as a finger pointing at the moon. The finger is not the moon and the teachings are not the Truth—they only point to it. Just as you can point at the one moon from many different places, so the Zen masters each point from their own unique perspective.

I asked myself what prevented me from being open and ready to receive the help of these masters. Was I blinded by ignorance? Had I immured myself for so long that I had forgotten I was inhibited from receiving? In the end I was forced to acknowledge that I was not ready to receive their guidance. This shocked me, as I thought I knew. Was it my limited understanding of myself that held me in the stream of humanity's influences? I was swept along, unable to see what was happening, until I realised I was conditioned by religious creeds and dogmas. I failed to see that my ignorance was deceiving me.

The cult, I remember, was such an authoritarian religious environment that I found it impossible to be aware of my motives, intentions and self-opinionated beliefs. So I went about with a 'holier-than-thou' demeanour unconsciously acquired from the Principal and the rest of the group. I remember so well, after one of the Sunday services open to visitors each week, one of those visitors saying to me: 'You know, you all look like Christian monks and nuns!' I remember feeling smugly content with this idea at the time. Now I can see how blinded I had been by my own self-righteousness.

Slowly, I realised that two kinds of conditioning, one negative and the other positive, bring a background of conflict into our early life. Consequently we are blinded to the effects of our conditioning, so that we are unable to see ourselves as we really are. Or is it that we have never been taught the real significance of the Divinity within? Or are we waiting for someone to tell us what to do? Or are we hoping to awaken from our dreamlike predicament in order to follow someone else?

When I realised that most human beings respond in much the same way to their emotions of fear, hurt, jealousy, anger, sorrow, hatred, ambition, pride, and a host of other psychological-emotional disturbances, it occurred to me that we might liken ourselves to constantly rotating kaleidoscopes. The only difference is that our kaleidoscopes never rotate in synchrony. In our ignorance, we don't see that our sixth sense—intuition and premonition—the only thing that could enlighten us—has been smothered by religious indoctrination.

Watching my neighbour's kaleidoscope, very conscious of my own behaviour, I realised unexpectedly and in a flash that I demonstrated the same patterns of behaviour as those I had observed in my neighbour's kaleidoscope. Being honest, I could see myself reflected as in a mirror, and watching closely, I caught myself deceiving myself again and again. It was by being more aware of my own behaviour that I grew more tolerant towards that of my neighbour.

By observing others and ourselves dispassionately and unreservedly, we gain a clearer picture of what it means to be part of the human family. Yet nothing in our relationships or interactions is permanent. No sooner has a thought entered our head than it has gone, and another arises. 'No sooner hath a day dawned than the evening cometh'. But I think what is most important is that when we do not recognise the Power of Divinity within ourselves, we cannot awaken to the real meaning of self-awareness and enlightenment. Indeed, when we do not realise the need for self-knowledge we are in poverty, and we are that poverty, as Jesus said.

I think the following profound words[20] spoken to Andrew Harvey by Thuksey Rinpoche of Ladakh, India, are a thought-provoking way to bring my autobiography to a near close.

Thuksey Rinpoche smiled as he said: "As long as there is Samsara, there will be an evasion of the inner perfection that is man's essence. This is perhaps the saddest of all the tragedies of Samsara, and the most painful. A man is starving in one dark room, while in another just across the corridor from him there is enough food for many lives, for eternity. But he has to walk to that room, and before he can walk to it, he has to believe that it is there. No one else can believe for him. No one can even bring the food from that room to him. Even if they could, he would not believe in the food or be able to eat it. The Dhammapada says, 'Buddha's neither wash away sins with water nor remove the suffering of beings with their hands. They do not transfer their realisation to others. Beings are freed through the teaching of truth, of the nature of things.' But to be taught, they have to want to listen, and to learn they have to have the humility to want to change.

[20] *A Journey in Ladakh*, by Andrew Harvey, published by Houghton Mifflin Company, Boston, USA 1983.

No one can make them listen or want to change. We are
free to become Bodhisatvas or consign ourselves to life
after life in pain. Often when men say they are helpless,
trapped, imperfect, they are really saying, 'I do not want
to endure my own perfection, I do not want to bear my
own reality.' Imperfection is more comforting, more human
than perfection. Many men want to believe that man is
imperfect because it makes it easier to live with their own
imperfections, more forgiving toward themselves. And
who can blame them? To understand that even despair at
oneself can be a deception, perhaps the most dangerous;
and to discover an inner power, that is completely good
and gentle, is frightening; it robs us of every comfort,
every safety in resignation or irony. Who can live naked
to his own perfection? And yet who, once seeing and
acknowledging his own perfection, could bear to try to
realise it in living? To see it is hard; to realise it within
life is the hardest thing. Somewhere men know that, and
that is why they cover up their knowledge. They prefer the
nightmare of Samsara, which they know, to the Awakening,
which they do not. And in a sense they are right. Once they
have acknowledged Reality, they will have to learn how to
die into it; they will have nowhere to hide any more, no
corner of the world in which to feel safe any longer. They
will have to "abide nowhere and alight on nothing."

And I would like to conclude with a communication from
Krishnamurti, who for me expresses much the same as
Thuksey Rinpoche only in different words what it means
for us to be *present—attentively alive*—to any experience
we meet in life. Being present is to recognise the God
within—the initiator of all Life. Then true communication
with others and ourselves is possible. For when we are not
'present'—attentively alive—we are not experiencing ex-

actly 'what is'—we are only living in the known side of things as we have always imaged them to be. Thus it is essential to die to the known—to all remembrances of Samsara as Thuksey Rinpoche said. Then we are fully present to die into the reality of the God within and nothing else. It is only in this attention that we are able to understand ourselves, as Krishnamurti points out:

And so it is important to understand oneself, is it not? Self-knowledge is the beginning of wisdom. Self-knowledge is not according to some psychologist's book or philosopher, but to know oneself as one is from moment to moment. To know oneself is to observe what one thinks, how one feels, not just superficially, but to be deeply aware of **what is**, *without condemnation, without judgment, without evaluation or comparison. Unless this takes place, not only at the superficial level, but right through the whole content of consciousness, there can be no delving into the profundity of the mind. Please if you are really here to understand what is being said* **it is THIS that we are concerned with and NOTHING ELSE**. *The mind is conditioned right through, there is no part of the mind which is not conditioned, and our problem is, can such a mind free itself?*

Through being conscious of what it means to self-discover I learnt that I had no alternative but to go forward, there was no turning back. I realised this fact from nature. One winter's day I was watching very attentively my big tree at the end of my garden when suddenly, I realised that the tree could not go backward it had to go forward according to nature's laws. It had no alternative but to meet the new cycle of growth that was forthcoming in the spring. And so it is with human beings, we too have our own cycles.

But it is only when we respond from our true nature that we find ourselves really focused—for is it not the essential nature of God underlying all phenomena that is always truly focused? Thus by responding to our True God Given Nature we are indeed in harmony with the Universal Laws. By obeying these very Laws that we are all interrelated to, and interdependent with, brings us dispassionately into focus with the 'what is' directly in front of us, whatever that may be, giving us all an opportunity to awaken to the love and compassion that dwells within in our hearts, and is the means of opening the door to freedom.

Nonetheless, I feel that this freedom can only be ours when we understand the following significant words proclaimed by Krishnamurti during the course of a conversation with regard to the fact that so many people have been wrongly conditioned to believe that there are several paths to truth.

There is no path to truth. Truth must be discovered, but there is no formula for its discovery. What is formulated is not true. You must set out on the uncharted sea and the uncharted sea is yourself. You must set out to discover yourself, but not according to any plan or pattern, for then there is no discovery.

Epilogue

It is interesting to pause a moment and consider what it means to be you—the entity occupying your skin, so to speak—not what you *think* that entity is. If we consider the quantum theory as reviewed by Fritjof Copra in his book *The Tao of Physics*, we recognise the field of Energy that holds everything together and makes human existence possible. This Immeasurable Force is untouchable, inaccessible, unseeable: quite unbelievably near—yet in its changing capacity so far away from our comprehension that we are oblivious to its Power. 'Not only is it the underlying essence of all material objects, but it also carries their interactions.' This is what the ancient Chinese Tao Masters called Tao—*The Nameless*. They referred to It as *Ch'i*. Japanese Masters of Martial Arts spoke of It as *Ki*.

As I observed myself with others, I noticed that this quantum energy force *Chi* became neutralised—unusable—when conflict arose. The untouchable positive energy force around and within was not available, because conflict made it a negative force: the self-inflicted, destructive energy that brings diseases, wars, destruction, horror and turmoil.

In nature we see order, where the quantum field of energy is active, interblending with everything in the Universe. It is only human conflict that, by interfering with this energy force, immediately invokes reaction in accordance with Laws that are both universal and eternal. The state of the world today reveals these laws in operation—upheavals, earth disturbances—conflicts of all kinds, crimes, disruptions, unruly behaviour in our young, etc, etc. So we can see the importance of self-knowledge.

The main thing that I found so intriguing was that my inner dissatisfaction had prompted me to take the course that I did. This brought me opportunities that would never otherwise have been possible. It is the extreme situations in which we find ourselves that can encourage both enlightenment and self-effacement, as the following account illustrates.

Parallels between living in a cult and living with Eskimos

It was after I had read *Kabloona* by Vicomte Gontran de Poncins that I saw a clear parallel between my own extreme circumstances in the cult and Poncins' voluntary experience with the Eskimos, each of us exploring our different hardships in unusual and confined living conditions. Clearly we were both searching for a deeper meaning to life. Certainly the experience gave me a different perspective on life.

Both of us had to make drastic changes in order to adapt to living in an environment totally different to anything experienced before or since. *Kabloona* is a true account of the psychological and physical experiences of living with a group of Eskimos. It strongly connects with my own true experience in the cult. We both learned that even the most sophisticated of us have predispositions that are hard to change. It was an extremely shattering time for me when I actually found myself in a cult living under incredibly harsh and unusual conditions, and at the same time being forced to accept the disciplined leadership of a fanatical teacher who ran her cult in a way totally alien to anything I had ever imagined possible. Equally, Poncins had to accept the extraordinary rigours of the bitter and unrelenting environment in which the Eskimos lived. We both had to let go of our connections to our family and everyone that we had previously known, in order to cope with the new and often 'challenging' environment.

Thus our experiences demanded deep fundamental changes in the way we looked and thought about human life. We both had to make a *volte-face* in order to survive. Perhaps the only real difference was that Poncins' experience was voluntarily planned to last a year whereas mine was definitely neither voluntary nor planned, but lasted nearly eight years.

Neither of us have regretted our experiences, indeed we learned a tremendous amount about ourselves, and in particular about those with whom we were associated and with whom we shared experiences. We both lived under exceptional pressures, neither of our experiences being comparable with those of ordinary lives in the 21st century.

Poncins learned from the Eskimos a totally different culture. He declared:

It was because of the simplicity and directness of the Eskimos' existence that I went into the Arctic to live with them; and living with them was not easy. Hardest of all was not the severity of the climate. The cold was a problem but a much more difficult problem was the Eskimos' mentality. A good part of this book, therefore, becomes of itself the story of the encounter of two mentalities, and of the gradual substitution of the Eskimos' mentality for the European mentality within myself.

The hardest part I had to face in the cult was separation from my family; yet in spite of my changed circumstances I was forced to subdue my mentality in favour of the mentality of the Principal and her group. My story, therefore, led me to discover what it meant to perceive the difference between being personal and impersonal, something that now plays such an important part in my life.

Poncins realised that Eskimos live in a shared world and he found them to be the happiest people he had ever met—although they were very primitive by our standards—maybe even Stone Age; but they understood what it meant to live harmoniously within their environment and to be fully self-responsible. They had a balanced intent toward their fellow Eskimos, all creatures and nature, through living in an orderly way within their Northern Arctic environment. Living in a tight-knit religious cult, I learned a totally different way of life based on rigid discipline, which eventually showed me that in the cult order took second place to obedience. Nonetheless, I began to understand very quickly that resistance of any kind whatsoever produced immediate conflict within my own mind, which made it hard for me to work in harmony with others. Yet I did not understand the significance of what was really happening to me or to what extent life in the cult was radically changing my outlook—indeed, not until long after I had left the cult.

Poncins observed that Eskimos never hurried, as we do in the West, yet their developed sixth sense guided and forewarned them of happenings long before they occurred. For example, one day when he was out fishing with his Eskimo friend, all of a sudden his friend started packing up to go home. Poncins could not understand such a move, as the sky above was intensely blue and the sea was calm as a millpond. However, they only just managed to reach the shore before a terrific electric storm spread over the whole area.

In the cult I learned that although I had partly developed my sixth sense very early in life, pride was interfering with any further development, as it became particularly evident when the Principal was castigating me.

Poncins also discovered that Eskimos learned the value of doing nothing in moments when it appeared to him immediate action was required. For example, when they had to leave one area for another, Poncins found that the Eskimos' closeness to nature gave them an instinctive awareness of when weather conditions were safe for moving. Again, through my experiences in the cult, I learned that by remaining still within myself, I could face the panic that the Principals' reprimand stirred within me when she disciplined me in front of the rest of the group. This inner stillness enabled me to approach such situations with less fear. In consequence my new life took on a less materialistic outlook; for example, clothes no longer held the importance that they once had when I was at home. Fashion was no longer even contemplated as a means to an end. Rather, by removing my mind from materialistic pursuits, l was able to face myself more realistically. It yielded inner space wherein I could eventually draw on presentiments that enabled me to see a much wider view. And in being less personal, I could be in harmony with myself, just as the Eskimos had learned to be.

These primitive people showed Poncins the value of living in harmony with the natural cyclic changes within any environment. The regularity of animals', birds' and insects' emigrational habits made Poncins acutely conscious and aware that cyclic changes are an essential part of all our lives. I learned, on the other hand, the vital need for disciplined order in my daily life, which drew my attention to the regularity of the cyclic movements that I noticed arose in the cult: sudden changes, for example. All would appear peaceful, then with no prior warning and for no apparent reason the group were called together to be disciplined by the Principal, so severely that it felt like bullets fired at random. This happened again and again. However, the whole experience for both Poncins and me proved to initiate an inner revolution.

Nevertheless, what eventually transpired was an extraordinary shock for us both, but the effects of these psychological ordeals awakened us to the reality of living within a totally different mental attitude. It became obvious that what we had endured could never be reversed, any more than the seasonal cycles in nature or the Universe can be reversed.

My understanding is that any attrition, any shattering of our ignorant behaviour, offers us the chance and the ability to begin to know ourselves. In fact, it is the only way to freedom.

Likewise, the first and best move towards understanding ourselves is to recognise that we do not know. To cling to fictitious values prevents release from false conditioning. I feel that it is essential for us to awaken from the state of ignorant behaviour that holds us imprisoned denying us the opportunity to transform our lives. To be enlightened is surely to be aware of the cycle of behaviour whereby we go round and round in circles looking for a way out of our delusionary human predicament. This enabled me to see myself as I really was and not as I thought I was.

Step by step on my homeward journey, I uncovered my patterns of ignorant conditioned behaviour, arriving at the first crossroad coming face to face with myself. But at this juncture, through perseverance, I noticed a new life coming into being—I realised that not to know or fear what lies ahead that is unknown—is freedom—very different from that greatest impediment, the false reasoning of unenlightened minds. Once my attention was drawn to the essential truth, that no one could help me but myself, I was forced to turn inwards. As Goethe said:

Freedom is the essence of Spirit. Freedom must be
preserved; without it, anything we stand for is jeopardised.
Alchemy is the science of transformation induced by Light,
the Light of the Spirit. The world is an Athanor,
an alchemistic oven, and we humans are here to ensure
that the 'cooking' is carried out according to the Law of Life
and not against it.

On my homeward journey I felt like an alchemist in quest of wisdom, who finds the path ahead strewn with untouched traces of the past; but as an alchemist, I was aware that without self-knowledge the path leading to the secrets of the Universe, to the Stars, could never be mine.

Perhaps this is why masters and sages of all ages knew the dangers of dabbling in esoterica—Mysticism, Occultism, Spiritualism, the Kabbalah, the deeper path of the Kundalini Yogi, Magic, Psychism, or any form of what we now term 'New Age' teachings—before there is real transformation of the 'self' through self-knowledge. It is interesting to note that Krishnamurti, whose teachings were recognised globally, never discussed the esoteric in his talks around the world. He emphasised the truth stated so poignantly by the Greeks: 'Know thyself and thou shalt know the Universe and its Gods'—and summed up so neatly by Alexander Pope:

Know then thyself; presume not God to Scan,
The Proper study of mankind is man.

When I considered what Alchemists have written and believed about the 'Subtle Energies' that provide cohesion to all things; I understood that fluidic radiance pervades all matter, both living and inert, from which physical structure is manifested, whether it be stone or metal, plants, animals or man.

These 'Subtle Energy Forces' determine the respective uniqueness and behaviour of everything. One intriguing example of how this manifests is within our body when special white cells instantly respond to a lesion in the skin, enabling a team-work of other cells to make the necessary repair. Much the same process takes place within a colony of ants in the insect world. Soldier ants immediately respond to the necessity of guarding a breach in their colony's wall caused by an intruder, until special ants are able to make the necessary repairs. This shows that all creatures and all of nature is structured and uniform to the same principal, that of the principal of a unity of ONENESS of Being.

Knowledge of myself enabled me to make an inner response to the silent intelligence within; that I like to think of as the God Given Power that created the form—the body, the mind and the sensing of the human being. This recognition gives the opportunity for the transforming of the egocentric will power into the ability to be open and ready to use the God Given Power of Energy. Learning to be aware of myself in action I learnt the value of being an impassive spectator—as Krishnamurti said: 'the observer is the observed.' There is no difference then between the objectified and the objective.

To abandon one's habits, ways of life, likes and dislikes, family attachments, even one's habit of continual movement of thought—especially image making—I found opens the door to an intelligent understanding of one's life. It seems, therefore, that we must direct our energies by deliberate action, rather than reaction caused by conditioning. However, I realised that this is not possible without a sufficient understanding of self-knowledge.

Once I awakened to my inner inbuilt capabilities I could understand the necessity of self-knowledge and realise that I was totally responsible for the whirlwinds of chaotic energies that in my ignorance I set into motion by my unruly conflicting emotional behaviour. Unable to quell the storms that I had created I was inevitably responsible for adding my conflict to the existing conflict around the world. Hence I could understand the recurrence of war, crime, disruption and corruption of every kind that inevitably follows such irresponsible behaviour.

Yet when I awoke to my inner instinctual capabilities, I found I could cope adequately and sanely in this somewhat unbalanced human world. In the realisation that true awareness emanates from vibrations superior to ours, I was conscious of my responsibility to be open to the guidance of the God Given Powers lying dormant within each of us. Thus I found it possible to rise above fear and pass beyond it, and at the same time understand the need to break through the barriers of 'self'?

We can never solve the world's problems by creating systems and believes—for is it not you and I who are responsible for creating human problems? Surely it is then our responsibility to transform ourselves and by so doing are we not solving the problems of humanity?

Only when I am in relationship with others have I the opportunity to truly know myself. The supreme value of relationships is that they afford us the opportunity to observe aspects of ourselves mirrored in others—a way of helping us to discover real love and compassion.

The most beautiful and profound emotion we can experience is the sensation of the mystical. It is the sower of all true science. He to whom this emotion is a stranger, who can no longer wonder and stand rapt in awe, is as good as dead—To know that what is impenetrable to us really exists, manifesting itself as the highest wisdom and the most radiant beauty, which our dull faculties can comprehend only in their primitive forms, this knowledge, this feeling, is at the centre of true religiousness.

Albert Einstein 1879–1955

What is so interesting is that when we have thought through what is troubling us or we find answers to our own inner enquiries we often find confirmation—this is what happened to me. I came across a short biography by A. Irwin Switzer III that confirmed an inner realisation that came to me after years and years of searching.

In this biography on the life of D.T.Suzuki (1897–1966), A. Irwin Switzer III, relates that Dr. D.T.Suzuki, who was regarded as the greatest Zen Buddhist of his time, brought Japanese Zen Buddhism to the West. It was due to his researching that he was able to make a reappraisal of the work of Yotaku Bankei (1622–93), uncovering his profound work on the 'Unborn' mind—a unique expression of Bankei's enlightenment, which only came to him after years of intense struggle.

The following words were written by Switzer to express what Dr. Suzuki understood from Bankei's teachings that corresponded to my own understanding.

The 'Unborn' mind is our own essence of mind. It is not a blind force, nor an irrational impulse; it is intelligence beyond logical calculation. The "Unborn' is the principle of order which directs the intellect to work in the world of practical affairs. To see the 'Unborn' mind is to realise that we are as we are and need not struggle to change our nature; what is needed is (for us) to accept our self-nature, forming no attachment in daily life.

This has been expressed before in many different ways, but none so poignantly as Bankei unfolded through the 'Unborn' mind. To me it uncovers what we have for so long ignored—the process of bringing into being the Essence of ourselves. A good analogy I discovered in Harry Benjamin's book *Basic Self-knowledge*, published in 1971 by Samuel Weiser, Inc., to quote:

> *Let us consider an egg. There is the yolk, the white and the shell. If we regard false personality (greed, hurts, fears, anger etc) as the outer hard shell, and personality (that which we make of our lives through self-realisation of the need to conduct our lives efficiently, supportively, with a warrior-like attitude of self-responsibility etc.) as the white of the egg, and the yolk as (the essence of our being waiting to be awakened into the bird, which can then break through the hard shell of our false personality) to emerge fully into the light of day as a living creature— a vibrant being.*

The yoke feeds on the white of the egg, as it grows into being, but in order to come into being the newly formed bird (or living vibrant human being) must break the shell of the egg (or false personality), so it can fly (or be free to leave no trace).

We have all been driven by the intellectual mind that we know, to the exclusion of that 'Unborn' mind (the God Given Essence of ourselves) that we do not know, causing a deep division within ourselves that has prevented us from finding the natural order that is our birthright. That is: if we only have the courage and perseverance to recognise the presence of this 'Unborn' mind. This we can only do from the stance of not knowing; then the 'Unborn' mind directs the intellect of knowing. Harmony and Order prevails and a human being enjoys an interblended life as a part of the whole of Creation.

However, I found that I still had to learn that cycles in human unfoldment comes around again when one least expects it. This is the time when one is thrown in at the deep end—being forced to face what one could not face during the initial cycle, doubtless due to ignorance and conditioning. When the cycles repeat, as they surely will, one either falls into the same trap or one has the courage to face what one could not face during the confrontation of the first cycle.

My repeated cycle forced me to look at myself in all honesty; knowing I had failed to do so during the initial cycle. Thus I could look at myself with no regrets—no blame or praise—no guilt or delusion. There was just an honest appraisal. I was now fully aware of my feelings at the time of the initial cycle—of my fears, my religious self-righteousness, my longings to become closer to the divine and my inability to stand on my own two feet. By escaping from the situation that I found myself in, I leaned on another following her ideas and dictates.

Now as I looked at what was right in front of me I saw a repetition of the first cycle resurrecting everything before me of that what I had been unable to face during the first cycle. Portraying to me all my actions and reactions that took place, in spite of myself, and the agony it caused. I took the opportunity offered by the repeated cycle to delve into myself so I could face the hard facts that I had been unable to face in the initial cycle, where I was escaping from what I could not bare to face by seeking refuge in the cult at the time when my children needed me the most. I saw my life as it was then in all its glaring tragic reality. And by not moving away from the remembrance of this early time I was able to have an insight into my background behaviour, which had been instrumental in shaping my childhood and adult life.

I recognised that in my childhood I had succumbed to the power and influence of my parents, my education and my environment, all of which came from conditioning and had the effect of causing me to be totally unaware of myself and my behaviour. Thus, in this repeated cycle that I was now experiencing, I was once again brought face to face with myself as I had been during that first cycle. I was seeing the images, the delusions, the desires, the urges, the dilemmas—and also what caused them—as I honestly and squarely opened my heart to the truth of my actions and reactions during that time.

I understood deeply the vital importance of the need for self-knowledge and self-awareness. I now realised the benefit of confronting my life as it is and not as it appeared to be from a purely external ignorant point of view. No longer am I concerned with advancing further up any ladder of human endeavour expressed as a possibility by others. I am content to search into my own inner nature to guide me. I now deal with what comes directly in front of me without fear or favour. I find that it is so good to be alive, so good to be unafraid to walk alone, yet willing to work together with others, facing life as it is. Ready every day to learn something new about what it means to be a human being.

Elisabeth Fraser, *2008*

The Eye of Truth

All the time I was writing this book I saw an eye whenever I was in need of help, when I had finished this, my autobiography, the eye moved. I have not seen it again. The above painting was given to me by one of the members of the Krishnamurti Foundation Centre, who in turn had it sent to him from an interested artist in Spain.

Glossary

IN THIS GLOSSARY are the meanings of the significant terms that have gradually developed through my struggles to understand my life with its ups and downs. So the meanings given below define what those terms came to mean to me and hopefully, from my definitions of them here, the reader will be able to follow my pathway. *Words* have a variety of meanings, one of which is implicitly selected by the context in which they are used. However, terms are different in that they are given one explicit meaning, which applies to all contexts in which they are used.

Awareness refers to the degree of accuracy of our conscious understanding concerning our total environment and the reality of the world in which we live. 'Basic awareness' means appreciating that something or someone exists, while "greater awareness' means an extension to include how the something or someone functions and is connected within our reality and environment. Awareness should not be confused with knowledge, which is a creation of the intellect and memory providing information about the something or someone. For instance, I can be aware of a church bell ringing from the sound I am hearing and a perception of what is happening, but it is from information in the memory about church bells that I am able to acquire knowledge as to how the church bells are made, what they are used for. However, awareness does not depend on knowledge or memory. Awareness is also vital when acquiring self-knowledge. Both self-awareness and self-knowledge being essential to those who endeavour to study themselves. The degree to which we are open-minded governs the extent to which we are able to acquire greater awareness about ourselves. Krishnamurti points out—that; 'awareness is from moment to moment and is not the accumulative effect of self-protective memories. Awareness is not determination nor is it the action of will. Awareness is the complete unconditioned surrender to what is, without rationalization, without the division of the observer and the observed'

Belief belongs to the mind and concerns what is true about a particular situation. Any action is in response to a perceived situation, which is the field in which the action takes place. Before any actions can be undertaken, however, it is normal to have a belief about what is real concerning the situation. Most of our beliefs reside in our subconscious mind, and most of them come from conditioning and indoctrination. For example, the Church has fostered beliefs that Jesus came down to save us, leaving many Church followers to believe that they have no responsibility for their actions other than believing that Jesus will save them if they repent. This is the usual understanding of the word belief. But one has to remember there may be a misinterpretation of the Coptic words giving an entirely different meaning to that word 'to give' as put forward by the Greeks to mean to save.

Bodhisattva refers to one whose essence is enlightenment—a being that compassionately refrains from entering nirvana in order to save others and is worshiped as a deity in Mahayana Buddhism

Conditioning refers to the process which makes us adopt a ready-made way of thinking about the things that exist in our environment and the reality of the world in which we live. We are conditioned when we absorb beliefs and ideas from our human environment without full appreciation of what we are adopting. The absorbed beliefs and ideas slide from our consciousness into our subconscious, which accepts them as though they were absolute truth and undeniable. Our vulnerability toward conditioning comes from our lack of self-knowledge and self-awareness and our ignorance of our behaviour patterns, so that we are drawn into thinking and acting as though we were mere automatons. Our conditioning starts in childhood and runs through our education, particularly our religious upbringing. These established beliefs concerning religion are of such a conditioned nature that we are unaware they have had a mind-boggling affect on our lives. We absorb what we read or hear through the media or what somebody else may tell us, which become a form of habit conditioning. Conditioning can be necessary as a form of discipline with regard to training.

Conflict refers to divisive behaviour in our relationship with other people and Nature. When we sound a self-limited ego note we immediately raise a similar self-limited note in others and this ego clash leads directly to conflict. When we become personal in our behaviour patterns toward others and Nature, we work to 'employ our authority and power over them.' Then conflict is provoked from our self-centred behaviour being used to enforce our will over others, or against Nature. In such a situation, our opinions supported by our ignorance of the whole situation causes us to revert to personalised thinking that inevitably brings conflict. Conflict is a seat of aggression, divisiveness and misery that always produces instability. Conflict does not just disappear into thin air—it is attracted to other conflicts already in existence—rather like 'black spots' on roads attract other accidents. Just imagine if there were no personal conflict in the world—in our homes and places of work—just think how much better it would be for our health and well-being. There would be no wars because no one would be stimulated by their egos to be on their personal defensive. Should anyone create conflict around themselves, there would be no one who would want to be provoked by that conflict, thus the *status quo*[21] 'what is' would be allowed to remain as it is.

Consciousness refers to the ability of something to respond to its environment. How it responds comes from the character of the consciousness. I am taking it to mean that there are three ways to view consciousness. 1) Ordinary consciousness through the five physical senses, referring to a mind-driven self-consciousness 2) sub-consciousness referring to an automatic response based on belief, mostly hidden 3) a deeper inner consciousness referring to a response based on true awareness.

Esoteric refers to something only intelligible to those with a special secret knowledge that is taught to initiates. Hence esoteric knowledge is formulated in terms to which only a select group has access. Many people use the word esoteric to refer to secret knowledge, usually of a religious nature, often referring to a doctrine that has no backing in logic. An example of esoteric knowledge is within *The Secret Doctrine* by Madame Blavatsky, who, along with Col. Alcott, established *The Theosophical Society*.

[21] See glossary 'What is'; it is used in a specific sense here.

Exoteric refers to knowledge of the sort that is verifiable, which can be understood by a layperson because it is logically founded. It is therefore the opposite of esoteric.

Identification refers to how we perceive ourselves in relation to others and our environment. The word—identification—comes from the Latin word *idem* meaning—same—and—*facere*—that means to make. Thus when I identify myself with something *I make the same—in my reference—the same as myself* or another. Basically too it means to make the same with things. I have used this term to express how we can be deceived by our thoughts. In our relationships we are mostly unaware that if we receive from another a hurtful remark or action, we immediately identify ourselves with that remark or that action or that person, because it attacks the image we have formed of ourselves. By creating images, we establish a space between ourselves—as the subject—and the one who has made the hurtful remark or action—as the object. Within this space thought moves to justify, condemn or escape from what it does not like, which is recorded in the memory and used by the memory to increase a hurt or establish a backing to enforce their beliefs. Also, in this space we use personalised thought to go backwards and forwards in our minds in condemnation and blame producing conflict and sometimes hatred. It is not necessary to make this identification. All it requires is total attention on ourselves, whereby the self is quiet, allowing the person who had made the hurtful remark or action to do so without any identified resistance from us. Then we make no identification or objectification whatsoever with the hurt remark - since we have remained quietly attentive and still with ourselves—i.e. not moving in response to the hurtful remark either verbally or non-verbally. In other words we are not affected in anyway by what has been said or done, although of course we hear what has been said, but we make no thought processes whatsoever to back indentification. Instead we allow the 'what is' to remain exactly as it is without wishing to alter, change or shape it in anyway.

Ignorance refers to a lack of both awareness and knowledge or mostly used by me as self-knowledge about us. As a consequence of which, we sooner or later fall into situations where we are brought face to face with the compelling need to dispel our ignorance. For example: it is considered that a person is ignorant if they do not know the implications of what they are doing, what they are saying, or how they are behaving. Academic learning does not prevent us from being ignorant of how we ourselves behave, or ignorant of the indoctrination that accompanies the learning. Many people who have little or no education are by no means ignorant of themselves. In fact they may be responding to their inner essence so they are not ignorant.

Impersonal behaviour refers to not allowing one's inner peace to be affected by anything said or addressed to us or about others or us. The moment we are affected by what others say or do to us we have taken what has been said to us in a personal way. That is: if we feel put down, then we rise to our own defence and against the other person for making remarks about us that we do not like to hear or accept. Being impersonal means that we hear what another says and we do not react personally to what has been said, but just listens very attentively to discover the truth within it, however brutal or insensitive the remark may be. We learn over many years to see everything as it is and allow it to remain so. In this way we do not encourage conflict and conflict does not envelop us. We note what has been said, but we do not try to alter, shape, or change it in order to fit it in with the way our egos see others or ourselves. Thus we are not drawn into conflict.

Indoctrination refers to the act of instilling beliefs, and concepts into another person's previously formulated ideas. Sometimes indoctrination specifically defines how its author desires the reader, viewer, or listener to think and act. Frequently, indoctrination is accompanied by conditions, often purposely set, that promote a passive state of mind and unthinking receptivity within the recipient, in the same sense as 'here is this pill, if you swallow it whole with no questions asked, it will do you good.'

Insights referred to by me in the book means a direct impression or inner immediate understanding of knowing—which comes into being uncalled for—but gives the immediate answer to exactly what is needed; without thinking or thought interfering. But the recipient knows instantly that it is right and acts on it spontaneously without question. Unfortunately these insights are not always acted upon because they do not seem to have any rhyme or reason why they should be, though I learnt to follow them implicitly.

Knowledge and Wisdom together refers to a blending of the material and spiritual aspects within our daily lives. As I see it, by relying totally on knowledge, which is always limited and put together through thought that is limited produces incompleteness in relation to the wholeness of anything. Then we are bound to remain materialistic and mundane, whereas, by embracing knowledge and wisdom together we strengthen our ability to provide a stable foundation on which to bring order to every aspect of our lives. Self-awareness based on self-knowledge leads to a union between knowledge and wisdom, and can bring about radical changes in one's consciousness. Knowledge, as I understand it, is acquired by focusing on the externally manifested aspect of a situation or phenomenon by limiting our input to our five physical senses and using the logical mind's ability to distinguish and discriminate among externally apparent aspects, in order to create an intellectual comprehension, whereas wisdom neither negates, nor is limited to, any intellectual cognition. Wisdom goes far beyond the intellectual grasp by perceiving the interconnectedness to everything else in the Universe, which touches what may be described as transcendental intelligence. In that way there is an attunement between knowledge and wisdom. This becomes the very ground on which our security rests when we study self-knowledge and self-awareness.

Karma refers to 'action'—the sum of all individual deeds, which ineluctably determine their experiences during this life and in the after life and future births.

Krishnamurti Teachings are available in books, CD-ROMs, DVDs audio and video tapes for sale at: Krishnamurti Centre, Brockwood Park, Bramdean, Hampshire SO24 OLQ
Tel. 01962 771 748; Fax 01962 771 755
Email: *kcentre@brockwood.org.uk*
Online bookings: *www.kfoundation.org*

There are several other main Krishnamurti Foundation Centres in India, Americas, Switzerland and Canada. There is also a worldwide network of Krishnamurti Foundation Information Centres around the world. Krishnamurti established schools in England, India, America and Canada. Krishnamurti held talks around the world for 50 to 60 years until 1985. He died on February 17th 1986 in Ojai, California at the age of 90 years.

Love is in the context of its use in this book referring to a Love exhibited by Holy Men and Women who have understood and exercised Compassion. You cannot have real Love without real Life; to me they are one and the same. Love is not expendable; it gives of Itself, just as Life does. There is no way that you can find love—It finds you just as Life does. Love can only come into being when the 'self' is abandoned. We do not understand LOVE because we place a personal construction on it—losing all the beauty of its BEING.

Naïveté, like 'ignorance', refers to being narrowly or shallowly ignorant about the way in which the world operates, about the way we conduct ourselves, and about our own behaviour patterns through our youthfulness and lack of experience. It can also refer to being ignorant of our essential nature so that we behave in a juvenile manner, unable to understand the effect of what we are doing or saying. Such behaviour leads to unsophisticated actions and unwise decisions of the kind that are usually associated with the very young, but are in fact often present in all ages. For instance, many of us will perhaps recall some time in our lives being conned by others too easily, simply because of our naïveté.

Narcissus refers to the Greek story that I have used to illustrate a specific meaning in my text. The story tells of a beautiful youth, Narcissus, who was the son of the river god Cephissus and the nymph Liriope. Narcissus saw his image reflected in a fountain and became enamoured by it, thinking it to be the nymph of the area. His fruitless attempts to approach this beautiful object drove him to despair and eventually his death. Narcissus was changed into the flower that bears his name.

Objectification refers to a specific way that the logical mind uses conceptual thought processes to relate to events and experiences. Objectification creates in the logical mind an image of a situation or person, who becomes reduced to an intellectual 'object' conception in fact—an illusion. And as such, the object is entirely disconnected from the reality of the person or situation. Objectification, as used in this way, suppresses our ability to see the way in which we act and react to the reality of any situation in the course of a relationship with others.

Pandora's Box *'Pandora, according to Hesiod... was made of clay by Hephaestus at the request of Zeus, who wished to be revenged on Prometheus for his championship of mankind. When this woman of clay had received life, she was endowed by the gods with every gift, so Zeus gave her a box, which she was directed to present to the man who married her. Hermes then conducted her not to Prometheus, who was too sagacious to accept her, but to Epimetheus, his brother. The latter, less prudent, married her and opened the box, whereupon there issued from it all the evils and distempers that have since afflicted the human race. Hope alone remained at the bottom of the box to assuage the lot of man.'* (Taken from the *Oxford*

Companion to English Literature, compiled and edited by Sir Paul Harvey, first published in 1932. Oxford University Press.)

Personal Behaviours & Behaviour Patterns refer to the personal way we respond to anything such as another person, a situation, or an object. The response is closely associated with our self-identity. For example, imagine someone rudely or brusquely cutting in front of your car as you are driving. By identifying yourself with the action you become upset and then you identify the feelings that have arisen in you with respect to the driver's actions. With respect to an object, for example, you see a car and feel how beautiful it is, and then you identify yourself with it, you have thus personalised it as a mind image and as a consequence your mind possesses it. On the other hand, by responding impersonally you see the person, object, or situation for what it is, and are thus able to leave it in its own space and at the same time retain your own space. In other words, you allow people or things to be the way they are without trying to alter, change or shape them to fit into what you think they are or want them to be or should be—which would be to indentify with them.

Personalised Thought & Personalised Thinking refers to the process of using thought in an egocentric way to formulate a meaning stemming from a personal identity. Thinking has three essential purposes 1) to help us manage our day-to-day affairs through memory as with driving a car; 2) to develop ourselves concerning the reality that exists within our environment; 3) projecting our mind into something we do not already know through intellectuality. Our feelings, used psychologically come from hurts or pleasure relating to a mosaic of concepts, from which stems our picture of what is real and what is false. We all have a picture or image of what is real and what is false, which totally limits our understanding of ourselves and everything else. So personalised thought is thinking that is specifically centred around ourselves in a personal psychological way. I specifically use the term 'personalised thought or thinking' to locate and reveal just how much we look at a reflected mirror-image of ourselves during our personal relationships and in our personal behaviour patterns. Personalised thought or thinking narrows our perception of 'what is' into a personal conception of what we think it means.

Psychological according to the dictionary means the scientific study of the human mind, mental make-up, attitude, and thought processes, as well as the mental inability or inhibition caused by emotional factors or psyche of a person. I am using all these terms, but mostly in connection with personal thought that stirs up our emotional hurts, hates, greeds, ambitions, anger, fears etc. I connect the psyche, which underlies the term psychology, to the inner positive emotional side of ourselves that is capable of an enormous expansion of awareness that allows us to reframe from entering imaginary fields of thought through which we identify ourselves in personalised thinking.

Samsara refers to the cycle of existence in which one is endlessly caught or propelled by negative emotions of the Karmic force of one's actions from one state of rebirth to another.

Self-awareness refers to being self aware in a way that is totally incompatible with thinking or intellectual knowledge. Self-awareness transports us away from ourselves. It can only be found through insights when we are open and ready to receive inner promptings from our Essence or God Given Powers within. Once we are truly aware about something or other, it is irreversible and we cannot go back on the awareness any more than a tree can go backwards in its growth cycle.

Self-centredness refers to our selfish behaviour patterns that we build up within for ourselves and exhibit to others. It is where the 'me's' or I's are most prevalent using our basic background behaviour patterns of conformity to express our personal demands and wants, but for the most part, we are unaware that we express these patterns in the way that we do, because of our conditioning. The result of this unawareness is that we react to situations and people from the limited point of view of our personalised behaviour. Self-centredness is revealed by the way we respond to others, and how they respond to us. The degree to which our self-centredness creates negativity depends on how we deal with our conceptual personalised thought processes. The more self-centred we are, the more hidden our real motives remain to us, and the more negative are our thoughts producing negative actions and reactions toward others and toward our selves and our environment. The problem is that our behaviour patterns can become so ingrained that we behave as though they were an essential part of who we are—we don't want to even let them go!!!

Self-knowledge refers to gaining accurate knowledge about how we behave and who we really are, which leads from the understanding of our everyday self and our biological structure. By careful self-study and observation of ourselves we come to learn how we tick, and the way in which our biological minds function through a constant form of image making. Achieving real knowledge of ourselves produces alertness in the way we act and react; this is the beginning of self-knowledge. As we awaken to its importance we discover the biological structure of energies that actives within us, and the way in which they are expressed in our disposition, our behaviour patterns, and our attitudes toward each other and ourselves. Then, we begin to recognise that others act as a mirror to ourselves in our relationships with them, and in recognising this, we are able to learn more and more about our own selves. However, all the self-knowledge that dispels our ignorance and naïvetè and awakens us to what it means to be a human being— cannot bring peace to our inner beings. This can only come through self-awareness, which we learn to perceive in our relationships with others. Firstly, by seeing we are not aware. Secondly, by perceiving that we are unable to be aware for most of the time. Thirdly, that we have been so conditioned that we don't know what awareness means. Fourthly, we are afraid to let go of what we have become used to thinking as the norm. Most of all we are unable to read or listen without referring to what we already think that we know which blanks our mind to anything and everything that we might discern when we can let go of all our conceptions.

Thought refers to the everyday patterns used in our everyday life for intellectual purposes. Such as learning how to drive a car, do our work or learn our lessons at school or in college. But the thought processes I am mostly using in my book are all about the misuse of thought processes through psychological disturbances produced by the incorrect us of thought. Thought is immensely powerful, but is subsequently just as destructive when misused. Psychologically there is no need to use thought, which occurs in the space between what is and what we think is what is. Example: I make a remark, which is taken to be hurtful by another. From the moment of the remark to the moment of the effect of the remark—is a space. Now this space is nearly always used by thought to be express silently—things such as "She shouldn't have said that to me—it was not true etc." Now it is not necessary to use thought here at all. If the receiver of the so called hurt remark had just allowed it to remain so, as she silently attentively acknowledged it, there would be no movement of thought and consequently no hurt. No registering in the brain as memory, so the space would not be used by thought, thus how could there be any memory of the occurrence to bring from the brain to add to any situation that might recur.

The Three Worlds refers to the Sanskrit—*Trailokya*, meaning the three realms. The Buddhists talk of it as 1) The world of sensuous desires; 2) The world of forms; 3) The formless world of purity.

The True Self refers to that which is never engaged in the outside activities beyond its inner being. There appears to be an irritant within that is the seat of the dissatisfaction that drives us onward and makes us think that sometime, somewhere, we must return home.

Truth refers to the quality of being true or truthful that is relative to our self-awareness. You cannot find Truth, it can only find you when you are ready to receive it, and even then only as you grow and change, for it comes within your heart. Truth will then find you in greater measure. However, absolute Truth is changeless. In this book the context of the word Truth relates to the struggle all human beings have to understand themselves in relationship with others and the Cosmos. We cannot bring Absolute Truth to ourselves any more than we can bring Absolute Love into Being. Our behaviour does that or does not do it.

View refers to how human beings perceive things within their environment. What they see becomes their mental picture of their world and its conditions. Our beliefs underlie and determine our views of what is real and what is false, although our view is often totally controlled by our conditioning and indoctrination. The degree to which we are aware of this potential control depends on our understanding of ourselves.

'**What is**' is used in my book as an expression used by Krishnamurti to express the Now in Being. His Teachings brought to mankind during the years between the 1920s and the mid 1980s. It holds a profound understanding of the Now in actuality—as a fact. By understanding ourselves we realise that the 'what is' is what we are, what is happening to us in the present moment of our lives as an actuality, where we can see ourselves as we really are and not as we think we are behaving. By living with the immediate 'what is' there is no self or me, no space or time, only the Absolute Power expressed through Dynamic Energy.

Bibliography

Anthony, Carol K.
A Guide to the I Ching,
Anthony Publishing Co., Massachusetts.

Blavatsky, H.P.
Isis Unveiled & The Secret Doctrine—Cosmogenesis,
The Theosophical Publishing Co, Ltd., 1888.

Barkel, Kathleen
The Dawn of Truth Vol 1 teachings of I-EM-HOTEP,
The Hermetic Philosophy Vol 1 & 2,
Rider & Co., London 1635/37.

Brandt, Johanna
The Grape Cure,
Ehret Literature Publishing Co., Inc Yonkers, New York.

Brinsley Le Poer Trench
Forgotten Heritage,
Neville Spearman London, 1964.

Men Among Mankind,
first published by Neville Spearman.

Robert Bauval & Adrian Gilbert
The Orion Mystery—Unlocking the Secrets of the Pyramids,
Heinemann London, 1994.

Benjamin, Harry
Basic Self-knowledge—Introduction to Esoteric Psychology,
Health for All Publishing, London, 1960.

Blofeld, John
Zen Teaching of Huang Po.
The Buddhist Society, London, 1947
—basis of D.T.Suzuki's rendering of *Sanskrit & Chinese.*
The Dawn Horse Press, California, 1932.

Brunton, Paul
In Search of Secret India,
Rider & Co., London, 1934.

In Search of Secret Egypt,
Rider & Co., London, 1935.

Alexia Carrel Man
The Unknown,
Hamish Hamilton London, 1935.

Alexandra David-Neel & Llama Yongden
The Secret Teachings in the Tibetan Buddhist Sects,
published by City Lights Books San Francisco, USA, 1967 and translated by
Capt. H.N.M. Hardy.

Dhopeshwarkar A.D.
Krisahnamurti and The Experience of the Silent Mind,

Krishnamurti and the Unity of Man,
Chetan Ltd., Bombay, 1961/2.

Durckhiem—Karlfried Graf Von
Hara. The Vital Centre of Man,
A Mandala Book, 1962. Translation George Allan & Unwin Ltd., London.

Dwight-Goddard
Self-realisation of Noble Wisdom—The Lankavatra Sutra.

Ellion Theodore
In Secret of Tibet,
Rider & Co, London, 1937.

Darkness over Tibet,
Mystic Travellers Series, first published 1938, Rider & Co, London.

Giorgio de Santillana & Hertha van Dechend
Hamlet's Mill. An Essay on Myth and the Frame of Time,
a Non Pareil Book, David R Godine, Boston 1977, reprinted from
Randhouse, Inc., 1914.

Fitzgerald Edward
translations of *Rubaiyat of Omar Khayyam.*

Frederic Lionel
Revolution in Consciousness—
this translation Routledge & Kegan Paul, London, 1984.

Govinda Llama Angarika
The Foundation of Tibetan Mysticism, Rider, London 1960.

Gurdjieff. G.I.
All and Everything: An objectively Impartial Criticism of the Life of Man,
Routledge & Kegan Paul, 1948.

Haeri, Shaykh Fadhlalla
Leaves from a Sufi Journal, Zahra Publications 1988.

Huang, Alfred A.
Taoist Master—*The Complete I Ching—A Definitive Translation*,
Inner Traditions, Rochester, Vermont, USA, 1998.

Hulme, Kathryn R.
The Nun's Story,
Frederick Muller, 1935.

Icke, David
...and the Truth shall set you Free,
Bridge of Love, 1995.

Feuerstein, Georg
Holy Madness,
Arkana, published by the Penguin Group, 1992;
first published by Paragon House, 1991.

Ikuko Osumi & Malcolm Ritchie
*The Shamanic Healer—the Healing World of Ikuko Osumi and the traditional Art of Seiki-Juitsu.*Rider Book published in Paperback series in 1987 by Century Hutchinson Ltd.

Jenkins, John Major
Maya Coismogenesis 2012,
Introduced by Terence McKenna.
The Meaning of the Maya Calendar End-Date,
Bear & Company, Santa Fe, New Mexico, 1998.

Kouzo Kaku
The Mysterious Power of Ki—The Force Within,
Global Oriental, 2000.

Jayakar Pupul
Fire of the 1995 Mind Dialogue with J.Krishnamurti,
first Published by Penguin Books India.

Krishnamurti, Jiddu
Exploration into Insight,
Victor Gollancz Ltd., 1979.

Dialogue with Professor Allan W Anderson, A Wholly Different Way of Living,
Published by Victor Gollancz Ltd.. London, 1991.

Love and Loneliness, Harper San Francisco, 1993.

Krishnamurti, Jiddu
On God,
Harper San Francisco, 1992.

Total Freedom—the essential Krishnamurti,
1996.

Education and the Significance of Life.

The Ending of Time with David Bohm.

Krishnamurti to Himself.

The Network of Thought.

On Learning and Knowledge

'*Surely freedom from the self... is the true function of Man*'.
Excerpts from J. Krishnamurti's talks and writings, Krishnamurti
Foundation of India, 64 Greenways Road, Madras 28, 1980.

In the light of Silence, all problems are dissolved,
Complied in 1992.Krishnamurti Foundation of India, 64 Greenways Road,
Madras 28, 1980. Highly recommended.

Landau, Rom
God is My Adventure, Ivor Nicholson & Watson, London, 1935.

Seven,
Ivor Nicholson & Watson, London, 1936.

Thy Kingdom Come, Ivor Nicholson & Watson, London, 1937.

Hendrik, Willem van Loon
The Story of Mankind,
George Harrap & Co., London, 1922.

The Liberation of Mankind
George Harrap & Co., London, 1926.

The Home of Mankind
George Harrap & Co., London, 1933.

The Story of the Bible
F. Fisher Unwin Ltd., 1924.

Lopez, Barry
Arctic Dreams Imagination and Desire in Northern Landscape,
MacMillan London Ltd., 1986.

Marais Eugene
The Soul of the Ape—The Soul of the White Ant,
Penguin Group, 1973. First published in GB, 1971. First Published in
Afrikaans, 1937.

Maeterlinck, Maurice
The Hour-Glass,
translated by Bernard Miall. George Allen & Unwin Ltd., London, 1936.

K.E. Maltwood
Glastonbury's Temple of the Stars,
published by John Watkins.

Mehta P.D.
Holistic Consciousness—Reflections on the Destiny of Humanity,
Element Books, 1989.

McGregor Ross, Hugh
Jesus Untouched by the Church, His Teachings in the Gospel of Thomas,
William Sessions Ltd., York, 1998.

Ni, Hua-Ching
The Unchartered Vogage toward the Subtle Light,
The Shrine of the Eternal Breath of Tao, 1985.

8000 years of Wisdom,
Seven Star Communications Group Santa Monica, 1983.

Nouy, Pierre Lecomte du
Human Destiny,
Longmans, Green & Co., London, 1947.

Between Knowing and Believing,
David McKay Co Inc., New York, 1964, first published in France in 1964.

Osbourne, Arthur
Ramana Maharshi and the Path of Self-knowledge,
Rider & Company, London, 1970.

Orage A.R.
The Teachings of G.I. Gurdjieff, The journal of a pupil,
Routledge & Kegan Paul, London, 1961.

Ouspensky P.D.
In Search of the Miraculous. Fragments of Unknown Teachings,
Routledge & Regan Paul Ltd., London, 1950.

Tertium Organum—A key to the Enigmas of the World,
Routledge & Paul, 1970.

Poncins, Vicomte Gontran de,
in Collaboration with Lewis Galantiere, introduced by Eric Linklater
Kabloona, Reader's Union Ltd., London, 1942,
by arrangement with Jonathan Cape.

Ray, Marie
Beynon Doctors of the Mind,
Robert Hale Ltd., London, 1950.

Rinpoche Sogyal
The Tibetan Book of Living and Dying,
A New Spiritual Classic, first published in 1992, published by Harper San Francisco, a Division of Harper Collins.

Reed Bika
Rebel in the Soul and Ancient Egyptian Dialogues between a Man and his Soul,
Inner Traditions International, Vermont USA, 1978.

Robinson, James M.
General Editor
The Nag Hammadi Library,
Harper San Francisco, revised edition, 1988.
Copyright 1978, E.J.Brill, Leidon, Holland.

Roget, Peter Mark, MD FRS
Roget's Thesaurus of English Words and Phrases,
Longmans, Green & Co London, 1929.

John Snelling
The complete guide to Tibet's Mount Kailas The Sacred Mountain,
East-West Publications, London and The Hague, 1990;
Classic Harper San Francisco, 1992.

Spalding Baird T.
6 Books on The Life and Teachings of The Masters of Far East,
De Vorss Publications, Camarilla, California. 1924, 1937.
ISBN 10 0875163637

Samuel, Athanasius Yeshue
Treasure of Qumran—My story of the Dead Seas Scrolls,
Hodder and Stoughton, 1968.

M. Nahum Stiskin
The Looking Glass God—A Study in Yin & Yang,
a Merloyd Lawrence Book, Delacorte Press, 1976.

Suzuki D.T., Erich Fromm & Richard de Martino
Zen Buddhism and Psychoanalysis,
George Allen & Unwin, London, 1960.

Tolle, Eckhart
The Power of Now,
Namaste, Canada, 1997; USA 1999.

A New Earth,
Penguin Group, Strand London, imprint by Michael Joseph.
Veith, Ilza
Introductory and translation of
The Yellow Emperor's Classic of Internal Medicine,
The University of California Press London.

Weber, Renee
Dialogues with Scientists and Sages—The search for Unity,
Routledge & Paul plc, 1986.

West, John Anthony
Serpent in the Sky—The High Wisdom of Ancient Egypt,
Quest Books Theosophical Publishing House, 1993;
previously published by Harper & Row, 1979.

Wilhelm, Richard
Translation rendered into English by Cary F. Baynes Spearman 1962.
Amherst Press Wisconsin, 1963, *The I Ching* or *Book of Changes.*
Published by Routledge & Kegan Paul Ltd., London.
First published in two volumes in 1951.

Watson, Burton
Chuang Tzu Basic Writings,
Columbia University Press, 1964.

Mo Tzu Basic Writings,
Columbia University Press, 1963.

Wing, R.L.
The I Ching Workbook,
First published by Doubleday, 1979. Then reprinted by Broadway Books,
New York. Reprinted by Broadway Books as First paperback edition, 2001.

Wood, David
Genesis,
The Baton Press, 1985.

Wood, David & Ian Campbell
Geneset Target Earth,
Bellevue Books, 1994.

Wei Wu Wei
Open Secret,
Hong Kong University Press, 1970.

All Else is Bondage,
Hong Kong University Press, 1964.

Fingers pointing towards the Moon—
Reflections of a Pilgrim on the Way,
Routledge & Kegan Paul, 1958.

Yazaki, Katsuhiko
Path to Liang Zhi Future Generations,
Alliance Foundation, 1994.

Yogananda Paramhansa
Autobiography of a Yogi Rider & Company,
first published, 1950.

Young, Arthur M.
The Reflexive Universe—Evolution of Consciousness.

The Way of the Sufi, The Magic Monastery,
Tales of the Dervishes on Sufism and
Learning How to Learn by **Idries Shah**
are recommended.

I also found *Muslim Saints & Mystics,* translated by
A.J. Arberry very helpful, and some of the articles in
The Leaves from a Sufi Journal, especially several articles
by **Shaykh Fadhlalla Haeri**. *The Sufi Mystery* edited by
Nathaniel P. Archer, and *Memories of a Sufi Sage* by
Hazrat Inayat Khan, were also very enlightening.

I highly recommend *The Mind of Krishnamurti,* edited
by **Luis S.R.Vas**, Jaico Publishing House, 121,Mahatma
Gandhi Road, Mumbai 400–001, India, 2007.

Printed in the United Kingdom
by Lightning Source UK Ltd.
135863UK00001B/1-9/P